THE STRANGE DEATH
OF THE BRITISH
MOTOR CYCLE INDUSTRY

THE STRANGE DEATH
of the **BRITISH**
MOTOR CYCLE INDUSTRY

STEVE KOERNER

Crucible Books

Frontispiece: During the 1930s, BSA was best known for building 350 cc and 500 cc single-cylinder machines such as the Gold Star. However, the company also produced the J12, a model that was fitted with a 500 cc V-twin engine (seen here). V-twin powered motor cycles were less popular in Britain than they were in the USA and certain parts of the British Empire. They were, however, favoured by some riders, including those who used motor cycle/side-car combinations. BSA ceased building V-twin models after 1940.

PHOTOGRAPH BY COURTESY OF JOHN OLSEN

The Strange Death of the British Motor Cycle Industry

Copyright © Steve Koerner, 2012

First edition

First published in 2012 by
Crucible Books,
an imprint of Carnegie Publishing Ltd,
Carnegie House,
Chatsworth Road,
Lancaster LA1 4SL
www.cruciblebooks.com

British Library Cataloguing-in-Publication data
A catalogue record for this book is available from the British Library

ISBN 978-1-905472-03-1 (softback)

Designed, typeset and originated by Carnegie Book Production, Lancaster
Printed and bound in the UK by Short Run Press, Exeter

This book is dedicated to the
memory of my parents,
Nicholas T. Koerner (1925–2001)
and Karin E. Koerner (1928–2005)

Contents

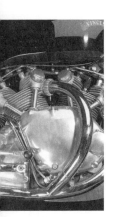

List of tables

Acknowledgements

I WOULD LIKE TO THANK the librarians, archivists and other staff at a number of research institutions that were consulted during the preparation of this book. In Britain, the Birmingham Central Reference Library, the Bodleian Library, the British Library (including the Newspaper Library at Colindale), the British Library of Political and Economic Science (London School of Economics), the Coventry City Library, the Coventry Records Office, the Guildhall Library (London), the Imperial War Museum, the Modern Records Centre (University of Warwick), the Parliamentary Archives, the Public Records Office (now National Archives), the Solihull Public Library and the libraries of both the University of Birmingham and the University of Warwick. In Canada, the British Columbia Archives, the Greater Victoria Public Library (Central Branch), the National Library and Archives (Ottawa, Ontario), the Prince George and District Library (Prince George, B.C.), and the University of Victoria library. And, in the USA, my thanks to the National Archives (Washington D.C.) for locating and sending me certain documents.

Recognition and thanks are due to Jamie Borwick, Managing Director of Manganese Bronze Holdings, for depositing archives relating to BSA at the Modern Records Centre, to EMAP, the Motor Cycle Industry Association and the Motor Cycle Retailers' Association for generously allowing me access to their various holdings and to Michael Miller for providing a copy of his unpublished paper 'The British Motor Cycle Industry before 1939'. Peter Watson has, over the years, provided a steady stream of ideas and suggestions which have much improved this book.

Special mention should be made here of Richard Storey, former Archivist at the Modern Records Centre, and the late Alistair Cave, former Works Manager at BSA's Small Heath factory, who both went to extraordinary lengths to preserve valuable company records and other documentation which, but for them, would certainly have been lost or destroyed. Without their timely action, the quality and depth of any book written about the history of the British motor cycle industry would be much diminished. I would also like to recognise and thank the various persons who agreed to be interviewed and who provided so much important information for this book.

Many very helpful comments and suggestions were also received from participants at a number of conferences and seminars where some of the themes raised in this book have been presented. These include sessions sponsored by the Association of Business Historians, the Business History Conference, the Economic History Society, the Institute of Railway Studies and Transport History, the Social History Society, the Japan Business History Society, Southwest/Texas Popular Culture Association, as well as the history departments of the University of Wales and the University of Birmingham and the Business History Unit at the London School of Economics.

Portions of this book have already appeared in the *Journal of Transport History*, *The International Journal of Motorcycle Studies*, various past issues of *The Classic Motor Cycle* and as chapters in the following books: *The Motor Car and Popular Culture in the 20th Century* (Ashgate, 1998) and *Canada and the End of Empire* (UBC Press, 2005).

I also very much appreciate the advice and encouragement received from a number of people during the research and writing of this book.

In Britain, my thanks to Jim Bamberg, Joanne Burman, Richard Coopey, Colin Divall, Terry Gourvish, Matt Hager, Fiona Lewis, Andrew Millward, Elfed Owens, Mary Ann Owens, Barbara Smith, Richard Temple, Jim Tomlinson, Margaret Walsh and Christine Woodward. In Canada and the USA, my thanks to Cameron Beck, Judith Brand, Kim Brittenham, Brad Brousseau, Hans Brown, Melodie Corrigal, Alan von Finster, Paul Harris, Bevin Jones, Steve Morrall, Karen Ochs, Mike O'Neill, Guy Robertson, Mike Shoop, Ed Youngblood and Jonathan Zeitlin. The section on the Japanese motor cycle industry benefited greatly from research conducted in Japan between 1998 and 1999 during the course of a Post-Doctoral Fellowship sponsored by the Japan Society for the Promotion of Science. My thanks especially to Hideo Ichihashi at Saitama University as well as Neil Cowie, Yu Cowie, Ronald Dore, Eamonn Fingleton, Yukio and Mariko Takeuchi, Kikuo Iwatate, Jun Otahara, Tatsuya Tsubaki, Hristofor Vankov and Takeshi Yuzawa. Thanks also to the Honda Motor Company, Kawasaki Heavy Industries, Suzuki Motor Corporation and Yamaha Motor Company for arranging visits to various motor cycle factories as well as providing access to their staff and respective archives.

This book is based on my Ph.D. dissertation which was completed at what was then the Centre for the Study of Social History at the University of Warwick. There I had the unfailing support of the staff and students including Brad Beaven, Kate Beaumont, John Dunlop, Jill Greenfield, Toby Haggith, Roger Laidlaw, Gwynne Lewis, Rainer Liedtke, Ros Lucas, Detlev Mares, Saho Matsumoto, Jim Obelkovich, Sean O'Connell, Carolyn Steedman, Birgit Strack and Lesley Whitworth. Last, but very certainly not least, much is owed to my tutor, Nick Tiratsoo, who oversaw my dissertation from beginning to end.

The generosity of the British Empire Motor Club, the BSA Owners' Club, the City of Toronto Archives, Mick Duckworth, Dan Mahony, Ed Moody and Ed Youngblood is much appreciated for having provided many of the photographs used in this book.

I would like to thank Crucible Books, its editor, John F. Wilson, and publishers, Alistair Hodge and Anna Goddard for their patience and forbearance as this book took shape and also Judith Franks for coordinating the collection of the photographs.

Finally, as always, any errors or omissions remain the sole responsibility of the author.

Steve Koerner, Victoria, BC, Canada,
January 2012

Abbreviations

AA	Automobile Association
ACU	Auto Cycle Union
AEU	Amalgamated Engineering Union
AMC	Associated Motor Cycles
ATS	Auxiliary Territorial Services
BCMCIA	British Cycle and Motor Cycle Industries' Association
BCMCMTU	British Cycle and Motor Cycle Manufacturers' and Traders' Union
BEF	British Expeditionary Force
BIOS	British Intelligence Objectives Subcommittee
BCG	Boston Consulting Group
BMC	British Motor Corporation
BSA	Birmingham Small Arms
cc	cubic centimetre
CDEEA	Coventry District Engineering Employers' Association
CIOS	Combined Intelligence Objectives Subcommittee
CSEU	Confederation of Shipbuilding and Engineering Unions
CTU	Cycle Trade Union
EEF	Engineering Employers' Federation
FBI	Federation of British Industries
FIAT	Field Information Agency, Technical
MAA	Motor Agents' Association
MBH	Manganese Bronze Holdings
MCIA	Motor Cycle Industry Association
MCC	Motor Cycle Club
MDW	Measured Day Work

MIRA	Motor Industry Research Association
MITI	Ministry of International Trade and Industry (Japan)
MRC	Modern Records Centre (University of Warwick)
MRPC	Monopolies and Restrictive Practices Commission
NA	National Archives (London England)
NVT	Norton-Villiers-Triumph
PIAE	Proceedings of the Institution of Automobile Engineers
RAC	Royal Automobile Club
RASC	Royal Army Service Corps
SMMT	Society of Motor Manufacturers and Traders
TGWU	Transport and General Workers' Union
TT	Tourist Trophy
TUC	Trade Union Congress
The Manufacturers' Union	British Cycle and Motor Cycle Manufacturers' and Traders' Union
UCS	Upper Clyde Shipyards
WMDEEA	West Midlands District Engineering Employers' Association

One of the classic British engines:
the Triumph Speed Twin (*see* page 273)

Introduction

I N DECEMBER 1969, as the British motor cycle industry was tottering on the verge of financial collapse, a brief was delivered to the Parliamentary Secretary for the Minister of Technology from the Motor Cycle and Cycle Industries' Association, an organisation that represented virtually all motor cycle and cycle manufacturers in Britain.[1] The brief, which was signed on behalf of the association by Lionel Jofeh, Managing Director of BSA's Motor Cycle Division – Britain's dominant manufacturer – provided the industry's explanation for its current predicament. The British motor cycle industry was once, the manufacturers claimed, 'at the top level of world production', but, since 1945, had been in long-term decline. This was caused in large part by the severe battering it had received at the hands of foreign competitors, first from Italy and Germany, and more recently from Japan.[2]

Jofeh and the other manufacturers were aware, the brief continued, of widespread criticism which accused them of having 'let the Italians and the Japanese steal our markets'. It was true that many of the overseas markets, indeed even the home market itself, once the exclusive preserve of British motor cycle manufacturers, had been taken over by their foreign rivals. The fault, they insisted, was not theirs. Rather, it was the result of government policy which during the critical years after 1945 had forced them to divert their output overseas, thus making it impossible for the British manufacturers to satisfy the strong home demand for motor cycles. This had left them unprepared to compete against the large numbers of imported motorised two-wheeled vehicles that flooded into the country after the mid-1950s onwards. Moreover, they had been hobbled for years by 'a severe restriction on the home market', in the form of regulations and tax, which had smothered consumer interest. Hence, even although 'mass demand existed', the manufacturers argued that they had been prevented from 'getting into gear to meet it because of artificial fiscal barriers'.[3]

Foreign rivals, by contrast, had enjoyed the full support of their respective governments, and benefited from being allowed 'unrestricted development and sale of the simplest form of transport available – mopeds, scooters and motor cycles'.[4] All this had placed the British manufacturers at a considerable disadvantage. While the Italian and Japanese home markets flourished, Britain's had grown at a slower rate than it was capable of doing.

1

This interpretation was supported by the most basic trade statistics. In 1950, for example, there had been 761,500 two-wheeled motorised vehicles registered in Britain, a total which had increased to 1,343,000 in 1968. By contrast, the number of motor cars registered had jumped from 2,307,379 to 11,078,000 over the same period of time. Furthermore, the slower rate of growth in motor cycle usage was aggravated by an actual overall drop in production. In 1950, 171,300 motor cycles had been produced by British factories, a total which had fallen to 84,000 in 1968. By contrast, imports, which had been negligible in 1950, had shot up to 111,700 in 1968.

Such was the manufacturers' case. However, six years later, an independent report commissioned by the Department of Industry to investigate the plight of the surviving British motor cycle manufacturers, came to very different conclusions. This report, authored by the Boston Consulting Group (BCG) and entitled *Strategy Alternatives for the British Motor Cycle Industry*, contained sharp criticism of the manufacturers' past performance. They had been, over the years, it charged, too preoccupied with 'a concern for short-term profitability', which had badly eroded their competitive position relative to their Japanese rivals.[5]

The BCG report further noted how lower investment and antiquated factories, which produced only a fraction of Japanese output, had contributed to the poor state of the British industry. Over 1974/75, for example, despite drastic restructuring and generous government subsidies, its entire output totalled 20,000 motor cycles, compared with over 2,000,000 from just one Japanese firm, Honda. The British manufacturers were particularly criticised for what was called 'segment retreat'. This was the process by which they reacted to the advance of their Japanese competitors, who initially built mostly small motor cycles with an engine capacity of less than 250 cc, but had gradually moved 'up' the market with larger and larger motor cycles.

As the competition increased, British manufacturers failed to develop new and improved light- to medium-weight models to counter those of their Japanese rivals, and simply vacated the various market segments one after another. By 1975 the British industry produced nothing smaller than machines in the 500 cc engine displacement class, with the majority of production in the 750 cc and 850 cc classes, and had nowhere left to retreat. Backed by a vastly greater manufacturing base, enhanced by modern factories and far larger research and development establishments, the Japanese now produced models that were considerably more sophisticated technically than those of the British, and had steadily encroached upon the British share of motor cycle markets around the world.[6]

The BCG report provided the justification for Prime Minister Harold Wilson's Labour government to cease subsidising the motor cycle industry, which had absorbed nearly £24 million of public funds since 1973.[7] Press coverage at the time confirmed a widespread belief that British motor cycle manufacturers were the architects of their own misfortune and did not deserve continued government support.[8] Indeed, since its publication, the report has gone on to be used at the Harvard Business School as a case study of entrepreneurial failure, and has been referred to for illustrative purposes in at least two studies of the problems confronting British manufacturing in general.[9] Popular business journals have been attracted to the subject as well. One noted that, throughout British business history, 'there can be few cases of industries collapsing so swiftly and so completely'.[10]

So what had happened? How could this industry, which had been the dominating force in world motor cycle production for decades, have failed so spectacularly, and what were the factors were caused the 'segment retreat' identified by the BCG report? And, more specifically, how can a book such as this answer these questions in a way others have not? In fact, since the collapse in 1975, the wreckage of the industry has come to be surrounded by a considerable literature describing its various aspects and some explanations for its demise. However, unlike, for example, studies of the automobile industry, very little originates from academic sources or even popular histories written for a broader reading audience. Nor has there been an in-depth follow-up on the Boston Consulting Group study.[11]

Foremost among the academic work is Barbara Smith's *History of the British Motor Cycle Industry, 1945–1975*, which shares many of the criticisms of British motor cycle manufacturers originally made by the Boston Consulting Group.[12] A few other published academic accounts address various aspects of the industry before [13] and after 1945.[14] There are also several unpublished dissertations that deal with particular companies including the Meriden Workers' Co-operative.[15]

While most published histories tend to be critical of the industry's management, there is at least one exception. This originates from the Centre for Policy Studies and places the blame for the demise of the industry squarely on the shoulders of successive British governments. It attributes the constant manipulation of domestic demand by fiscal regulation, combined with a disastrous rescue attempt in 1973, for the weak performance of the industry after 1945.[16]

Particularly reliable are the small number of published memoirs that have originated from industry veterans, mainly former managerial or sales staff who are sharply critical of those corporate decision-makers who inhabited the industry's boardrooms.[17] These books contain some insights into the inner workings of specific firms, the industry generally, and the causes of its collapse. They do, however, need to be treated with some caution. This literature, as Barbara Smith warns, 'engenders nostalgia, inter-personal vituperation and shame that so much was lost so negligently'.[18]

In fact, the vast bulk of the literature published about the British motor cycle industry is directed towards a popular audience, one mostly comprising motor cycle enthusiasts. In turn, much of this literature is made up of histories of individual firms, such as Triumph, BSA, Matchless, Norton and Veloce (Velocette), hardly ever of the industry as a whole. These vary considerably in quality, but as a rule are far more concerned with describing sports events and, more commonly, the various technical aspects of the motor cycles themselves than they are business histories. Nor, as a rule, do they address the causes of the end of the industry in any depth.[19] Ironically, British motor cycles now seem to be the object of greater attention, as an integral part of the burgeoning 'industrial heritage industry', than they ever enjoyed while the factories still operated. Indeed, over the past three decades, the literature written for motor cycle enthusiasts has grown at a prolific rate.[20]

In a more general sense, motor cycles, whether manufactured in Britain or elsewhere, have attracted widespread attention, extending well beyond the ranks of enthusiasts. A recent show at the Guggenheim gallery in New York City entitled 'The Art of the Motorcycle', for example, drew tens of thousands of visitors and is currently touring internationally. That has also resulted in a 'coffee table' type book which understandably focuses more on design than on history.[21] Nor have the people who ride motor cycles been neglected. Motor cyclists, particularly the self-styled 'outlaws', have exercised considerable fascination, with both a popular as well as an academic audience, albeit more for North American than British readers.[22] There is also a strong and enduring interest in works of the 'true crime' genre related to motor cyclists and associated gang activity that reaches across both sides of the Atlantic.[23]

What all the literature, academic, popular or otherwise, lacks is a larger historical context, particularly for the years before 1945. This book seeks to fill the gap, and indeed it is no coincidence that its title quite consciously alludes to George Dangerfield's classic account of the unravelling of Edwardian England, *The Strange Death of Liberal England*.[24] Here, however, the intention is merely to explain the end of one industry, not an entire era.

This book will present an analysis based on a longer historical perspective in order to provide a fuller understanding of the various forces that caused the eventual collapse of the industry.[25] Such an understanding of the industry's final demise presupposes a thorough examination of its history during the pre-war era. During this period the British motor cycle industry consolidated its position as the world's leading producer, but at the same time adopted a manufacturing strategy that involved producing larger, comparatively expensive models which catered to a fairly limited market, one made up mostly of younger, working-class, male customers.

The industry chose this course of action in large part because of how it perceived the motor cycle market, both in Britain and abroad. During the 1920s and into the 1930s, however, some in the industry believed it should try to begin manufacturing smaller, cheaper models that would appeal to a wider range of consumers. These industry critics maintained that the smaller models would, among other things, attract female consumers, who had been hitherto an insignificant part of the market and had the potential to transform and enlarge the market.

Instead, as will be shown, the manufacturers were reluctant to consider alternatives to their traditional male market, one that preferred the larger, often sports-oriented motor cycles. They were also unwilling to take on the engineering and managerial challenges implicit with taking on a higher-volume 'small bike' manufacturing strategy. However, sticking with their lower-production 'big bike' strategy had implications for the manufacturers that reached well into the post-war era and would indeed become a major factor in the ultimate failure of the British motor cycle industry in the late 1960s and early 1970s.

In order to conduct such an analysis of the history of the British motor cycle industry, this book has drawn on a variety of sources, many not used before. In particular, extensive reference has been made to the records of the Motor Cycle Industry Association, only opened to researchers since the 1980s. This archive, currently on deposit at the Modern Records Centre at the University of Warwick, contains a comprehensive collection of minutes, guardbooks and other documentation which provides in-depth information about the industry for the entire period covered.

Unfortunately, the remaining archives of individual firms are not remotely as well preserved, nor have they been extensively used by other industry historians. Fragments of various financial records for BSA and Triumph have survived along with most of the former's Directors' Minute Books. Information on other firms has been obtained from either the secondary literature, the business and popular press or from annual reports on deposit at the Guildhall Library in London. Finally, the government's side on issues concerning foreign trade negotiations and on motor vehicle legislation was revealed in documents on deposit at the Public Record Office, now the National Archives (NA) in London.

Use of this newer material casts a different light on the industry's history. This book will argue that the collapse of the British motor cycle industry had far more to do with internal weaknesses and, more specifically, the consequences of the production strategy adopted during the inter-war years than it did with later, foreign competition. There is no one overriding cause; instead, a number of variables will be examined, ranging from managerial 'culture' (especially how those in the company boardrooms perceived markets), to government policy, labour relations and foreign competition to the peculiarities of the motor cycle market, both in Britain and abroad. No single factor can explain the death of the motor cycle industry adequately; rather, there were a variety of reasons, some external but most from within.

Finally, this book seeks to make a modest contribution to the burgeoning literature on the subject of British economic decline as a case study of a comparatively minor industry but one that for decades dominated world markets.[26] Moreover, it will take up the invitation contained in the conclusion of a more recent summary of literature on British economic decline. We are asked, in 'place of generalisations about "British" attitudes and "British" institutions', to produce 'close, empirical inquiries into actual British enterprises and their decision-makers'. What follows proposes to do just that.[27]

This book will especially focus on and analyse three major episodes in the history of the industry that were pivotal to both its initial development and ultimate fall. The first, and most important, is the drastic fall in the demand for motor cycles which occurred after 1929 and which lasted until 1939. The response of the industry to this crisis, how it tried to re-stimulate demand, and in particular its growing dependence as comparatively low-volume manufacturers of heavy-weight (350 cc to 500 cc engine displacement classes) motor cycles became a defining characteristic. Indeed, this characteristic would colour its responses to future changes in the market right through to its death throes during the early 1970s.

The second episode began in the years after 1945 when, with their pre-war competition temporarily knocked out of action or otherwise unable to satisfy demand for cheap personal motorised transport, British manufacturers were in a position once more to assert their world-wide supremacy. That they failed do so was the result of factors both in and out of their control. The third and final episode covers the period when international rivals, initially Germany and Italy and, subsequently and most important, Japan, resumed production and gradually undermined the position of British manufacturers, first at home and then abroad. By the early 1970s, the end of the industry had become virtually unavoidable.

These episodes will be examined chronologically. The opening chapter will provide some background information about the industry and describe its structure, some of the more important firms involved and the character of their management. It will review the relationship between the manufacturers and their dealerships as well as the trade association which governed the industry's internal functions including a tightly enforced system of retail price maintenance. Finally, there will be an examination of the causes for the crisis in demand that affected the industry from the late 1920s to 1939 and how the various manufacturers tried to overcome it, particularly by trying to enlarge their market to include more women.

The second chapter covers the war years between 1939 and 1945 and analyses government policy, especially what was termed 'Concentration of Production', which transformed the industry during the time in question. It will also review the use of the so-called 'Shadow Factories' as an important addition to its productive capacity along with how the manufacturers coped under the pressure of enemy bombing attacks, the military use of motor cycles during the conflict and the start of post-war planning.

Chapter 3 describes the period of reconstruction between 1945 and 1951 and explains how the industry and its various component firms converted back to peace time production in the context of post-war 'Austerity' era Britain. It will examine how some new export markets were opened but others lost; the sales strategies of individual companies; the potential gains offered through technology transfer from Germany via the Reparations Programme; and the industry's response to the Attlee Labour government's efforts to promote efficiency and standardisation.

The fourth chapter, covering the period between 1951 and 1956, addresses the impact of increased affluence in Britain – in particular the impact of greater numbers of cheap automobiles – on motor cycle sales. It will also show how public opinion began to turn against motor cycles, not the least because the mounting numbers of road accidents. Such social disapproval dampened the market, this at a time when there was a determined challenge to the industry's long-standing retail price maintenance system. Finally, it will explain how, for the first time, the home market was faced with growing numbers of imports, albeit mopeds and scooters rather than orthodox motor cycles.

The fifth chapter covers the period 1956 to 1961, especially the state of the industry in terms of factories and capital investment. At home, several companies introduced new models in order to counter the continuing influx of imports. Yet, mopeds and scooters aside, the industry was alarmed to discover that fewer and fewer consumers at home purchased British motor cycles, a reflection in part of the continuing public antagonism over motor cycle accidents and the perceived anti-social behaviour of the so-called 'Teddy Boys on Wheels' and 'Rockers'. Elsewhere there were changes throughout export markets, including a failed attempt by British manufacturers to open up the Japanese market and the closing down of the formerly lucrative Australian and Argentine markets, developments offset by the growth of the spectacularly successful North American market.

The sixth chapter follows two main developments, one being how the industry struggled through a home market sales recession that lasted for much of the 1960s, so severe that it even became the subject of a brief parliamentary debate. Poor home sales meant that the export trade became even more important than previously. Under these conditions, some firms performed less successfully than others, such that by 1970 essentially only two remained in business. The second development was the emergence of a comparatively new issue, increased levels of shop-floor labour unrest, although this mostly affected only one company, Coventry-based Triumph.

The final chapter explains the background of the Japanese motor cycle industry and then how, during the post-war era, it grew within twenty years from insignificance to a point where it threatened Britain's position as the world's premier motor cycle producer. During the 1960s, Japanese motor cycles soon appeared in large numbers on the British home market, thanks to the Anglo-Japanese trade agreement which removed the tariffs and import quotas which had previously protected British manufacturers. As the home market was gradually taken over by imports, the British motor cycle industry became more and more dependent on the export trade, especially the North American market. BSA, the larger of the two remaining manufacturers, tried to find a way out of its plight by launching an unexpected sales offensive against its Japanese rivals.

A brief epilogue outlines the collapse of virtually the whole industry in 1975, with the exception of a workers' co-operative near Coventry which carried on for a few more years. However, this was not the end of the industry, thanks to the rebirth of the Triumph motor cycle company since 1990. Once again Britain is producing competitive motor cycles, but now its output is at best marginal by international standards. Nonetheless, this modest motor cycle revival occurred when the British automobile industry, at least that part of it not wholly owned subsidiaries of foreign manufactures, has virtually disappeared.

Finally, a note on terminology: throughout this book the more traditional term 'motor cycle', which was commonly used in Britain from the birth of the industry through to the end of the 1960s, will be used in place of the modern spelling of 'motorcycle'.

CHAPTER ONE

British supremacy,
1935–1939

I N DECEMBER 1934 a special issue of the popular journal, *The Motor Cycle*, was devoted to the theme of 'British supremacy'. The issue was a celebration of the ascendancy of the British motor cycle industry over all international rivals. This supremacy could be seen, various articles in the issue claimed, in a number of ways. Not only were British motor cycle companies producing more than anyone else, but they were also represented as being ahead of all others in terms of design and workmanship.[1] In the sporting field especially, British products were described as particularly successful, winning race after race, both on home and foreign tracks.[2] Was there any truth behind these claims, or were they merely the puffing of some over-enthusiastic or perhaps xenophobic trade journalists?

The British motor cycle industry had emerged from the bicycle industry at around the turn of the century and, for a time, evolved alongside the motor car industry (production of motor cars only outstripped that of motor cycles in 1924). During the First World War, the industry suffered a setback when much of its productive capacity was diverted into munitions work, allowing American motor cycle companies to move into Dominion and Empire markets. After 1919, however, production grew rapidly, and British companies were able to regain the markets their American competitors had won during the war. By 1925 Britain was the world's undisputed volume producer and the biggest exporter, shipping abroad more motor cycles than all other rivals combined.[3] Indeed, such was the formidable reputation of British motor cycles, for example, that it was remarked they overshadowed the domestic competition in continental trade shows. In Italy, for a time, even Il Duce was accompanied by an escort of British-built motor cycles.[4]

Moreover, although the British motor cycle industry produced far less than its motor car counterpart, 125,000 units compared to 160,266 (worth £5,161,000 compared to £32,869,000) at the beginning of the 1930s, it was arguably a more successful industry in terms of international acceptability and prestige.[5] While motor car sales tended to be concentrated in the home, Empire and Dominion markets, British motor cycles sold in many areas where the former did not, a point that was remarked upon at the time.[6] In 1927, a reporter with the *Daily Telegraph* was moved to write:

> It is depressing to the motorist travelling on the Continent to meet so rarely a British-made motor-car, but everywhere the British motor-cycle is upon the roads, and the foreigner willingly concedes its superiority. In design, lightness, and efficiency it beats everything.[7]

In terms of the proportion of machines exported, the motor cycle industry far outdid its automobile counterpart. In 1929, for example, 62,377 out of a total 147,000 motor cycles, or approximately 42 per cent of production, was sent abroad. By comparison, that same year, the automobile industry exported only 23,891 out of a total of 182,347 cars, or 13 per cent of production (see tables 1 and 2). The contrast between international motor cycle and

Table 1 *British motor cycle registrations, production, imports and exports, 1919–1939*

	Registrations	Production	Exports	Imports
1919	114,722	65,000	8,330	1,481
1920	287,739	100,000	21,304	4,277
1921	373,200	80,000	8,104	2,130
1922	377,943	60,000	7,280	965
1923	430,138	80,000	16,156	1,011
1924	495,579	110,000	37,911	402
1925	558,911	120,000	47,114	867
1926	628,955	120,000	48,121	775
1927	681,410	160,000	53,000	149
1928	712,583	145,000	59,906	76
1929	724,319	147,000	62,377	103
1930	724,319	126,000	42,689	236
1931	626,649	74,700	23,247	108
1932	599,904	70,400	19,537	16
1933	562,656	52,200	17,731	16
1934	548,461	58,500	16,807	20
1935	521,128	64,700	18,000	–
1936	510,242	55,200	20,500	–
1937	491,718	82,014	25,400	200
1938	499,265	65,100	19,800	200
1939	–	66,400	18,900	100

Sources: BCMCMTU, *Review of the British Cycle and Motor Cycle Industry*, 1935; Michael Miller, 'The British Motor-Cycle Industry before 1939' (unpublished); and SMMT, *The Motor Industry of Great Britain*, 1939.

Table 2   *British motor car production, registrations, exports and imports,*
1919–1938

	Registrations	Production	Exports	Imports
1919	109,715	–	–	–
1920	186,801	–	4,294	–
1921	245,882	–	1,966	–
1922	319,311	–	1,338	12,992
1923	389,767	71,396	3,256	14,429
1924	482,356	116,600	11,007	10,800
1925	590,156	132,000	17,711	31,781
1926	695,64	153,500	14,858	10,923
1927	800,112	164,553	16,139	18,194
1928	900,557	165,352	18,192	22,582
1929	998,489	182,347	23,891	21,520
1930	1,075,081	169,669	19,226	9,751
1931	1,103,715	158,997	17,104	2,118
1932	1,149,231	171,244	26,942	2,762
1933	1,226,541	220,779	33,802	3,679
1934	1,333,590	256,566	34,877	10,851
1935	1,505,019	311,544	44,193	13,563
1936	1,675,104	353,838	51,173	12,323
1937	1,834,248	389,633	53,655	18,609
1938	1,984,430	342,390	44,130	–

Source: *The Motor Industry of Great Britain*, SMMT, 1939.

automobile producers was striking. Although the Americans overwhelmingly dominated the motor car manufacturing league, making over 5,000,000 units in 1929 compared to barely 200,000 units by number-two producer Britain, the situation was reversed with respect to motor cycles. The 147,000 units manufactured in 1929, compared to America's 31,900, meant that Britain was well ahead.[8]

It was also true that the motor cycle industry was far more secure in the home market, for although both industries were protected by the McKenna Duties, the motor car firms had more need of the tariff wall. In 1929 a mere 103 foreign motor cycles entered Britain compared with 21,520 foreign motor cars. During 1937 only 200 foreign motor cycles arrived compared to 18,609 cars.

A motor cycle for everyone

What was the industry producing during the 1930s? British motor cycle companies were notable for their varied and extensive product lines. British consumers had the widest choice of motor cycles anywhere in the world, ranging from small, single-cylinder machines to large displacement twins and even four-cylinder models.[9] As one industry leader boasted, it was 'literally true to say that there is no class of public or size of pocket which is not adequately catered for'. However, British consumers seemed to have a particularly marked preference for large, single-cylinder machines in the 350 cc and 500 cc displacement classes (see table 3). No doubt these larger machines were also necessary in order to haul the many sidecars on the road.[10]

Table 3   *Motor cycles registered during the year ending 30 September 1926*

	1933	1934	1935	1936	1937	1938
Solo motor cycles:						
up to 150 cc	21,068	25,703	27,124	30,703	31,809	32,867
150 cc–250 cc	131,706	137,193	134,904	136,500	135,469	131,620
over 250 cc	244,554	220,608	197,319	188,913	182,873	172,964
Combo units:						
up to 150 cc	24	13	27	45	58	51
150 cc–250 cc	1,315	1,634	1,241	1,295	996	930
over 250 cc	144,636	140,589	131,041	124,159	114,999	105,219
Tricycles	19,353	22,716	24,911	24,165	21,374	18,724
Total	562,656	548,461	516,567	505,779	487,578	462,375

Source: Ministry of Transport, 'Return showing the number of mechanically propelled vehicles registered for the first time under the Road Act, 1926'.

This inclination towards larger displacement motor cycles had been established right from the beginnings of the industry. In 1913, for example, models available to British consumers were in the 170 cc to 600 cc range, with the majority in the 350 cc to 500 cc classes. In 1921 the smallest engine displacement size on the market was still only 211 cc, and even as late as 1925, only one firm offered a machine under 100 cc (a 98 cc Alcyon). The predilection for larger sized motor cycles is suggestive of the fact that they often provided a cheaper substitute for the far more expensive motor cars, as well as being used for sports and touring purposes. Until the mid-1920s, even a small motor car cost between £250 and £500, while a good-quality 500 cc motor cycle side-car combination cost around £150.[11] Little wonder that a visiting American automotive engineer observed that motor cycles 'held the same position in England as Ford in America', and more specifically, 'that the class of people who possessed Fords in America have motor cycles in England'.[12]

The structure of the pre-war motor cycle industry

What was the structure of this highly successful industry during the period in question? In certain respects, the motor cycle industry shared some common characteristics with its motor car counterpart, having started with a vast number of firms of varying sizes and then slimmed down during the late 1920s and early 1930s. For example, in 1925 there were approximately 120 firms in Britain manufacturing motor cycles; by 1939 this total had fallen to 32.[13]

As in the motor car industry, several of the larger motor cycle companies, a so-called 'Big Six',[14] dominated, followed by a number of medium-sized firms, several of whom extensively used proprietary parts (mainly motors). There were also specialised firms who built expensive sports and touring machines, as well as three major proprietary engine manufacturers, the most prominent being Wolverhampton-based Villiers Engineering. Although there were companies, such as Rover, that built both cars and motor cycles at the turn of the century, these links had been largely severed by the 1920s.

Most of the firms in the industry were privately owned, and only a few of them were registered on the stock market. In marked contrast with the motor car industry, ownership and management was exclusively British and would remain so during the entire period covered by this book. The industry shared a number of general supply and accessory firms with its motor car counterpart, such as Dunlop for tyres and Joseph Lucas for electrical components, although the motor cycle factories were capable of producing a great deal of in-house work, a point noted at the time.[15]

The 'Big Six' accounted for a very large proportion of the industry's production. Indeed, it has been estimated that two firms alone manufactured slightly over 60 per cent of gross output.[16] Of the 'Six', BSA (Birmingham Small Arms) was the clear market leader (a position it had held since the early 1920s), producing between 12,000 and 18,000 machines per year for much of the 1930s, or around 20–25 per cent of total British motor cycle output.[17] As for the others, they continually jockeyed for the number-two position, which regularly changed from year to year.[18] All of the 'Big Six' were located in the Midlands, more particularly the Birmingham/Coventry/Redditch area, with the exception of Matchless (Associated Motor Cycles – AMC – after 1937) which was based in London.

Matchless had been founded by the Collier family in the late nineteenth century, originally as a bicycle maker, and had branched out into motor cycles by the turn of the century. In the late 1920s Matchless manufactured a full range of machines, from 250 cc to 1000 cc engine displacement, with a particular emphasis on the 350 cc to 500 cc, single-cylinder classes. It also supplied motor car companies such as Morgan with proprietary engine units.[19]

During 1932, with the sponsorship of the Ariel Motor Co., which provided him with one of their 500 cc Red Hunter machines, J. Graham Oates rode 4,000 miles across Canada, mostly over poor and sometimes almost non-existent roads. Motor cycle companies, then and now, often used such sponsored rides in order to underscore the robustness and reliability of their machines.

COURTESY OF ED MOODY

Mr. Graham Oates on his "Red Hunter"

ARIEL

12,000 MILES OF UNPARALLELED RELIABILITY

"OUTFIT RAN PERFECTLY THROUGHOUT"

This Ariel combination (weighing over 800 lbs.) travelled farther north in Canada than any rubber-tyred vehicle.
5,000 miles in 9 days. Temperature below zero.
1,500 miles in 56 hours. Atrocious roads.
Capable of a mile a minute at the conclusion of the most gruelling test to which any motor cycle has been put.

Ariel does it again!

In 1931 a rival manufacturer, AJS, a Wolverhampton-based firm which had diversified into radios and commercial vehicles, went into receivership. Matchless picked up the motor cycle end of the business, shut down the Wolverhampton factory and moved the production facilities to its factory in Woolwich, east London. There Matchless continued to manufacture, side by side, two essentially identical lines of motor cycle, one badged as Matchless, the other AJS, a practice it would follow until the mid-1960s. This policy, commonly known as 'badge engineering', was also carried on by other motor cycle companies.[20]

Throughout the late 1920s, Matchless was profitable. In 1929, for example, it returned healthy profits and distributed dividends of 12½ per cent. Profits declined at the onset of the Depression, although by 1934 the company was able to pay out dividends of 5 per cent. Recovery was due, in part, to the company's proprietary engine work (which also included aircraft components) and to its re-entry in the bicycle trade.[21]

Another major firm was Ariel Motors, based in Birmingham. Founded by Charles Sangster during the late nineteenth century as a bicycle and bicycle components manufacturer, by the 1920s it had evolved into the more diversified Cycle Components Manufacturing Company. Owned by Sangster, the firm had expanded into motor cycle and motor car production, along with a variety of other related activities. However, Cycle Components Manufacturing Company was hit hard by the Depression and went into receivership in 1931. Charles Sangster's son, Jack, who was then general manager of the motor cycle and automotive end of the business, was able to negotiate an arrangement with the receiver whereby he took over the rights to motor cycle production along with a good part of its plant and equipment.[22]

This advertisement, dating from sometime in the 1920s, promotes a Triumph motor cycle side-car combination unit.

Jack Sangster, who would in time become the industry's single most dominant figure, had been educated at Hurstpierpoint College in West Sussex and served an engineering apprenticeship at the Triumph motor cycle factory in Nuremberg, Germany. After the war, he worked in the motor car industry (he designed the Rover Eight) and then returned to his father's company. Under his direction, the new firm, Ariel Motors (JS), was established at a factory in Selly Oak, Birmingham. The company produced a wide range of motor cycles, mostly single-cylinder machines from 250 cc to 995 cc engine displacement but also an innovative four-cylinder machine which was produced in limited numbers.[23]

The Triumph Cycle Co. also had its origins in the bicycle trade. Founded by a German Jew, Siegfried Bettmann, who had immigrated to England from Nuremberg in the 1880s, the company subsequently moved into motor cycle manufacturing in the early 1900s. Based at a multi-storey factory in the centre of Coventry, Triumph offered a limited range of machines, mostly in the single cylinder, 250 cc to 500 cc classes. During the 1920s, Triumph commenced motor car manufacture so that its factory simultaneously produced motor bicycles, motor cycles and cars. It was the latter which brought the company down. An ill-fated decision to manufacture higher priced models left the company's finances in a shambles. In 1934 it carried over a huge debt from the previous year and appeared to be on the edge of bankruptcy.[24]

The Enfield Cycle Co. was founded as a bicycle manufacturer during the late nineteenth century in Redditch. A contract to provide rifle parts to the Royal Small Arms factory in Enfield led to the adoption of the name 'Royal Enfield' for its bicycles and later motor cycles. The company was led by Managing Director Robert Walker Smith, whose son Frank was Assistant Managing Director. After the former's death in 1933, Frank Smith became Managing Director, a position he would hold for the next thirty years. Enfield produced a modest but comprehensive range of models, from a 250 cc, single cylinder machine to a 1000 V-twin. Like the other manufacturers, however, its best sellers were mostly single-cylinder models in the 350 cc to 500 cc classes.[25]

Norton was probably the lowest-volume producer of the 'Big Six'. Founded by James L. Norton at the turn of the century, it had at first supplied the bicycle trade but quickly moved on to motor cycles. Although initially owned privately by Norton, the company had experienced severe financial troubles in 1913. It was picked up in an auction by Bob Shelly, owner of R.J. Shelly, a machining concern that was a major Norton creditor. Shelly was in turn owned by C.A. Vandervell & Company, a leading magneto manufacturer and an important Norton supplier. Although James Norton stayed on the company board, Charles Vandervell became Chairman of the renamed Norton Motors Ltd, which continued to be privately owned.[26]

The Isle of Man TT races are among the oldest and most demanding motor cycle sporting events in the world, where the island's bumpy and varied road circuit pushes both machine and rider to extremes of performance. The manufacturers often claimed that the technology developed for the highly tuned competition machines would ultimately trickle down and improve their everyday production models.

Of all the major producers, Norton had the most limited model line up, mostly in the 350 cc to 500 cc range, all single-cylinder machines.[27] It was also the one most oriented towards motor cycle sport. Indeed, this company probably fielded more successful race track participants in Britain or anywhere else. Between 1926 and 1939, at least one Norton finished in the top three places at the Isle of Man TT, at that time the world's premier road race event.[28]

Industry management and motor cycle sports

Norton was not unique in its close involvement with the race track. There were important implications for nearly all firms relating to sporting success. Many thought that there was a close linkage between the industry, motor sports and consumers. One technical journal noted that there were 'undoubted commercial advantages that follow upon success in this [the TT] and other trials of a sports character', and indeed it was judged a 'ruling factor'. As a trade journal observed, emphasis on sporting events was 'a useful device in breaking down sales resistance'. Thus, a firm whose motor cycles did well at the TT was almost certain to enjoy improved sales shortly afterwards.[29]

A second aspect of race track activity that attracted the industry was its role as a surrogate form of research and development. It was generally acknowledged that the TT was in effect a 'testing ground', acting as a means of improving motor cycle performance and reliability under the most severe of conditions, a conviction that many in the industry would hold for decades to come.[30] Brakes, frames and transmissions and road-holding qualities in general had, it was believed, all been improved as a direct benefit of the trial and error process that had taken place during race after race. As one expert asserted during a meeting of the Institution of Automobile Engineers, 'there can be no possible doubt that road racing has come more to improve the breed than any other single item'. Moreover, in the absence of any extensive research and development facilities, the track was, many believed, an excellent substitute.[31]

It was also true that many throughout the industry's management were keen motor cycle enthusiasts. Brothers Harry and Charles Collier, sons of Matchless founder Henry Collier, who would become the company's joint managing directors, regularly rode motor cycles. Indeed, Harry Collier raced semi-professionally and had a distinguished career at the TT. Donald Heather, a Matchless company director during this time, was unusual among the industry's senior management by virtue of his higher education (an engineering degree from London University). He also regularly rode a motor cycle and attended sports activities. At Ariel Motors, owner Jack Sangster had a successful career as a trials rider before the First World War and subsequently continued to ride whenever possible. Enfield Cycle Managing Director Frank Smith was also an active motor cyclist and James Norton raced semi-professionally for several years before 1914 and during the early 1920s, as part of a publicity campaign to increase sales in South Africa, rode one of his company's motor cycle side-car combinations across the country.[32]

The industry's top leadership was proud of its personal involvement and dedication to motor cycling. Indeed, managers often made a point of letting their customers know that they too shared an equal interest in motor cycle activities, especially sports. In 1939, for example, a number of managing directors rode their motor cycles in a procession to the Donnington race track at the season's opening. Attending these events undoubtedly gave the industry's leaders an opportunity to mix with many of the people who either already owned their motor cycles or might soon be buying a new model. No doubt it also gave them a first-hand insight into any upcoming changes in market demand. However, one suspects that they would have been there anyhow, commercial advantage or not.[33]

Leadership at BSA

While the other 'Big Six' firms were frequently owned and managed by motor cycle enthusiasts, BSA was the notable exception. No doubt this owed much to the fact that BSA had always been far more than a motor cycle manufacturer. Originally founded in the mid-nineteenth century as a small arms manufacturer, it had subsequently expanded into bicycles and then motor cars (Daimler and Lanchester), steel, machine tools and other businesses, which gave it access to resources unavailable to the other firms.[34]

The differences between BSA and the other 'Big Six' firms were also reflected in its board, which often included well-known figures from business and political circles. The various chairmen during this period, Sir Hallewell Roger (1906–28), Sir Edward Manville (1928–32), Arthur Pollen (1932) and Sir Alexander Roger (1932–40), were all engaged in a variety of activities besides BSA. Two of them, for example, were MPs, and all the others held senior positions with national banks or organisations such as the Federation of British Industries (FBI).[35]

Sir Patrick ('Paddy') Hannon was typical in many ways. He served on the BSA board between 1923 and 1957 and was vice-chairman for a good portion of the period. He was especially well connected in the political world. A long-time parliamentarian, Hannon represented the Moseley district in Birmingham for the Conservative Party between 1921 and 1950. He was a close associate of Neville Chamberlain, the future prime minister who had also been on the BSA board as Managing Director of BSA Cycles, which covered both the motor cycle and bicycles subsidiaries, during the early 1920s.[36]

Other board members during this time had similar backgrounds. Lord Eugene Ramsden, long-time Unionist MP for Bradford North, was Chairman of the National Union of Conservative and Unionist Associations during 1938–39 and a director of the Lloyds Bank. Sir Francis Joseph was President of the FBI in 1935 and a director of the Midland Bank. Commander G. Herbert, who was Managing Director of BSA Cycles, left the company in 1935 to become a director of Standard Motors, where his brother-in-law R.W. Maudslay was chairman and founder. Although he was not actually on the board for most of the 1920s and 1930s, former director Dudley Docker, one of Britain's leading business figures, remained highly influential, and was often consulted about company affairs.[37]

Nor was the question of leadership all that separated BSA from the other firms. Not only was it the industry's biggest producer, but it also offered the most comprehensive model line-up available in Britain, or anywhere else for that matter. This breadth of production was a point of some pride to the company and Chairman Hallewell Roger once informed shareholders that the secret of its success was the ability to provide a 'thoroughly reliable range of machines of almost every kind, fit for any purpose, by any person of any age in any country and at almost any price'.[38] (See table 4.)

Table 4   *Type of BSA motor cycle sold, by displacement size, 1929–1938*

	up to 150 cc	150 to 250 cc	over 250 cc	Total
1926	–	11,057	18,042	29,099
1927	–	8,878	19,125	28,003
1928	–	4,851	14,927	19,778
1929 *	–	4,884	18,871	23,755
1930	–	6,320	18,713	25,033
1931	–	1,880	10,514	12,394
1932	–	357	12,216	12,573
1933	–	3,455	7,524	10,979
1934	1,501	5,995	7,532	15,028
1935	776	5,118	7,836	13,730
1936	650	6,593	8,848	16,091
1937	9	6,679	11,875	18,563
1938	2	4,759	8,824	13,585

* First nine months of 1929 only.

Source: MSS 19A/2/37 (Modern Records Centre).

Yet by the beginning of the 1930s BSA seemed to be drifting into serious financial difficulties. Although the company paid out a dividend of 5 per cent for the year ending 31 July 1930, that was the last time for several years that shareholders saw any direct return on their investment. The Depression hurt the company, but much of its trouble seems to have been generated by general disorganisation and, more particularly, bitter dissension among board members.[39]

Relations between Chairman Manville and Percy Martin, Managing Director of the Daimler motor car subsidiary, were particularly strained. At one highly emotional meeting, Manville was reduced to tears after a dispute with Martin, although he was then rounded on by Arthur Pollen, for 'upsetting the whole internal organisation of the company by his impulsive and dictatorial methods'.[40] In a letter written in 1933, Hannon recalled that board business over the past few years had been 'conducted in such an atmosphere in which, to put it mildly, feeling of mutual confidence and accommodation was not a conspicuous feature'.[41]

Both Pollen and Martin soon left the company, and the new chairman Alexander Roger was able to convince his fellow board members to work together more effectively. However, the company still appeared to function at less than full potential. The various subsidiaries, although disparate, could have been combined into a more cohesive group of mutually reinforcing units. This did not happen. In 1937 Chairman Roger circulated a memorandum to other board members noting that the various subsidiaries were not only separate geographically, but 'in essence their products are so diverse as to enable one to say they have little or no relation to each other'.[42] As will be seen later, poor coordination within the various parts of the BSA Group would remain an intractable problem right up until the end.[43]

The remaining motor cycle companies were a mixed bag. Many of the medium-sized firms produced a fairly extensive product line in their own right, albeit often at a higher price than those of the 'Big Six'. Companies such as Velocette, Douglas and Rudge provided fairly sophisticated larger displacement machines, many of which catered to racing enthusiasts at correspondingly higher prices. There were a number of firms, such as Francis-Barnett, James and Excelsior, which manufactured lighter weight machines and were heavily dependent on several proprietary engine manufacturers, especially Villiers Engineering.

As with the larger companies, these firms tended to be owned and managed by motor cycle enthusiasts who often were directly involved in the design, production and testing of their own products. Three examples illustrate this point. Eric Barnett, son of Francis & Barnett founder Arthur Barnett, joined the firm in 1920, being appointed a director eight years later. A keen enthusiast, he participated in sports events such as the Scottish Six Days trials and the Colmore Cup. Ernest Humphries was the long-time managing director of OK Supreme, a family-owned firm. As early as 1899, he was building his own motor cycles, one of which was raced in the 1912 Junior TT. Finally, virtually the entire Goodman family, owners of Velocette, were dedicated motor cycle enthusiasts. Brothers Percy and Eugene Goodman were, respectively, managing director and works director. The former was a familiar sight on various race tracks, a tradition kept up by Eugene's son Peter, who headed the company's competitions team until he was injured while racing in 1948.[44]

Henry Richard Watling, 1885–1961

One of the British motor cycle industry's most significant personalities, H.R. Watling was the Director of the British Motor Cycle and Cycle Manufacturers' and Traders' Union between 1919 and 1953.

He qualified as a solicitor in 1906 and several years later became legal counsel for the Roads Board. Like so many of his generation, Watling's career was interrupted by the outbreak of war in 1914. He joined the British army and served in the trenches with the 16th West Yorkshire regiment. Along the way he reached the rank of Major, a well-earned title that he would continue to use for the rest of his life.

Upon demobilisation in 1919, Major Watling was hired by the Manufacturers' Union as its Director. Created in 1910, this was a kind of federation of firms who were engaged in the motor cycle and bicycle trades, representing manufacturers as well as makers of proprietary items and accessories.

To the general public, the Manufacturers' Union was best known for organising the annual Motor Cycle Show, as its successor, the Motor Cycle Industry Association, does to this day.

However, behind the scenes, the Manufacturers' Union also ran a controversial system of retail price maintenance, one that Major Watling had been instrumental in creating. This system also regulated business dealings throughout the industry and set out the conditions for retailing motor cycles in Britain. These had been put into effect by the industry during the late 1920s in order to dampen down what was considered to be 'harmful' or 'disruptive' competition, although some critics thought retail price maintenance simply amounted to price-fixing.

For decades Major Watling was the Manufacturers' Union's chief enforcer. Besides ensuring that retail prices stayed in line, he also inspected motor cycle shops to ensure the premises were kept tidy and stocked with sufficient parts and accessories. If they were not, Watling administered the punitive measures that were brought against the miscreants.

Major Watling's job involved other duties as well. He was a key figure in the negotiations that the industry conducted with government departments including the Ministry of Transportation and the Board of Trade. Major Watling was responsible for arguing the industry's case on legislation and taxation and enjoyed some degree of success, such as when Philip Snowden, the Chancellor of the Exchequer, gave tax breaks for smaller motor cycles in the 1932 budget.

However, Watling scored his greatest successes helping to develop the industry's export markets. He made a number of visits abroad in order to drum up business for British manufacturers, especially around Continental Europe. Long before anyone else, Watling saw the potential of opening up the North American market and made a comprehensive tour of the region as early as 1927. Unfortunately, for reasons beyond his control, it took until after 1945 before British motor cycles sold in any significant numbers there.

Major Watling was well respected but not always admired. He defied conventional wisdom through his outspoken criticism of the industry's deeply ingrained devotion to motor sports. Nor was Watling afraid of taking other unpopular stands, such as during the 1930s when he championed the cause of female motor cyclists, taking a position that put him well outside the industry's mainstream.

Motor cycle dealers resented Watling's close scrutiny of their operations and sometimes called him a dictator. There were others, particularly civil servants and politicians, who came to dislike his brisk and sometimes less-than-diplomatic manner. Indeed, there were certain Whitehall officials who probably would rather have not had any contact with him at all.

Still, the fact that he stayed in his job for 34 years speaks for itself, and Major Watling's influence on the British motor cycle industry was probably second only to its leading executive, Jack Sangster (see page 54).

The British Cycle and Motor Cycle Manufacturers' and Traders' Union

The industry was represented by a trade association, the British Cycle and Motor Cycle Manufacturers' and Traders' Union ('the Manufacturers' Union'), whose membership included virtually all enterprises connected in one way or another to the production or retailing of bicycles and motor cycles.[45] The Manufacturers' Union, based in Coventry, had a number of functions including organising the annual motor cycle show (open only to its members for display purposes), representing the views of the industry with respect to legislation and taxation, general parliamentary activities and other dealings with government including the matters of tariff and import rates. The Manufacturers' Union arranged for intelligence reports on overseas markets and general advertising campaigns, as well as technical coordination through bodies such as the British Motor Cycle and Cyclecar Research Association. The Manufacturers' Union also worked closely with the Auto Cycle Union, a branch of the Royal Automobile Club (RAC), to regulate approved sporting events.[46]

The Manufacturers' Union's chief executive body was the Management Committee, composed of representatives elected at the Annual General Meeting. It met on a regular, usually monthly, basis. There were also subsidiary groups such as the Motor Cycle Manufacturers' Section, along with similar bodies for proprietary article manufacturers and exporters, designed to deal with problems specific to those members. The Manufacturers' Union's president, elected from among delegates at the annual general meeting, was usually a senior executive from one of the affiliated firms. In fact, virtually every significant managing director served as the Manufacturers' Union president at some time. There was also a small permanent staff, headed by a director. Between 1919 and 1953, the director was Major H.R. Watling, a man who became well known to manufacturers and retailers, as well as Whitehall civil servants, through the course of his duties.[47]

At the heart of the Manufacturers' Union's authority over the industry was the Bond and an interlocking series of Agreements that all members had to sign as a condition of membership. The Bond required all members to follow the rules of the Manufacturers' Union, preventing them from participation or support of any advertising, commercial shows or sporting activity which it had not officially sanctioned. Infractions of union rules would invariably result in stiff fines and other penalties, which were enforced through the offices of an associated organisation, the Cycle Trade Union (CTU). The CTU had available to it an arsenal of measures to punish breaches of the Bond and Agreements, including fines and placement on a 'Stop List' (that prevented other Union affiliates from having any dealing whatsoever with a wrongdoer).[48] The Bond also set the terms and conditions of the allowable discounts and rebates that could be offered by manufacturers to their retailers, as well as by the retailers to the public.[49]

In essence this system, reinforced by the agreements between the Manufacturers' Union, manufacturers, component makers and factors, prevented any motor cycle from being sold at a lower price by any retailer. It also prevented, among other things, a retailer from selling motor cycles acquired from a manufacturer who was outside the Manufacturers' Union and vice versa. This system had been created in the mid-1920s as a response to falling profit levels. Starting as an agreement limited to several firms, by the 1930s it had been adopted as a means of stabilising the industry by all Union affiliates.[50]

Was this price maintenance in fact price fixing? The Manufacturers' Union did not think so and vehemently asserted that price maintenance was fair and voluntary, created in the best interests of all concerned, whether they be manufacturers, retailers or consumers.[51] The manufacturers' protests to the contrary notwithstanding, even though the Manufacturers' Union's files do not contain much material directly relating to price fixing, there remains strong evidence that it did in fact take place until outlawed during the 1950s.

The Manufacturers' Union was a profit-making institution in its own right, thanks to its sponsorship of many successful annual motor cycle shows. Union bank balances were always well into the black, and throughout nearly all the period in question, it possessed financial resources measured in tens of thousands of pounds, which continued to grow year by year. For example, in 1934 its balance was £69,561, a total which had jumped to £77,888 by 1939.[52]

Public interest in the industry was catered for by a popular motor cycle press aimed primarily at enthusiasts. Two magazines, *The Motor Cycle* and *Motor Cycling*, dominated the market, although there was also a weekly industry journal, the *Cycle and Motor Cycle Trader*, which had a circulation restricted to the manufacturers and retailers, a fact which made its pages echo with more frankly stated opinions than were found in the other two.[53] The two popular journals enjoyed a close relationship with the industry. It was not uncommon, for example, for their editors to be invited to important Manufacturers' Union meetings in order to put forward their views. Nor was it unusual for members of the press to jump to the industry or back again.[54]

Foreign competition between the wars

During the inter-war era, the British faced two major international competitors, the USA and Germany, who each offered very different products to their clientele. The American industry had been robust until just after the First World War, when it had made significant incursions into

A range of British-made motor cycles on display at the 1914 Canadian National Exhibition in Toronto. Despite being part of the British Empire, unlike other Dominions such as Australia, sales of British motor cycles in Canada only reached substantial levels after 1945.

many important British export markets. American firms were subsequently devastated by the appearance of cheap cars, notably the Ford Model T, which had flooded on to the roads after 1913, severely undercutting both their home market and competitiveness abroad.[55]

When the Manufacturers' Union Director, Major H.R. Watling, visited North America in 1928 he found the American industry in steep decline, mostly because of the growing numbers of cheap cars. He also discovered that American motor cyclists suffered from a correspondingly poor image. They were often referred to by many of the general public as so-called 'greaseballs', men who, Watling wrote, 'invariably looked dirty, dusty and disheveled – a subject of scorn amongst men and a matter for mockery amongst women'.[56] Consequently, by the late 1930s, only two companies, Harley-Davidson and Indian, had survived. While the American motor cycle market had shrunk radically in size, the two companies continued to have some limited, albeit wavering, success in overseas markets, mainly in the Americas and British Dominions such as Canada and Australia. Because American motor cycles were invariably large, powerful (and higher priced) machines designed for long distances and rough roads, they were popular in underdeveloped areas such as the outback and prairies.[57]

The German industry, a leader before 1914, had gradually progressed during the 1920s and, in terms of overall production, had actually overtaken the British industry in 1929. However, aggregate figures were misleading, since much of Germany's powered two-wheel production comprised small-capacity machines primarily in the 50 cc to 100 cc range, which was in turn a reflection of relatively lower domestic purchasing power in their home market. Consequently, these machines were popular with the middle classes, acting in effect as a substitute for light-weight motor cars.[58] The German industry included a greater number of firms than the American, but offered a more diversified product line, although less extensive than the British. Devastated by the 1929 crash, it quickly recovered after 1933, thanks to the supportive nature of National Socialist transport policies. German production overtook the British once again in the middle of the decade and this again reflected the success of the cheaper, small capacity machines (see table 5).[59]

Table 5   *Production totals for the three major motor cycle manufacturing nations*

	1925	1929	1933	1935	1937
Britain	120,000	146,700	52,200	63,100	82,014
Germany	55,980	201,000	53,400	123,100	171,239
USA	45,000	31,900	7,400	14,110	17,700

Sources: *Review of the British Cycle and Motor Cycle Industry*, Coventry: BCMCMTU, 1925; Imperial Economic Committee, Thirtieth Report, *Survey of the Trade in Motor Vehicles*, London: HMSO, 1936; US Strategic Bombing Survey, *German Motor Vehicle Industry*, Washington, Munitions Division, 1947; Harry Sucher, *Harley-Davidson – The Milwaukee Marvel*, Sparkford: Haynes, 1990; *idem, The Iron Redskin*, Sparkford: Haynes, 1990.

Sales crisis in the home market

If there was real substance to the claims of 'British Supremacy' in the motor cycle world, it was equally true that the industry suffered from a number of serious weaknesses which could not be glossed over. Indeed, its supremacy had been undermined from the late 1920s onwards, and by 1935 the industry found itself in the middle of a severe crisis.

In brief, home and export markets had suffered a massive drop in sales and motor cycle usage. Between 1929 and 1934, overall production had halved, from 120,000 to 60,000 units; meanwhile, the number of motor cycle registrations (the index of the motor cycles in actual use in Great Britain) had declined from an all-time high of 790,000 to 540,000 units; and exports had virtually collapsed, falling from 62,377 to 16,807 units (although, in relative terms, British exports still remained greater than those of her rivals). Of course, some of the drop could be attributed to the world-wide depression, which had hit other businesses equally hard. Yet the motor car industry, while suffering initially, had recovered by 1935 and was enjoying record sales. What was happening in the market? Why had British and overseas consumers stopped buying motor cycles at the previous rate?

For some time the motor cycle had enjoyed certain advantages over the automobile. In this purchase price was one key factor. Until the early 1920s even a smaller new motor car cost between £250 and £500, a cyclecar (a three wheeled automobile-like vehicle) approximately £220, while a good-quality 500 cc motor cycle combination sold for around £150.[60] Little wonder that when, shortly after 1918, a visiting American automotive engineer observed motor cycles 'held the same position in England as Ford in America', and 'that the class of people who possessed Fords in America have motor cycles in England'.[61]

Motor cycle owners also paid lower taxes. In 1924 one motor cycle advocate boasted that the would-be motor cyclist need only pay an annual road tax of £4 (compared to £6 for a motor car); then there was the advantage of lower fuel consumption.[62] Moreover, many believed the garaging issue provided an additional advantage for two wheels over four.[63] At a meeting of the Institution of Automobile Engineers during the early 1920s, for example, one participant claimed that the majority of the working classes 'will, for the sheer joy of using the open road, purchase something. The motor cycle with the detachable side-car is the only machine they can possibly have for convenient garaging,' and would remain popular 'as long as mankind is forced to live in houses with restricted accommodation,' a common feature for those living among Britain's crowded urban areas.[64]

Even the fact that a motor cycle often demanded relatively more mechanical maintenance than a motor car was not necessarily considered a drawback. As another proponent of motorised two-wheeled transport noted: 'The motorist is content with a much lower standard of performance than the great majority of motor cyclists. The car, to its owner, is simply a means to an end, an invention for comparatively rapid movement, expected to function with as little attention as the train receives from its passengers.'[65] On the other hand, motor cycle ownership involved specific costs of its own:

Although this Toronto motor cycle shop seems prosperous, like its counterparts back in Britain, by the mid-1920s motor cycle sales had begun to suffer in comparison with those of automobiles. Consumers preferred the latter in terms of price, their superior passenger carrying capacity and overall convenience.

COURTESY OF ED MOODY

motor cyclists had to purchase riding gear, such as gloves, a riding coat, rain gear and boots, which were unnecessary for car owners.

Two major factors underlay the shift in consumer preference away from the motor cycle. One was the continued decline of motor car prices, especially with models such as the Austin Seven and Ford Y. In contrast, those of motor cycles had remained relatively constant, so eroding their original price advantage.[66] The second factor was the continuing technical improvements occurring in the motor car industry: electric starters, all-metal bodies (providing better weather protection) and vastly improved suspension systems were just some of features now frequently added as standard to even economy cars.[67]

By comparison, motor cycles had remained technologically unchanged and continued to demand more of their operators. They had to be kick-started; there was no effective protection against inclement weather; suspension systems were questionable; and they were by nature inherently unstable.[68] Carrying capacity, even with a side-car, was still less than that offered by the smallest standard motor car. Despite the best efforts of designers, motor cycle riders and their pillion companions remained far more vulnerable to injury than if they were in a motor car.

Motor cycles had also suffered in relation to motor cars in terms of social acceptability and prestige. Ownership of a two-wheeled vehicle simply did not have the same cachet that increasingly came with ownership of four-wheeled transport. Writing in a popular journal, one motor cyclist had to admit that his chosen mode of travel put him at a disadvantage. 'I must agree,' he noted, 'that occasionally people in business are rather inclined to look down their noses at a fellow who turns up on a motor cycle.'[69] Although the industry did its best to promote continued use of its products on the grounds of cheaper running costs, this appeared to have become a losing battle.[70]

It was the matter of price that was probably the most important determining factor in the choices British consumers made between a car and a motor cycle (with or without a side-car), notwithstanding hire/purchase schemes and low deposits. As the motor car industry adapted more and more to American-style systems of mass production, the type of motor car bought by British consumers changed. There was a sharp increase in the sales of models with ratings of less than ten horse power. Indeed, between 1929 and 1936 the numbers of these machines registered for road use increased by 236,353 to 842,514, that is by 256 per cent.[71]

Higher volume production was followed by lower prices. Moreover, there was also a concurrent development which was probably just as, or perhaps even more, damaging to motor cycle sales. This was the growth of the used car market, which seriously undercut the economy appeal of the motor cycle.[72]

This comparison was especially acute in the competition between motor cycle side-car combinations and light cars such as the Austin Seven (users of solo motor cycles would not necessarily be as tempted to switch their machines for a four-wheeled vehicle). In the late 1920s, there was still a distinct price advantage between a 350 cc motor cycle combination and a used eight-horse power car. Ten years later, however, this difference had nearly vanished. Indeed, registration figures of motor cycle combinations show a consistent deterioration, far more acute than those of solo motor cycles (see tables 6 and 7).[73]

Table 6   *Motor cycle combination and Austin Seven prices compared,*
1922–1928

	Austin Seven £	BSA 550 cc £	Triumph 550 cc £	Ariel 500 cc £
1922	225	142	155	125
1923	165	100	115 17s.	107
1924	155	85 10s.	107	90
1925	141	87	88 5s.	77 10s.
1926	145	74	82 17s.	71 10s.
1927	145	n/a	67 12s.	71 10s.
1928	125	66 10s.	–	66 10s.

Source: Roy Church, *Herbert Austin. The British Motor Car Industry to 1941*, London: Europa Publications, 1979.

Table 7   *Comparisons of prices of new motor-cycle combinations with*
second-hand cars: selected years

Sales Season	1929/30	1931/32	1933/34	1936/37
Comparison I				
1. Price of a new 350 cc combination	£63.3	£64.7	£66.0	£68.1
2. Price of a 2-year-old 8 hp car	£81.2	£73.1	£66.1	£66.6
Comparison II				
1. Price of a new 500 cc combination.	–	£72.9	£74.7	£79.3
2. Price of a 3-year-old car not exceeding 10 hp	–	£72.2	£65.4	£68.5
Ratio: 2:1	n/a	.99	.88	.86

Source: M. Miller, *The British Motor-Cycle Industry before 1939*.

Much the same phenomenon was occurring in key overseas markets as well. In Australia and New Zealand, for example, motor cycle retailers informed British manufacturers that sales had been hurt by four-wheeled competition. In one instance, an Australian dealer described how increasing numbers of second-hand Austin Sevens were threatening the motor cycle trade. However, he warned, it was the '2nd hand American car market' that most impeded motor cycle sales. Formerly, he continued, 'it was the custom of many motor cyclists to buy first a solo machine, then a side-car outfit, and eventually a motor car. A large percentage of them now begin by purchasing solo machines, and sooner or later acquire cars without becoming buyers of sidecars.'[74] Nor was this process exclusive in what were then called the 'White Dominions'. A report received from East Africa at around the same time noted that: 'In the old days most chieftains rode Sunbeam bicycles and the sons rode Raleigh bicycles. Nowadays, the Raleigh is common amongst the natives and the Chieftains use American cars, whilst the sons ride motor cycles.'[75]

While motor cycle manufacturers saw the top end of their markets, at home and abroad, eaten away by cheaper cars, they also encountered a similar problem at the bottom end. During the late 1920s, there was a phenomenal increase in bicycle usage in Britain, and by the mid-1930s there were thought to be anywhere up to fourteen million of them in use.[76] At an average price of between £3 and £5 each, bicycles met a need for personal transport among those in urban or suburban areas who were not satisfied with public transport. No doubt many of these commuters could not afford either a car or a motor cycle.[77]

Critics of the British motor cycle industry

Critics of the state of the industry were found in three general groupings. First, there were those inside the industry, whether from particular firms or from the retail end of the business, who thought that more motor cycles could be sold, given a change of attitude from those who manufactured and distributed them. Second, there were technical people such as engineers and press commentators disturbed by the lack of progress in the industry, who made numerous and unfavourable comparisons between Britain, Italy and Germany. Finally, there were those offended by the fundamental character of motor cycles, especially their noise as well as the manner in which their riders operated them. These latter critics tended to be ordinary citizens, members of organisations such as the Anti-Noise League and the Pedestrian Association, although they also included sections of the trade and business press, the judiciary and parliamentarians.

The criticism boiled down to two major issues. Growing numbers of the public had become increasingly irritated by the level of noise created by motor cycles during sports events, never mind during normal use or in the hands of over-enthusiastic riders. Government officials received complaint after complaint about the noise and disruption caused by rallies, trials, beach racing and so forth. There was also public uproar about the hazards of pillion riding, the high fatality rate among young motor cyclists, as well as the dangers they created for other road users by reckless riding habits or who

THE STRANGE DEATH OF THE BRITISH MOTOR CYCLE INDUSTRY

otherwise made a nuisance of themselves, including those riders popularly known as 'Promenade Percys'.[78]

The latter point was addressed by H.A. Tripp, Assistant Commissioner of the Metropolitan Police, when he gave evidence before the Select Committee of the House of Lords in May 1938 on the theme of 'The Prevention of Road Accidents'. Tripp attributed the dangers of motor cycle riding to the very nature of the machine itself: serious injuries were inevitable, 'largely on account of the vulnerability of the motor cyclist'. Another group of critics who caused the industry much irritation were the coroners. Indeed, manufacturers were often deeply offended by their findings, which were full of harsh condemnations against the supposedly reckless behaviour of young motor cyclists and the correspondingly high level of fatal accidents. In 1934 Major Watling had actually petitioned the Lord Chancellor, urging him to prevent coroners from including such gratuitous criticism in their reports.[79]

The search for the 'Everyman' motor cycle, and the elusive female rider

Fundamental to the future of the industry was the debate over the 'economy' or, as it was called within the industry, the 'Everyman' motor cycle and its attendant theme, the potential for gaining female consumers, which had been the subject of much controversy for years. This criticism really turned on the issue of what the market was or, more to the point, rather what it could become. Critics maintained that it could be much enlarged if only the industry would adopt a more progressive approach to what they made and how they marketed their products. This was especially true for the manufacturers of 'economy' motor cycles, since some press commentators saw the small machines as the industry's salvation.[80]

The question of how the industry could convince women, who made up only a small proportion of Britain's motor cycling population, to buy more of their products posed an especially difficult problem. Throughout the 1920s there had been a concerted effort by the popular motor cycle press to make motor cycling more appealing to women. One of the earlier attempts to try and bring them into the market was undertaken by several aviation firms, who had no previous experience in motor cycle production but wanted to use their excess plant capacity created at the end of the war. These companies produced unusual products that fell half-way between the traditional motor cycle and an automobile.

One of these, the 'Ner-a-Car', was created to appeal to would-be car buyers by incorporating many features that its manufacturer, Sheffield-Simplex, believed were missing from standard motor cycle models. It had a small engine with an automobile-like chassis, combined with bodywork that would provide protection against inclement weather and road dirt.

For a woman who wanted to ride a motor cycle, one of the few opportunities to do so, at least for those lacking either independent means or a generous husband, was in the armed forces. This photograph, taken sometime during the First World War, shows a woman motor cyclist with the Women's Royal Air Force, seated on a Cylno motor cycle side-car combination.

Sheffield-Simplex hoped the Ner-a-Car would attract those who did not want a full-sized motor car but were reluctant to buy a motor cycle. The company especially hoped to find a market among women, and this was reflected in how they were depicted in the advertising used.[81]

However, it was the scooter that had been built with women specifically in mind. Scooter advertising portrayed women using them not only for leisure purposes but also to help in various activities such as shopping. By and large, because of the purchase cost and running expenses of these vehicles, most of the women who bought them were fairly affluent. Adventurous working-class women would very likely have had to make do with a bicycle or to enjoy motor cycling vicariously as spectators at sports and competition events.

Soon afterwards, many of the more traditional motor cycle manufacturers began to produce a new type of machine. A reporter from *The Daily Mirror*, for example, who had attended the 1921 Motor Cycle Show at London's Olympia exhibition hall, commented favourably on a new range of lightweight models built specifically for women. These were, he enthused, 'the daintiest and prettiest little vehicles imaginable ... perfectly adapted for shopping excursions as for long runs in the country and to the sea'.[82]

Some publishers saw a possible sales market of their own in trying to interest women in motor cycling. A book entitled *Motor Cycling for Women* appeared in the late 1920s with an introduction written by Major H.R. Watling, director of the industry's trade association, the British Cycle and Motor Cycle Manufacturers' Union.[83] Watling took the opportunity to welcome the appearance of such a book, which contained chapters covering topics such as 'Our First Side Car Tour', 'Frocks and Frills' and 'On Choosing a Mount', as representative of 'the growing interest in motor-cycling amongst women, who with acute feminine intuition, appreciate the part that a motor cycle can now play in their lives'.[84]

Other books, also written by women for what one suspects was mostly a female market, appeared and described how they used a motor cycle to go touring to far-away destinations. In 1925, for example, Clare Sheridan's account of her travels, together with her brother Oswald Frewen, riding a motor cycle side-car combination from Britain to Bolshevik Russia appeared under the title *Across Europe with Satanella*.[85] Among other things, Sheridan

The Motor-Pony was an example of how after the First World War the industry tried to target female consumers and so increase sales of motorised two-wheelers.

The Ner-A-Car was another one of the British motor cycle industry's novel engineering concepts from the post-1918 era that failed to find a market.

went into some detail explaining how she overcame the various obstacles and challenges encountered along the way, with the implication that, if she could do it, so could other women as well.

The motor cycle press also joined the campaign to encourage women to take up two-wheeled motor transport. Both *The Motor Cycle* and the *Motor Cyclist Review*, two leading popular journals, appointed female contributors to write articles for a female readership. Mabel Lockwood-Tatham, for example, wrote a column entitled 'Through Feminine Goggles' in the former publication, and the latter carried 'Entirely for Eve' authored by 'Cylinda'.[86] These articles were filled with practical advice about motor cycling apparel and suggestions about the types of machines available for purchase by aspiring female motor cyclists. Other columns and features contained information about maintenance, touring, and holiday destinations.

One such column was written by sisters Betty and Nancy Debenham, both ardent motor cycle enthusiasts who also participated in sporting activities such as trials events. They stressed the benefits of motor cycling as a leisure pursuit for young women that would not compromise prevailing social concepts of femininity:

> Motor-cycling is an ideal hobby for the tired business girl. She can seek health and pleasure during her precious week-ends by exploring the countryside and the seaside. She can gather her violets and primroses from the woods instead of buying them in jaded twopenny bunches, and her whole week-end's holiday need only cost her the price of her return fare to Brighton.[87]

Not long afterwards, the Debenhams addressed the issue of physical strength, or rather the lack of it, which was thought to be one of the main reasons so few women bought and used motor cycles. Remarking how difficult it was to kick-start a motor bike, they claimed that many of the new motor cycles were now designed to ensure that virtually any woman could easily use them. Earlier, they conceded:

> ... the motor cycle was something for young giants to urge into pulsating life, but that was many years ago. Today there are wonderful little machines which start with the very first kick and with most precocious appetites for roadfaring.[88]

Manufacturers also adopted other strategies to increase sales among women. In 1923, for example, they planned a 'rally for lady motor cyclists', and at least two firms pointedly used women, instead of men, to publicise their machines. In one instance, Dunelt, a smaller Birmingham-based company, arranged for a young German woman, Suzanne Koerner (no

One not especially realistic photographic depiction of female motor cyclists, *circa* 1935. Despite the efforts of some manufacturers to increase sales to women after 1918, they made up only a small proportion of riders during the inter-war period and for long after 1945.

SCIENCE AND SOCIETY PICTURE LIBRARY

relation to the author), to ride one of their light weight models from Berlin to its Midlands factory during the winter of 1927. The success of her journey, which was reported by the trade press, demonstrated yet again that being female was no impediment to operating a motor cycle successfully, even in the most unfavourable of circumstances.[89]

In the other instance, bicycle-maker Raleigh, which was still making motor cycles during the 1920s, provided a light weight machine to Marjorie Cottle, a leading motor cycle sports rider and then probably Britain's best-known female motor cyclist, to use on a well-publicised 1,400-mile journey around the country. One trade paper, *The Garage and Motor Agent*, was particularly enthusiastic about Cottle's promotional activities on behalf of the motor cycle industry. She was, it declared, 'undoubtedly one of the trade's most useful propagandists'. Not only did she demonstrate that physical strength was not crucial for operating a motor cycle, but 'the fact that Miss Cottle always manages to look nice when engaged in her exploits, and not the least like a professional motor cyclist, produces the best possible impression on the public'.[90]

Despite widespread social disapproval, there were always women willing to ride motor cycles. In this undated photograph (probably pre-1914), a Mrs William Porter, together with her slightly apprehensive looking male passenger, gets ready to head off on her British-built Douglas motor cycle side-car combination to a destination somewhere in Toronto, Canada.

COURTESY OF ED MOODY

British motor cycle manufacturers also encouraged women to participate in various motor cycle sports activities. This had been a well-tried and successful method for promoting sales among men, and no doubt they believed it was a strategy that could succeed with women as well. In 1926, indeed, the industry's trade association went as far as to honour a number of popular female competitions riders at a banquet held during the annual London motor cycle show. Press releases announcing the event were sent to *The Nursing Times*, *Home Notes* and *Women's Weekly*, magazines not normally associated with either motor cycles or motor cyclists. These publications were invited to send reporters in order to give the event the fullest possible exposure to a female audience.[91] Reaction of the guests at the banquet was very positive about the future for women and motor cycling. Miss Margaret Bedington, for example, a district nurse and a prominent private rider on the trials and competitions circuit, was quoted by the *Daily Sketch* as saying that she hoped 'to see the day when every girl – and especially every nurse – will be a motor cyclist'.[92]

Despite all the publicity, however, the campaign to increase sales of motor cycles to women ended in failure. By the end of the decade, even the Manufacturers' Union's redoubtable director Major Watling had to admit that probably only a paltry 25,000 of Britain's estimated 700,000 motor cyclists were female.[93]

So why did so few women respond to the manufacturers' marketing campaign? For the most part, it was likely the result of what seems to have been a deeply ingrained public prejudice against the practice of women riding motor cycles because it was thought to be unfeminine, or simply outside proper 'ladylike behaviour'. In fact, dedicated motor cyclists such as

Marjorie Cottle were acutely aware of such attitudes and tried to counter them by highlighting positive aspects of motor cycling for British women. For example, in an article which appeared in a 1928 edition of the *Evening Standard*, she confided to her readers that:

> Once, not so very long ago, the woman motor-cyclist was regarded as something of a crank or a freak. Times have changed, and motor-cycling as a sport is becoming more and more popular with women. It has been conclusively proved that motor-cycling is not harmful to women.[94]

Cottle then went on to explain why motor cycle riding was good for women on the grounds of what was then a more traditionally accepted language of 'femininity':

Marjorie Cottle (*right*) on the job at a motor cycle show sometime during the 1930s. One of the era's most talented sports riders, either male or female, Cottle faced hostility and discrimination from race organisers simply because of her gender. Here she demonstrates the features of a BSA motor bike to some show attendees.

© BSA OWNERS CLUB

Girls will find that motor-cycling brings health. It will give them honest, fresh-air complexions. It will make them hardy and strong, and although the powder puff is not a part of the girl motor-cyclist's make-up it can always be hidden away for use when occasion demands it.

Despite such assurances, the continuing social prejudices against women riding motor cycles created a defensive attitude among even some of the most determined female enthusiasts. As Mable Lockwood-Tatham explained in the pages of *The Motor Cycle*, 'It seems that the fact of a girl being a rider of a motor cycle immediately labels her as being "mannish" – admittedly an unpleasant characteristic – uninterested in frocks and frills, careless of home life, and devoid of any desire for women friends.'[95]

'No women need apply'

These attitudes provided at least a partial basis for the outright discrimination practised against women motor cyclists and which probably deterred many of them from participating in various activities, especially recreational and sports events. For example, only a few months before being honoured for her many competition victories at the manufacturers' banquet, Marjorie Cottle was banned from participating in a racing event for no other reason than her gender.[96] The ban was implemented despite the fact that many thought Cottle was an excellent rider. Indeed, at a recent race at the Scott Trial, *The Motor Cycle* noted that she had successfully finished the gruelling course 'while burly men had given up from sheer exhaustion'.[97]

Cottle's forced exclusion from these sports events was not an isolated instance, as the careers of other successful female motor cyclists such as Theresa Wallach, Florence Blenkiron, Faye Taylour and Jessie Innis suggest.[98] Similar exclusionary practices were apparently also employed against female motor cyclists in North America.[99] Consequently, judging at least from coverage in the motor cycle press, women seemed to have largely dropped out of most competition events by the early 1930s. In fact, women had already been barred from holding membership in the Motor Cycle Club (MCC) as early as 1910 and would not be readmitted until 1946 and only then as a form of recognition for their contribution to the British war effort.[100]

Practices which separated women from motor cycles extended far beyond British roads and racetracks. In the late 1930s, for example, Norton openly boasted about how it kept the number of women employed at its Birmingham factory to a minimum. Not to do so would, the company proclaimed, compromise the existing high standards of craftsmanship.[101] Whatever the validity of such claims, it is also true that when the senior executives from a number of British motor cycle manufacturers held a special meeting during the summer of 1935 to discuss the general decline in sales and usage, they expressed puzzlement and dismay about the low numbers of women riding motor cycles either in sporting events or indeed anywhere else.[102]

At the root of the problem were widespread social preconceptions of femininity and masculinity. Because of the very nature of riding a motor cycle, it taken for granted in many quarters that its successful operation depended upon physical strength and stamina as well as a reckless bravery in the face of danger and risk. At the time these were not widely believed to be feminine attributes. As Sean O'Connell has noted, when racing an automobile, men, far more than women, could demonstrate how they could 'gain pride, respect, [and] assert and confirm [their] identity by pitting themselves against fear'.[103] If this was the case for automobiles, it was even more so with respect to motor cycle sport. Due to the long-standing emphasis on racing and the glorification of power and speed, so well exemplified by the Isle of Man TT races, the industry had created an aura of masculinity around the motor cycle, acknowledged, if not always admired, by enthusiast and non-enthusiast alike.

As noted above, manufacturers found motor cycle sport had become important for selling their products and were deeply concerned about anything that might compromise that relationship. Many factories committed significant resources into preparing and entering their motor cycles into major race events such as the TT, and were convinced that winning competitions translated into higher sales. In fact, this was a point well recognised both inside and outside the industry. In 1925, for example, *The Times* observed:

> The importance of the Isle of Man races to any of the manufacturers represented can hardly be exaggerated. Many firms devote the greater part of their energies to the attempt to win in one or more of the classes, while scarcely a firm in the trade can plead complete indifference to the commercial value of a good performance. Some makers owe much of their prosperity to early prominence in the Tourist Trophy races?[104]

Moreover, *The Times* continued, it was also widely believed that sporting events made for better motor cycles: 'Competitions serve an important purpose as they encourage and intensify technical progress,' a sentiment that would continue to be widely held throughout the industry for decades to come.[105]

Seen in that light, broadening the motor cycle market by bringing in greater numbers of women was seen as a threat to the industry's continuing sales to what was understood as their core market of young men. Consequently, any campaign designed to increase the numbers of female motor cyclists also had the potential to undermine that very same aura of masculinity so important in maintaining existing sales among traditional male motor cyclists. In practice, this put one section of the industry at cross-purposes with the other. It prevented any sort of coherent sales campaign from emerging and was at the heart of the British motor cycle industry's inability to increase its market by recruiting more female customers. The implications of the failure to attract female customers during the 1920s would become evident twenty years later when large numbers of Italian scooters, which were especially popular among women, started to arrive in Britain.

Over-reliance on the racetrack

There were others, however, who noted more generally that the industry's continuing emphasis on sports was by its very nature a self-limiting strategy when it came to enlarging the market. Indeed, those women who rode motor

Motor cycles at the Liverpool docks about to be loaded on to a ferry destined for the Isle of Man TT races sometime in the early post-1945 era. For many, these races were as much a social occasion as a sporting event, just as they had been during the pre-war years, an opportunity to see and be seen by fellow motor cyclists from around Britain.

cycles often did so for much the same reason as their male counterparts. As one observer noted, instead of creating a new type of consumer, most female riders 'are all more or less of the sporting class, who use motor cycles for the pleasure they provide rather than for business or shopping purposes'.[106] That point, in turn, raised the question of whether or not the industry should change its current manufacturing strategy, shift the focus away from performance motor cycles, and start instead to concentrate on providing British consumers with a utility, or so-called 'Everyman' model.

This was a point that was also much discussed during the late 1920s. *The Motor Cycle*, for example, criticised the industry for having overly catered to 'the needs of the sporting athletic rider'. Manufacturers should try and improve comfort and economy instead of always stressing how fast their motor cycles could go. The journal challenged them to develop a cheap, reliable and low-powered machine, and offered a prize of £500 for the company that could provide one.[107] Manufacturers' Union Director Major Watling also championed the cause of this type of motor cycle. Writing in another popular journal, he stressed how such a machine would increase the size of the motor cycle market by appealing to non-motor cyclists, those he defined as 'the parson, retired civil servant, the business man and the clerk'. In private correspondence with manufacturers, Watling was even more emphatic. While sports-oriented buyers were 'comparatively few', the number of 'utility' buyers was 'illimitable'.[108]

Few manufacturers took up this challenge. In large part, the problem was that, in the absence of any effective marketing surveys, no one in the trade really knew who exactly was buying motor cycles and why.[109] There were two schools of thought. In public, especially after its failure to create more female customers, the industry confidently asserted that their market was made up mostly of young working-class males, who primarily used motor cycles to commute to and from work.[110] The growth of suburban housing estates and new factories outside of city centres had facilitated this development. Some within the industry regretted the association between the working class and the motor cycle. As one journal observed, the problem seemed to be that the industry had now slipped down-market in comparison with its motor car counterpart: 'Cars are Harrow, bikes are Borstal.'[111]

The critics remained unconvinced. Was a large, 350 cc to 500 cc motor cycle – the industry's biggest selling product – really necessary for day-to-day commuting? After all, one could quite as easily (and more cheaply) reach the local factory on a small 150 cc (or less) machine. Nor did this take into account the fact that motor cycle use had a strong appeal to many who were hardly working-class commuters, even if they made up only a minority of the market. Indeed, many enthusiasts' clubs probably had fairly socially diverse memberships.[112] On the other hand, throughout this period, *The Motor Cycle* regularly carried news about the Public Schools Motor Cycle

Club as well as kindred groups such as the Oxford University MCC.[113] These were unlikely to have been bastions of proletarian membership. Nor could T.E. ('Lawrence of Arabia') Lawrence, then probably Britain's best known motor cycling enthusiast, have been thought of as a typical factory commuter.[114]

Sporting events were often the focus of attention for large groups of motor cycle enthusiasts, and these, too, attracted spectators from varied social backgrounds. The *New Statesman* reported that at the TT, 'universities and public schools vie with the garage hands and Birmingham stockbrokers in their interest'. Crowds on the island were said to be teeming with 'thousands of youngsters in Harris tweeds with club ties; as many North Country artisans with their sweethearts; and the greedy efficient people who sell cycles in every city and town from Land's End to John O'Groats.'[115]

These races attracted much of the critics' ire. They pointed to the industry's near-obsessive preoccupation with sports functions such as the TT, events characterised by an emphasis on speed and good handling that generally required large and high-powered motor cycles. This accent had in turn a corresponding and, some thought, detrimental influence on motor cycle design and expended resources that could have been used to develop more utilitarian models. One trade journal blamed the industry for devoting 'an excess of energy to the sporting element of motor cycling, with its resultant excess of noise, lack of flexibility, and limited appeal'.[116] Major Watling, another critic of over-reliance on the race track, actually counselled abandoning the 1931 TT. What was the point, he wrote privately, of focusing so much attention on an event which provided only 'temporary advantage to not more than two firms'?[117]

By 1935 the industry appeared to be at a crossroads. As one correspondent wrote in the *Motor Cycle and Cycle Trader*, the industry could not continue to have it both ways. It would have to choose between building the big, often sports-oriented, motor cycles or the smaller commuting machines: 'You can make your sporting machine, you can make it fast, but so far you can't make it quiet. You can make your motor cycle for the million, but the million just isn't there for a single-track vehicle.' Instead, the industry was urged, 'Let us drop this power-bike idea. Let us make a car on two wheels.'[118] Such was the choice: either the industry would continue to stagnate, catering to its traditional, restricted market, or it could attempt to break into a new stratum of potential customers.

The British motor cycle industry answers its critics

How did the industry and its constituent members respond to the crisis and so attempt to confound the critics? On 9 July 1935 the Manufacturers' Union scheduled a special Management Committee meeting to discuss the alarming drop in motor cycle registrations and exports. The mood of industry leaders was not only dampened by low sales. The month before, for the first time in years, a foreign machine (an Italian Moto Guzzi) had won the Senior TT. A stinging blow had been dealt to British racing prestige.[119] At the meeting, a brief was tabled by Union Vice-President Eric Barnett which summarised the crisis facing the industry. He highlighted several issues which underlay the decline in sales: perceived safety hazards associated with motor cycle operation; competition from small, economy motor cars; the noise which accompanied motor cycle use; and high insurance premiums.

Barnett was convinced that sensationalist press reporting was one of the main reasons the public had turned away from the industry. Road accidents, he said, 'always seem to be given the fullest prominence in the newspaper reports and the existing prejudice is thus intensified'. This had, in turn, resulted in fewer younger consumers. British parents were becoming 'more and more averse to their boys riding motor cycles: while the girls, who seemed likely to swell the ranks of motor cyclists a few years ago, have practically faded out of the picture.'[120]

After a lengthy discussion, the committee resolved to set up two sub-committees to study the points raised by the critics, especially the noise and safety problems, as well as ways to increase sales. With respect to technical matters, the Manufacturers' Union began to devote some of its financial resources to scientific research to discover better ways of silencing motor cycles. By the late 1930s, the Ministry of Transport seemed to be satisfied with the progress that was being made. In the commercial field, however, the Manufacturers' Union had less success, even though some efforts were made to coordinate advertising and to launch a co-operative insurance scheme to counter high premiums. These efforts were initially successful, but they seem to have mostly ended inconclusively by 1937, a development which prompted further criticism from within the industry.[121]

Most of the attempts made by the Manufacturers' Union to enlarge the market came in the form of attacks on the government's formula of taxation by weight and engine capacity, which it claimed discouraged the public from buying smaller motor cycles and was therefore a serious barrier to increased sales. Another point of contention was recently implemented legislation requiring motor cycle drivers' licences, tests and compulsory third-party insurance, the latter point being thought the cause of the high insurance premiums. The government might well have introduced these requirements out of concern for the public interest but, as far as the industry was concerned, they were simply further deterrents to sales. The Manufacturers' Union's solution was to urge the British government to follow the example of its French and German counterparts and either substantially reduce or simply remove all tax and regulations on motor cycles of less than 200 cc.[122]

Edward Turner (1901–73)

Born in Walworth, south London, the son of a mechanical engineer, Edward Turner seemed destined for a life in manufacturing. After gaining experience working at his father's engineering works, Turner went on to study wireless radio technology at the Marconi School. During the First World War he did a stint as a wireless operator with the merchant marine.

Back in civilian life, Turner opened a motor cycle shop in London and within a few years had designed and built his own prototype machine, the so-called 'Turner Special'. That put him in contact with Jack Sangster who, impressed with the brilliant and dynamic young Turner, hired him to become Chief Development Engineer at his Ariel Motors factory in Birmingham.

In 1936, after helping Valentine Page design the ground-breaking four-cylinder Square Four, Sangster transferred Turner down to Coventry to manage the revival of the recently acquired Triumph factory. There, among other models, he designed the Speed Twin, one of the most significant machines in motor cycle history.

Turner had a natural flair for attractive design work and a keen instinct as to what would succeed in the motor cycle market, one which was, as he would later say, dominated by 'fashionable young men'. He also had the skills to manage one of the most productive manufacturing teams in the motor cycle world. He had, however, a mercurial and abrasive personality ('hopelessly egotistical' in the words of colleague Bert Hopwood) and was highly demanding of those who worked for him.

Nonetheless, by the late 1940s, in no small part because of Turner's leadership, Triumph had become Britain's most successful motor cycle company. As leading shareholders, both he and Sangster became personally wealthy when BSA bought Triumph in 1951 for £2.4 million. His expanded bank account notwithstanding, he also grew resentful towards Sangster and was once heard to remark bitterly about 'the faceless one who prospered greatly by my brilliance'.

Bitter or not, in 1956, after Sangster became Chairman of BSA, Turner joined the board of directors and was appointed head of the Automotive Division with responsibilities for the motor cycle subsidiaries as well as Daimler cars. There he turned his hand to automobile manufacturing and designed a new 2.5 litre V-8 engine that was fitted to the Daimler SP250 sports car.

After Daimler was sold off to Jaguar in 1960, Turner continued on as chief of what had become the BSA motor cycle division. However, as the years went by, he became less and less effective, in part because of the onset of diabetes but also as a consequence of his increasingly truculent nature. He retired in 1964 although stayed on the BSA Group board in a non-executive capacity until 1967 and even afterwards continued to work for the company as a private design consultant.

Edward Turner.

If this was what was being done at the industry level, what actions did the individual firms take to increase their sales? Did they try and respond to the proposition that there was a wider market waiting to be tapped if only the right kind of motor cycle was offered? In fact, barring several notable exceptions among smaller firms, it appears that they virtually ignored the critics' suggestions.

Industry leader BSA, for example, was undoubtedly in the best position to discover whether or not the market was capable of expansion. However, instead of developing a new light weight model, when it came to promoting its newest offering for the 1935 season, the company chose to emphasise a medium-weight sports/enthusiast model, the Empire Star, a high-performance 500 cc single-cylinder machine which had made a sensational debut on the racetrack and cost £65 10s. By 1939, the company had actually dropped its only small-displacement machine (in the 150 cc class) from the catalogue.[123]

BSA was not the only manufacturer to continue building the larger motor cycles. The dramatic recovery of Triumph after 1936 also demonstrates how manufacturers judged where market demand was strongest. Nearly on the verge of bankruptcy, Triumph had been purchased by Jack Sangster, who appointed Edward Turner, a promising young designer at Ariel Motors, as the new managing director of the newly named Triumph Engineering Company. Turner completely revamped the factory. The model line-up was pruned down to several single-cylinder machines in the 250 cc, 350 cc and 500 cc classes, all fitted with sports specification engines. Most significantly, in 1937, he led the design team that produced the 500 cc twin-cylinder Speed Twin. This high-performance machine, which was a smash hit among sports riders, cost £76 15s. It was unlikely to be the kind of machine that would open a new market of non-traditional motor cyclists, but it certainly made handsome profits for the company, which jumped from £7,000 in 1936 to £35,000 in 1939.[124]

In fact, constructive responses to the critics were restricted to the smaller firms, such as Coventry-based Francis-Barnett. For the 1935 season it offered a line-up of seven motor cycles ranging from 150 cc to 250 cc, two of which were variations of the Cruiser model. The Cruiser seemed to incorporate many of the features that critics said a motor cycle should have in order to broaden its appeal. It carried a 250 cc motor capable of speeds of up to 50 mph, which was enclosed in order to prevent oil from soiling the rider. It had a form of weather protection to keep the rider dry, a silencing system better than most, and was priced at a modest £37 5s. Although selling reasonably well and gaining, no doubt, some welcome profit for the company, it never became the breakthrough to a new market that some had hoped.[125]

By the 1938/39 season, a number of companies (none of them from the 'Big Six') was offering a line-up of auto-cycles (mopeds). Indeed, British consumers seemed to react favourably to them, and there was a modest

Francis-Barnett 1938 PROGRAMME

STAND No. 31

- The Show's most progressive Motor Cycle

THE 249 c.c. CRUISER H45

Fitted with Villiers deflectorless piston engine employing petroil lubrication and flywheel magneto. Complete with 4-speed gearbox, large petrol tank, leg shields and total enclosure of units. This model is fitted with Miller 6 v. dynamo lighting set and is a fast and reliable touring mount capable of covering very long distances at high average speeds.

PRICE £45 - 0 - 0

Six models are available to suit every taste, ranging from 148 c.c. at £28-10-0 to the 249 c.c. Cruisers at £42-10-0 and £45-0-0 respectively.

ALL MODELS FITTED WITH JAEGER SPEEDOMETER AT 50/- UNLESS OTHERWISE SPECIFIED.

Telegrams : FRANBAR, COVENTRY.

Tel. 5034

FRANCIS-BARNETT LTD. LOWER FORD STREET COVENTRY

The shape of things to come ... but never did. This photograph of a Francis-Barnett Cruiser is taken from a late 1930s Motor Cycle Show catalogue. The Cruiser was a sophisticated utility motor cycle designed for commuters, one that many had urged the industry to produce. Unfortunately sales failed to meet the company's expectations.

© MOTOR CYCLE INDUSTRY ASSOCIATION OF GREAT BRITAIN

interest in the small-capacity machines. Because of the outbreak of the war, it is impossible to determine how successful these might have become.[126]

Some thought that the manufacturers' cautious approach seemed to have been vindicated when, by the late 1930s, sales appeared to have stopped falling and even to have picked up slightly. What was confusing about the figures was that, while production increased from 55,200 units in 1936 to 82,014 the following year, motor cycle registration numbers dropped from 510,242 to 491,718 over the same period. This seeming contradiction was difficult to interpret. Some suspected that committed motor cyclists were still buying new machines while others simply discarded theirs, being unable to find a place for them in the used motor cycle market. Others in the industry simply dismissed the validity of government statistics.[127]

Competition from Germany

Even as the home market began to stabilise, the industry became increasingly concerned about what remained of its export market. It was becoming more difficult to export because of foreign tariffs and import quotas. In Spain, Poland and Denmark, for instance, formerly important destinations for British motor cycles, manufacturers complained that trade barriers prevented them from selling as many machines as they could have done otherwise.[128] Consequently, exports became increasingly oriented towards Empire and Dominion markets. While sales there had accounted for 41 per cent of exports in 1929, this proportion had grown to 59 per cent by 1935 (see tables 8 and 9).[129]

Table 8 *British motor cycle exports, 1929–1938*

	Australia/ New Zealand	Europe	North/South America	Other	Total
1929	15,170	28,934	839	17,434	62,377
1931	1,231	11,763	834	9,419	23,247
1933	2,749	6,128	1,173	7,681	17,731
1935	5,985	4,473	647	6,969	18,074
1937	10,833	6,197	1,177	7,143	25,350
1939	5,526	7,569	1,121	4,739	18,955

Source: MSS 204/13/1/1 (Modern Records Centre).

Table 9 *British exports to selected markets, 1925–1938*

	Australia	Holland	Switzerland	Sweden	Germany	India	USA	Canada	Total
1925	10,233	1,183	1,591	765	2,751	1,386	0	22	47,114
1928	8,724	1,298	3,648	4,279	6,111	1,902	43	126	59,906
1929	11,597	1,826	2,853	2,853	5,410	1,963	56	378	62,377
1930	5,314	1,891	2,065	2,940	2,429	1,570	47	433	42,689
1935	5,060	1,410	258	253	131	618	61	394	18,074
1936	7,298	1,350	132	285	212	379	92	402	20,460
1937	8,568	739	77	321	292	628	166	572	25,350
1938	6,344	1,156	99	348	338	719	114	362	19,769

Total sales of British motor cycles to Empire and Dominion markets:

1935	10,827
1936	13,599
1937	15,824
1938	11,487

Source: MSS 204/13/1/1 (Modern Records Centre).

Many in the industry believed that this situation had become aggravated by a series of bilateral trade agreements negotiated by the Board of Trade. The British government, the manufacturers insisted, had to do more to protect their interests. However, as board officials explained, matters were actually far more complicated. In 1936, for example, when the Manufacturers' Union protested at low import quotas that had been agreed to during a set of negotiations with Argentina, they were told to keep their objections private. Trade talks, motor cycle manufacturers were informed, had reached a 'delicate situation' because of Argentinian concerns over Britain's preferential treatment of Australian meat. The blunt fact was that the Board of Trade's chief priority was to ensure a cheap supply of imported Argentine products, rather than to export more British motor cycles.[130]

An even more serious threat to exports was the prospect of vastly increased foreign competition. Spurred on by various forms of government incentives, the German motor cycle industry launched a vigorous and successful campaign to sell its products in traditional British markets, especially in Holland, South America and parts of Asia, much to the alarm of the British industry (see table 10).[131]

Table 10   *British and German motor cycle exports, 1933–1937*

| | British | | German | |
	No.	£	No.	£
1933	17,731	670,712	2,006	64,090
1934	16,497	648,998	1,904	75,999
1935	18,074	701,938	5,702	179,682
1936	20,460	799,414	14,612	377,736
1937	25,350	1,026,776	31,708	596,246

Source: *Memo 47/38: Germany: Export Trade in Bicycles and Motor Cycles.* BCMCMTU Guardbook, MSS 204/3/1/44 (Modern Records Centre).

The Manufacturers' Union complained bitterly to government ministers that they were unable to compete effectively with their German rivals because of legislative handicaps. This reflected the considerable difference in attitude between the two nations regarding motor cycles. As one popular journal reported, when Reichs-Kanzler Adolf Hitler opened the 1935 Berlin Motor Cycle Show, he was at 'pains to stress the national importance of motor cycling and the motor cycle industry'. In contrast, had a British politician been in his place, the journal sardonically remarked, he could not have resisted 'the temptation to indulge in a peroration about road accidents, controlling the motor cyclist or even abolishing him'.[132]

British manufacturers were convinced that the German government did more than simply provide their industry with encouraging words. Not only did the German manufacturers receive various subsidies which enabled them to sell their products at prices the British found difficult to match, but because of the lack of regulations affecting their motor cycle market (compulsory insurance and drivers' licences for light weight motor cycles had been waived) they were able to concentrate on fewer models and benefit from larger and longer production runs, thus keeping their unit costs comparatively low. As a result, the British industry insisted, sales of German machines were growing at their expense.[133]

Whitehall officials were not moved. Civil servants reminded industry representatives that German exports were predominantly in the 'ultra-light' (auto-cycle or moped) category, in contrast with the larger and more expensive British motor cycles. As one confided in an internal memo, the real problem seemed to be that Germany had 'produced a motor cycle which the world wants and we appear to have lagged behind'.[134] This view was shared by others. One trade journal noted that overseas buyers 'don't want what we want them to want. If the German national were placed as we are, and if cars in America were not so cheap as they are, our export trade in motor cycles would be worth a small packet of snuff.'[135]

In order to counter the German incursions, British manufacturers began a series of price cuts in order to maintain their competitiveness. The Germans responded with cuts of their own, and so commenced a price war which both sides came to see as mutually destructive. The British motor cycle industry was not alone in this struggle; many other industries also engaged in fierce competition with German rivals, a fact that quickly came to the attention of the FBI and the Board of Trade. The outcome was a complex series of negotiations between British and German industries, conducted under the sponsorship of both governments, with the aim of reaching what amounted to a set of international cartel agreements. This process culminated in the so-called 'Dusseldorf Agreement' of March 1939. Although the British and German motor cycle industries, which were an integral part of these negotiations, reached agreement in principle with respect to pricing and market share, events later that year prevented their consummation.[136]

Trouble in the factories

The reluctance of British motor cycle manufacturers to make a determined entry into the lightweight market could be traced back to the debacle the industry had suffered when it had tried to sell scooters in the early and mid-1920s.[137] Industry leaders might have believed that such designs had been tried out before and had been a failure, making them unwilling, especially under the economic conditions then prevailing, to take another gamble. It must have seemed far better to stick with the tried and true. The other problem was that, failing volume production, the smaller-displacement machines by definition equalled smaller profits, a point of great concern to the industry.[138] Assuming that the industry had wished to change its overall orientation, perhaps the only way open to it at the time would have been to narrow down the number of models on offer and to reap the benefits of larger and longer production runs, following the German example. But for a number of reasons this would have been a very difficult strategy for the British industry to pursue at this time.[139]

To begin with, many in the industry simply did not believe they should be building motor cycles on any kind of larger scale production basis, and indeed the sentiments of BSA's chairman, quoted above, about catering to all segments of the market, were quite typical. Nor were they a recent phenomenon. When he delivered his evidence to the Committee on Industry and Trade in March 1925, Major H.R. Watling claimed that, because the industry was so 'fiercely competitive', it had been segmented into 'groups which concentrate on special designs for special classes of users, for the user seems to be as individualistic as the manufacturer'. Under those circumstances, he continued, 'it is useless to think of "mass" production for the industry in general'.[140]

This attitude remained entrenched right to the end of the inter-war period, and was reflected in the often old-fashioned production technology to be found in the factories. At the Triumph company factory in Coventry, for example, all through the 1920s and well into the 1930s, there was no assembly-line track. Instead, motor cycles were built individually and completed on separate work platforms within a large central assembly room.[141] Much the same situation prevailed at BSA where, as a reporter from the journal *Automobile Engineer* noted during the late 1930s, 'no attempt had been made to introduce the continuous flow principle' in its motor cycle factory at Small Heath in Birmingham.[142] In fact, BSA does not appear to have installed a moving assembly line until as late as 1936.[143]

One trade publication, arguing in favour of current practices, stated outright that mass production methods, by definition, would depreciate the industry's high standards of manufacturing.[144] The Norton company, for one, quite openly proclaimed that it was very proud of the fact that it did not have a moving assembly-line track at its Birmingham factory. Much like its policy against employing women, Norton believed that to convert to that type of production would compromise its well-established standards of quality and craftsmanship.[145] The major firms seemed content to continue building their mostly bigger single-cylinder machines in comparatively limited numbers, even if this meant regularly under-utilising factory and plant.

Another factor that prevented the industry from boosting output was the lack of adequate quality control in the factories. Indeed, there were serious problems in the market with regard to defective motor cycles. For example, in 1936 A.B. Bourne, editor of *The Motor Cycle*, informed members of the Manufacturers' Union's management committee that he was afraid to publish all of the some 10,000 letters he had received from irate customers, since 'publication would have a damping effect upon other readers' enthusiasm'. This type of criticism was not at all exceptional and, in 1939, the Manufacturers' Union actually created a special committee to investigate a range of problems, ranging from persistent oil leaks to faulty electrical equipment.[146]

It is doubtful, therefore, whether the industry possessed either the facilities or the skilled management and production engineers that would have enabled it to have expanded to the volume necessary to service a larger market. There were also those who noted that any company that made a serious effort to change production programmes would be faced with very significant retooling costs. As one industry expert observed:

The management is loth to make radical alternations in design, since such alternations are bound to involve expense in the purchase of new machinery and perhaps in the reorganisation of certain departments [so that] … with few notable exceptions, the improvements during the last few years have been concerned chiefly with details like tank finish, tool case construction and showy details like instrument panels.[147]

Against these obstacles, the manufacturers did possess certain advantages. Labour militancy, significantly, was not an obstructing factor to any restructuring of their factory practices. Although trade unions had been strong in some motor cycle firms before and after the First World War, they had been gravely weakened by the Depression. Thus, when Jack Sangster took over Triumph he immediately instituted a pay cut on a 'take it or leave it' basis, which was met without resistance. Previously, workers there had been among the most militant in the industry. In fact, there is no record of labour unrest at all during the 1930s, although there were disputes in certain of the component industries such as tyre manufacturing. If strikes were virtually non-existent, it was also true, however, that many of the manufacturers did experience shortages of skilled workers as a result of the higher wages being paid in the aeronautics industry as the pre-war rearmament programme progressed.[148]

Another potential barrier to any overhaul of the industry's productive capacity was the availability of capital. Yet BSA, AMC and Enfield Cycles all reported rising dividends at the end of the decade, and the private companies were almost certainly profitable. For example, after years without dividends, BSA paid out 10 per cent on ordinary shares in 1938, while AMC's dividends jumped from 5 per cent to 10 per cent between 1937 and 1938.[149] Much of the increased profitability was created by the government's rearmament programme, which resulted in many lucrative military contracts, some of which involved motor cycles, while other companies were involved in component manufacturing for the aircraft and armaments industries. Moreover, during the late 1930s several manufacturers made a series of expenditures to enlarge their factories, although it is unclear how much this was related to motor cycle work as against unrelated rearmament contracts.[150]

For its part, the industry had no trouble identifying the root cause for the much diminished motor cycle market. Government legislation was again fingered as the main culprit for dampening potential consumer demand. But was there any truth to the complaint that the industry was over-taxed and regulated during the 1930s? Could the government have done anything else, lacking hard evidence from the industry that relaxation of legislation and lowering of tax would increase sales, and under pressure from various quarters to retain the laws? In fact, Neville Chamberlain, who was either chancellor of the exchequer or prime minister for a good part of the 1930s, had been Managing Director of BSA Cycles during the early 1920s and would surely have had some understanding of (and perhaps sympathy for) the industry's problems. Yet the legislation remained fundamentally unchanged. Although the 1932 budget did alter the tax structure, to favour sales of motor cycles under 150 cc capacity, this was not sufficient to satisfy the industry; nor did it help significantly to generate demand for these light-weight machines.[151]

Despite all the criticism of their production programmes, there were those in the industry who remained unconvinced that there was a market for anything other than what was already being produced. To substantiate their case, all they need do was point to the type of motor cycles that were actually moving off showroom floors. After all, when the small motor cycles were offered to the public, they were not purchased in any great numbers. On the other hand, the big 350 cc to 500 cc models were consistent best sellers.

However, had the companies done really all they could to expand their market? How much were they spending on advertising and where? The industry was particularly disappointed in its failure to convince women, among other non-traditional consumers, to buy its products. Yet this could only be done by reaching out to the kind of people who had never before considered buying a motor cycle, but might if they were pitched a convincing case. On the evidence available, it is not at all clear that the industry was prepared to take such steps to widen their market.

The fact is that neither the Manufacturers' Union nor the various firms increased their advertising budgets, which lagged far behind those of the motor car and even the bicycle industries; nor did they make an effort to place advertisements in magazines outside the enthusiast press that were read by the kind of potential consumers they hoped would buy their products (see table 11).[152] Nor, for that matter, did the industry continue to use the services of a publicity company hired in the late 1920s in order to counteract negative press coverage.[153]

Table 11   *Advertising expenditure by the cycle, motor cycle and motor car industries, 1935–1938*

	1935	*1936*	*1937*	*1938*
Cycles	£160,985	£200,446	£223,335	£173,912
Motor cycles	£36,441	£38,821	£39,206	£34,823
Motor cars	£901,089	£877,141	£911,726	£853,799

Source: Statistical Review of Advertising, 1935–1938.

Finally, although the industry did sponsor some limited technical research, via the Institution of Automobile Engineers, into the problems associated with large-displacement machines, this work had a very restricted scope.[154] Aside from models produced by the smaller firms, very little was done to examine how best to construct an inexpensive, low-powered motor cycle which would have enabled the industry to appeal to a new type of consumer. There certainly was money available to them at the time to have conducted such work. On this point, the critics were not adequately answered.[155]

If considered a question of sound, although conservative, business practice, one must conclude that the industry had effectively dealt with the circumstances that confronted them during the 1930s. Their strategies seemed a fairly rational response to the huge drop in sales, and the industry was able to hold on to a stable and traditional market and, most important, it continued to make money. By 1939, helped in part by its restrictive trading rules as well as its incipient commercial agreement with the Germans, the industry had created a nice cosy environment for itself which removed any real pressure, external or internal, for change.[156]

It may never be known with any certainty whether or not there ever was a serious possibility of cultivating a large-scale motor cycle market in Britain during this time. The point is that the industry was simply not committed to discovering if one, in fact, existed. Instead, the most successful company of this period was looking abroad for the real growth in sales. In May 1939 Triumph Managing Director Edward Turner gave an interview in which he explained his firm's strategy for the near future:

> We are not endeavouring to take a lion's share of the home market. Such a course obviously postulates undue internal competition which is possibly not for the good of the industry as a whole. We prefer to concentrate upon the best grade of machine with a view to extending our sales not only in this country but in every market in the world.[157]

Turner's optimism about the sales potential of Triumph motor cycles might have been well placed, but within a few weeks both he and the rest of the industry would have more pressing matters to think about.

John 'Jack' Sangster (1896–1977)

For decades the British motor cycle industry's single most important figure, Jack Sangster was born in Birmingham. His father, Charles Sangster, was a bicycle manufacturer who owned the Ariel Cycle Company and had diversified into motor cycles prior to the First World War. Young Jack had gone to work with the family firm and was later sent for further training as a motor engineer on the Continent.

After wartime service with the British army, Sangster was taken on by the Rover Car Company where he designed a successful 1000 cc (8 horse power) automobile. In 1923 he rejoined the family firm, now known as Components Manufacturing Company, which produced both cars and motor cycles. Hit hard by the Depression, the company was put into receivership. However, Sangster, who had by then amassed some personal wealth, was able to purchase the motor cycle end of its subsidiary, Ariel Motors, based at Selly Oak in Birmingham.

Under his management, Ariel was soon back on its feet and once again became one of Britain's leading motor cycle producers. Success was a reflection of Sangster's considerable business and managerial abilities. Bert Hopwood, never one to dole out praise promiscuously, called him 'this needle-sharp man'. Sangster was especially renowned for his skill as a talent-spotter. During the late 1920s and early 1930s, for example, Ariel employed Valentine Page, Bert Hopwood and Edward Turner, undoubtedly the most capable designers to be found anywhere in the industry.

In late 1935 Sangster was presented with a new business opportunity. The financially stricken Triumph Company was on the point of bankruptcy. Sangster moved quickly and within a short time had purchased it for a reported £28,000, surely one of the greatest bargains in motor cycle history. Sangster transferred Turner over to the new business as its manager, and the company was soon operating at a profit.

During the war Sangster sold Ariel to BSA and again proved himself a formidable business negotiator. BSA had initially offered £80,000

but ended up paying him £376,000! In 1951 he did even better by selling Triumph to BSA for a remarkable £2.4 million, a deal which also gave Sangster a seat on the BSA Group board of directors.

There Sangster bumped up against BSA's Chairman and Managing Director, the inept and scandal-prone Sir Bernard Docker. The two were soon in conflict, a situation that was resolved in May 1956 when Sangster engineered a non-confidence vote which abruptly ended Docker's career at BSA. Sangster took his place and remained there until 1960.

Unfortunately, Sangster's career, which until then had been an unbroken string of business achievements, ended on a sour note. Although he stayed on BSA's board in a non-executive capacity until nearly the end, he seems to have done little to avert the disaster created by Eric Turner, the man Jack Sangster hand-picked as his successor.

COURTESY OF THE IVOR DAVIES COLLECTION

CHAPTER TWO
The war years, 1939–1945

S OON AFTER THE OUTBREAK OF WAR between Britain and Germany in September 1939, the motor cycle industry fell under government control for the coordination of war production. In this case the Board of Trade (Industrial Supplies Department) presided, and as the war dragged on the degree of control became tighter and tighter. One immediate effect of hostilities was the cancellation of the Motor Cycle Show that had been scheduled for November, as well as the imposition of petrol rationing. The so-called 'Licence to Acquire' placed severe restrictions on the private sales of motor cycles for all but urgent or essential use.[1]

The government 'concentrates' motor cycle production

Like many other British industries, the motor cycle industry was 'concentrated'. What this meant was that the government became responsible for the transfer of 'resources from peacetime to wartime purposes and of ensuring that the available manpower and productive capacity of the nation were fully used'.[2] In the case of the motor cycle industry, some firms would continue manufacturing motor cycles, while many of the smaller companies would be shunted off into general munitions work. However, the vast majority of the productive capacity of the industry was engaged in the manufacture of motor cycles.

Thus five of the 'Big Six' were set to work producing motor cycles for the British and Allied governments, although Velocette (outside the 'Big Six') was allowed to manufacture both military (especially for the French army) and civilian machines for export only. BSA, being far more than a motor cycle manufacturer with its diverse engineering interests, was also a prime contractor for the British (and Allied) governments, producing under licence, among other things, rifles (Lee-Enfields), light automatic weapons (the Sten gun) as well as aircraft machine guns (Browning) and

Paratroopers collecting their folding 'Welbikes' from equipment canisters after a drop somewhere in England, *circa* 1943. Most motor cycles used by the British armed forces were in the 250 cc to 500 cc range, but they also used smaller speciality bikes such as these.

© IMPERIAL WAR MUSEUM

cannon (Hispano-Suiza). Its motor car subsidiary Daimler built a line of armoured vehicles for the army as well as aero engines for the Royal Air Force (RAF). The company's workforce ballooned from several thousand to nearly 28,000 employees spread out over a number of factories throughout the Midlands.[3] This is not to suggest that other members of the 'Big Six' were restricted only to motor cycle work. Some branched out into other types of manufacture as the war wore on. Enfield Cycles, for example, went into precision instrument production, and at various times Triumph also built tank tracks and small engines for aviation purposes.[4]

Not all of the smaller motor cycle manufacturers were prevented from continuing their accustomed production, at least during the first two years of hostilities. Firms such as Cotton, Norman and Francis-Barnett were encouraged to build machines for the export trade and for an extremely limited home market. Union Director Major Watling even suggested, in light of the major firms' preoccupation with military work, that the minor companies should consider producing larger (250 cc capacity and up) machines for sale abroad.[5]

Indeed a form of volume exports did continue, at least up until 1942, with particular emphasis on the so-called 'hard currency' nations, such as the USA and Canada, in place of those within the 'Sterling Area'. Under overall government direction, Export Groups, which were staffed by industry personnel, were created to stress co-operation (to be brought about by coercion if necessary) within the industry, and were given a wide-ranging brief. Not only would they fix export prices to ensure competitiveness with the manufacturers, but also seek out raw materials and arrange for timber for packing and shipping. Export licences were required, which ensured that the motor cycles went only to the favoured currency areas. Moreover it was expected that 75 per cent of production should go abroad, otherwise the raw materials might not be forthcoming.[6]

Motor cycle Blitzkrieg

From the very beginning, however, the top priority was equipping the British military. In the months after September 1939, during the so-called 'Phoney War', there was, in comparison to the activity that followed the Dunkirk evacuation, a fairly lackadaisical mobilisation. However, the level of motor cycle orders had still risen steeply after the 1938 Munich Agreement and reached 9,000 in 1939, a result of a decision to expand the army from five to ten divisions. Pressure for more production grew after September as the British Expeditionary Force (BEF) was sent over to France in order to counter an expected German invasion.[7]

At that stage in the war, the General Staff saw motor cycles as providing a varied role on the battlefield. They would mostly be used for communications purposes, the favoured means for dispatch riders to travel back and forth between headquarters and the front line, but also to shepherd truck convoys and, perhaps more controversially, take over the role once played by horse cavalry to reconnoitre ahead of the main body of the army.[8]

Accordingly, most of the motor cycles manufactured for the military were in the single-cylinder 350 cc plus class. These machines were more or less the same as those that had been produced before

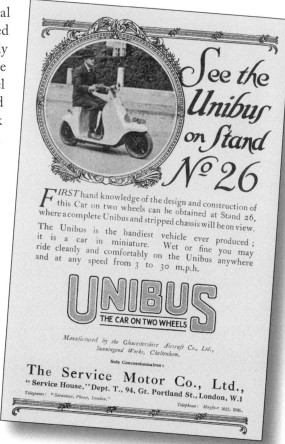

See the *Unibus* on Stand № 26

FIRST hand knowledge of the design and construction of this Car on two wheels can be obtained at Stand 26, where a complete Unibus and stripped chassis will be on view.
The Unibus is the handiest vehicle ever produced; it is a car in miniature. Wet or fine you may ride cleanly and comfortably on the Unibus anywhere and at any speed from 3 to 30 m.p.h.

UNIBUS
THE CAR ON TWO WHEELS

Manufactured by the Gloucestershire Aircraft Co., Ltd., Sunningend Works, Cheltenham.

Sole Concessionaires:

The Service Motor Co., Ltd.,
"Service House," Dept. T., 94, Gt. Portland St., London, W.1
Telegrams: "Servalvco, Phone, London."   *Telephone: Mayfair 3025, 3026.*

'The Car on Two Wheels' – another unsuccessful effort from the early 1920s to try and develop a new market for motorised two-wheelers among non-motor cyclists.
© MOTOR CYCLE INDUSTRY ASSOCIATION OF GREAT BRITAIN

the war in the sense that they were essentially civilian models modified to meet military specification. Norton, for example, one of the major pre-war contractors, supplied its 16H model, a 500 cc single-cylinder side-valve machine that was also available in a similar form to the public. These were mostly all designed as solo machines, although the army also expressed an interest in motor cycle/side-car combinations. To this end Norton developed a variation of the 16H which had a powered side-car wheel.[9]

The other companies provided their own different versions of the 16H, and, as the army was soon to discover, this created a great deal of practical servicing difficulties. It not only had to purchase and stock parts in numerous and widely dispersed depots for the non-standardised motor cycles, but train maintenance staff in repairing a number of different types of machines.

Auxiliary Territorial Service (ATS) women learning motor cycle mechanics at an armed forces workshop somewhere in England during 1942. With the men overseas, many women joined the military and filled non-traditional jobs such as these.

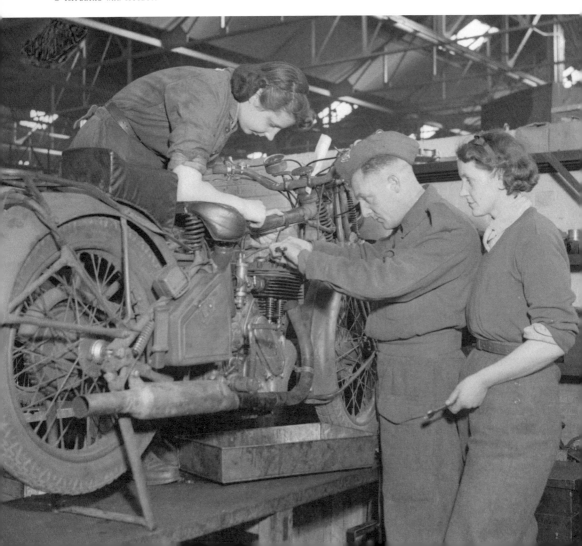

The lightning German successes in France and the Low Countries during May and June 1940 seem to have caught the public's imagination and excited much speculation about the use of motor cycle troops by the Wehrmacht.[10] Major Watling later claimed that he had been told by returning members of the defeated BEF that a key part of the devastating Blitzkrieg assault were the German motor cycle units, who had been 'here, there and everywhere', causing disruption and disarray among Allied ranks. One British newspaper went as far as to state that the German armed forces contained a large body of motor cyclists, which had been instrumental in breaking through the French armies and seizing the Channel ports.[11]

When Major Watling met with a member of the General Staff shortly after the evacuation of British army at Dunkirk, he repeated the industry's familiar complaint that, in contrast to Britain, Germany had actively encouraged the use of motor cycles, both in and out of the military, during the previous decade. Now, he insisted, the full effects of what the Manufacturers' Union considered to be Britain's punitive tax and regulatory provisions were finally being felt. The crushing defeat on the Continent was, according to him, at least in part directly attributable to this pre-war neglect of the motor cycle industry.[12]

Soon after, Watling had a meeting with Sir John Reith, the Minister of Transport, and was able to repeat the industry's criticisms of government policy. In this case the problem was the less than satisfactory level of training being given to the growing numbers of motor cycle operators, especially in the ARP (Air Raid Precautions) units and the Home Guard. This poor-quality training created far more accidents than was necessary, although the blackout was responsible for a good share of them. He was also concerned about the below-standard training of motor cycle repair units, which had created a high degree of attrition among the reserves of machines.[13]

Blitz on Britain

After the Dunkirk evacuation, with a good portion of the army's stocks of motor cycles (as well as much of its other equipment) left behind on the beaches, the industry worked flat out to re-equip the military.[14] In fact, it appears that production during 1940 reached what would be its highest peak for the rest of the war. This was also the year when the industry received its worst damage from enemy action. In mid-November the Luftwaffe launched a major raid against Coventry, which devastated the centre of the city. One of the factories hit was Triumph Engineering, which happened to be located nearly adjacent to the gutted cathedral. Fortunately, casualties among the workforce were comparatively low, and although many of the machine tools and other equipment were later salvaged, virtually all stock,

Bogged down in north-west Europe. An army despatch rider receives assistance from a young boy on a muddy Dutch road, sometime in late 1944. In both world wars, motor cycles performed an important role for the army, particularly carrying messages between units and shepherding road traffic.

along with the precious blueprints and business records, went up in flames, and the factory was left a pile of rubble.[15]

Triumph was able to restart very limited production at nearby Warwick until a new purpose-built factory could be erected in Meriden, a village midway between Coventry and Birmingham. Although work on this factory began in mid-1941, Triumph's output was much reduced until 1943, when the Meriden plant was finally able to go into full production. Why Triumph received this factory when it had not been a military producer on the scale of either BSA, AMC or Norton before the war and ranked well behind them even after September 1939 is not well explained in either published or unpublished accounts. For whatever reason, the new factory (albeit equipped largely with plant salvaged from the bombed-out Coventry works) provided Triumph with a valuable asset and gave it, no doubt, a considerable advantage over the other firms in the post-war era.[16]

Only a few days after the Coventry Blitz, the Luftwaffe hammered Birmingham with a series of heavy bombing raids. BSA's Small Heath factory was badly hit, although the damage seems to have been largely restricted to the armaments section and did not directly affect the motor cycle assembly areas.[17] However, the raids evidently had a shattering effect on worker morale. Indeed it was alleged in confidential Home Office correspondence that BSA management had seemingly taken few precautions against the raids.

After the raids, it came to be widely believed that the workforce had been poorly provided for in terms of an early warning system, that the bomb shelters were deficient, and that the damage had been made worse by the failure of management to remove inflammable materials from around the factory, which provided ready tinder for the German incendiaries. For long afterwards, many in Birmingham believed that the casualties suffered were actually much worse than the authorities would admit. Consequently, it was difficult to convince some workers to attend the factory, never mind work normal shifts, and production was badly disrupted for some time after the November raids.[18]

The other major manufacturers do not seem to have suffered from bombing to the same degree, although the Velocette factory in Birmingham was hit, albeit without major damage. Even AMC, located as it was in the Woolwich area of south-east London, apparently continued to produce straight through the 1940 and 1941 bombings. Nor was it stopped by the V1 'Flying Bomb' and V2 rocket attacks in 1944 and 1945. Smaller manufacturers such as Francis-Barnett and Coventry Eagle were also bombed out of their Coventry factories. The James works in Birmingham was badly damaged as well by enemy action. The Manufacturers' Union headquarters building, near Coventry railway station, was destroyed during the November 1940 raids. Its operations were subsequently relocated for the duration of the war to Kenilworth, a small town several miles away.[19]

Wartime production

Despite the growing intensity of the overall British war effort, motor cycle production did not actually expand much beyond the 1939/40 levels, and even though annual output was greater than anything achieved during the 1930s, it still fell far short of the 1929 peak. Several factors underlay this failure to expand to full potential. First, because of the drastic contraction of the domestic and export markets during the early 1930s, the six major manufacturers did not necessarily share the same productive capacity that the industry had possessed in 1929. Certainly the total number of producers had dropped. Although the industry was servicing a far smaller market than before, it is arguable that their factories might have become more efficient. Norton, for example, had refused to convert to an assembly-line system, believing this would compromise its craftsmanship and quality standards. By 1939, however, under pressure from increased military contracts, it hired an engineer from BSA and made a number of improvements to its factory procedures, including the installation of an assembly track.[20] Moreover, there had been drastic contraction of the home market, understandable under the circumstances of total war. Motor cycle registrations had dropped from over 400,000 in 1939 to just over 100,000 by 1943, thanks no doubt to severe petrol rationing, the 'Licence to Acquire', as well as contracting supplies of materials, among other things.[21]

By July 1941 the British army had decided, on the basis of battlefield experience, to scale back the use of motor cycles from its earlier projections. Evidently this question, or so a senior officer informed Major Watling, had been carefully considered by the General Staff, including Chief of Staff Alanbrooke, and the unanimous view was that 'the motor cycle could only usefully be employed for communications – not for offensive use'. Moreover, even the Germans, hitherto enthusiastic proponents of the aggressive use of motor cycles, had been reducing their deployment as well. This was probably a result of high losses suffered by motor cycle troops over the past campaigns and no doubt many in the German High Command were concerned about their applicability on the vast and inhospitable Russian front. Thereafter, like the British and other Allied forces, German motor cycles would be mostly used for dispatch purposes and truck convoy duties.[22]

Finally, and most important, the military motor cycle simply could not compete either in terms of safety for its operators or for general versatility with light armoured vehicles such as the Bren Gun carrier and, even more so after America's entry in the war in December 1941, with the four-wheel-drive 'Jeep', a machine which could fill many of the roles that had been customarily performed by motor cycles. Hence, as far as the General Staff was concerned, there was not the need to order motor cycles in the quantities that some had thought would be necessary at the beginning of the war. In some ways, the situation was analogous to the problem that the industry faced in the late 1920s and early 1930s when inexpensive motor cars had begun to undercut the economy appeal of the motor cycle among the middle class and parts of the working class. Again, the industry could not seem to come up with an adequate response, although under these circumstances there might not have been one to employ.[23]

In the meantime, the export trade began to flag under the pressures of war.[24] One notable problem was the fact that the reputation of British via-a-vis German motor cycles had suffered during the pre-war years. In early 1940, for example, when the British attempted to increase sales of motor cycles to the then neutral Dutch market, they discovered that the Germans had become very difficult to dislodge. The British consul general in Rotterdam wrote a report which noted that, thanks to pre-war neglect on the part of British manufacturers, the Germans had moved in and had achieved 'practically a monopoly' of the local motor cycle trade. Not only were the German models 'more convenient' for users, but because of an export discount of 20 per cent, spare parts were cheaper, and delivery was faster, while, most important, 'the quality of their materials is A.1'.[25]

The report was highly critical of the record of British manufacturers in Holland. Their machines were 'old fashioned compared to the German product', a result of 'the conservatism of British manufacturers who have ignored German competition for years and are now beaten by it in the Dutch market'. Moreover, unfavourable comparisons were also drawn by retailers about the superior level of service received from German manufacturers. Indeed, it seemed 'the British manufacturers have no interest in their agent so long as he pays up (mostly in advance)'. Little wonder British motor cycle companies had trouble making progress in this important market before 1939.[26]

Nonetheless, elsewhere, especially in distant overseas markets, the German presence had begun to fade away. This was mostly the result of demands from their own military, combined with an effective Allied blockade of German ports, although overland routes to the East remained open for some time. As for the industry's military production, there is no indication that British motor cycle companies had any difficulty supplying the armed forces with a sufficient supply of machines. Indeed, unlike other sections of industry which produced four-wheeled and tracked transportation for the military, the motor cycle manufacturers were able not only to meet all British requirements but also to supply the Canadian army.[27]

Standardising design

The profusion of different models provided by the five British producers – all with mostly incompatible spares – continued to drive service quartermasters to distraction. By way of a letter from the Ministry of Supply, several firms were informed that the War Office 'has expressed very strongly the view that the numbers of solo motor cycles at present in service use is excessive and that one design should be adopted as soon as is practicable'. By early 1944 matters had reached the point where a meeting between the Ministry of Supply and the leading executives of the industry was called in order to discuss the matter.[28]

The ministry's position was quite clear: the military was fed up with trying to maintain all the different types of motor cycles used by its various branches and wanted the industry to develop a single, standardised model.[29] For their part, the industry representatives objected, since such a design would require at least two years to develop, never mind the trouble of trying to find the necessary special jigs and tools for the extra work under difficult wartime conditions. Worst of all, the manufacturers complained that, as far as they were concerned, a standardised model built specifically for the military would be 'useless in other directions', with no direct commercial applicability. Norton managing director Gilbert Smith wanted the government to drop its plans and instead allow the motor cycle industry 'to use the very limited design capacity left to [it] to perfect their post-war attacks on Home and overseas markets'.[30]

In order to break the impasse, Jack Sangster proposed a compromise. Companies would use an existing model that all the manufacturers were already familiar with and then make all the necessary modifications. The ministry replied that, as far as it was concerned, there was no suitable existing design, and the manufacturers were pointedly reminded that 'in relation to post-war problems and development of export trade, the motor cycle industry was in a far better position than certain other industries'. The government had been no more demanding than it had with the motor car industry, which was also heavily committed to aircraft production. The required labour and materials would be made available; it was now up to the motor cycle manufacturers to get on with the job and have a prototype ready by 1946. If not, members of the ministry warned, the industry would be forced to come up with a suitable design.[31]

Planning for the post-war world

In the meantime, as early as 1941, under prodding from the Board of Trade, the industry had begun to consider the question of post-war planning. This had three aspects. First, the industry would list the requirements needed from the government in order to facilitate speedy re-conversion from war-time to peace-time production. Second, it would describe what measures it intended to take to re-open export markets; and, finally, manufacturers would undertake a programme to develop new motor cycle designs.[32]

In the meantime, the government set a production target for 1942 of 50,000 motor cycles. A commitment of sufficient labour as well as extra machine tools to be imported from the United States was made, although this was not always fulfilled. The position of the various manufacturers varied: Ariel, for example, was 'entirely controlled by the labour position'. There were also worries about shortages of machine tools, despite earlier assurances to the contrary. BSA said it needed more, but admitted that, even if they were provided, it might not be able to find sufficient operators because of a shortage of skilled workers.[33] Watling stressed that the industry's situation

Pre-war racing and trials riders Sgt J.S. 'Crasher' White and Sgt Freddie Firth joined the army as motor cycle riding instructors. They are shown here at a Royal Army Service Corps (RASC) driving and maintenance school in the English Lake District, *circa* October 1942.

was complicated by the fact that it was structured horizontally rather than vertically. This meant that there would likely be potential bottlenecks caused by a dependency on specialist component makers.[34]

Among all these problems, one hopeful sign for the future was the growing potential of the export trade. Now that the Allied blockade had cut off the Germans and Italians from their overseas markets, unprecedented opportunities awaited British manufacturers. In Mexico, for example, after 1939 the removal of German competition left the field wide open. Although during the 1920s and early 1930s this market had been dominated by the American producers, the Germans had broken through to a whole new range of customers with their light-weight machines, such as the 175 cc single cylinder Wanderers and Maicos, which were especially popular in urban areas. Britain could inherit this market, if only it could emulate the nature, quality and price of the machines the Germans had sold there.[35]

Indications were also favourable for future expansion in the USA. German products had not been popular there previously, since American tastes tended to run towards the large Harley-Davidsons and Indians. Market investigations conducted by the Department of Overseas Trade in California and the cities of New Orleans and Philadelphia, which had been forwarded to the Manufacturers' Union, suggested that there might be a demand for British-built machines once hostilities had ceased. They were warned, however, that expanding sales would not be an easy task. In northern California, for example, demand was thought weak, 'principally because a good second-hand car is cheaper than a new imported motor cycle'. This news had little evident effect on Triumph's managing director, Edward Turner. In the midst of war, he was busily cultivating his pre-war contacts in Los Angeles with an eye to a build-up of exports when the time was right.[36]

Yet this good news was tempered with caution. Shortly after the American entry into the war in December 1941, British industry generally was warned about the implications of a changed export environment in the post-war era. During a speech to a conference of export groups in late January 1942, the President of the Board of Trade informed them that in future there would be far closer economic collaboration between Britain and the USA, which might result in a 'possible division of export markets'.[37]

The implications of this development, in the view of the Board of Trade, was that there would have to be a greater level of 'co-operation and understanding' among the manufacturers themselves if they wished to increase exports. They would now have to accept that the 'general tendency of export business in the future would be on a collective basis instead of [an] individual basis'.[38] Later on, Watling drew the obvious conclusions with respect to the future of the Manufacturers' Union and why it was so important to have a membership embracing the entire industry: 'All that has been said and written of post-war organisation of Trade makes it extremely probable that the Government will expect Industry to negotiate on all matters affecting marketing, sales, propaganda, production and export on a collective basis.' Furthermore, manufacturers could expect to have materials allocated by the government through the trade organisations.[39]

The motor cycle industry was also warned that the British Imperial Preference system might have to be abandoned. Certain Dominions, especially Australia, had already indicated their intention to start up secondary industries that would compete with British imports. This might also have implications with respect to the kind of exports Britain could send abroad. Perhaps it might be best for British manufacturers to concentrate on producing 'high grade products' and leave the 'cheaper products' to be made in the 'markets in which there was comparatively cheap labour'.[40]

These changes were being brought about largely because of increased dependency on American imports shipped in under the Lend-Lease Agreement. Although this agreement was essential to the continuation of the British war effort, Roosevelt's Lend-Lease administrator Edward Stettinius was putting heavy pressure upon the Board of Trade to curtail what little export trade remained between Britain and other nations. After the war it was feared these restrictions might well carry on. The Americans had also raised the question of creating a form of joint planning and the allocation of markets between themselves and the British.[41]

In early 1942 the Board of Trade canvassed the industry to determine what the problems it thought might impede a speedy conversion to civilian production. Considering the wartime conditions, the industry's response was quite optimistic. In contrast to the bicycle industry, which was only 25 per cent engaged in its normal production, the board was informed that 75 per cent of the motor cycle industry was devoted to more or less regular manufacture, albeit nearly all destined for military use. Production was by then limited to seven firms, and the civilian and export trades had declined severely. Still, once the hostilities ended, the board was advised, full peace-time production could be reached in only 'a few months', as long as enough raw materials, specifically steel, aluminium, alloys and brass, were made available.[42]

To questions about improving its complement of research and design staff, the industry could only reply that there were 'enquiries to be made'. In terms of new models, the ministry was informed that at least one firm was thinking about producing a light-weight two-stroke machine, with an engine capacity of between 100 to 125 cc, and there was also the possibility of a four-stroke 175 cc model.[43] Although the industry anticipated a strong demand abroad for British motor cycles (in fact, it was believed demand would be well in excess of supply), it did expect some sort of help from the government. The time would soon come, argued the manufacturers, for the government 'to modify their attitude towards the industry and give real encouragement to production and research in technical problems and design rather than confine their contacts to the introduction of restrictive measures'. No explanation was provided, at this time at least, about what was meant by 'real encouragement'.[44]

The industry attached some importance to the Imperial Preferential Tariff system, although it noted that commercial relations with the Germans, previously the industry's biggest competitors, had become 'definitely friendly' just prior to the outbreak of war. The favourable trade agreements extended beyond the boundaries of the Empire. For example, the one negotiated with Argentina just before the war had been 'of very definite advantages to the industry', especially when there had been fierce competition with the Germans.[45]

Preparing for peace

During this period there was also some internal discussion about how best to prepare for peace-time production. At least one senior industry leader, Triumph managing director Edward Turner, reflected publicly on the opportunities that would be open to motor cycle manufacturers after the war and urged the industry to appeal to a broader market than it had previously. In a paper delivered to several chapter meetings of the Institution of Automobile Engineers, Turner expressed the belief that the motor cycle industry, so badly hit by the decline in home and export markets during the 1930s, could now bounce back if only the right kind of motor cycle were produced.[46]

Turner's remarks, all the more telling coming as they did from the managing director of a firm whose market share had actually increased in the three years before the war, repeated many of the criticisms levelled at the industry since 1929. Motor cycle design, he admitted, had been uninspired and far too oriented to the racetrack: the industry had been 'almost entirely supported by the sporting elements and consequently restricted in its appeal'. Turner did not advocate forsaking sporting events completely, nor abandoning the sports enthusiasts; after all, he conceded, races such as the TT had a role in stimulating design at the top end of the market. What he had in mind, however, was a motor cycle that 'will attract, by its utility, the ordinary pedestrian'.[47]

But, as became evident in the remainder of his paper, Turner was unclear exactly what he meant by the term 'economy' motor cycle. Like other critics, Turner stressed the need for quiet running, easy starting and handling and some form of weather protection in order to appeal to potential but less dedicated motor cyclists. However, he was reluctant to commit himself to specifying just what kind of machine the ideal motor cycle would be. Although Turner saw the virtue of incorporating these features in motor cycles of all sizes, he stopped short of actually urging the industry to try and create a mass market by manufacturing the 'autocycles' or other small-engined motor cycles such as Germany had done before 1939.[48]

Turner's article did precipitate a brief debate within the industry about why it had been unable to produce a successful 'economy' motor cycle and what the future direction should be. Donald Heather, then an AMC director, dismissed any hope of producing a 'utility' motor cycle. Many different versions had been tried, he reminded those present at the London chapter discussion, but they had all failed: '... the fact remains that we have always come back to the sports type, not because the industry has not shown an interest in the utility machine or has not attempted to make it, but because the sports market is, in fact, the dominant market.'[49]

Turner replied that it was about time the industry faced facts. Look at the basic statistics, he urged. Registrations and production had declined consistently since 1930: 'That would rather indicate that a lot of people were not too satisfied with the service they were getting from their machines, and that they were going in for cars (as the great majority of them did) or preferred to ride bicycles.' Over the years, the motor cycle had slipped badly when compared to other forms of transport, and the decline had to be arrested: 'We should not be satisfied merely to carry on the industry as it is, but should try to develop it and make more people motor cycle minded.'[50]

Others present at the meetings found further defects in the record of the 'utility' motor cycle. Bertram Marians, managing director of Phelon and Moore (manufacturers of Panther motor cycles), criticised the poor advertising of the industry compared to motor car companies. Another participant blamed 'the innate conservatism' of the British public, which had failed to buy 'several advanced designs'. However, Turner himself conceded that not enough effort had gone into producing products of high quality: 'We have lost literally thousands of customers through the years because of the utility machine falling to pieces, sometimes before the owner paid for it.'[51]

Did any of the companies take up Turner's suggestions and try to develop an improved motor cycle design? As before 1939, BSA was preparing the most extensive model line-up, which would be offered in two phases after the war. The first would be a number of essentially pre-war vintage designs, 250 cc, 350 cc and 500 cc models, as well as reconditioned military machines. The second range was to be far more comprehensive, covering a 98 cc auto-cycle (badged as 'New Hudson') plus models in the 250 cc, 350 cc and 500 cc capacity. BSA was also studying a Harley-Davidson with the intent of producing an 800 cc twin-cylinder model and was considering manufacturing 250 cc and 500 cc shaft-drive machines, one of which was to be based on a captured German model.[52]

Other firms were working on new designs of their own, none of which differed greatly from their pre-war offerings. Douglas, for example, capitalising on its work during the war producing aircraft components, was readying a 350 cc transverse 'flat' twin, unlike anything else in Britain at the time, although not to be marketed until 1947. AMC was the first British manufacturer to incorporate hydraulic front forks (until then virtually all the manufacturers used the so-called 'girder' forks that were generally thought inferior) based on those used on certain pre-war German motor cycles.

However, the company also decided to drop its 250 cc and the large-capacity twin-cylinder models and to concentrate on the 350 cc and 500 cc machines. Norton's prospective 1945 line-up comprised just two models, both using designs from 1939. A large displacement twin-cylinder machine, designed to match the Triumph Speed Twin, was also under consideration.[53]

And what did Edward Turner's Triumph company have planned? Ironically, although its motor cycles were as technologically advanced as any in Britain, they were virtually all directed at performance-oriented customers. In 1945 the smallest projected machine was a 350 cc model, and three variants of the 500 cc twin-cylinder machines were planned. They might have met, in part, the criteria Turner had earlier defined for rider satisfaction, but they were 'utility' or 'economy' machines in only the very broadest possible sense.[54]

The Manufacturers' Union was very interested in taking advantage of the suspension of peace-time trading to reorganise the home market. In 1943 the Union and the Motor Cycle Section of the Motor Agents' Association (MAA) formed a special joint committee, composed of equal representation by manufacturers and retailers, in order to begin making arrangements for trading in Britain once the war ended. There were a number of items which both parties wanted reviewed.[55]

The retailers in general were unhappy about the large numbers of shops around the country that had built up during the 1930s. There were, they maintained, 'too many dealers in relation to the number of machines sold'. This was caused by the manufacturers having sold some of their machines to 'dabblers', dealers who were not really committed to the trade. They wanted the rules tightened up with respect to what kind of shops could sell motor cycles. Another point of concern was control of the prices of second-hand machines and of the allowances given on vehicles traded in on exchange. This was considered to be 'essential'.[56]

The manufacturers wanted an overhaul of the rebate system they administered, although there was some division on this point. They were also adamant on maintaining their right to appoint their own dealers, 'dabblers' or not. Another point the manufacturers wished to promote was a standardised discount, based on a two-tier dealership system, to apply across the trade and cover all types of motor cycle. This, they believed, would 'provide the best incentive for the trade to sell more motor cycles'.[57] Both parties were especially concerned to deal with the issue of high insurance premiums. The retailers considered this issue to have been 'unquestionably … one of the greatest sales deterrents in the past'. It was agreed to have the committee investigate the feasibility of having an industry-wide insurance plan implemented, with the backing of the Manufacturers' Union. Several alternatives were reviewed, although no decision was made before the end of the war.[58]

Making the transition from war to peace

Over the winter of 1943/44, with the war clearly going in favour of the Allies, the industry and government entered into a more intense phase of post-war planning. In a memorandum dated 9 May 1944, intended as a response to a Board of Trade questionnaire distributed in the previous year, the Manufacturers' Union provided a comprehensive overview of both its current problems and expectations for the future.[59]

This was not as optimistic an appraisal as their earlier memorandum. Worries were now being expressed that, although a minority (approximately 30 per cent) of the manufacturers thought that the transition from war to peace-time production would be comparatively painless (assuming, of course, sufficient supplies of labour and materials), this was not the case for the remainder. They would face a difficult task, 'owing to the practical restrictions upon design and development since the outbreak of war'. This would mean that the industry would be looking to the government for help in terms of the release of technicians and other specialist personnel, provision of research equipment, as well as new plant and training for other labour. The manufacturers were also very anxious about the 'excessive wear and tear' inflicted on their factory and plant and hoped for government relief.[60]

What sort of specific proposals did the industry put to the Board of Trade in order to enable it to 'overcome existing difficulties'? Top of the list was a request to modify the Essential Works Orders (EWOs) to give the firms 'a greater control over labour' (they did not explain how this was to be accomplished), which 'might eliminate difficulties with respect to shortages or excess of personnel to the advantage of both employer and employed'. The early return of the skilled labour, displaced during the course of the war effort, was deemed essential if the manufacturers were to provide 'a higher standard of performance and economy and easier maintenance'.[61]

Suggestions were also made regarding re-employment of returning soldiers and 'directed' labour, as well as the importance of what was termed 'key' personnel. On the 'supply side', the industry wanted existing tool room plant put at their disposal as soon as possible at the conclusion of military contracts, and the provision of 'cheap money' to allow for needed capital expenditure. They also hoped to be allowed to buy surplus government plant 'at prices equitable to the purchasing manufacturer' as well as 'further concessions' with respect to income tax allowances for depreciation of plant and machinery.[62]

On the question of re-opening the home market, the industry urged the 'complete and speedy' abolition of the Purchase Tax which was thought 'to restrict the volume of sales in the Home Market and thus retard economy in production and reduction of price to the consumer'. With respect to sales abroad, the government was asked to take 'emphatic and immediate steps' to ensure 'the prompt re-establishment of export trade' with a minimum of limitations. Moreover, it was assumed that the Americans would be requested to drop 'the harassing restrictions of Lend-Lease'.[63] However, potential export success was being jeopardised by certain government departments.

Criticism, for example, was voiced about the effectiveness of the Export Credits Guarantee Department. Its insurance was considered too expensive; department staff were too conservative in accepting risks offered by exporters; and service was 'slow and cumbersome'. The industry realised the opportunities offered in the post-war export market and anticipated being able to replace German and Italian manufacturers in their previous commercial strongholds. To this end, the government was asked to impose controls on their pre-war competitors and thus ensure, over a transitional period at least, that British industry would be protected from the 'unfair competition' that had characterised the latter part of the 1930s. If this could be done, the promise abroad was considerable: with 'the improvement in the standard of living and the comparatively high cost of other forms of mechanical transport', future circumstances 'should give UK Motor Cycle Manufacturers a valuable opportunity in other Overseas Markets'.[64]

However, the memorandum contained a surprising admission of internal divisions over how best to re-open overseas markets. The Manufacturers' Union itself was in favour of some form of collective market research that would be coordinated centrally. However, some constituent firms were dubious about this on the grounds that such a policy was not 'practicable'. It might yet be possible for individual firms, or limited combinations of firms, to act in unison, but nothing had been planned yet.[65] The submission also contained a prediction that later would be shown to be, at best, wildly optimistic. Encouraged by its modest expansion since 1939, when annual production was greater than any single year since 1929, the Manufacturers' Union claimed that, within one year of the upcoming Armistice, assuming sufficient skilled labour and materials, it could produce 500,000 motor cycles and parts for sale at home and abroad. This prediction was based, again far too hopefully, on the experience it claimed to have gained in supplying the war effort. In light of the fact that the pre-war peak reached in 1927 was only 160,000 units, this was a highly ambitious, if not rash, self-imposed target.[66]

The industry now began to focus seriously on the practical problems of improving the export trade to the United States. It was a potential market which held much promise but was also one where the British manufacturers – with the exception of Triumph and Ariel – had little experience and few contacts among existing motor cycle distributors. Then in May 1944 a fortuitous development occurred. The British Consul-General in Chicago was approached by A.R. Child, local manager of the Lockheed

Aircraft Company, who indicated that he wished to become the American representative for British motor cycle manufacturers.[67]

Child presented a glowing picture of the sales potential of North America. In his opinion, because of difficulties they would experience converting back to peace-time production, the sole American manufacturers, Harley-Davidson and Indian, would be unable to produce for the civilian market for two years after the end of hostilities, and the British now had a golden opportunity to step in and fill the gap. Child thought that American consumers, who had not bought motor cycles in any great numbers since the 1920s, were ready for the kind of machines Britain could produce, whether the sophisticated Ariel Square Four or the speedy and agile twin-cylinder Triumphs, which would be a welcome contrast to the larger but slower and less manoeuvrable American models.[68]

Child declared that he could resolve any problems the British might have with tariffs and currency exchange and that freight rates overseas would be competitive with continental rail charges. Best of all, because of his previous association with Harley-Davidson, Child possessed what he described as 'wide personal friendships with many of the most important motor cycle distributors'. Child presented himself as just the man to make the connections they would need in order to break into the American market.[69]

At about the same time, the Manufacturers' Union was approached by the automakers' industry association, the Society of Motor Manufacturers and Traders (SMMT), which wanted to know whether or not there was any interest in combining the resources of the two organisations in terms of creating a co-operative arrangement for an export campaign. The proposed scheme was targeted at Empire and Dominion territories such as Australia, South Africa and India, but also included South America and the Middle East. At long last it seemed as if the industry was serious about laying the groundwork for a new, revamped worldwide sales and distribution network, and now had the means before it.[70]

Sorting out problems

In late 1944 the Anglo-American armies were crossing France and had begun to approach German territory itself. There was now little doubt that in a matter of months the war in Europe would be coming to an end. At this point, two specific issues came to preoccupy the attention of the industry. The first was how the government might smoothly wind up the wartime controls and disengage from its military contracts and so allow the manufacturers to resume full civilian production. The second focused on what would now happen to the large stocks of surplus motor cycles. Both issues contained plenty of potential for continued friction between the government and the industry.

Industry representatives had an opportunity to put many of their concerns about the post-war situation to Board of Trade representative Captain B.H. Peters, in the course of two meetings held during the summer of 1944. At these meetings the manufacturers claimed that they would have little difficulty converting to peace-time production, again assuming they were supplied with enough labour and material. Major Watling recognised that exports would be 'a very high priority', although Union President Gilbert Smith made it clear that the industry wanted government controls removed as soon as possible. They also urged the lifting of Purchase Tax on both motor cycles and bicycles on the grounds that they were not a 'luxury' but rather 'an essential means of transport for workers'.[71]

There were matters concerning export markets which also needed the speedy attention of the government. Not only would the current restrictions have to be lifted, but there were certain aspects to international agreements which were complicating the industry's efforts to re-enter overseas markets. Under the Lend-Lease agreement, for example, Australia, Britain's most important export market, had been allocated to American motor cycle manufacturers. This would have to be altered or removed altogether as soon as possible. But there were also many opportunities now opening to the industry. India, which held large sterling balances as a result of wartime financial arrangements, had an especially good potential.[72]

There were other problems which pressed upon the industry. The question of cutbacks in government orders of motor cycles first arose in late 1944. Watling had expressed his concern to a Board of Trade official about rumours flying around the industry to the effect that government contracts would soon be coming to an end. The rumours were denied, but Watling used the opportunity to make clear his objections to the fact that production schedules had been set by the Ministry of Supply without first consulting either the manufacturers or, for that matter, the Board itself. He also noted that some of the manufacturers were now reluctant to seek approval from the government to begin producing prototypes of new civilian models, since they feared that to do so might be interpreted as an admission of a labour surplus, with all that implied under the prevailing circumstances.[73]

There followed a series of meetings between the Manufacturers' Union and various government ministries to negotiate the terms of the conversion to civilian production. At one held during late November 1944, Watling vented his ire at Colonel R. Grantham, a senior representative of the Ministry of Supply. Although the India Office had indicated that they were 'very anxious' to resume importing motor cycles, Watling complained to Grantham that his ministry would only allow the export of light-weight models, a type that the Indians apparently did not want.[74]

Several weeks later, at a conference at the Board of Trade, Grantham delivered some good news. Service requirements were dropping off, he announced, to such an extent that the industry would be able to resume peace-time production, 'on a considerable scale', as early as July 1945. Capacity would be released to the individual firms on a proportional basis and phased in over the forthcoming months. Edward Turner, who was present at the meeting on behalf of Triumph and Ariel, wanted to know if permitted exports would now include the heavy-weight models, his firms' speciality. This would be allowed, he was informed, but the priority export targets were to be Allied and Continental markets.[75]

In January 1945 a meeting between the Ministry of Supply and the Manufacturers' Union thrashed out many of the detailed problems. Colonel Grantham, who was chairing the meeting, informed industry representatives that, following a discussion with the Board of Trade, it was decided that his Ministry would now be responsible for civilian motor cycle manufacturing, although the Board would still continue to administer the export licences. Grantham confirmed that by the end of the following June the current War Office delivery rates would be cut by 40 per cent. Moreover, the manufacturers could use their extra capacity to ship abroad as many motor cycles as they were able to produce; indeed, the Ministry was 'anxious that the export of motor cycles should be as high as the availability of labour would allow'.[76]

In turn, Grantham wanted each firm to forward to his Ministry their estimates of the numbers and type of machines they wished to export. These would be examined by Ministry personnel who would issue material allocations accordingly. The industry was more or less free to choose their export destinations, subject to continuing service commitments and urgent orders, although Canada and the Middle East were two locations where 'special conditions' prevailed (presumably because of currency or remaining Lend-Lease restrictions).[77]

Nonetheless, by the end of January, the industry had formulated its own post-war production programme which it hoped to develop, subject to supplies of materials, especially rubber. The programme envisaged a total of 35,000 machines, the majority in the 250 cc and over engine capacity class, for the remainder of 1945, starting at the end of hostilities.[78] At the Ministry of Supply, staff were busy evaluating the applications from the firms who wished to export. The Ministry had also worked out a fairly detailed analysis of the industry's productive capacity and employment levels.[79]

However, the industry found itself becoming increasingly frustrated with the slow pace that restrictions, especially the hated Licence to Acquire, were being lifted from civilian production.[80] In April a telegram signed by Watling was sent to the Ministry of Fuel and Power which stated that, since the industry was about to recommence civilian production, it was imperative that both the Licence to Acquire be scrapped, and the basic petrol ration increased, in order to encourage sales of motor cycles to potential customers in the home market. Not only was there a growing demand for motor cycles in the home market, but increased numbers of them on British roads would help take some pressure off over-worked public transportation systems. If no changes were forthcoming, Watling warned, the Manufacturers' Union would make this a political issue.[81]

A meeting was scheduled on 11 May at the Board of Trade in order to resolve the industry's continuing problems. Watling stated at the outset that the Manufacturers' Union was 'frankly anxious and irritated at the delay in removing obstructions in the way of their civilian trade'. He firmly stated the Manufacturers' Union's major requirements: the need to increase the basic petrol ration; to give the industry the discretion to resume servicing its former export markets (especially in continental Europe, now starved for personal transport); to revise the motor cycle tax structure; and, finally, to remove the Licence to Acquire, in order to allow the home market to develop fully.[82]

Industry representatives were especially angry about what they considered unnecessary continuation of export restrictions. W. Corbett, a representative from Douglas motor cycles, for example, told the Ministry of Supply and Board of Trade officials present that, even though his firm had a number of outstanding orders from Australia and New Zealand, they could not be fulfilled because of lack of co-operation from the British government. Such limitations would hobble the industry's ability to maintain their export programme.[83]

Like the other manufacturers, The Douglas company saw a strong correlation between an expanding home market and a healthy export trade. Corbett claimed that, during the pre-war period, Douglas had sold 30 per cent of production abroad, but that under the right conditions this figure could now be increased to 50 per cent. He argued that 'practically no profit is made on exports' and instead much would depend on the home market, since foreign sales tended to fluctuate from year to year and the domestic trade absorbed production when exports were weak.[84]

W. Binney, Principal Assistant Secretary of the Board of Trade and chairman of the meeting, expressed some scepticism about this assertion of the inter-relationship between exports and the home market. After all, he reminded industry representatives, 'cost was surely related to output irrespective of the distribution between markets'. But he said that the officials present would do whatever they could to expedite matters for the motor cycle producers.[85]

In Watling's view, the best way to administer the home market was simply to leave it all in the hands of the industry. Together with the existing high prices and limited petrol supplies, the market itself would then regulate sales. There was no need for the Licence to Acquire system to stay on. However, a Ministry of War Transport official noted that, over the previous two years, only ten applications in total of motor cycles had been turned down, so 'it could hardly be claimed that the system was restricting the home market'.[86]

Another particularly sensitive matter for the industry was the question of the disposal of surplus military motor cycles. Evidently, after the First World War the industry had been able to convince the government of the day to scrap the surplus military stock instead of releasing it on to the open market. However, it seemed unlikely that this would happen a second time. Manufacturers' Union President Gilbert Smith noted that both the Treasury and what he termed 'public opinion' would not 'easily be persuaded' to allow this to happen once more. The Manufacturers' Union would, he declared, develop other alternatives.[87]

For its part, the Board of Trade was beginning to find the growing numbers of military motor cycles, now surplus to requirements but under its jurisdiction, to be particularly irksome. Because of wartime government contracts, the manufacturers had produced far more motor cycles since 1939 than they would ever have done under normal circumstances, and, as one memorandum noted, disposal of these machines was a time-consuming task. One factor which made disposal so difficult was what was termed the 'peculiar' nature of the home motor cycle market. First, this was because of the decline in motor cycle sales before the war (attributed to the greater appeal of light motor cars) which might continue after the war, and, second, because sales would be limited by the fact that this was a 'pleasure market', one 'to some extent confined to the sporting youth section of the community'. Finally, continuation of petrol sales would hardly be an incentive for members of the public to want to buy personal motorised transport.[88]

Earlier on during the war, the Board had already become apprehensive of what would happen to motor cycle prices after the end of hostilities. The problem was thought to be more acute for used rather than new motor cycles. Even in 1942 a Board official had told Watling that his Ministry feared 'the likelihood of exorbitant prices being asked for motor cycles' and was investigating the possibility of the application of controls. However, by 1944, circumstances seem to have changed drastically. Another Board official told Watling that they were open to the Manufacturers' Union's suggestions. Indeed, as far as he was concerned, the entire matter of disposals was 'a blank piece of paper upon which they could write'.[89]

The manufacturers advanced several proposals. Gilbert Smith thought that surplus machines could be stored in the vacant factories that were scattered around the countryside and could be drawn upon as needed and absorbed into trade channels. Edward Turner had a simple solution: send off as much of the surplus as possible to what he called 'backward territories'. In fact, he believed this was also a shrewd marketing ploy that could pay dividends later on, since ownership of these motor cycles would subsequently 'arouse in such people a desire to continue to acquire them'.[90]

A solution to the problem was reached in the spring of 1945. The whole question had become complicated by the fact that, far from being a sellers' market, the home market was depressed because of continued petrol rationing, which undercut the attraction of ownership, irrespective of price. The Manufacturers' Union convinced the government to allow the individual firms to buy and re-condition used military motor cycles, at a predetermined figure, and then gradually to release them onto the market.

A ceremony marking the delivery of the 400,000th motor cycle, in this case a Triumph, to the War Department. During the Second World War British motor cycle production far exceeded any other single nation including the USA and Germany. Not only was the British industry able to supply its own forces but also those of Commonwealth nations such as Australia and Canada.

COURTESY OF THE IVOR DAVIES COLLECTION

There does not seem to have been any wholesale scrapping of surplus British motor cycles, nor price hikes to the levels feared, although there were to be problems regulating the flow of reconditioned machines.[91]

As the war drew to a close, it was clear that the British motor cycle industry had regained an undisputed position as world leader in the trade. Between 1939 and 1945, it had produced more motor cycles than any other country, in excess of 400,000 machines by May 1945.[92] (See table 12.) German production, in contrast, had totalled 307,436 machines of all types over the period 1940–44. Arguably the Germans often showed more innovation in their designs, but with many of their factories destroyed by bombing and the nation now about to fall under Allied occupation, no one seriously thought they would pose a threat for some time to come.[93] As for the other continental producers, they may not have been as badly damaged as the Germans, but they all suffered from the war to one degree or other.

Table 12   *British motor cycle production, September 1939 to December 1944*

	Sept. 1939/Dec. 1940	*1941*	*1942*	*1943*	*1944*	*Total*
Ariel	4,098	7,197	8,946	8,792	7,527	35,560
AMC	10,556	12,812	16,435	16,726	14,567	71,096
BSA	24,758	21,758	21,876	19,753	18,427	106,572
Enfield	8,422	9,199	9,637	8,960	10,354	46,572
Excelsior	–	–	636	3,205	–	3,841
James	–	–	–	2,222	2,610	4,832
Norton	23,880	18,924	15,112	10,814	9,553	78,283
Triumph	9,018	840	2,563	8,246	10,709	31,376
Velo	666	554	797	130	–	2,147
Misc.	–	19	–	966	451	1,436
Grand total	81,398	71,303	76,002	79,814	74,198	382,715

Note: these figures may or may not include civilian production destined for dollar export countries.
Source: PRO AVIA 46/192.

The USA, which had emerged in 1945 as an economic and military superpower, still lagged well behind Britain as a motor cycle producer. During the war, the combined volume of the Harley-Davidson and Indian companies amounted to 130,044 machines or just barely over one quarter of Britain's military output. Nor had they been beset by the same degree of material shortages or had their operations disrupted by enemy action and seemed to be in a better condition to increase market share. However, there was no evident sign that they intended to extend their model range beyond their pre-war offering or had any plans for post-war marketing.[94]

The British manufacturers wasted little time in introducing their peace-time models to the public. Triumph actually announced its 1945 line-up while the British army was still fighting its way to Berlin, and this development was followed by one from AMC only a few weeks before VE day. However, these motor cycles would not be available to the public until after government permission had been received. Moreover, several of the firms had shown an interest in examining captured German machines for possible incorporation of their features in upcoming models of their own.[95]

Still, at least one disquieting note was recorded. The *Motor Cycle and Cycle Trader* let the manufacturers know its misgivings about their peace-time plans. True, Britain was again back on top with a seemingly freer hand than before to expand into markets all over the world, but on what basis would this be done? A correspondent writing in that journal saw the potential for growth in the small 'economy' motor cycle category, and this was especially important if the industry wished to service the strong demand for cheap, basic personal transport on the Continent.[96] Yet the British manufacturers seemed no more inclined to follow this advice than they had been in the 1930s. True, the motor cycle industry seemed to be entering a period of prosperity, but the fundamental question remained largely unanswered: how long would these happy circumstances last?

CHAPTER THREE
Revival and complacency, 1945–1951

THE SIX YEARS AFTER THE WAR provided the motor cycle industry, like much of British industry generally, with unparalleled opportunities for an expansion of sales both at home and abroad. These opportunities were considerable, as British manufacturers were now well ahead of their foreign competitors in terms of production and design. Yet the challenges facing them were also daunting. British motor cycle firms were now subject to frequent disruption of their supplies of labour and raw materials, a condition that was to be their bane for several years to come. Moreover, after the June 1945 General Election, the industry also had to assess the attitude of a whole new set of ministers. There was now the uncertainty of discovering where the industry stood in relation to the newly elected Labour government's reconstruction plans. An internal debate commenced as to how the manufacturers could best prepare for the future.

Recovering from war

During the course of a series of meetings in the first half of 1945, the Manufacturers' Union set itself several goals for the years that would follow the defeat of Germany: first, to convert to civilian production as quickly as possible; second, to re-open export markets, especially those that had been lost to the Germans during the 1930s and during the war, thanks to foreign competition in export markets and later through the terms of the Lend-Lease programme;[1] third, to complete designs for new models and get them into showrooms quickly, at home and abroad, in order to maintain and enlarge existing ownership; and, finally, to acquire new plant and factories where needed, through the anticipated Reparations Programme.[2]

This final point was an especially sensitive one in light of the fierce rivalry that had been waged between the British and German motor cycle industries during the 1930s. The industry believed it now had the opportunity

Triumph motor cycles participating in the 1946 celebrations held in London marking victory over the Axis powers in the Second World War.

to investigate German factories thoroughly and to pick up plant and designs, virtually, they hoped, on demand. British manufacturers thought they would also be able to discover just how the Germans had been able to launch and maintain their pre-war export drive which had so alarmed industry leaders. Many British manufacturers firmly believed that this success was less the result of the superior quality of German designs or their manufacturing techniques but instead the result of state-sponsored subsidies.[3]

When Germany capitulated in May 1945, the motor cycle industry was more fortunate than other British industries. Although some of its factories had been bombed during the conflict, nearly all the damage had been repaired or replaced, and Triumph, for one, actually emerged from the war with far better facilities than it had started out with in 1939. Moreover, unlike the motor car industry's 'Big Six', who had been required by the war effort to drop their regular production programmes and had become heavily committed to aircraft and other military work, the major British motor cycle companies had continued building their main line of products, albeit modified for the armed services. For this reason, for them reconversion would likely be fraught with fewer problems in terms of retooling for peace-time production.

Nonetheless, there still remained the difficulties of procuring sufficient quantities of materials and labour. Unlike the motor industry, motor cycle manufacturers were not at first subject to the same degree of tight export quotas, although intimations to this effect had been received by certain manufacturers, even before the war had ended. In January 1945 BSA, for one, had been told that materials and labour would only be forthcoming contingent on production for export.[4] However, as late as May 1946, the industry had yet to receive firm export guidelines from the government. At that point, Triumph Chairman Jack Sangster led a Union delegation to the Board of Trade and concluded a verbal agreement that ensured 50 per cent of production would go abroad.[5]

In fact, the industry claimed its exports had consistently reached this target both before and after Sangster's agreement. By early 1946, for example, Norton was already exporting 75 per cent of its output, mostly to Canada and various South American countries. In September 1947, a letter was received from the Ministry of Supply notifying the Manufacturers' Union that, pursuant with guidelines put down for four-wheeled motor vehicles and bicycles, henceforth the motor cycle industry would have to increase its proportion of exports to 75 per cent. In another communication, the Ministry informed the industry that it had approved its 1948 production programme at the level of 150,000 machines, assuming adequate supplies of materials and labour.[6]

The manufacturers unanimously agreed to meet this new export target, by way of a series of monthly increases of 5 per cent, commencing that October. Union members were also relieved to hear news of a recent speech made by Board of Trade President Harold Wilson, delivered in Birmingham, where he had promised the motor cycle industry priority deliveries of coal and steel. They were disappointed, however, to learn later in October that they would not qualify as a priority industry for labour supplies.[7]

British motor cycle manufacturers were mindful of the situation they had faced immediately prior to the war when German competition had eroded many previously secure overseas markets. However, now they faced a radically changed trading environment and one that could work very much to their favour. It was obvious that, after the sustained aerial bombing and extensive ground fighting which had destroyed large parts of its industrial plant, Germany would not be in any condition to challenge Britain industrially for some time to come. Many manufacturers hoped that the Germans would now face punitive limitations on production, in order to retard any quick recovery in overseas markets. Italy, the lesser pre-war competitor, was not treated as a former enemy, having dropped out of the Axis in 1943. Yet it would still need time to reorganise its battered industries.[8] Therefore, the only conceivable competition would have to come from the Americans, whose industry had been progressively fading away in export markets long before 1939 and who seemed to be preoccupied with supplying its own domestic market.[9]

The structure of the post-war industry

There had also been some changes in the structure of the British industry during the war years. The 'Big Six' had persisted to 1939 but did not survive the war. It had become, for all intents and purposes, the 'Big Five' after BSA bought Ariel Motors from Jack Sangster, along with the rights to the defunct New Imperial name, in October 1944.[10] Production continued at Ariel's Birmingham factory but now under the overall direction of the BSA Board of Directors. Although the sales agreement promised a degree of autonomy for the firm, this would diminish progressively year by year.[11] Ariel was not the only motor cycle firm picked up by BSA before 1945. Cash rich because of its numerous and lucrative military contracts, BSA had gone off on a wartime buying spree. Prior to the Ariel sale both New Hudson and Sunbeam had been purchased in 1943, the latter from AMC. The BSA Group, which was the largest producer before the war, became by 1945 the dominant and pre-eminent firm within the industry.[12]

Two other well-known pre-war names did not survive the war. Rudge-Whitworth, a Coventry-based quality producer, had been bought by music giant EMI and production moved to a new factory in Hayes, Middlesex. However, the planned resumption of motor cycle production was disrupted by the war, and the factory was instead put to work with other types of manufacture. After the war EMI decided to keep Rudge shut down, although it would later produce a reasonably successful motor attachment for bicycles, the Cyclemaster. Brough-Superior, the low-production, high-quality firm favoured by the well-heeled or celebrity riders such as T.E. Lawrence, was concentrated into munitions work during the war and simply never resumed production after 1945.[13]

The 'Big Five' British motor cycle manufacturers were either in a position to produce new or revamped models immediately or at least had something moving through their development offices.[14] Triumph was probably the best prepared of all the British firms to move quickly and exploit the export market. This company had experienced great success with its innovative and pace-setting 500 cc vertical-twin cylinder model, the Speed Twin. Although it was not specifically designed as a 'National Champion' for export markets, in the way that the Standard Motors Vanguard automobile had been, this machine certainly gave the company a strong competitive advantage in the

This motor cycle trials event, sponsored by the British Empire Motor Club, was held somewhere in Ontario, Canada, during the 1930s, much like other similar activities then taking place around North America. However, before the Second World War, British motor cycles were more often seen in Canada than they were in the USA.

COURTESY OF ED MOODY

post-war era.[15] Introduced over the 1936/37 season, this motor cycle had put Triumph well ahead of the pack and left the other firms scrambling to develop equivalent models of their own.

Thus Triumph, based since 1942 in their Meriden plant on the outskirts of Coventry, which was then probably the most modern motor cycle factory in the world, lost no time switching to civilian production. Not only was the Meriden works designed for dedicated motor cycle production, but the company had, for the most part, been able since 1942 to stick to their regular line of manufacture for the British armed forces. Hence, converting back to civilian-based manufacturing was not too difficult.[16]

More important, Triumph was probably the firm best positioned to move into the American market, the most promising in the world. Indeed, owner Jack Sangster had shown an interest in the USA before the war when both his Triumph and Ariel companies had begun to send small numbers of machines there. Moreover, Triumph Managing Director Edward Turner was especially keen about sales prospects in the USA, especially on the west coast.[17] Before the war, Turner had met an American lawyer and fellow motor cycle enthusiast, Bill Johnson, who was willing to set up a Triumph dealership in Los Angeles. This was to be the start of a growing foothold there. It is a reflection of Triumph's commitment to the American market that Jack Sangster allowed Turner six months off every year in order to travel to the USA and drum up sales. As will be seen, Triumph sales in the USA, mostly larger displacement machines, began to rise steadily.[18]

Triumph's orientation to larger displacement motor cycles made sound business sense. For an operation of its size, producing approximately 10,000 units per year, profits were more related to charging the highest possible price on individual machines as opposed to turnover gained from producing in large volumes. In 1947, for example, the factory produced, among others, 2,288 of its 500 cc T100 models, worth £266,904, and 3,630 of the 350 cc 3T models worth £350,721. Notwithstanding the higher turnover gained from the smaller machines, Triumph actually cleared £56,985 profit on the T100s compared to £49,619 for the 3Ts.[19]

Triumph may have been the first off the mark with the Speed Twin, but the other major firms were soon to follow with their own machines. AMC and Royal Enfield both introduced large displacement twin-cylinder models designed to compete directly with the Triumph. Norton was slower to produce a vertical twin, sticking to the big singles either out of loyalty or because of a shortage of funds for expansion or retooling. The latter constraint was rectified shortly after the conclusion of the war, when the company applied for government authorisation to build an addition to its Birmingham factory.[20] Nonetheless, thanks to their many racing victories, as well as much publicised patronage from celebrities such as entertainer George Formby, the Nortons had an aura of glamour that gave them a cachet over and above most other motor cycle brands.[21]

The other larger scale manufacturer, Royal Enfield, was still located at its long-time base at Redditch, although it continued to have access to a wartime underground munitions factory near Bradford-on-Avon, which would ultimately be used for motor cycle production. Although it too would produce a twin-cylinder model, a proportion of the company's production remained the traditional larger displacement single-cylinder machines.[22] This is not to suggest that all the British motor cycle industry produced were big displacement machines. Royal Enfield, for one, had a version of its 125 cc light-weight machine which had been used by British paratroopers during the war and was introduced in 1946. Most of the other firms, in and out of the 'Big Five', manufactured at least one 250 cc model, and, as before the war, smaller firms such as James, Francis-Barnett and Cyc-Auto produced a series of smaller machines, starting at the 98 cc engine displacement class.[23]

As the industry's largest firm, it was not surprising to discover that BSA had the most diversified and ambitious post-war programme.[24] By 1945 the company had several new designs ready for production, although in order to keep machines in the showrooms production of pre-war machines continued for some time after the end of the war. These models included some using the New Hudson and Ariel names, ranging from small BSA or New Hudson single-cylinder machines to the massive Ariel four-cylinder 'Square Four'.[25] These also included the inevitable 500 cc parallel vertical twin-cylinder model but also an innovative 500 cc shaft-drive machine, whose features undoubtedly owed something to the captured German BMWs and Zundapps. The 500 cc vertical cylinder twin, named the A7,

The Norton Dominator

This 500 cc twin-cylinder motor cycle began as Norton's answer to the ground-breaking Triumph Speed Twin (see page 273). Developed by designer Bert Hopwood, the Dominator was a startling change of direction for a company that until then had been best known as a builder of single-cylinder models.

Although perhaps Hopwood's most famous design, he never seemed particularly impressed with his creation, dismissing it as a 'stop-gap' that was forced on him by Norton's board of directors. What he had in mind was a far more radical and technically advanced machine, one that the company's finances simply could not afford at the time.

Despite this, the Dominator, and its derivatives, would continue in production for nearly three decades. Designed in 1947 and launched the following year, the Dominator gradually evolved, with its engine size progressively increasing to 600 cc, 650 cc and then, under the name Atlas, to 750 cc. Greater size and power, however, had their own drawbacks. The larger the engine, the greater the vibration, to the detriment of rider comfort and reliability, as nuts, bolts and other bits and pieces often shook loose the faster it was ridden. Shortly after 1966, when Norton and its parent, AMC, were taken over by Manganese Bronze Holdings and transformed into Norton-Villiers, the Atlas was given a makeover. Company engineers developed an ingenious way around the problem of vibration: a new, so-called 'isolastic' suspension system, placed the existing engine, gearbox and rear forks into a new independent sub-frame that was attached to the main frame by way of rubber mountings. The worst of the vibration problem was solved and achieved cheaply with a minimum of new parts.

The new bike, named the Commando, was not, except for its new suspension system, larger engine and some cosmetic styling changes, significantly different from the Dominator. Nonetheless, it had a spectacular debut in 1967 and also enjoyed some racetrack success. The Commando's greatest success, however, was with North American motor cyclists. By the early 1970s, the lion's share of sales were in the USA and Canada, and its engine had become even bigger, increased from 750 cc to 850 cc.

However, greater size could not disguise this motor cycle's age and the 'isolastic' suspension was not really a substitute for a proper re-design. Consequently, the Commando began to look more and more an anachronism when compared to the far more sophisticated Japanese motor cycles such as the Honda CB750.

Still, sales carried on until the liquidation of Norton-Villiers-Triumph in 1976 when production of the Commando finally ceased. Even more remarkably, and a testament to the soundness of Hopwood's original Dominator design and its enduring popularity, several attempts have been made to manufacture modern versions of the Commando, most recently by a company in the USA, although to date none appears to have had any real commercial success.

was targeted at a more sports-oriented market, to compete directly against Triumph's Speed Twin.[26]

In contrast, the shaft-drive machine, which would be badged under the recently acquired Sunbeam name, was given an entirely different image. Building on the Sunbeam marque's pre-war reputation as a comparatively expensive, high-quality 'gentleman's' motor cycle, it would enable the company to stake out the upper level of the market.[27] The company also found itself with an abundance of manufacturing capacity. The main factory at Small Heath, Birmingham, may not have been as modern as Triumph's Meriden operation, but it had been repaired and improved after the bomb damage of 1940 and 1941. Moreover, BSA had also managed a new 'Shadow' munitions factory in nearby Redditch, which would later be converted to motor cycle production.[28]

Hence, the company was able to develop a dual manufacturing strategy of continuing to produce pre-war models at Small Heath and then gradually to introduce new machines over the next year as they became available. At Redditch in the meantime, Sunbeam manufacture would commence as soon as possible. These facilities were complemented by a metal-plating firm, Monochrome, which had been bought by the group in 1946 along with Metal and Plastics Components.[29]

The one gap in BSA's plans was for an inexpensive light-weight motor cycle. Although the company had manufactured a 150 cc machine during most of the inter-war era, it had been dropped from the line-up towards the end of the 1930s. The company had developed a prototype autocycle model at the Small Heath factory just before the outbreak of the war, as a belated effort to re-enter the light-weight utility market. However, the sole copy had been destroyed during the 1940 Blitz, and engineers had been set to work devising a replacement. It was hoped this machine would have great potential in post-war Britain, undoubtedly starved for personal transport and which would have need of highly efficient, economy transport.[30]

BSA and Triumph were not the only firms to benefit from the acquisition of new war-time factories. Other Midlands motor cycle producers, such as James and Francis-Barnett, also suffered war damage and were relocated in renovated buildings. Francis-Barnett had even bid for a reconditioned Ministry of Supply building in Kenilworth, Warwickshire. It was ultimately sited in new quarters just outside Coventry city centre. The Coventry-Eagle Motor Company had been a smaller producer of bicycles and light-weight motor cycles before the war. During the war its factory had also been knocked out by the Luftwaffe. In 1945 it acquired the use of a new 'shadow' factory at Tile Hill near Coventry and announced an ambitious production programme. In the event Coventry-Eagle never did resume production of motor cycles, deciding instead to concentrate on bicycles.[31]

Among the smaller firms, more specialised sales strategies prevailed. the

Vincent Company, for example, had been formed in the late 1920s by Philip Vincent, a Harrow School and Cambridge University engineering graduate, unusual qualifications for a manager in the motor cycle industry. Vincent's father, who was a wealthy cattle rancher in Argentina, helped bankroll the company. During the inter-war years the company gained a reputation for building, albeit in small numbers, expensive high-performance racing and touring machines.[32]

In early 1946 Vincent acquired a former 'shadow' aero-engine factory in Stevenage, which complemented an existing works. During the war, although the firm had been diverted into general munitions and non-motor cycle work, time had been found for design work to revamp the existing line of large, sports- and touring-oriented 500 cc and 1000 cc machines. With hostilities concluded, Vincent was ready to produce a much-improved line of high-powered, expensive road burners. After only a short time its 1000 cc Rapide model, followed by a specially speed-tuned variant, the Black Shadow, put Britain far in advance of its potential American rivals in the top end of the market.[33]

Vincent is a good representation of what British motor cycle companies produced for the high end of the market, but there were a number of other smaller firms interested in developing the economy end. As during the inter-war period, these machines were mostly the products of firms outside the 'Big Five'. Veloce, the Birmingham manufacturer of Velocette motor cycles, which had made a reputation for its expensive sports-oriented machines, startled the industry by debuting its LE (Little Engine) machine at the 1948 Show. In the words of company director Eugene Goodman, Veloce had 'designed a machine that will not only make a great appeal to motor cyclists but one that will extend the market by attracting many people who want economical and trouble-free transport'. In this way the company hoped to carry on where the Francis & Barnett Cruiser of the 1930s had left off.[34] Other smaller companies were also active in this market. The James Company, which built machines mostly in the 125 cc range using proprietary Villiers engines, managed to procure a large order from the American market in 1945, through a distribution agreement with Hambros Bank. Two companies, Swallow and Brockhouse, built, respectively, the Gadabout and the Gorgi, which were early versions of the scooter, although they were not to be remotely as successful as the Italian Vespa or Lambretta.[35]

Meeting the expectations of the government

Even though many of these machines were diverted to overseas markets, the Manufacturers' Union did not display the same public vehemence in opposing government export quotas as did the SMMT. There was, for example, little of the open hostility shown by motor car manufacturers when

The Vincent Black Shadow

The Vincent Black Shadow might well be the most famous motor cycle ever built. The Vincent company, a small-scale manufacturer based in Stevenage, was founded by Philip Vincent in the late 1920s, originally as Vincent-HRD although later after the war simply as the Vincent Company. Born into an Anglo-Argentine family, Vincent left South America for Britain, where he attended Harrow School and also received at least some university-level training in mechanical engineering. With financing provided by his father, Vincent stayed on and went into motor cycle manufacturing through the purchase of the HRD company.

Together with Australian designer Philip Irving, Vincent and his small factory produced a limited number of high-performance motor cycles that were powered by 1,000 cc V-twin engines.

Diverted into munitions work during the Second World War, Vincent resumed production after 1945. Two models especially brought the company vast publicity and a legion of admirers, the Rapide, a fast touring machine and its glamorous sister, the Black Shadow (the name referred to a special baked-on black finish which coated the engine). These motor cycles were built to exceptionally high engineering standards. In the judgement of motor-journalist Mick Ducksworth, such was the level of their mechanical sophistication, the Vincents actually incorporated 'solutions to problems that didn't exist'.

They were also capable of astonishing performance and could easily achieve 120 mph and more, doing it with blistering acceleration. Indeed, the Black Shadow still dazzled motor cyclists years later. American writer Hunter S. Thompson, who tested one in the early 1970s, claimed, with a touch of hyperbole, that the Black Shadow was so fast it could, 'out-pace an F-111 [jet fighter plane] until take-off'.

Thanks to machines like the Black Shadow, Vincent had an outstanding export record, selling its motor cycles around the world. However, possibly because of Vincent's family background and business connections, the company became disproportionately dependent on the Argentinian market. When imports there were severely curtailed in the late 1940s, Vincent suffered a massive blow, one from which it never really recovered despite determined efforts to diversify sales elsewhere and even to try out other forms of manufacturing. The company struggled along, finally going out of business in 1955.

The Black Shadow remains one of the finest achievements of the British motor cycle industry.

Stafford Cripps announced the details of their export quotas in 1947. The motor cycle industry was far more inclined to get down to the job of making as many motor cycles as possible for sale abroad without the same degree of grumbling. The Manufacturers' Union was, however, quite insistent that the tax structure for motor cycles should be completely reformed.[36] This was a now familiar refrain, one which the Manufacturers' Union had been repeating to various governments ever since the time when Winston Churchill had been Chancellor of the Exchequer in the late 1920s. Using many of the same arguments as the SMMT, the Manufacturers' Union maintained adamantly that a healthy export market must rest on a strong and secure home market. This, they claimed, would only come about if the existing tax system were changed as the industry had suggested during the 1930s. They remained convinced that there was a latent demand in the home market, which would be tapped by light-weight motor cycles, but which would only be successful if the tax were lowered.[37]

Not only did the government fail to heed such appeals, but when in 1947 the horse-power tax on motor cars was abolished and replaced by one based on engine capacity, nothing whatever was done to change the motor cycle tax. In response to petitions launched by both a standing joint committee made up of representatives from the MAA, RAC and Automobile Association (AA) as well as one directly from Jack Sangster on behalf of the Motor Cycle Manufacturers' Section of the Manufacturers' Union, a Treasury representative informed them that the current tax structure would remain unchanged.[38] The decision was defended on the grounds that, while it was true that the new flat-rate scheme for the motor car industry was designed as an incentive to pare down the multiplicity of models and thus promote the export trade, there was no 'close analogy' with the motor cycle industry. As matters now stood, there were only two tax steps up to the 250 cc engine capacity stage, while for larger capacities there was already a flat rate. Hence, it could hardly 'be regarded as restrictive of design'.[39]

The Manufacturers' Union was angered by what was considered favouritism shown towards the motor car industry and the destruction of the historical linkages between the two industries that had been implicit in the old tax system. It made dire predictions about what would happen to the home motor cycle market should the government not alter the tax laws, a development that would inevitably hurt the export trade.[40]

Old problems return

Why had the government disregarded the petitions submitted by the motor cycle industry? The truth was mostly likely that, in contrast with the motor car industry, the motor cycle industry was simply not big enough and did not share anything approaching the same scale of manufacturing or employment. Although the motor car industry was a focus of attention in the government's export drive, their motor cycle counterpart was considered something of a poor sister. For example, it was not even mentioned in the Ministerial Subcommittee on Industrial Problems' influential paper, 'Post-War Resettlement of the Motor Industry', an odd omission since the Minister of Reconstruction, Lord Woolton, would shortly become a member of BSA's Board of Directors.[41] No motor cycle manufacturer was represented on the National Advisory Council for the Motor Manufacturing Industry, nor was any parallel organisation created for them. In private, civil servants condescendingly referred to motor cycle manufacturers as an 'old fashioned Midlands industry' whose views could be more or less safely ignored. There also seems to have been a degree of antagonism between the occasionally cantankerous Union Director Major Watling and certain influential Whitehall officials.[42]

An additional factor complicating the status of the motor cycle industry was a renewal of unfavourable press coverage of motor cycle accidents. Although throughout the 1940s motor cycles had been welcomed as transport in an economy starved of motor vehicles, public and subsequently government opinion began to turn against the growing number of road fatalities. The growing death rate was not only a reflection of the fact that there were more and more machines on the road but also, in part, the result of the industry's continuing orientation towards the large, high-powered motor cycles.[43]

If Britain remained loyal for the most part to this type of motor cycles, the same could not be said about the Continental manufacturers. By 1948 it was becoming increasingly obvious that, starting with Italy, they were well on the way to recovery and making rapid progress with small-engined motor cycles. This was part of a continuing trend in Continental nations, which under their post-war conditions required the cheapest possible motorised transport. Britain was lagging in the field of small light-weight capacity, a development confirmed in 1948 when an Italian machine won the Isle of Man Lightweight TT races.[44]

Post-war German reparations

Yet the attention of the industry was focused elsewhere, and these warning signs were ignored. Because of the intense nature of Anglo-German competition before 1939, the British industry was keenly interested in the future state of its German counterpart. In fact, the question of German reparations takes up a large place in the history of the British motor cycle industry during the early post-war era. Despite initial optimism, the efforts of the British industry to benefit from the military defeat of Germany proved to be a story of endless frustration. After several years of repeated appeals to the British government, only one firm was able to take advantage of German technical advances.[45]

The industry had anticipated access to Germany plants some time before the end of the war, and detailed planning had begun during a meeting at the London headquarters of the Engineering Section of the Foreign Office (FO). Representatives from the Manufacturers' Union met with FO officials in June 1945 to discuss a number of related issues. The FO Section's Deputy Director General, E. Harle, explained that the present situation allowed 'an opportunity for UK Industry to inform itself as to the development of German Industry – its production – and economic and financial methods'. Union members were also informed that, in future, it was to be the policy of the British government to control German industry and any potential export trade 'to a very considerable extent', even to the point where it would be maintained at what was described as 'something above starvation standard and no more'.[46]

For its part, the FO needed the Manufacturers' Union to identify specific targets among German industry, in particular which factories, models, technologies and financial information it wanted to have examined. The Manufacturers' Union delegation provided three nominees to serve on joint government/industry investigation teams, as well as naming a number of firms, among them BMW, NSU, and Zundapp, for on-the-spot scrutiny.[47] These teams were given a mandate to uncover information about the costs of individual factories and, more specifically, how they related to actual export prices in markets such as Holland and India, which had been penetrated so successfully before the war. The teams were also given direction to locate motor cycle models, which were to be 'thoroughly examined' with the 'patent position' in mind, as well as to look generally at tariffs, subsidies and 'currency manipulation' not just for the motor cycle industry but for light engineering generally.[48]

With Germany defeated and a large section of the country occupied by the British army, the motor cycle manufacturers must have thought that it would now be comparatively easy for this formerly secret information to be made available through the teams. However, the practical operation of reparations would become much more difficult – and politically charged – over the following years, than it appeared in the heady weeks after VE Day.[49]

Co-operation between the British and the Americans in this matter had commenced in 1944 in the form of the Combined Intelligence Objectives Subcommittee (CIOS), a group that was subordinated to the Supreme Military Command of the Western allies, SHAEF. After July 1945 CIOS was dissolved and replaced by the British Intelligence Objectives Subcommittee (BIOS) along with an Anglo-American counterpart, the Field Information Agency, Technical (FIAT). The United States Strategic

Bombing Survey undertook its own study as well.[50] The Manufacturers' Union had nominees that were among the various BIOS teams which followed up behind combat units as the fighting progressed and commenced rummaging around the remains of factories throughout the western part of the Reich. They also sought out documentary information and whenever possible arranged interviews with the former managers and technicians in order to ascertain details of the pre-war achievements of the German motor cycle industry.[51]

Notwithstanding professions of inter-allied co-operation in the exploitation of German industry, there arose a growing rivalry not only between the Western allies and the Soviets, but also between the British and American investigating teams. By early 1946 the Manufacturers' Union had to admit that so far it had very little to show for the Reparations Programme, thanks to the actions of its wartime ally. In February it expressed disappointment that certain motor cycle prototype models had not yet been obtained. Reference was made to 'unaccountable delays in delivery of [the machines] due it was believed to the action of the US authorities'.[52]

The position of the British industry with regard to German motor cycle manufacturers was greatly weakened by the fact that most of the primary factories were either in the Soviet or American sectors. For example, the Americans had prevented British teams from entering a targeted factory in Nuremberg, despite previous agreements allowing them access. When they finally did gain entry, it was only to discover that the motor cycle engines they had hoped to examine had already been shipped to the USA. This was not the only instance of obstruction. At the BMW plant in Munich, the remaining German personnel refused entry to a BIOS team under American instructions. Nor were the Soviets any more co-operative about allowing access to the DKW plant near Chemnitz in eastern Germany.[53]

Still, despite much frustration, the British persisted. In 1946 a large number of reports had been published by the BIOS covering its investigations into a variety of commercial sectors, including several on the motor cycle industry. These were supplemented by reports from FIAT and the US Strategic Bombing Survey. The reports were distributed widely throughout British industry. There was also a travelling exhibition of examples of representative German equipment, including motor cycles, which visited several British cities during 1947.[54]

The reports provided little comfort for those in the British industry who wished to attribute the pre-war success of their rivals only to government assistance or to brush off the potential danger of resurgent German competition. True, the reports did confirm the degree to which the Reich government had subsidised individual firms before 1939. BMW, for one, whose pre-war racing successes had so alarmed British manufacturers, had been encouraged by government funding, on the grounds that international competitions were a matter of prestige, worth subsidising 'at any cost'. It also confirmed, as British manufacturers had suspected all along, the existence of additional subsidies which enabled German motor cycles to be exported at low cost.[55]

Yet the reports also documented evidence of disquieting technical advances on the part of the Germans, of a nature that could not entirely be written off as the result of surreptitious government subsidies. The state of some of the factories, for instance, elicited grudging praise from the investigators, which by implication, did not always reflect well on the production facilities back in Britain. The German works were described as 'well equipped', with 'practically all machine tools inspected being modern and of the latest type'. These tools were singled out for especial attention, and it was remarked that few of them were belt-driven or line-shafting models. The conclusion reached was that 'as an average, [they were] considerably more modern than that in an average, similar factory in Great Britain'.[56]

The investigators also remarked on the presence of apprenticeship schools, which in many cases were attached directly to the factories. Moreover, what was termed an 'outstanding feature' of the German industry was the high level of standardisation being adopted, 'which is in sharp contrast to the British Motor Cycle Industry'. This had been accomplished as a result of a conscious policy of the Reich government, implemented and supervised by the military. This meant that the various firms, in stark contrast to the practice followed in Britain before and after the war, each manufactured a limited range of models.[57]

It was this policy, it was suggested, that had been the foundation of the German export success. Standardisation had given them 'considerable manufacturing economies' allowing for a 'large proportion' of factory equipment to be single-tooled and provided continuous production. This was the formula that enabled them to produce the large numbers of inexpensive, small-capacity machines which had so bedevilled British exporters.[58]

The reports contained many admiring references about German research establishments. Particular note was made of the 'close relationship' between the universities and the motor cycle industry.[59] Whether or not this was a root cause of higher German motor cycle sales was not stated, but the investigators did concede that, in general, 'we should judge that the "average" German motor cycle was of a cleaner and more pleasing appearance than the average British motor cycle'. This was telling criticism, authored as it was by some of the leading figures in the British industry.[60]

Despite these positive reports about the achievements of the German industry, which carried an implicit message that British manufacturers would have much to gain from the Reparations Programme, the Manufacturers' Union's leadership ultimately arrived at a very different conclusion. In April 1946 Union Director Major Watling wrote to manufacturing members informing them that, from what he could gather from the BIOS reports, there was not any plant or machinery in Germany worth acquiring. No explanation was provided for this interpretation, which appeared to be at such variance with what the reports had concluded; nor is it easy to understand why Watling dismissed these reports so easily. In light of the lack of co-operation from the other two occupying forces it may well have been that there was little else Watling or the industry could have done. He did, however, agree that there was 'a number' of new and/or experimental motor cycle engines that should be examined. He also expressed hope that BMW's factory research and racing records would be open for perusal by Union members.[61]

There is another possible explanation for the failure of the British motor cycle industry fully to exploit the possibilities offered by the Reparations Programme. According to Ministry of Supply personnel, upon querying the industry about its lack of interest in acquiring the latest in German motor cycle technology, the Manufacturers' Union had replied that it had no future plans to make any 'bids for plants'. Under current circumstances, the Ministry had been informed, the industry 'considers there is adequate capacity already in the UK for production needs'.[62]

Shortly thereafter, Major Watling produced an unpleasant surprise to those manufacturers who had hoped that German competition was now a thing of the past. Watling wrote that he had recently been informed that the Allied Control Commission was now considering the 'resuscitation of the German motor cycle industry', albeit only to the total of 10,000 machines per year and even then with capacities restricted to no more than 250 cc. Watling reported further that, when he had questioned the policy, he had been informed by an unnamed Board of Trade official that this was a decision based on hard-headed practicality. If left de-industrialised, he had been told, Germany was in danger of becoming 'a "slum" nation in the midst of plenty'. Limited production, on the other hand, would 'allow Germany to earn sufficient foreign exchange to keep her in a reasonably contented frame of mind'. Hence, the Reparations Programme would be cut back.[63]

As it was, only BSA was to benefit from German technology to any appreciable extent. Thanks to the Reparations Programme, this company gained the rights to the design as well as the tooling for a DKW 125 cc model. This machine was thereupon renamed the 'Bantam' and proved to be the cheap light-weight machine the company had earlier sought to produce on its own. Moreover, it was acquired virtually without any research and development costs.[64] The circumstances under which BSA acquired the Bantam are unclear, if not mysterious. No mention of the sale is contained in either the Board of Directors' minute books or in any other surviving company documents.[65] Nor are there any explanations to be found in government records. Nonetheless, after 1948, when the Bantam was first available for export, BSA enjoyed a big advantage over other manufacturers. In fact, this model would subsequently become the single most successful 'British' motor cycle of all time.[66]

The export drive

In the meantime other plans went ahead. Foremost among these was the direction of the export drive. It would be determined, firstly, by the ability of consumers in a particular market to afford to buy British-made motor cycles and, secondly, to the inclination of various foreign governments to accept the free import of these machines into their countries. By the end of the decade, the British motor cycle export drive had scored some notable successes, although, as we shall see in a later chapter, disturbing signs were already appearing of a repetition of the closure of markets that had so disrupted the export trade in the 1930s.

The problems did not always originate overseas. In early 1946 the Manufacturers' Union was informed that domestic control over the industry had passed from the Board of Trade to the Ministry of Supply (Engineering Industries Division). For Union Director Major Watling, who had, among other things, represented the industry with government departments since 1919, this was an unwelcome development. He feared that the new supervision would be 'more rigid and inelastic' than the Board of Trade's had been and that greater demands would now be placed on individual firms with respect to producing statistical information relating to their manufacturing programmes and development plant for both home and export markets. This information, Watling had been informed by the Ministry, was necessary to enable it to help with 'bottle-necks' in labour and materials supplies. Government officials had also told Watling that, now the Essential Works Orders had been abolished, new methods would have to be developed for directing labour into the industry.[67]

Watling was not alone in this jaundiced view of the Ministry. BSA's Brotherton, for example, was equally unhappy over the transfer of jurisdiction from the Board of Trade to the Ministry of Supply. He did not relish having to deal with it over supplies of materials such as chrome. He also expressed scepticism over its ability to reconcile the differing needs of small, medium and large firms, whose interests, he observed, were 'somewhat at variance'. In his opinion, labour, or rather the lack of it, was identified as the chief 'stumbling block', preventing the production outputs that would satisfy Chancellor of the Exchequer Cripps' export targets. Brotherton noted, in common with other industry executives, that the first priority should be the expansion of the home market, which would then be the foundation of a successful export trade. As he observed sourly, however, it would be 'too much to expect some of the academically minded gentlemen in the government to understand this very salient point'.[68]

Nonetheless, the industry was willing to continue to co-operate with the government's export targets, but as they informed an FBI special conference held during the spring of 1946, certain problems would first have to be addressed and sorted out without delay. Three in particular exercised Major Watling: difficulties calling up key workers, especially tool makers; complications involved in getting licences to extend existing buildings; and what Watling called the generation of 'unnecessary statistics'.[69]

The materials situation not only failed to improve but began to deteriorate seriously at this time. At a meeting of the Group Management Committee for the Bicycle and Motor Cycle Industrial and Export Groups (a carry-over from the wartime organisations), members heard a glum assessment from Major Watling about the prospects for 1947. A report had been received from the Ministry of Supply which envisaged a 50 per cent reduction in the manufacture of steel products.[70]

This bad news was quickly followed by word that the steel shortages that had been plaguing the industry for all of 1946 would continue and would 'seriously affect' distribution, forcing the Ministry of Supply greatly to reduce existing materials allocations.[71] At this rate, the industry's self-imposed target of 500,000 machines a year was not going to be achieved for some time to come, if ever. Then came the power cuts over the winter of 1947, which shut several factories down completely and put severe restraints on those that were able to keep operating.[72]

The continuous shortages experienced by the industry, shared by all manufacturers in Britain that year, caused the Manufacturers' Union to consider whether or not to stage a Motor Cycle Show that autumn. Because conditions had been so unsettled since 1945, there had yet to be a post-war Show (the last had been held in 1938), and many looked forward to an opportunity to get the widest possible publicity for the various new lines of motor cycles which would be symbolic of British recovery.

A meeting of the Manufacturers' Union's Council dealt with this question. Most of the industry's senior managers, including Donald Heather, Eric Barnett, Bertram Marians and Jack Sangster, were present. Those in favour noted that, even if the materials shortages meant they could not supply their distributors, the Show would still give them an opportunity to explain their problems personally. Far better, it was said, to meet the trade face to face rather than 'continually send out letters of regret'.[73] Manufacturers could also renew their overseas contacts, disrupted by the many years of war, while the presence of different marques could only stimulate manufacturers to improve their quality and specifications. Not the least, it was argued, the Show was a prestigious event, and, after all, the current 'sellers' market' would not last for ever. The Show would proclaim the fact that, despite all the problems, 'Great Britain is getting on her feet again, and is not falling behind other countries'.[74] The arguments against were that, given the inability to deliver orders, staging the Show would be potentially 'embarrassing' for the manufacturers. Moreover, members were reminded that, at present, none of them had anything new to display. Hence, better to delay another year by which time circumstances would probably improve. In a close vote, the Council decided not to proceed.[75]

There was to be no abandonment of general publicity. Overseas distributors were informed that the Show had been cancelled for what were tactfully termed 'production difficulties'. However, they were assured, the much anticipated TT races would go ahead on schedule. As one trade journal put it: 'No other motor cycle races have ever captured the heart of the enthusiast like the TT, and successes in them have made the names of British machines known wherever motor cycles are ridden.'[76]

Several months later, the steel situation had deteriorated further. Manufacturers were bitter over the fact that, although they claimed to be willing and able to expand production, materials shortages were blocking the way. In a brief to the Minister of Supply, the Manufacturers' Union stated that they should receive 'special consideration' because of their high export potential and the fact that they could earn a disproportionately higher return of foreign currency than other steel-consuming industries. The Minister was reminded that, if in the past British motor cycles were 'pre-eminent', now in the post-war era, they were 'supreme' and that demand 'from all over the world was enormous'.[77] Even having suffered from the materials cuts, the Manufacturers' Union insisted, British motor cycle production increases were remarkable, especially when compared with pre-war figures. On a best monthly basis, they argued, the optimum total the industry had achieved before 1939 was 2,120 during 1937. This had jumped to 6,650 in May 1946, the best post-war month so far.[78] This performance could easily be outdone if only the industry were given sufficient supplies.

The worst was yet to come. In the summer of 1947 the government, in the interests of preserving scarce dollar reserves, abolished the basic petrol ration. This decision appalled members of the Manufacturers' Union. True, Britain had to protect its economy and international position, but this measure, they insisted, was far too draconian. The manufacturers deplored the fact that the ration cut would now prevent the conduct of motor cycle sports such as racing and trials events. These, they stated, were essential for maintaining public interest in the industry at home and also out in the export markets. Not only would removal of the basic petrol ration strangle the home market, but, for all intents and purposes, also eliminate the industry's beloved sports programme. One member went as far as to stress its importance to the industry by way of a parallel between the racing machines and horse-racing as well as 'the exports of blood stock'.[79]

In mid-September, Norton Motors Managing Director Gilbert Smith led a delegation on behalf of the MAA (Motor Cycle Section) and related organisations to meet Prime Minister Attlee and protest the petrol ration cut. The Prime Minister was warned of the disruptive effect of the move on the home market, not only among consumers but the retail trade as well. The critical importance of motor cycle sport was emphasised yet again. C.A. Lewis, secretary of the British Motor Cycle Racing Club, told Attlee that the industry's exports were 'to a surprising extent' based upon racetrack victory, primarily as publicity. 'Our successes,' Lewis said, 'have demonstrated in a way that no catalogue could, the good qualities built into these British machines.' 'Racing and competitive events,' he added, 'are the backbone of the motor cycle industry and the backbone of these events is the basic petrol allowance.' Attlee's response was not recorded.[80]

Motor cycle sport

Continuing sporting events were not the only reason why motor cyclists should continue to receive petrol. After all, the industry claimed, once personal motorised transport was put out of action, unbearable pressure would be placed on bus and tram services, as well as the railways. With their higher fuel efficiency, especially with the light-weight machines, surely motor cycle use for regular commuters should be maintained, not eliminated? The Manufacturers' Union resolved to enlist the help of the RAC and to lobby Labour MPs. Prudently it was agreed to petition the government at least to allow 'a general and modest' basic ration for all motor cyclists, rather than make a case for a special allocation for sports events.[81]

As it had before the war, the industry played on the theme of the contribution of motor cycles to the general well-being of the nation, as cheap and efficient personal transport, which particularly benefited working people. However, its inclination to emphasise the use of the big sports machines was never really sidelined. When the occasion demanded, the industry insisted over and over that its products were designed for everyday use, and indeed this argument was the essential premise of its case for tax reform.

Yet, enormous energies were spent to protect and promote professional racing events. In the final analysis the industry always seemed to fight the hardest, and to place the greatest emphasis in its dealings with the government, on issues that touched on the use of their cherished high-powered sports motor cycles. As one critic noted at the time, the result was a major diversion of resources away from developing small utility-oriented machines.[82]

This predilection can be illustrated by the campaign the industry waged over 1947 and 1948 for the re-opening of the Donington Park race track.

Prior to the war, Donington and Brooklands (the latter, a track near London, was taken over for military purposes after 1939 and was never restored to its original use) were the prime locales for racing in England. After 1945, Donington continued to be used by the armed forces as a storage depot, much to the chagrin of the motor cycle industry, who claimed that there was now no proper facility for race testing. This was, it was maintained, not simply a matter of the industry indulging the whims of enthusiasts. At issue, so Major Watling explained in a letter to the Parliamentary Private Secretary to the Secretary of War, were solid commercial interests, specifically the continuing ability of the industry to maintain the export trade. According to Watling, future success in world markets was contingent upon maintaining Britain's reputation as the leading manufacturer of the large-displacement sports motor cycles.[83]

Watling warned those in government circles that it was 'not always appreciated' that this success 'can only be based on … [the] unique record of successes against the best machines which the Continent can produce'. As usual, the government was cautioned that the export trade was sustained by a 'satisfactory Home Trade'. This, in turn, could only be as good as there were 'models produced of a character approved both by Home and Overseas riders'. If they were to remain competitive, the machines in question needed

Motor cyclists getting ready for the start of a race at the Lindsay Fairgrounds, Ontario, Canada, early 1942. Because of tighter petrol rationing, this was one of the last sports events to be held before the end of the war.

COURTESY OF ED MOODY

Motor cycle racing on Wasaga Beach, Ontario, *circa* late 1930s.

to be tested properly on a track such as Donington, which would allow them to be pushed to their full potential.[84]

This letter was followed up by a brief sent out on 11 February 1948 to the Interdepartmental Committee on Services' Land Requirements. The value of Donington was hammered home yet again. It was an ideal track as it incorporated sections with 'suitable high speed stretches, followed by abrupt turns and changes of gradient where it is possible to test almost to destruction every important element which goes into the design of the modern motor cycle'.

Without the reopening of Donington, the manufacturers argued, there would simply be no other facilities available elsewhere in Great Britain suitable for motor cycle testing, thereby forcing them to seek alternatives on the Continent. The Motor Industry Research Association (MIRA) track at Nuneaton, the motor cycle manufacturers insisted, did not meet their needs. Overseas buyers wanted 'an exceptionally high efficiency engine', and what might be considered adequate for motor car testing was not satisfactory for the kind of performance and high speed required by the typical motor cycle. The MIRA track might be suitable for the motor car industry, but only Donington fully met the necessary specifications of motor cycle manufacturers.[85]

At great effort, the Manufacturers' Union was ultimately successful in having Donington restored to its original function, thanks in part to the intervention of BSA Deputy Chairman Patrick 'Paddy' Hannon, who was also an MP for a Birmingham constituency.[86] The episode does raise some questions about the consistency of their stance on other related matters. It flew in the face of arguments they used with the Treasury about taxation, specifically the point made about revising rates to encourage the use of cheaper, small-displacement motor cycles. It is unclear how use of the Donington track, used almost exclusively for the larger racing machines, could do anything to promote the use of smaller, less powerful motor cycles, except perhaps in the most indirect fashion.

When it came to issues such as enlarging the export trade and seeking to open up new markets, the government and the industry worked in reasonable harmony, without an undue degree of friction.[87] There may have been frustration over steel allocation cuts and petrol rations but, once restored, the industry's production rose and the tension abated. In two areas, however, retail price maintenance and production efficiency, the Labour government's initiatives created a serious breach between it and the manufacturers, simultaneously stirring up considerable debate within the industry.

Retail price maintenance

The industry was very sensitive about retaining its ability to control the minimum price level at which motor cycles could be sold to the public. It lay at the heart of the Manufacturers' Union's complex network of trading agreements, as summarised in chapter one. In late 1947 the Board of Trade created a Committee on Resale Price Maintenance (popularly known as the 'Jacob Committee' after its chairman) to investigate the status of such arrangements throughout British industry.[88]

Like similar clubs in Britain and elsewhere, during the post-war era the British Empire Motor Club actively promoted motor cycle sports activities around Ontario, as this poster attests.
COURTESY OF ED MOODY

Alarmed, the Manufacturers' Union's Council discussed this development during its first meeting of 1948. Major Watling informed members that he had been told that the purpose of the Committee was to determine whether or not resale price maintenance should be either prevented or regulated, in the interests of the 'maximum economy and efficiency in the production and distribution of goods'. As far as Watling was concerned, this issue had already been examined thoroughly by the Board of Trade Committee on Restraint of Trade (the 'Greene Committee') in 1930.[89] Indeed, he had appeared before that committee and believed its findings had vindicated the Manufacturers' Union's trading agreements. Watling thought that the intent of the Jacob Committee was to examine 'whether unnecessary numbers of people were being attracted into the Retail Trade and its high profit margins'. The Council thereupon gave a mandate to Watling to defend the Manufacturers' Union before the Committee.[90]

In July 1948 Major Watling appeared before the Jacob Committee to answer questions about the Manufacturers' Union's policies regarding prices and other internal matters, an experience which led to occasionally acrimonious exchanges between the parties. In a wide-ranging enquiry, committee members probed a variety of aspects of the relationship between the manufacturers and their distribution network. Under pressure, Watling remained adamant in his defence of the Manufacturers' Union's trading agreements and their importance in underpinning the prosperity of the entire trade.[91]

Jacob himself questioned whether, failing the manufacturers' control, if prices were left freely to find 'an economic level', this would necessarily lead to disaster throughout the industry. Watling was unequivocal in his response, stating that resale price maintenance 'was the best method of ensuring equity for all sections of the trade, and for the public'. There was, he insisted, no 'price ring' in place. Quite the contrary, the trading agreements were necessary to protect prices, in times of what he termed both 'excess' supply and demand.[92] Under relentless questioning from Jacob, Watling conceded that, although he claimed the discount provided to dealers was negotiable, in fact it was fixed at 20 per cent. This was administered irrespective of the number of motor cycles sold, on the grounds that it promoted fairness among the dealers geographically dispersed throughout Britain.[93]

Asked to provide an example of how the industry's trading agreements benefited the public directly, Watling suggested the manufacturers' newly instituted free after-sales service was evidence of the manufacturers' good corporate citizenship. Offered by dealers after 500 miles' use, Watling claimed this service had been created in the public interest and was covered by existing profit margins. Jacob was sceptical. In his mind, it 'applies a standard to the purchasing public which comes as a surprise to me'. Nor, under further questioning, could Watling document instances of owner misuse that would justify the service. Instead, he stressed the importance of the good name of the industry, 'the finest reputation in the world'.[94] Jacob was equally sceptical about Watling's repeated claim that the agreements benefited all concerned. The fact that they were administered by manufacturers and retailers did not appear to work in the common interest. It was a case, he commented, that 'if only the public were represented, it would include everybody'. When Watling protested that there was nothing in the agreements which 'adversely affects the interests of the public', Jacob concluded that 'I suppose that must be really a matter of opinion'.[95]

The Committee's final report outlined the factual circumstances of these trading arrangements.[96] No action on behalf of the government followed, perhaps because it was already preoccupied enough elsewhere and wished to avoid a full-blown battle with industry over the issue of prices and internal agreements. At around the same time, the Manufacturers' Union responded to a query from the Chancellor of the Exchequer to the FBI about a programme to limit prices and profits. The FBI had, in turn, begun to contact its members to ascertain their views on the subject. The Manufacturers' Union's Council adopted a firm position in opposition to this initiative, on the grounds that it was simply impracticable to control retail prices. The Council did, however, say that it was prepared to advise its members to fix their prices at the current levels, as long as production and distribution costs outside of their control remained unchanged.[97]

Indeed, the Council proceeded to formulate counter-proposals of its own. The industry might co-operate with a government prices and profits programme, but only if it also addressed some other, purportedly related issues. These included a general increase of working hours throughout industry, a reduction of government expenditure and the subsequent release of redundant civil service workers to industry, as well as sponsorship of a campaign against 'damage, theft and pilferage' in the workplace, although the latter had not been previously referred to as a major problem being faced by the industry.[98]

Improving productivity

The prices and profits campaign may never have reached fruition, but it was to be followed shortly by another initiative. During the autumn of 1947 the Manufacturers' Union heard of a government proposal which, if implemented, they believed would seriously undermine their untrammelled right to manage their enterprises as they best saw fit.[99] Watling had been advised by the employer members of the Ministry of Supply's Engineering Advisory Council that the Minister was concerned that every effort to ensure maximum production efficiency be exercised. He was convinced, Watling was told, that there was currently 'scope for improvement'. As the Major reminded Union Council members, if not enough progress were attained, the Ministry had the power to create a Development Council to see that it was.[100]

The Manufacturers' Union's leadership resented this level of examination of the inner workings of its members' factories. There was, it claimed, already a high level of co-operation within its ranks, not only among top-level managers when the Manufacturers' Union's Council and the Motor Cycle Manufacturers' Section convened, but also through proceedings of the Technical Committee.[101] This committee thought its work would stand well in comparison with its motor car industry counterpart. It had, it was claimed, been active for over 20 years and in that time 'undoubtedly eased production problems by the issue of numerous recommended Data Sheets'.[102]

Later in the month, the Manufacturers' Union's Assistant Director Hugh Palin reported to the Council that he had met with employer members of the Engineering Advisory Council, who had assured him that, failing higher levels of productivity from the industry, the threat of an imposed Development Council was a definite prospect. This may or may not have been a realistic assessment of ministerial intentions, but the Government's initiative precipitated the most wide-ranging debate from within the motor cycle industry about its manufacturing practices that had ever taken place, or would occur, prior to the final collapse in 1975.[103]

The Manufacturers' Union's line, that it was already doing enough to promote production efficiency without additional governmental prodding, did not take long to fray. Major Watling reported to the Council that he had attended a meeting sponsored by the FBI, which had been addressed by motor car manufacturer William Rootes, who had explained how the SMMT had been promoting production efficiency in his industry. Not only did they encourage managers to visit each others' factories, but there were plans maturing to ensure a greater interchangeability of accessories and components.[104]

This news provoked further debate during the Manufacturers' Union's governing Council meeting of December 1948. President George Wilson asked members what action they should take in response to the Minister's initiative, in case they were asked to account for their actions later on. The responses to his query showed that not everyone thought the industry was doing enough. Donald Heather, Managing Director of AMC, spoke out first in what would turn out to be the majority view. He dismissed Rootes' advice as irrelevant to their industry. There was, in his mind, a 'fundamental difference' between the two industries. In particular, Heather noted the 'complete contrast' in their relative international standings: the American motor car industry dominated the world yet American motor cycle makers looked to Britain for new designs and lagged far behind in terms of production.[105]

BSA's Cycle Division Managing Director James Leek did not dispute Heather's assertion directly. He did, however, say that there were some aspects of the SMMT's programme that could be emulated to their own benefit. He observed that its internal committees were composed of fairly high-level staff – often the heads of firms. The Manufacturers' Union's Standardisation Committee, in contrast, was made up of designers and drafting-room personnel, none of whom had any substantial influence over company policy. Triumph Chairman Jack Sangster agreed with Leek and explained that he did not believe the Manufacturers' Union's committees really touched on what he termed the industry's 'real problem'. It might be true that the industry operated reasonably well, yet 'we must be prepared to do everything possible to make ourselves even more efficient'. As it turned out, however, Sangster and Leek represented only a minority opinion among the industry's leadership.[106]

Still, this was not an issue that could be sidestepped by the Manufacturers' Union for very much longer. Looming behind the rhetoric was the danger of direct government intervention. In late January 1949 the Manufacturers' Union issued an internal position paper which outlined a possible strategy. There were, it said, two aspects to the problem: first, the matter of production efficiency at the level of the individual factory; and, second, improvements which could be gained at the industry level through more inter-firm co-operation and general standardisation. Yet, in terms of concrete action, the Manufacturers' Union does not seem to have done much to encourage such internal co-operation among its membership. Indeed, its virtually sole accomplishment in this matter was to have distributed an FBI booklet on 'Standardisation'. By January 1949, only one member had made an enquiry on the subject, and that had already been referred back to an outside research group.[107]

Despite earlier scepticism expressed about following the example of the SMMT, attention was drawn to the continuing achievements of its Production Efficiency and Standardisation Committee. Much useful information, it was claimed, had been exchanged during its regular monthly meetings. These meetings also facilitated discussions to further the use of common accessories and components and the pooling of technical information such as blueprints and the peculiarities of jigs and tools. The committee sponsored factory tours and encouraged the secondment of technical staff to help out suppliers. Surely the motor cycle industry could learn at least something from the practices of its four-wheeled counterpart.[108]

At the January 1949 Council meeting, Union President Wilson commenced discussion on the necessity of forming a special committee, having had the benefit of attending an FBI Conference on Production Efficiency held the previous month. He was convinced that the government expected 'some positive action by the Industry', and it was not enough simply to expand the jurisdiction of their existing Standardisation Committee. What was now needed was an entirely new committee, with a membership drawn from the highest levels of the industry. In this he was supported by BSA's James Leek, who believed it was now 'essential' to take quick action. In Leek's opinion, although it might be true that the industry was currently the unchallenged world leader, this condition could not last for ever. Now, as their overseas competitors recovered from war damage, 'everything must be done to preserve this position as there would undoubtedly be difficult days ahead'. He implicitly agreed with the Minister in thinking that the industry 'offered considerable scope for work to eliminate unnecessary overlapping'.[109]

Wilson and Leek received further support from Jack Sangster, but it was soon evident that the majority of the Council did not share their enthusiasm for this project. Not only was there considerable disagreement about what exactly needed to be improved, but there existed a strong sentiment that, after all, their industry was internationally supreme, had been for as long as any of them could remember, and there was no reason to suppose that it would not remain so well into the future. Moreover, it was evident that the majority of those present were irritated that the government should implicitly question their competence and skill as managers and businessmen. Who were they to criticise those who oversaw such a successful export industry?[110]

Nonetheless, members bowed to the inevitable by forming a Production Efficiency Committee of their own. It was composed of the most senior members of the industry, including George Wilson (a bicycle company executive), Jack Sangster, Gilbert Smith, James Leek and Donald Heather. There were also senior representatives from component makers such as Villiers Engineering and Dunlop Tyres. Yet, this decision was in a sense a deceptive sign of the industry's resolution to face up to the vital questions of how to improve its overall efficiency. In fact, the Manufacturers' Union's Council remained just as deeply divided on the issue as the newly formed Production Efficiency Committee.[111]

With this lack of common purpose, the potential effectiveness of the Committee was seriously compromised even before its first meeting on 7 February 1949. At the top of the agenda for the Committee's consideration was an invitation to the Manufacturers' Union from the Anglo-American Council on Productivity to send teams to the USA in order to study the latest production methods. During the meeting, the invitation was rejected out of hand, although BSA's James Leek again spoke out in favour of more preparation on the part of the motor cycle industry and stressed the need to modernise and anticipate resurgent foreign competition.[112] For Leek the status quo was no longer good enough. He warned the Council that 'it was dangerous for the Industry to be complacent about their efficiency'. He also advocated industry standardisation with respect to certain components such as hubs and front forks.[113]

However, Leek again represented a minority viewpoint. AMC Managing Director Donald Heather, speaking for the majority, thought that launching a rationalisation drive within the industry was actually a threat to the continued prosperity of the industry. Too much standardisation, for example, would he said 'prejudice the individuality of each manufacturer, and would undermine the present proper competition' among them. It was the need for robust internal competition that must preclude 'too close a consultation' between the various firms.[114]

Subsequently, other members made known their objection to information exchange with the Americans. It was stressed that 'the UK product and the UK production methods were considerably ahead of the US'. Thus, there should be no exchange of teams between the British and American motor cycle factories. In conclusion, the Committee agreed that 'a visit to the USA would produce nothing of any great value'. The Government was informed accordingly.[115]

As far as the other recommendations of the Minister of Supply were concerned, the Committee curtly disposed of them. Union Director Watling was instructed to prepare a press release informing all and sundry of 'the high degree of efficiency already achieved in the Industry' as well as its dominance in world export markets. Thus, the industry's leaders saw no need to implement any searching evaluation of their factories and production facilities. Instead, any improvements in what the Government termed production efficiency would rest with each firm, and any technical problems could be forwarded to the Committee for reference to the appropriate outside agency. The Manufacturers' Union, they agreed, would undertake to inform its membership of the work of their Production Efficiency Committee and to disseminate relevant information received from the FBI, SMMT, MIRA and the British Standards Institute. As far as the Manufacturers' Union was concerned, that was that. There was nothing more to be done about either Production Efficiency or the Anglo-American Council on Productivity.[116]

The following year Watling reported on a recent meeting with the Minister of Supply. The Minister had stressed his anxiety that the engineering industries 'should do everything possible to increase their production efficiency by means of standardisation and simplification'. In their reply, members of the Manufacturers' Union's Council declared that they, in their collective minds, had done all they could to bring these issues to the attention of their membership. Moreover, it was felt that 'the Industry generally has gone as far as it possibly can along the road to Standardisation'. For the British motor cycle industry, the book was closed on production efficiency.[117]

Nothing lasting was to come out of this episode. In a short space of time, the newly formed Standardisation Committee went back to dealing with the comparatively minor technical issues that its predecessor had been addressing before the Government raised their concerns. Yet the manner in which the Manufacturers' Union reacted to this question was highly significant for the future of the industry. Surely, if there was ever a time after the war when the industry could have made a collective effort to prepare for the future, this was it. Instead, an unparalleled opportunity was allowed to slip away.

The industry's leadership saw matters differently. For members of the Manufacturers' Union's Council, the fact was that British motor cycles remained superior to all others, in terms of performance, especially at sports events. Moreover, British factories continued to outperform all rivals, and the export trade continued to be dominated by their products. There seemed no reason for the industry to question its current manufacturing practices, never mind change them.

Danger ahead

Yet, in 1949, the signs of change were there for those inclined to look. Germany had resumed production, albeit limited. In Italy production was well under way to reintroduce what had been originally a British invention, the motor scooter. Even the year before, many of the leaders of the British motor cycle industry had witnessed the unhappy sight of light-weight Italian motor cycles storming back to victory at the Isle of Man TT. One trade journal warned the industry that it was making a serious error neglecting the development of smaller machines. These were of 'vital importance' to the long-term prospects of motor cycle use in Britain. Otherwise, there was a danger that the public's perception of the motor cycle could return to the pre-war situation of 'being regarded almost entirely as a sporting [machine] for the young and adventurous', with all the implications such an attitude would have for maintaining a self-limited market.[118]

Unlike their British counterparts, Italian companies such as Innocenti (maker of the Vespa) and Lambretta had produced machines of their own design which were both technically sound and financially successful. Indeed, they had become so popular on the Continent that in 1949 the Douglas company bought the rights to manufacture the Vespa at its Bristol motor cycle factory. The move, which did not arouse much notice at the time, was an important indication of upcoming shifts in consumer tastes after 1950.[119]

As the reconstruction period drew to a close in 1951, the British motor cycle industry could look back at a mixed record of accomplishment. It had, considering the constraints of the time, done a reasonable job of recovery. The manufacturers' annual output had fallen far short of predictions

During the 1950s and 1960s scooters and mopeds became increasingly popular in Britain and elsewhere in Western Europe. Advertisements often stressed their practical assets, particularly ease of parking, for use around town, and frequently depicted female models as these photos demonstrate.

They do look cuter on a scooter!

POWER PRETTILY

Parking problems simply don't exist when you travel this modern way. Rain or shine, town or country, these sturdy little run-abouts will get you there—and with a minimum of fuss. What other means of transport will so conveniently take you shopping, or to that special hair appointment, or on any other of the thousand-and-one different errands that crop up daily?

Nowadays Miss 1962 demands her own personalised means of getting about—no more strap-hanging on crowded bus or tube for her! A lift into town with the boy friend—or perhaps borrow the family car?—very useful, no doubt . . . But the independent-minded girl of today must have a means of transport to match her own sleek good looks.

THE SPORTING TOUCH
Here again in a happy golfcourse trio — the moped is well to the fore!

made during the war, but this was because of a combination of unrealistic expectations as well as certain conditions, such as the supply of materials, over which they had little control. Other than the BSA Bantam, the benefits of the Reparations Programme had also fallen well below expectation. Moreover, little had been gained from the industry's examination of German production methods and acquisition of plant. After 1948 the Germans were free to develop new models without fear of expropriation by the occupying Western Allies. In light of the politics of the Reparations Programme, the disappointing results could not be blamed entirely on lack of initiative on the part of the motor cycle industry.

Ironically, the era ended as it had begun at the conclusion of the war, with a surprise acquisition by BSA. Again, this involved a firm owned by Jack Sangster, who decided to sell off Triumph Engineering in order to spare his family death duties.[120] The industry's structure was now further narrowed. Although the news was not widely disseminated to the public, the shock of Sangster's sale of Triumph to its greatest rival must have been considerable. Once more, Sangster screwed every possible penny he could from BSA. The buyout cost £2,450,000 cash (Sangster had paid approximately £28,000 for Triumph in 1936), and the deal also included a seat on the BSA Group board for Sangster himself.[121]

One might be tempted to draw a parallel between the Triumph sale and the Morris–Austin merger, which created the British Motor Car Company, which was to take place the following year. Superficially, there appears to be some justification to think there was. All the firms concerned were major forces in their respective fields, and the consolidation of assets was widely thought to be a positive development for the future of their industries.[122]

However, there the similarities end. While, in the motor car industry, several strong competitors remained, not only American-owned Ford and Vauxhall, but also Rootes and Standard, the motor cycle industry was different. The BSA/Triumph combine, along with subsidiaries Ariel and Sunbeam, now had a clearly dominant position among British motor cycle manufacturers. Although firm and reliable production figures are always difficult to determine, it is likely that total BSA Group production amounted to at least 60 per cent of the industry's total output. Between them, AMC and Norton probably accounted for a large portion of what remained. In future, the other firms were to be pushed further and further to the margins of the industry or bought out in turn themselves. From now on, for better or worse, whatever happened to BSA would determine the future of the entire British motor cycle industry.

CHAPTER FOUR

The window of opportunity, 1951–1956

H AVING EMERGED from the difficulties of the immediate post-war years, British motor cycle manufacturers now appeared poised for a period of vast and sustained expansion. With no foreign competition as yet evident, the industry was in a highly advantageous position from which to supply inexpensive motorised transport to a world well on the way to full economic recovery. The path was now cleared to realise its highly ambitious and self-imposed post-war production goals. Although a short period of material shortages, brought about by the Korean War and the rearmament programme, restricted production between 1950 and 1952, thereafter the industry was generally able to procure most of its requirements.[1] Yet this era ended on a far less optimistic note than it had begun. As we shall see, however, one positive development could be found at BSA. The industry's leading firm, plagued by a long-running leadership crisis, had finally resolved it with a dramatic boardroom putsch.

Spreading affluence

As Britain gradually moved out of post-war austerity, the sales situation in the home market was improving rapidly. Increasing affluence assisted greater levels of motor vehicle ownership, to which many in the working classes now aspired. Many agreed with Winston Churchill's appeal, made during the 1950 general election campaign in reply to an earlier remark made by Labour cabinet minister Aneurin Bevan, which insisted that British voters were not necessarily, "'lower than vermin" because by their skill and thrift they have earned and saved enough money to buy a car or motor cycle'.[2] The sense of optimism was also boosted by production levels, which had increased from 49,000 units in 1945 to 171,700 in 1951. During the same period, motor cycle registrations had jumped from 312,844 to 859,034 and exports, which brought in badly needed hard currency, had rocketed from

As late as the 1950s BSA produced the most extensive range of motor cycles anywhere in the world, but perhaps here diversity was taken to an extreme. This New Guinea tribesman is mounted on a light-weight Bantam, the single best selling motor cycle the company ever produced. It found markets around the world albeit mostly in the British Commonwealth.

© BSA OWNERS CLUB

4,000 to 91,000. The industry remained the world's largest producer, and although former rivals might be recovering steadily, none of them was as yet strong enough to present a direct challenge to the British.

Indeed, one could suggest that during this period there was a 'window of opportunity' to consolidate a worldwide primacy. The years 1951 to 1956 were arguably a time when the industry had the resources and the time to prepare for the onslaught of overseas competitors, as its rivals recovered fully from war-time damage.[3] This was a period bounded on one side by BSA's purchase of Triumph Engineering and, on the other, by the 1956 sales recession, the first of the post-war era. Nonetheless, during this time, three substantial problems emerged to plague the industry. Cumulatively these prevented it from taking full advantage of the favourable conditions to expand in the way its leadership had hoped.

The first of these was growing public concern about the perceived anti-social behaviour of some motor cyclists. More significantly increased levels of motor cycle road accidents became a serious sales deterrent and also complicated the industry's efforts to convince the government to relax tax and regulations. The second was the gradual loss of export markets, a result of factors both within and without the manufacturers' control. Third, and most important, was a shift in the character of the British home market, particularly the popularity of the scooter, both imported and built under licence by domestic manufacturers, a factor which the collective leadership of the industry was slow to appreciate.

BSA's rising star

In 1951, these problems were still easy to overlook. For most of the manufacturers, the major problem was still that of trying to meet the incessant demands from their customers at home and abroad. If any single firm was representative of the potential of the industry at this time, it was BSA. This was certainly the judgement of its Chairman Sir Bernard Docker, who was convinced that the future for his company was full of boundless promise. During an address to shareholders at the 1951 Annual General Meeting, he commented on the booming state of trade which faced his corporation in markets around the world. He defined the primary challenge facing the company and its various subsidiaries as achieving 'production and still more production'.[4]

Docker's remarks were more than mere rhetoric, and on one level at least his optimism seemed to be well founded. This was a company that employed 20,000 workers in a number of locations around Britain and abroad, including an armaments factory in South Africa and a Canadian machine tool subsidiary. Its various interests had for many years spanned a wide range of engineering products, diverse but complementary, covering steel, machine tools, firearms and earth-moving equipment.[5]

Indeed, BSA was able to supply many of the goods that were in demand during this period of economic recovery. Among other things, it produced utilitarian bicycles, some of the most expensive and luxurious limousines available in Britain, along with a range of buses (supplied to metropolitan fleets at home and abroad) and armoured fighting vehicles, allowing it to cater to the whole spectrum of motor transport. Everything was manufactured, in fact, except for cheaper, economy-class motor cars. Nor was the motor cycle side of BSA neglected, and the company continued to account for nearly 50 per cent of total British production.[6]

BSA had in fact maintained its position as the world's largest motor cycle manufacturer, offering what was undeniably still the most extensive and comprehensive product range of motorised two-wheelers anywhere. In 1951 BSA and its subsidiaries manufactured over 20 individual models, an even more varied range than during the pre-war period. Its output included everything from the 98 cc auto-cycle made under the New Hudson name, the 175 cc Bantam entry-level motor cycle, acquired from the Germans through the wartime Reparations Programme, to the four-cylinder 1000 cc Ariel Square Four. These machines were diverse, mostly well engineered, and covered virtually the entire market spectrum.[7]

Among the other models produced was the highly successful 650 cc twin-cylinder machine, the 'Golden Flash', introduced after 1945 to counter the big Triumph models that were so popular in export markets, particularly the USA. Subsequent derivatives of the Golden Flash would continue to be built until 1972. BSA also manufactured the highly successful single-cylinder 500 cc Gold Star which swept race tracks around the world. In between, the company produced a number of machines in varying configurations, built up around engine capacities of the 250 cc, 350 cc and 500 cc classes.[8] In 1953, as recognition of the relative importance of motor cycles within the BSA Group, they were split away from BSA Cycles (which included bicycles), and BSA Motor Cycles Ltd was created. The other motor cycle subsidiaries, Ariel, Triumph and Sunbeam, continued to operate with varying degrees of autonomy.[9]

Moreover, BSA was well equipped with factory and plant in order to produce this extensive range of motor cycles. The main factory on Armoury Road at Small Heath, Birmingham, manufactured most of the motor cycles, along with a diminishing number of rifles, and also performed some general engineering work. This capacity was complemented by a former government-built 'shadow factory' at nearby Redditch, which produced the engine for the Bantam and the high-priced Sunbeam models as well as undertaking sundry subcontracting work.[10]

After 1944, BSA also owned the Ariel Motors plant at Selly Oak, Birmingham, which produced a smaller but still comprehensive line of models, including the giant Square Four. In 1953, responding to expanding demand for the so-called 'clip-on' (a small engine which could be attached to a bicycle frame as an auxiliary power unit), BSA introduced the Winged Wheel. This unit, which extended BSA's two-wheeled range

Bantam to Golden Flash. Claiming to be 'King of the Queen's Highway' was no idle boast on the part of BSA. In the mid-1950s when this advertisement appeared, BSA and its subsidiaries Ariel and Triumph offered one of the widest ranges of motor cycles to be found in Europe or anywhere else.

even further, was manufactured at its bicycle factory at Montgomery Street in Birmingham.[11]

After 1951 BSA's most important motor cycle subsidiary was Triumph Engineering Co. BSA included Triumph's highly successful range of large-capacity twin-cylinder models as part of the overall line-up, although Triumph continued to maintain its previous separate identity. Indeed, with the general public BSA deliberately played down its purchase of the Triumph brand, in the interests of fostering competition between the subsidiaries, an important sales factor among enthusiasts who were often fiercely loyal to individual marques. As he had before 1951, Triumph's Managing Director Edward Turner was allowed to run his enterprise with virtually a free hand.[12] Moreover, Triumph continued as a manufacturer of large-displacement motor cycles, although two smaller models, one with a 150 cc engine and the other 199 cc, were also introduced in the early 1950s. Indeed, the 199 cc model would become increasingly important after 1956, although later on Triumph's production would consist mostly of machines in the 500 cc and larger displacement category.[13]

During the early 1950s BSA was working close to full productive capacity, now well in excess of the best pre-war figures. During the 1951/52 season the Small Heath factory alone churned out at least 65,000 machines of various types, a total never again surpassed by it or any other British motor cycle company. The subsidiaries probably accounted for another 30,000 to 35,000 units. According to its surviving records, Triumph alone produced on average between 20,000 to 22,000 machines annually throughout most of the 1950s.[14]

Yet, beyond the slick, flashy covers of the company reports and prospectuses, at a deeper, less evident level, the BSA Group was a troubled organisation. The sources of this malaise, which were remarked upon privately by certain Board members, had very little to do with motor cycle production.[15] In brief, the crucial underlying weakness was that the top management of BSA was simply not up to the job of directing and co-ordinating the activities of such a vast and diverse enterprise. At the time, much evidence about the true state of the company was submerged by the acrimony surrounding Chairman Docker and his wife Norah's increasingly unstable and eccentric behaviour and their personal excesses. Lacking either the talent or the dynamism of his late father, Dudley Docker, a man closely associated with BSA for many years and who had manoeuvred his son into the chairman's office in an act of blatant nepotism, Sir Bernard was unable to achieve the harmonious working together of the company's many parts.

Still, in the years after the war, it must have been easy to overlook these weaknesses when the BSA Group's products were in such demand. This was especially true for the special alloy steels made by its subsidiaries Jessops and Saville. These were key components in the manufacture of the turbines needed for one of Britain's newest industries, jet engines, used on high-profile aircraft such as the Comet. This product placed BSA in the forefront among some of the most promising developments in British engineering.[16]

So what went wrong? The most obvious and intractable of all BSA's difficulties was the Daimler motor car subsidiary. This key division had not flourished after 1945. It had enormous difficulties finding a place in the home market and had a dismal export record.[17] For his part, Docker blamed the Attlee government's 'vicious' Double Purchase Tax on 'luxury' motor cars. This tax, he complained, was a 'monstrous handicap to the sales of such cars' and had prevented Daimler from becoming a viable concern.[18]

The fact was, however, that Daimler's main product line, largely old-fashioned and expensive limousines, simply did not have sufficient customer appeal for the company to operate its factory on an economic basis. In 1950 the BSA Group Board decided to break out of this impasse by adopting a new automotive manufacturing strategy.[19] This committed Daimler to a range of smaller, less expensive models in a determined bid to appeal to Britain's growing numbers of middle-class motorists. Even though considerable resources were spent upgrading Daimler's Coventry factory in order to produce the new models, the results were disappointing. By early 1956, Daimler's continuing losses threatened the entire BSA Group, and Chairman Docker's position with his fellow Board members had become increasingly precarious.[20]

Although far more successful than Daimler motor cars, the motor cycle division produced its share of disappointments. Sunbeam, the 'Gentleman's motor cycle', upon which such high hopes had been placed, was not only high-priced but was also plagued by serious quality-control problems, mostly the result of a badly flawed design. It never quite lived up to the standards of its German BMW inspiration. In consequence, far fewer machines were sold than hoped, and this model was ultimately dropped in 1956.[21] The Ariel Square Four had a far longer production life than the ill-fated Sunbeam, but it was an aged design, dating from the early 1930s, and had its own inherent design problems. The Square Four also suffered from its relatively high cost, which restricted its appeal further. It would be finally dropped from the factory's production programme in 1959.[22]

On the other end of the product range, the bicycle motor attachment also failed to live up to expectations. Begun as a response to changing consumer tastes for light-weight power units, the 'Winged Wheel' was produced too late to really exploit the cycle attachment market.[23] On the other hand, the light-weight Bantam, the big capacity twins and the more traditional single-cylinder machines (the 500 cc 'Gold Star' was a particularly successful racetrack machine) were consistent money-spinners which would continue to earn revenue for years to come.

As the leading shareholders of Triumph, Jack Sangster and Edward Turner had one of the most successful partnerships in the industry even if it was antagonistic in nature from time to time. Here they are shown admiring a Triumph at the 1955 Motor Cycle Show, several years after the company had been sold to BSA and Sangster elevated to its board of directors.

From 'Big Six' to 'Big Four'

If the state of the industry's leader, BSA, was not as good as surface appearances suggested, what remained of the one-time 'Big Six' of motor cycle manufacturers? By 1953 this had shrunk to the 'Big Four', itself a highly misleading concept since, between them, BSA and Associated Motor Cycles (AMC) accounted for between 65 and 75 per cent of the industry's output and made the motor cycle industry one of the most concentrated in Britain.[24] Now firmly established as the industry's number two producer, AMC had followed BSA's example by diversifying production through the acquisition of smaller firms. Unlike BSA, it remained a dedicated motor cycle producer. During this time AMC launched several important takeovers that enabled it to extend its limited model range without having to add to its existing facilities. This was important since AMC's output consisted mostly of the larger capacity Matchless and AJS models, either the traditional single- or the newer twin-cylinder machines.[25]

In 1947 AMC picked up the Coventry-based Francis-Barnett, another medium-sized producer of smaller machines. Acquisition of this firm enabled AMC, in the words its Chairman, to take 'an active interest in the light weight motor cycle field, with particular regard to export markets which were largely supplied by Germany in pre-war days'. The pattern was continued in 1950 when AMC acquired James Cycle, another medium-sized producer of light-weight models, based in Birmingham. Both these companies gave the parent company some presence in the light-weight market which formerly it had lacked.[26]

The management of the Woolwich factory, the core of AMC, had an intensely conservative conception of both motor cycles and motor cyclists, which was manifested in the manufacturing programmes. This consisted of the larger displacement single- and twin-cylinder Matchless and AJS models which were built largely for the traditional segment of the market. This conception was also reflected in the outlook of Managing Director Donald Heather. In his opinion, the majority of people who bought motor cycles were dedicated enthusiasts, many of whom were oriented towards sporting events. According to fellow executive Bert Hopwood, Heather refused to believe that substantive technical improvements were necessary. Indeed, Heather evidently doubted it was worthwhile even trying to produce a more mechanically reliable motor cycle, having once commented that 'most motor cyclists love to spend their Sunday mornings taking off the cylinder head and re-seating the valves'.[27] For a time, his strategy seemed vindicated by the fact that the company worked at full capacity during this period, barely able to meet either home or export demand, a point that shareholders were often reminded of by the company chairman at AMC's annual meetings. The policy was also reinforced by a high rate of return on capital and a series of generous dividend payouts.[28]

The most important single post-war acquisition AMC made was its 1953 purchase of Norton Motors, along with its sister firm R.T. Shelley, an automobile accessory maker, for a reported sum of £900,000. Like the earlier purchases, this Birmingham-based firm was only loosely integrated within AMC's corporate structure. S.R. Hogg, AMC's chairman, explained the Board's strategy of diversification to the shareholders at the subsequent Annual General Meeting:

> The great reputation which is attached to the names of Matchless, AJS and Norton, in the field of high grade sporting motor cycles, and to the names of Francis-Barnett and James, in the lightweight motor cycle markets, will give our Group a strength and prestige which cannot be matched by that of any other organisation in the motor cycle industry.

Hogg went on to declare that the addition of Norton would 'greatly strengthen the group in dealing with the competition we will have to face in the future, not merely from other British manufacturers, but also competition from the European motor cycle industry'.[29] Whether or not these acquisitions would be enough to meet that competition was a question that would soon be answered by British motor cycle consumers.

The smaller firms struggle on

The industry's two remaining larger companies struggled along with varying degrees of success. Neither came anywhere near BSA or AMC in terms of production levels, although they did try to adopt various innovative production strategies in order to maintain sales.

Royal Enfield remained committed to motor cycle and bicycle production but had also branched out to manufacture diesel engines and small engines for motorised bicycles. It continued to fill specialised government armament contracts at its old wartime underground factory near Bradford-on-Avon. From its main factory at Redditch, the company built its mainly large (350 cc to 500 cc) traditional single-cylinder machines, although it did also have a smaller displacement (125 cc) model to rival the BSA Bantam along with a popular 250 cc sports machine. Royal Enfield also built several large twin-cylinder models, although these never sold in great numbers. In response to tariff walls and import quotas, it was the only British motor cycle firm to establish an overseas manufacturing facility, by way of a licensing agreement with an Indian company based at Madras.[30]

The second company, Douglas, suffered from a period of upheaval and was put under receivership in 1948. It was later bought by Westinghouse Brake and Signal Company in 1956. Nonetheless, it maintained a limited line-up of motor cycles, although its real 'bread and butter' was a licensing arrangement negotiated with the Italian Piaggio company to manufacture the Vespa scooter. The latter proved to be a profitable venture and one which kept the firm abreast of changing consumer tastes in the home market and probably saved it from its earlier financial problems. Scooter production continued into the 1960s, while orthodox motor cycle production ended in 1957.[31]

Two of the well-established smaller specialist firms, Veloce (Velocette) and Vincent, had shown considerable design flair in their post-war models. Yet they, too, performed below their own expectations and experienced serious troubles, sufficient to cause one of them to go out of business during the period in question.

Vincent continued to produce the big 1000 cc twin-cylinder models which regularly broke speed records around the world. These machines are still considered to be benchmarks of engineering and design excellence. Nonetheless, the Vincent company found that it had boxed itself into a very limited market consisting of well-heeled enthusiasts. There were simply not enough of them willing to pay the steep prices – some £366 for a 1000 cc Rapide model in 1954 – which was necessary to keep the factory running on an economic basis.[32]

In 1948 the company suffered a major and ultimately fatal blow when Argentina adopted stringent import quotas and higher tariffs. This was a disaster for Vincent, as it had become highly committed to the Argentinian market, with much business having been developed in, among other things, supplying motor cycles to the country's military and police forces. From then on the company limped along as best it could.[33]

Vincent did not give up without a fight. It tried an imaginative, flexible response to the changing market and falling sales of the big twin-cylinder models. It produced a 48 cc cyclemotor (the Firefly) and later went into a partnership with the German NSU company. This project involved importing and assembling under licence NSU's light-weight motor cycles as well as its popular Quickly moped, but using at least 51 per cent British content, thus enabling them to be badged and sold as 'Vincents' throughout Britain and the Commonwealth. Ultimately the company also tried building three-wheel cars, engines for pilotless target aircraft, lawnmowers and even a water scooter. This was all to no avail, and in 1955 Vincent ceased production of motorised two-wheelers. After the company went out of business, owner Philip Vincent blamed competition from smaller, cheaply priced cars for the decline of his firm.[34]

The other specialised company, Velocette, continued to build its larger capacity single-cylinder models, primarily catering to a sports-oriented market of enthusiasts. The 1948 launch of its utilitarian 'Little Engine' or LE model was planned as a way of opening up a larger market of commuters. Although designed and manufactured to a very high standard, the LE never lived up to the hopes of its designers. The problems were essentially two-fold. Firstly, because of the LE's demanding specifications, which required expensive materials and manufacturing, it was priced beyond the pockets of the everyday commuter. Secondly, even though the LE was supposed to appeal to non-traditional consumers (its advertising slogan was 'Car-Like in Conception'), the approach to marketing was very orthodox. Although designer Philip Irving had urged the company to take out advertisements in publications such as *Tatler*, *Hoof and Horns* and *The Illustrated London News*, in the interests of reaching potential customers who would not read the established enthusiasts' journals, he failed to convince the board of directors to follow his advice. Instead, he was told 'that it was not my job to sell the machine but to design it'.[35] Such handicaps, combined with its unusual appearance, seriously undercut any chance of mass appeal. In 1950, for example, although the company had predicted sales of 14,500, actual production was only 2,800 units. Even

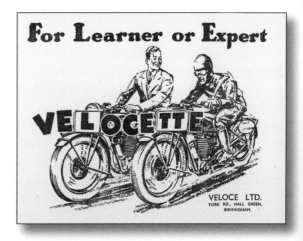

The slogan 'For Learner or Expert' used in this Velocette advertisement is slightly misleading insofar as their motor cycles were designed and built to unusually high standards and so tended to be purchased by more discerning and certainly wealthier riders.

Velocette LE ('Little Engine')

The Veloce Company, better known by its trade name, Velocette, was based in Hall Green, a suburb of Birmingham. For years the company produced a line of larger (350 cc to 500 cc) single-cylinder machines, often for a market of sporting enthusiasts. However, after the Second World War Velocette veered sharply off in a different direction and produced the so-called LE (Little Engine), a model specifically designed for commuters.

Initially introduced in 1949 and advertised as the 'Motor Cycle of Tomorrow', the LE was full of unorthodox and innovative features. It came with a 192 cc twin-cylinder, water-cooled four-stroke engine and had pressed steel body work which enclosed its mechanical parts. In order to enhance its appeal for potential non-motor cycling customers, it came equipped with a car-type hand gear changer and a hand operated centre stand. Unlike most British-made motor cycles of the era, which were powered by a final chain drive, the LE used a shaft drive for cleaner operation.

The LE was a huge gamble on the part of Velocette. It was so different from its other motor cycles that the factory had to be re-tooled at great expense. Nonetheless, despite all the innovation and technical sophistication, the LE was a commercial disappointment.

In part, this was a reflection of its comparatively high price. In 1952, for example, an LE cost £173, while the more conventional light-weight BSA Bantam was priced at £94 and a 125 cc Vespa scooter at £149 16s. However, it was also true that this machine was probably simply too much of an oddity to appeal to the average motor cyclist, either in Britain or abroad. Nor, on the other hand, was it the breakthrough model its creators hoped it would be among the general public, even after several post-production upgrades. Consequently, LE production failed to reach the levels expected. Indeed, far from being a money-spinner, the LE probably barely paid for the new tooling necessary for its manufacture.

However, the LE did achieve one unanticipated success. It became quite popular with British police forces, becoming known as the 'Noddy' bike since police riders, who needed both hands on the handlebars, were allowed to nod at, instead of saluting, their superior officers as they rode by. Thanks mostly to these police fleet orders, the LE remained in production right up until the end of Velocette, which closed its doors in 1971.

though production continued for years afterwards, sales of the LE never really improved.[36]

As before, there continued to be a number of smaller firms catering to various market segments which used proprietary two-stroke engine units, particularly those made by Villiers Engineering. Access to these power units enabled such companies to stay in business and complement the mainly large-capacity machines produced by the major firms. These lower-output companies built models in batches and targeted a variety of consumers, including commuters but also those participating in scrambles, trials and other sporting events.[37] One of them, Greeves, was virtually the only notable new market entry after 1945. Some of the others, responding to changed market conditions, would go into scooter manufacturing.[38]

Motor cycle road accidents on the rise

Smaller-sized, slower motor cycles might have implied fewer problems in terms of accidents on British roads, yet instead the exact opposite occurred. During these years, public opinion was increasingly inflamed over what was perceived as carnage on the highways as the numbers of motor cycle accidents and deaths mounted steadily.[39] Public concern about road safety focused mainly on riders, primarily young men and their mainly female pillion passengers, but also extended to the general behaviour of motor cyclists towards other road users.[40]

As they had twenty years before, growing numbers of motor cycles equalled more accidents. Initially, in the years after the war, this had not been a pressing problem. Motor cycles were seen as just another form of transport at a time when there was only limited access to personal motorised transport. In fact, it was not until 1953 that there were once again as many motor cycles on the road as there had been in the pre-war peak of 1929. The lower number of motor cycles, at least compared with motor cars, was probably the cause of a correspondingly lower accident rate.[41] (See table 13.)

Public indifference began to erode as motor cycle registrations and accident levels gradually built up. While indications are that many of these motor cycles were probably used largely for commuting purposes, the sporting aspect remained as strong as it had been before 1939.[42] During the summer of 1951 Francis Jones, a columnist with the industry's journal, *The Motor Cycle and Cycle Trader*, warned that public opinion was beginning to shift against motor cycles and motor cyclists. Jones opined that the 'gravest problem facing the industry at present' was the 'continuing increase in motor cycle accidents'. He also passed on information that he had picked up from a contact with the Metropolitan Police that, in the face of a 90 per cent increase of motor cycle accidents, the manufacturers might be confronted with 'repressive' legislation such as the compulsory use of helmets.[43]

Table 13 *British road accident fatalities, 1950–1960*

	Pedestrians	*Pedal cyclists*	*TWMV**	*Others*	*Total*
1950	2,251	805	1,129	827	5,021
1951	2,398	800	1,175	877	5,250
1952	2,063	743	1,142	748	4,706
1953	2,233	720	1,237	900	5,090
1954	2,226	696	1,148	940	5,010
1955	2,287	708	1,362	1,169	5,526
1956	2,270	650	1,250	1,197	5,367
1957	2,225	663	1,425	1,237	5,550
1958	2,408	668	1,421	1,473	5,970
1959	2,520	738	1,680	1,582	6,520
1960	2,708	679	1,743	1,840	6,970

* Twin-wheeled motor vehicles.
Source: *Department of Transport Road Accidents, Great Britain 1992*, London: HMSO, 1992.

The sporting ethos endures

Yet, in spite of the growing number of accidents and fatalities, many in the upper ranks of the industry, along with workers on the factory shop floor, remained stubbornly loyal to the primacy of racing, with the emphasis on fast, powerful motor cycles of between 350 cc and 500 cc engine capacity, as the underlying criterion of success. Although criticism was building in the press about the high level of accidents that occurred during the Isle of Man TT races, others viewed the hazards of competitive sport as an unavoidable evil.[44] In 1953 recently retired Union Director Major Watling, for one, took a decidedly philosophical approach to these deaths. They were regrettable, he agreed, but in the end were a 'grievous burden that had to be shared by all as the price of progress'.[45]

The fact was that the sports ethos continued to permeate the industry at virtually every level. Each June, as they had for years before, members of the industry's senior management would make their regular pilgrimage to the Isle of Man to attend the TT races. It seemed to be almost an obligation for the managers to see and to be seen at Britain's premier race meeting.[46] Nor was it only boardroom members who cheered on the racers from the grandstands. Racing results were often broadcast over the Woolwich factory's public address system and, on at least one occasion, AMC gave nearly 200 of its employees the day off to allow them to go up to 'The Island' and attend the Senior TT race. By its own account, the company even gave preference to enthusiasts in its shopfloor hiring policies. Managing Director Donald Heather was once quoted as saying that, all things being equal, motor cycle enthusiasts actually received preference when it came to recruiting workers at the AMC factory.[47]

Nor was it unusual for company chairmen to emphasise the importance of racing to their shareholders. At the 1955 Annual General Meeting, for example, AMC chairman S.R. Hogg proudly announced further victories of the Group's motor cycles at the TT. He assured his audience that these successes 'have undoubtedly helped greatly to maintain the prestige of our products, while the knowledge which we obtain of the performance of our machines under the strenuous conditions of open competitions, is of great benefit to our Technical Staff in their constant efforts to improve the quality of our products'.[48]

Other industry leaders made a regular point of stressing the importance of motor cycle racing as a form of research and development. Gilbert Smith, then Managing Director of Norton Motors, speaking in 1951 at a luncheon sponsored by the Manchester Motor Trades, left no doubt about the central place of racing for his firm and, by implication, for much of the rest of the industry:

> We do not race for fun, or merely for publicity. Our racing machines are travelling laboratories and our riders are, in fact, research workers. All these activities help to improve the standard machines.[49]

This theme was repeated elsewhere. For example, one article, published in a journal circulated among overseas distributors of British motor cycles, put strong emphasis on the close correlation between success on the race track and continuing high sales levels. Moreover, it was maintained that British motor cycle design had been in essence created by racing, and this in turn affected the way it was seen and appreciated by motor cycle buyers around the world:

> There is usually something distinctive in the feel and handling of a British machine, something that has resulted from the years of development and experience gained through a continuous series of sporting successes at home and aboard, as well as through factory testing and experiment.[50]

The manufacturers' orientation to motor cycling sports activity found other ways of expression. Not only did they produce movies highlighting this theme – BSA released two alone in 1955 (*Stars in Action* and *Gold Star*) – but petroleum and accessory companies also made their contributions. Castrol produced two colour movies in 1952 (*Motor Cycle World Championships* and *European Motor Racing*) and another (*Round the TT Course with Geoff Duke*) in 1953. Dunlop Tyre Co. released its own production (*Twistgrip*) in 1952.

As before the war, the pages of virtually every issue of the two main popular motor cycle journals, *The Motor Cycle* and *Motor Cycling*, continued to be full of coverage of sporting events: everything from grass track and speedway to scrambling and road racing. There were also other forms of literature devoted to sports. BP, for example, produced an annual review of the Isle of Man TT races in a popular paperback book format. Shell produced a guide to *European Motor Cycle Racing*, and BSA distributed a review of its own racing victories.[51]

Even the British government played its part in promoting motor cycle sports. In 1955 the Central Office of Information produced a fourteen-minute feature about various forms of motor cycle sport entitled *Tough on Two Wheels*, which was released to cinemas throughout Britain in co-operation with MGM. There is no evidence that movies were ever released dealing with non-sports themes, advocating, for example, the advantages of commuting.[52]

Nor did these films lack appreciative audiences. In one instance, a motor cycle dealer in Cambridge arranged a showing of several films on the Isle of Man TT races, which had been loaned to him by Shell-Mex and BP. The hall where the movies played was packed for two days running with hundreds of attentive enthusiasts.[53]

Such expressions of loyalty to sport were not shared by all within the industry. Columnist Francis Jones warned again of the possible repercussions from what he called 'the high performance obsession' as well as 'the belief that motor cycling is essentially a form of sport'. Success on the race track probably did have a positive impact on sales figures, at least among dedicated motor cyclists and enthusiasts generally. It is more debatable whether or not racetrack prowess directly assisted in the design of better commuter machines or attracted non-enthusiasts. There was, however, little doubt that this emphasis on sport exacted a high price in terms of public opinion.[54]

Such was the case when a correspondent for an insurance industry trade journal visited the 1951 Motor Cycle Show. He was clearly impressed with the quality of the machines on display, but was doubtful about how safely they would be operated. It was true, he noted, that they were well built and 'are perfectly "safe" in themselves – just like razor blades, gunpowder, matches and atom bombs are "safe"'. From the perspective of the insurance industry, he concluded there were 'far too many youngish fellows who buy powerful solos and promptly set out to test, *on public roads*, whether their machines will *really* clock 100 mph and more'.[55]

Was there any truth to claims that British motor cyclists were as sports-oriented and 'speed mad' as the industry leaders and their critics seemed to believe, or were such assertions blown out of all proportion? This is a difficult question to answer since the industry did not commission profes-sional marketing surveys at this time. However, in early 1954, a Gallop poll was conducted which provides an informative profile of British motor cyclists, even if it does not completely resolve the question of the primacy of sport during the 1950s.

Among other things, the survey reported that there was close to a 50/50 split between those who claimed they used their motorised two-wheelers (the survey included moped and scooter users as well as motor cyclists) for transport, as against those who used them for pleasure or as a hobby. In terms of sports orientation, 40 per cent indicated that the Isle of Man TT was the main focus of their interest, followed by scrambles (22 per cent), other road races (13 per cent), dirt track racing (11 per cent), reliability trials (7 per cent), grass track racing (6 per cent) and speed record attempts (1 per cent).[56]

But the most revealing aspect of the poll was the answers to the questions put to the respondents about whether their next purchase would be either another motor cycle or a motor car. Some 36 per cent of current motor cycle owners indicated they would buy a motor car, 48 per cent another motor cycle of indeterminate size and only 1 per cent a moped or scooter. The poll clearly suggested that a large proportion of Britain's motor cyclists saw themselves in a temporary 'half-way house' on the way to motor car ownership.[57]

More reliable data about motor cycle owners appeared several years later in an academic study. This work, based on a social survey published in 1953, reinforced what more impressionistic observations had revealed much earlier. According to the survey, owners tended to be male (95 per cent) and mostly under 35 years of age (very few motor cycles were owned by people over 55). These owners were mainly in skilled manual labour occupations, with total incomes of between £200 and £399. By contrast, rates of motor car ownership tended to increase proportionately with income, rising steeply among those with total incomes over £600.[58]

Rider safety

Whatever their income level or social class, it is likely that many, possibly a majority, of motor cyclists had some interest in motor cycle sports, and this in turn might have had some effect on riding behaviour. It is also likely that rising levels of dissension and indeed accidents with other road users resulted, at least to some extent. More significantly there had been a vast increase of all road vehicles on a road system that was incapable of handling the volume of traffic. There were many in the industry who agreed that this was a problem which they would soon have to address.[59]

As highly vulnerable road users, motor cyclists naturally suffered a correspondingly higher accident rate. In the words of one consulting surgeon, J.S. Horn, 'how many motorists can drive for five years without having a slight bump hard enough to dent a mud wing? They get away without injury – but the same bump to the more vulnerable motor cyclist is enough to kill him and his passenger.'[60]

The government became so alarmed that details about the extent of these accidents were provided directly to Prime Minister Anthony Eden. In fact, as early as 1951, the accident rate had attracted sufficient attention for the Ministry of Transport to warrant the setting up of a special sub-committee of the Road Safety Committee to study motor cycle accidents.[61] At one of its meetings Major Watling vigorously defended the industry's record in the area of safety and refused to concede that there was anything wrong with British-built motor cycles. Although he insisted that they were not inherently dangerous, the manufacturers had already taken measures on their own initiative to improve them. He gave the example of further standardisation, such as handlebar control levers, as proof of their commitment to this goal. Motor cycles, Watling insisted, 'were quite safe if properly handled'.[62]

There was one aspect of motor cycle safety which was particularly sensitive. The manufacturers were highly defensive about the question of helmet use, which they perceived as an implicit admission that motor cycle accidents could result in serious head injury. In fact, they went as far as to ban a poster designed for the 1955 Show, which depicted a motor cyclist wearing a helmet, on the grounds that it was 'undesirable'. Ministry of Transport personnel discovered that many motor cyclists were very resistant to measures designed to protect them. This was particularly true of helmet use. Ministry officials noted that, despite the fact that 50 per cent of all motor cycle accidents involved head injuries, there was 'a psychological difficulty in that young men (who form a substantial part of the motor cycling public) tend to regard crash helmets as something effeminate'.[63]

Nor did everyone share Major Watling's confidence in the safety of contemporary motor cycles, or more specifically the competence of the riders. For example, C.B. Hewitt, Deputy Secretary of the Institute of Automobile Assessors, wrote to the sub-committee and specifically criticised the riders as the root cause of the high accident rate.[64] And some civil servants had become so exasperated by the safety problems surrounding motor cycle use that they actually contemplated giving away a number of sidecars in the hope of slowing down solo motor cyclists.[65]

The government's concerns about levels of motor cycle accidents were set out in the sub-committee's *Report to the Minister of Transport on Motor Cycle Accidents*, published in 1952. The *Report* made a number of observations about the hazards of operating motor cycles on British roads. Because of the inherent lack of protection for either rider or pillion passenger, the danger was termed 'extremely serious'.[66] As evidence, it was noted that during 1950 some 37,390 motor cyclists and their passengers had been either injured or killed, compared with 32,771 in 1938. The *Report* did, however, note that at least a part of the rising toll of motor cyclists was a reflection of higher levels of motor vehicle traffic on congested roads.[67] It was also observed that close to 50 per cent of accident victims were young men between the ages of 19 and 27. The *Report* stated that many of these young male riders had female pillion passengers and may have yielded to the 'temptation' to 'show off by driving at excessive speed', and this was yet a further hazard contributing to these high accident rates.[68]

The numbers of motor cycle accident fatalities, especially among young men, continued to mount throughout the following years. In 1951, the year petrol rationing ended, some 117 motor cyclists aged between 15 and 19 were killed in accidents (compared to a total of 887 killed by all causes in the same age group). According to a survey conducted in 1958, motor cycle accident fatalities had climbed to 298 (compared to 835 in the same age group killed by all causes). Even more significantly, another study commissioned in 1957 noted that motor cyclists riding machines of less than 250 cc had a lower accident rate than those using larger sized models. Scooterists, it was noted, also had a lower accident rate.[69]

Bad behaviour

All this had a considerable impact on press coverage, which now became ever more negative and sensationalist, of the perils of motor cycle riding, especially with respect to the larger, more powerful models. As during the late 1920s, motor cyclists once again believed themselves to have become an endangered species. One motor cycle dealer reported that he had been dismayed to hear an episode from the popular BBC radio programme, *The Archers,* which contained critical comments about motor cycles. In Bournemouth, the local police chief was supposed to have called motor cyclists 'perfect pests'. In his mind the problem seemed to be related to the age of the riders and the nature of their machines: 'Many of the young riders are on high-powered machines which they cannot handle and don't understand and they will gad about the town on them instead of going off into the country.'[70]

The effect of this detrimental publicity did more than simply give motor cyclists a bad name on radio serials or around seaside resorts. The primary result was the creation of ill-will among politicians and civil servants, the very people the industry would increasingly depend upon for co-operation over issues such as the export trade and the revision of legislation. Equally important, it also had the effect of once more causing anguish for parents of potential motor cyclists, which the industry itself had already identified as an important damper on sales in the home market.[71]

The industry did not stand by passively amid this barrage of criticism. The Manufacturers' Union hired a full-time public relations officer (PRO) in order to try and influence press coverage or at least to refute the negative coverage whenever possible. The Manufacturers' Union worked together with the RAC and the ACU to set up motor cycle training programmes around the country to defuse some of the concern about young riders buying powerful motor cycles without adequate preparation. Moreover, as evidence of their commitment to safer motor cycling, the Manufacturers' Union decided to arrange for the publication of a booklet entitled *Road Craft*, which would accompany each new motor cycle sold.[72]

The Manufacturers' Union even sponsored the production of a feature film, which was released throughout Britain and later Australia and North America. Made at the cost of £12,000 and entitled *The Black Rider*, it attempted to depict motor cyclists in a positive light, to soften the image often highlighted in the press reports.[73] The Manufacturers' Union also sponsored a pavilion at a number of events designed to attract large numbers of young people. For example, it displayed a wide range of models, from mopeds to large-displacement sports machines, at both the Hulton Exhibition (a show organised for British youth) and at the Boy Scouts Jubilee Jamboree.[74]

Scooter fashion

The safety issue created severe problems for the manufacturers, but far more ominous was a longer-term trend only just becoming discernible in the early 1950s. This was a far-reaching shift in consumer tastes, which began several years before, away from the traditional medium- and heavy-weight machines to lighter weight models. The significance of this development, amounting to a fundamental re-alignment of buying habits, was one that most of the major manufacturers failed to appreciate until it was too late.

One factor in particular underlay this shift in public tastes. Living standards had improved since 1945, but there was still a shortage of personal motorised transport, aggravated by the motor car industry's inability to satisfy home market demand, due to high export quotas. There were also those consumers who wanted more than a bicycle, may not have wanted a full-sized motor cycle, but could not afford a motor car. The trend was reflected in changes in the type of motor cycles being registered for road use. In 1948, for example, there had been 210,688 machines with engine displacements up to 250 cc and another 245,121 machines in the larger capacity classes. By 1952, however, the machines under 250 cc had grown to 465,151, compared to 314,871 of the larger models. By 1956, there were 778,659 of the smaller machines and only 352,788 machines over 250 cc registered. The growth in machines of the lightest weight category, those with engines of less than 60 cc displacement (mopeds and cyclemotors), was particularly marked. In 1950, there were 29,297 of this type on the road. Two years later, the numbers had swollen to 120,472, and in 1956 they reached 246,443. (See table 14.)

Table 14   *Number of motor cycles for which licences were current at any time during the quarter ending 30 September, between 1946 and 1952*

Capacity	1946	1947	1948	1949	1950	1951	1952
Solo units:							
up to 60 cc					29,297	79,473	120,472
60–150 cc	77,349	87,332	97,195	129,890	157,677	178,755	205,914
150–250 cc	114,735	118,779	113,493	126,568	130,191	129,156	138,765
over 250 cc	183,744	222,907	245,121	281,286	305,885	314,871	326,448
Total solo:	375,828	429,018	455,809	537,744	623,050	702,255	791,599
Combo units:	73,521	84,594	87,000	96,727	106,370	120,316	130,229
Tricycles and others:	12,965	14,824	14,462	19,099	22,292	25,192	26,999
Grand total:	462,327	528,415	559,313	653,635	751,738.	847,801	948,860

Source: Ministry of Transport, *Return showing the number of Mechanically Propelled Vehicles.*

This growing demand created an opening for the motor cycle industry. During the late 1940s and throughout the 1950s some of the smaller, more dedicated producers made many, albeit clumsy and tardy, efforts to respond to changing public tastes in motorised two-wheelers.[75] As described earlier, at the end of the 1930s, a number of smaller British firms from outside the established industry had tried to develop what was then known as the 'ultra-lightweight' market. The pre-war 'autocycles' (an early form of moped) were replaced after 1945 with the so-called 'clip-ons', small engine units that could be attached to bicycles. This was a shift in production which one trade journal called the 'most interesting development' in the motorised two-wheeled industry that had been seen for years.[76]

EMI, for example, had purchased Rudge-Whitworth just before the war and built a new factory in Hayes, Middlesex. Although it never resumed production of the traditional, large-capacity Rudges, it did enjoy considerable success with the Cyclemaster – a clip-on variant, well known by its motto, 'The magic wheel that wings your heel'.[77] By 1950 there were ten firms building such units, many of them small-scale producers, some all-British in construction, others using foreign components. Still, it was remarked that the British were still far behind Continental manufacturers in the light-weight field.[78]

The basic 'cyclemotor' and 'clip-on' were familiar concepts to the British industry. However, the more sophisticated imports which began to flow in from the Continent after 1950 were a different matter altogether. These were purpose-built motorised (50 cc or less engine) bicycles, which became known as 'mopeds'. By 1955 one trade journal noted that British manufacturers had fallen behind their Continental rivals, having failed to react quickly enough and come out with their own domestically produced mopeds. As

Ironically, as early as 1919, Britain had already developed and produced the world's first scooters. Unfortunately, these machines were poorly designed and failed in the market. Later, and not for the first time, someone else took a British invention and turned it into a commercial success. The result was machines such as the Lambretta scooter seen here.

© MOTOR CYCLE INDUSTRY ASSOCIATION OF GREAT BRITAIN

The Lambretta 125 c.c. Motor Scooter is here !
★ A revelation in Safe, Reliable, Economical transport for you and your family ★ 140 m.p.g. ★ Enclosed Transmission of advanced design. ★ Also Light Delivery Trucks with open or closed bodies. You must see them.

Lambretta

LAMBRETTA CONCESSIONAIRES LIMITED
28 OLD BROMPTON RD., LONDON S.W.7
Head Office :   Phone : PARK 5928
Lloyds Bank Chambers, 64 High Street, Epsom, Surrey
Phone : EPSOM 1206

early as 1953 there were already 500,000 of these units in use in Italy while only an estimated 175,000 were found on British roads.[79]

Nor, in the immediate post-war years, had British bicycle firms entered the moped market. Initially, they believed that increased moped sales would not necessarily shrink the bicycle market. Instead, the dominant opinion among bicycle industry managers was that mopeds 'seem to have appealed to an entirely new public who have not hitherto been attracted to two-wheeled transport'. Like their motor cycle counterparts, within a few years, the bicycle industry would also come to revise this judgement on the moped.[80]

The real threat, however, arose from the growing levels of imported scooters. This machine, which differed in several significant ways from the orthodox motor cycle, was created among the economic shambles of post-1945 Italy, where much manufacturing industry had been destroyed during the war. Ironically, as described in chapter one, the scooter, which had been invented and then abandoned by the British during the 1920s, was now vastly refined by Italian engineers and subsequently by their German counterparts.[81] It had been designed and manufactured by non-traditional firms, particularly those emerging from the Italian aeronautics industry. These firms had been forced to find new uses for their factories, and cheap personal transport held particular potential.[82]

Scooter use in Italy grew rapidly after its introduction in 1946. It became a social phenomenon, virtually unprecedented in motorised transportation. Production increased dramatically, and scooters were soon seen on streets and roads all over Europe.[83] To many it may have seemed to be the realisation of what critics in Britain during the inter-war period had been urging for so long and unsuccessfully, a true 'Everyman's' motorised two-wheeler.[84]

Much of the popularisation of the scooter was helped by imaginative promotion by continental manufacturers such as Germany's NSU (who built Italian machines under licence for several years), which, among other things, organised special summer camps for scooterists.[85] Perhaps the strongest point about the scooter was precisely that it was not a motor cycle, making it especially popular with middle-class riders in general, and women in particular.[86] In other words, its appearance created an entirely new stratum of consumers. Ironically, it took these exported scooters to bring about the belated realisation of the British industry's own abortive 1920s campaign to try and interest women in motorised two-wheeled transportation. This was a point certainly well recognised from the beginning by the British producer of the Vespa if not by the rest of the industry.[87]

Although they had been long aware of developments in Italy, the initial response of British motor cycle manufacturers to the growing popularity of these unorthodox, light-weight machines, which began to appear in the home market around 1950, was amused contempt, quickly followed by frustration and anger.[88] In 1956, for example, Claude McCormack, Managing Director of Douglas, recalled the reaction of the industry, several years before, to the announcement that his firm would be manufacturing Vespa scooters under licence. They had, he said, laughed at his prediction of the coming popularity of the scooter among British consumers. Instead, he claimed, 'the motor scooter proved to have a remarkable "boy meets girl" appeal. It created an entirely new market – safety and economy on two wheels.'[89]

This attitude was mirrored elsewhere in the industry. Many established motor cycle dealers displayed overt hostility to scooters and even refused to service them. Indeed, the market began to split into two discrete parts, one made up of 'conventional' motor cyclists, both enthusiasts and commuters, many of whom were prepared to put up with comparatively poor quality control and to carry out their own mechanical work, and the other consisting of the new 'scooterists' who were less likely to be mechanically inclined or able or willing to perform their own servicing.[90]

For several vital years the majority of the industry's top managers simply did not appreciate the implications arising from the growing popularity of scooters and other light-weight models. To men such as Donald Heather, Gilbert Smith and Jack Sangster, who had moved into executive positions in the industry during the inter-war period, the scooter must have brought back memories of the 1920s sales fiasco. Now, once again, their inclination was to write it off as another passing fashion. As before, there would be a short period of experimentation followed by inevitable disillusionment, and consumers would go back to the traditional larger displacement, orthodox motor cycles. Consequently, there was deemed to be no pressing need to change manufacturing programmes.[91]

There were those at the time who did realise what was happening and who tried to draw it to the attention of the manufacturers. In 1953 Francis Jones, the industry's long-time gadfly, wrote that they had not been 'quick off the mark with cyclemotors', and were 'still more dilatory about motor scooters'. Jones was not alone in his assessment. Several months later, in a well-publicised paper he read before a meeting of the South Birmingham Motor Cycle Club, George Beresford, a commercial artist, criticised the industry for design conservatism. Had the manufacturers, he claimed, been more receptive to developments on the Continent, 'there would now be at least twice as many motor cycles registered in this country as at present'.[92] Similar judgements, moreover, were being made in the broadsheets and the business press.[93]

Despite those who criticised the industry for its inaction, there were others in the technical and popular motor cycle press who supported the position of industry leaders. Bob Holliday, an editor of the popular journal *Motor Cycling*, made it clear that he was not impressed with the 'tissue-paper-wrapped brick-bats thrown at our manufacturers for their alleged conservative nature'. He believed that, far from being detrimental, the fact that British motor cycle makers had failed to copy some of the features of these best-selling Continental imports or to alter their production programmes was, under the circumstances, a sound decision.[94] Holliday went on to describe what he thought was the overall strategy of the British industry:

> There are features on foreign machines which are good, and which we could very well copy, but in the main I would say that the British methods of making haste slowly is to our advantage in the long run. In this country we make motor cycles to sell, and if possible, to sell for hard currency. We are well aware that we have growing competition abroad, but our factory directors must know what they are doing for their own sales' returns tell them what is wanted throughout the world and, judging by the general reception given to their machines at Earls Court, they cannot be so far off the beam.[95]

In the event, as during the late 1930s, it was the smaller firms, such as Excelsior, Mercury and Norman, which first tried to respond to changing consumer tastes. However, their small production runs must have hampered their ability to compete on the basis of price. There were also problems with design, and the British-made products were manifestly not as attractive as the foreign machines. In contrast, Douglas, which built the Vespa under licence, and the Lambretta Concessionaires thrived. Indeed, by 1957, it was estimated that most of the estimated 115,000 scooters in use were foreign made, and Britain had become one of Lambretta's best export markets.[96]

Retail price maintenance under threat

Higher levels of imports were not the only problem facing British motor cycle manufacturers. In the early 1950s a new threat re-emerged, one that was to destroy the industry's carefully constructed home market trading scheme. The government's *Report of the Committee on Resale Price Maintenance*, released in 1951, did not recommend substantive changes to the Manufacturers' Union's trading agreements, nor were they ever investigated by the Monopolies and Restrictive Practices Commission. Nonetheless, the industry remained apprehensive of any move to change its well-entrenched trading system which, they doggedly maintained, was in the best interests of everyone, manufacturers, retailers and consumers alike. The *Motor Cycle and Cycle Trader*, for example, claimed that if the then Labour government implemented its plans to abolish price maintenance, it would result in a reversion 'to the law of the jungle'.[97]

The subsequent publication of a *White Paper on Retail Price Maintenance*, which suggested that the government might challenge their trading agreements, caused great consternation among industry leaders. Major Watling had warned Union members that the government 'proposes to abolish both individual and collective minimum Price Maintenance, giving the Manufacturer only the sole right to state his *maximum* retail price and leaving Dealers free, if they so wish, to sell the product at a lower price'.[98] That, Watling continued, was not all. He understood that the government also wanted to 'control other types of trading arrangement which now discipline the Retail Trader and which might result in a restriction of competition'. Watling suggested that the Manufacturers' Union follow the lead of the motor industry and ask for a special exclusion from the proposed legislation on the basis of a promise of better after-sales service to consumers.[99]

The Manufacturers' Union continued to insist that its trading rules benefited the community at large. In a brief to the Board of Trade, Watling claimed that, should the Bill currently before Parliament become law, the real victims would not be the manufacturers but rather British consumers. Watling maintained that one of the keystones of the Manufacturers' Union's campaign to make motor cycles safer was its free after-sales service, which was an obligation agreed to by all retailers party to the Resale Price Maintenance scheme. Abolishing resale price maintenance would endanger this campaign and make for more dangerous traffic conditions.[100] Moreover, if enacted, the legislation 'would inevitably lead to price competition amongst dealers which could only be at the expense of the standard of service laid down by the Manufacturer, and expected by the public'. This would also result 'in the entry into the Trade of what are often described as "kerb-side dealers" who offer no service to the public, who frequently deal in notes, and who have been a major factor in seeking to undermine the Covenant Scheme in the Motor Car Industry'.[101]

A year and a half later, the Manufacturers' Union replied to an official query from the Monopolies and Restrictive Practices Commission (MRPC) about its price maintenance scheme. Although the Manufacturers' Union tried to avoid the jurisdiction of the Commission and stall for time, by July 1955, following a report by the MRPC the month before, Union Director Hugh Palin realised that their trading agreements would have to be changed. Palin was especially concerned about critical press reports that had recently appeared on what was termed the 'Star Chamber' proceedings of the CTU, the Manufacturers' Union's enforcement body. In early 1956, the Manufacturers' Union was faced with the likely passage in Parliament of the Restrictive Trade Practices Bill and reluctantly proceeded to wind up the CTU, which was certain to be made illegal, and to modify the existing agreements to avoid any inconsistency with the legislation. Thereafter, manufacturers would find it more difficult than before to retain control of retail prices, discounts and other trade terms.[102]

The export drive falters

Whatever its troubles in the home market, the industry could always congratulate itself on mounting export earnings.[103] For many years after 1945, these had been a consistent success story. From only 4,000 units in 1945, the industry sent abroad 74,000 machines in 1950. The following year a peak of 91,700 motor cycles left Britain, an all-time record never again exceeded (see table 15). Thereafter, exports declined progressively until the 1960s. There were several reasons why British motor cycles had become more difficult to sell overseas.

It was true that the rearmament programme that accompanied the Korean War created scarcities of certain critical materials, especially steel, which hampered production, albeit only for two or three years.[104] There were also problems increasingly encountered with protectionism in hitherto favourable markets. For example, Argentina had been targeted in 1948 as a prime motor cycle export market.[105] At first these hopes seemed to be realised, and motor cycle shipments rose sharply during this period. Only 271 machines had been sent in 1938, a total that jumped to 1,956 in 1947 and then reached a staggering 9,410 (or close to 20 per cent of total British motor cycle exports) the following year. In 1949 Argentina had agreed to issue least 10,000 import licences, and the future there for British exporters looked secure.[106]

However, this highly promising market abruptly crashed shortly afterwards when the Argentinian government abruptly withdrew most of the licences.

Table 15 *British motor cycles exports, 1945–1951*

	Aust./NZ	*Europe*	*USA*	*Canada*	*Other*	*Subtotal*	*Total*
1945	626	1,560	283	20	1,459	3,948	3,948
1946	6,438	12,492	8,199	1,238	19,861	48,228 (5,248)	54,889
1947	9,971	29,366	9,933	1,612	19,340	48,706 (6,661)	55,367
1948	17,413	8,759	7,670	2,389	29,062	65,293 (9,843)	75,136
1949	24,501	6,664	3,001	3,959	18,597	56,722 (8,547)	65,269
1950	23,348	13,705	8,535	5,098	17,685	68,377 (5,588)	73, 965
1951	28,377	19,287	8,185	2,876	28,316	87,041 (4,658)	91,699
1959	2,535	7,769	12,834	1,387	18,160	n/a	42,685

Figures in brackets indicate total exports of motor cycles of less than 100 cc capacity.
Source: MRC, MSS 204/13/1/1.

According to the Argentinians, the cancellation of agreed-to quotas was caused by internal financial difficulties, especially their fast-sinking sterling balances. However, as Major Watling noted sourly to manufacturers afterwards, there did not seem to be a shortage of either French or Italian currency.[107]

In the years to follow, Argentinian imports never reached anything like the 1947–48 levels; in 1956 they had dropped to a miserly 5 machines.[108] Subsequently, other nations began to accept fewer motor cycles than they had before. Once again, sterling shortages were blamed. Egypt, Denmark, Brazil and Finland – previously good markets – all clamped down on imports during the early 1950s.[109]

The most dramatic example of the problems facing the industry in world markets was in Australia, which had consistently been the single most important destination for British motor cycles since long before the war. On average, it had absorbed up to a quarter of the industry's exports on a regular basis.[110] Then, starting in the mid-1950s, this lucrative market began to falter. Dismayed British motor cycle manufacturers were informed that Australia had its own sterling crisis and would begin to limit imports severely. Soon afterwards, thanks to the choking off of this market, the Manufacturers' Union estimated it had to find, at great difficulty, new markets for some 18,000 machines (see table 16). These restrictions were later eased off, but Australia would never again be as significant an export market as it had been before.[111]

Table 16 *British motor cycle exports to the USA, Canada and Australia, 1951–1964*

	USA	Canada	Australia
1951	8,195	2,876	n/a
1952	7,095	1,407	6,872
1953	5,136	2,031	6,678
1954	8,172	1,595	9,474
1955	9,598	1,196	6,692
1956	13,651	2,562	3,925
1957	12,383	1,411	4,490
1958	10,601	1,228	2,271
1959	12,834	1,387	1,921
1960	12,285	1,043	1,632
1961	7,998	741	932
1962	10,022	642	1,090
1963	14,898	702	1,236
1964	20,977	596	813

Source: Data contained in MSS 204/13/1 and various issues of the BCCMCMTU and BCMCIA *Quarterly Reports* (Modern Records Centre).

Some senior members of the industry realised that the easy selling of the post-war era had ended. During 1952 Gilbert Smith, Managing Director of Norton, claimed in an article entitled 'The Honeymoon's Over', that export sales would be much more difficult to sustain.[112] His views were followed by an editorial in *The Motor Cycle and Cycle Export Trader* entitled 'Return to Normal'. The journal warned manufacturers that the 'post-war wave of unrestricted buying is over'. Consumer spending would now be less plentiful, and value for money was essential. Henceforth, they would have to work harder for their sales.[113]

Foreign competition revives

Nonetheless, many industry leaders believed that the shrinking export markets were actually a reflection of poor representation on the part of the British government. The manufacturers were convinced that the industry was losing out in the series of bilateral negotiations that had been concluded for a number of key markets since 1945.[114] What particularly incensed them was their conviction that Board of Trade negotiators were agreeing far too easily to restrictive quotas and tariffs. A tougher set of negotiators, they insisted, might have saved them valuable sales.[115]

There were also concerns about their declining status among Whitehall officials and their Ministers. This conviction was re-enforced when motor cycle manufacturers discovered, to their intense irritation, during a meeting with the Dollar Export Board in May 1950, that they had been lumped into the same category as perambulator makers, a seemingly less critical industry.[116] Nor was the Federation of British Industries much help. Major Watling was convinced that the FBI 'seemed anxious not to be too critical of the Board of Trade and other Government departments' and would not effectively stand up for their members.[117] Increasingly, the industry seemed friendless among Whitehall's corridors of power.

A stiff letter summarising the industry's grievances on the trade negotiations had already been sent to the then President of the Board of Trade, Harold Wilson, via Federation of British Industries' Director-General Norman Kipping, in 1949.[118] However, as Board personnel told Wilson, after he had asked for an investigation into the Manufacturers' Union's complaint, these quotas and other import restrictions were difficult to alter since the countries involved were either anxious to protect their own domestic industries or wanted to preserve sterling balances. There was only so much that British government negotiators could do in order to convince their foreign counterparts to make any significant concessions.[119]

Growing foreign competition was another factor that began to complicate British motor cycle exports. The manufacturers worried about incursions by Continental rivals, such as the Italian Moto Guzzi and Austrian Puch firms (albeit in the light-weight motor cycle class), into British export markets. The British were convinced that these competitors had unduly benefited from American aid programmes such as the Marshall Plan and now had an unfair advantage. Thanks to this largesse, so they claimed, their rivals' factories had been rebuilt and re-equipped, 'to an extent which would be quite impracticable and uneconomic for a British firm'.[120] Another foreign rival, Czechoslovakia, exported lightweights into Australia, directly competing with the BSA Bantam. The Czech machine was much cheaper, even after taking into account a 17½ per cent import duty on non-British motor cycles.[121]

There were other less obvious problems slowing the sale of British motor cycles overseas which the industry was aware of but had not mentioned in their briefs to the government. One enthusiast's journal complained, for example, about how the poor appearance of displays of British motor cycles at a show on the Continent had hurt the reputation of the industry generally.[122] Overseas retailers continually complained of shipping delays, sloppy paperwork, badly packed motor cycles, poor servicing and a general shortage of spare parts. British manufacturers were also slow to provide their service manuals in languages other than English, even after repeated requests to do so.[123] More significantly, market reports prepared by the Manufacturers' Union's own representatives highlighted factors which had little connection with either the effectiveness or determination of British trade negotiators. In fact, the biggest obstacle to sales was the fact that foreign tastes in motorised two-wheeled transport had been steadily shifting away from the kind of products being produced by British factories.

The Dutch market is one example of how these changes in consumer preference adversely affected British exports. For example, during 1953 a highly critical article published in the Dutch motor cycle enthusiast's journal, *Motor Kampioen*, had been drawn to the attention of the Manufacturers' Union. It declared that, while it may have once been true that British motor cycles were supreme, this was no longer the case. German and Italian machines were now more and more successful, especially on European racetracks, not just in the light-weight classes but even in the 350 cc to 500 cc engine classes, normally the preserve of British machines. This had made a considerable impact on Dutch consumers. But instead of trying to improve their products, the article concluded, British manufacturers seemed content to rest on past laurels and had not developed more competitive models.[124]

Several years later a report prepared for the Manufacturers' Union observed that the demand for the heavy-weight British motor cycles in Holland was declining in favour of the mopeds and light-weight models being manufactured by its Continental rivals. A number of causes were responsible for the decline. The report noted 'changes in the standard of living of the section of the public interested in this type of transport, but more especially ... the fact that insurance rates for such motor cycles have increased considerably ... whilst prices in the second-hand car market have considerably declined' and thus 'the operating costs of a heavy-weight motor cycle and a small second-hand car do not differ appreciably'. Sales to Holland, which had reached 3,642 in 1946, had dropped to 343 in 1958.[125]

Switzerland, another key British export market, was also buying fewer of the heavy-weight motor cycles. One of Europe's few remaining hard-currency markets that for many years had no import quotas, Switzerland had previously been well disposed to British motor cycles.[126] However, by 1951, this too had changed. In part, this was the result of new import restrictions, designed to protect Swiss currency reserves, but there was also an increased consumer interest in light-weight machines, particularly Czech Jawas and Austrian Puch models in the 125 cc to 250 cc classes. These, British manufacturers were warned, were not only cheaper than their machines but better designed as well.[127]

Moreover, they had also been cautioned that the Swiss were becoming impatient with the poor mechanical reliability of British motor cycles. For example, at a dinner sponsored by Triumph Engineering for its overseas agents held in November 1951, Managing Director Edward Turner heard sharp criticism voiced by a Swiss retailer. In future, Turner was told, motor cycles dispatched to Switzerland must be 'trouble-free, neater and cleaner'. In his reply, however, Turner airily dismissed these disquieting words. Swiss retailers, he said, had to understand that 'there was a wide gap between the

Table 17   *British exports to selected markets, 1945–1950, 1958 and 1959*

	Australia	Holland	Switzerland	Sweden	Denmark	India	USA	Canada
1945	619	893	2	14	61	128	283	20
1946	5,808	3,642	910	1,950	3,000	2,887	9,044	1,414
1947	9,295	113	2,424	2,261	75	3,284	10,232	2,171
1948	18,880	1,495	4,381	804	321	3,158	8,178	3,790
1949	25,107	1,468	3,541	299	591	2,542	4,267	5,404
1950	22,171	2,097	4,448	3,653	480	1,419	8,582	6,225
1958	2,271	343	164	693	116	2,784	10,601	1,228
1959	1,921	321	228	423	178	3,136	12,834	1,387

Source: MSS 204/10/1/1 (Modern Records Centre).

conceptions of a model and the delivery thereof in quantity'. While foreign competitors might promise more, only his company exhibited what they could actually deliver.[128]

Notwithstanding Turner's confidence, several years later another market report noted that there had been a continued decline in Swiss motor cycle registrations, the most serious drop being for models larger than 250 cc engine capacity, the mainstay of British exports. Higher insurance premiums were blamed, and it now cost as much to insure a 500 cc motor cycle as a small car. Moreover, like their Dutch counterparts, Swiss consumers were also buying greater numbers of mopeds and other lightweights, models which did not constitute a significant part of British exports to that market. Swiss sales, which had peaked in 1950 at 4,448 units, had slumped to just 164 eight years later.[129] (See table 17.)

Imports flood into the home market

As the industry began to readjust to the unhappy combination of more difficult trading conditions at home and abroad, British motor cycle manufacturers were increasingly vexed with the growing flood of imports, which began after 1952. Even though the foreign machines did not challenge the domestic producers directly, being mostly light-weight models and scooters, it was nevertheless galling to see the inroads imports were making in British showrooms, hitherto the exclusive preserves of domestic producers since before 1914.

The manufacturers were acutely aware of these rising numbers of imports, coming at a time when domestic sales had begun to lag. In April 1956 Manufacturers' Union Director Hugh Palin wrote a confidential memo to members of the Manufacturers' Union Council and expressed his alarm over the industry's trading conditions. Comparing 1954 production totals with those of 1955, he noted a slight decline in output, from 184,057 to 182,603 units, although exports had slumped from 70,254 to 60,473 units. During the same period there had been a dramatic increase in imports, which had jumped from 7,057 to 46,277 units. Most of these were mopeds and scooters – and indeed 41,457 of them had an engine capacity of less than 50 cc.[130] (See table 18.)

Table 18   *British motor cycle registrations, production, imports and exports,*
1945–1975

	Registrations	*Production*	*Imports*	*Exports*
1945	312,844	49,000	n/a	3,948
1946	467,058	84,200	n/a	54,900
1947	533,783	116,600	n/a	55,350
1948	560,107	130,800	n/a	75,136
1949	655,200	154,800	n/a	65,270
1950	761,500	171,300	n/a	74,000
1951	859,034	171,700	n/a	91,700
1952	962,210	153,000	1,600	70,300
1953	1,052,864	153,000	2,400	63,100
1954	1,256,568	184,100	10,900	70,300
1955	1,276,894	182,600	59,900	60,700
1956	1,349,282	126,700	48,200	58,800
1957	1,497,050	175,000	115,000	50,400
1958	1,546,183	139,700	75,500	36,700
1959	1,764,535	234,300	173,000	42,700
1960	1,795,000	193,600	134,700	44,100
1961	1,790,000	144,200	82,100	32,700
1962	1,779,000	99,800	69,300	29,000
1963	1,755,000	101,300	146,700	32,400
1964	1,741,000	99,600	186,200	34,300
1965	1,612,000	95,200	81,300	44,500
1966	1,407,000	94,700	48,700	60,700
1967	1,350,000	94,800	90,400	57,000
1968	1,228,000	84,000	111,700	65,900
1969	1,128,00	71,200	43,200	60,200
1970	1,048,000	69,800	76,700	56,400
1971	1,033,150	85,500	119,500	48,100
1972	1,075,770	43,600	165,400	46,300
1973	1,122,820	55,100	202,700	49,700
1974	1,154,461	27,400	243,600	23,600
1975	1,281,576	26,900	278,600	21,000

Source: SMMT, *The Motor Industry of Great Britain*, 1976 and data provided by the Motor Cycle Retailers' Association.

The imports kept on flowing into Britain. In 1956 some 18,500 foreign mopeds and 24,000 scooters entered the home market, which meant that around two-thirds of the up-to-150 cc engine capacity class now originated from overseas manufacturers. In 1955 one half of these units had been imported. Yet, at the same time domestic production (including exports) dropped to 126,700 units and overall sales slumped to 150,228.[131] The industry was now in the worst sales recession since the war. The lower sales caused substantial redundancies through the industry. During the spring of 1956, AMC sacked 200 workers, followed by 300 at BSA and another 400 at proprietary engine maker Villiers Engineering. Managers attributed their cutbacks directly to the government's credit squeeze.[132]

This situation greatly disturbed the industry which now turned to the government for help. A submission to the President of the Board of Trade made in 1955 blamed legislative and fiscal measures for restricting the manufacturers' competitiveness both at home and abroad. Firstly, they attacked the 'crippling' effect of the Purchase Tax on sales and asked that it be reduced if not eliminated completely. Not only would this improve the state of their industry, but it would be for the greater good of the public, easing traffic congestion and reducing the nation's consumption of expensive imported petrol.[133]

Secondly, no doubt mindful of growing public hostility towards the higher-powered motor cycles, the Manufacturers' Union asked that legislative concessions apply only to the light-weight models, particularly the mopeds. As they had before the war, the manufacturers drew attention to the far greater use of mopeds on the Continent, especially in Germany. This, they insisted, was the result of the active encouragement of moped use by foreign governments. German moped riders, for example, did not have to carry licences or even take tests and paid much lower insurance premiums. They even received an income tax concession if they used their machines for commuting to work.[134]

In contrast, British laws treated mopeds on the same basis as the larger motor cycles, making them far more expensive to operate and so dampening consumer interest. The government could both improve accessibility to a cheaper means of motorised personal transport for a larger number of people as well as help the industry by stimulating more sales, if only it would adopt laws of a Continental type. On the other hand, if the present situation continued, the manufacturers warned, the industry would go on declining, and foreign rivals, particularly Germany, would overtake Britain as the world's leading motor cycle producers.[135]

These arguments were subsequently raised during meetings held between industry officials and civil servants. However, the advice that Ministers received from civil servants largely ran against the case being made by industry representatives. These views seemed well established by 1951. It may not have been said openly at the meetings, but a strong bias against motor cycles and motor cyclists had re-emerged in private correspondence between

Ministry officials. This attitude was very detrimental to the industry's case for legislative reform. The civil servants' judgement had become deeply coloured by the industry's reputation for building fast, high-performance motor cycles, which were considered hazardous for the riders themselves and the public at large.[136]

No matter how often the manufacturers insisted that they only called for the relaxation of these laws solely to provide the public with cheap and low-speed mopeds, the civil servants suspected an ulterior motive. This stiffened their resolve against any concessions being made to the industry. As one department official, who favoured continuing to cover mopeds by existing legislation, minuted his Parliamentary Secretary:

> I think it would be fair to summarise the departmental view as being that this is right because any departure from the strict rule might result, through the ingenuity of scientists and engineers, in the production of a vehicle which, while technically entitled to exemption, would, in fact, be highly lethal and at the same time have an unfair advantage against the ordinary motor vehicle. It is possible to imagine, for example, the production of an extremely powerful small engine, to be attached to a bicycle, capable of very high speeds and of being as great a potential danger to life and limb as the most powerful motor cycle.[137]

Once more, the manufacturers found themselves in a dilemma of their own making. Their emphasis on the heavy-weights models, along with the cultivation of a market that consisted essentially of enthusiasts, may have provided a firm bedrock of consumers, but it was, by definition, self-limiting. Now, once again, it thwarted their efforts to enlist the support of the government.

Boardroom putsch at BSA

Even if the industry's attempts to change moped legislation had failed, at least one company appeared to be dealing effectively with its internal problems. In 1956 BSA's leadership question had finally been resolved. At a Board meeting held on 31 May, a majority of his fellow directors voted to remove Sir Bernard Docker from his position as the Group's Managing Director and Chairman, a decision that was later upheld at a rambunctious Extraordinary General Meeting. The official explanation given was that forcing him off the board was necessary as a result of Sir Bernard's scandalous behaviour. This included an earlier conviction for violations of currency control regulations while abroad (which in 1953 had also caused him to resign from the board of the Midland Bank), his and Lady Norah's increasingly bloated personal expense accounts and, most notoriously, the misuse of their extravagant gold-plated Daimler company limousines. All that, together with accusations of boardroom nepotism and the chronic and the seemingly endless losses at Daimler, made Docker's continued tenure undesirable.[138]

However, the real reasons for Sir Bernard's forced departure, never made public at the time, were less concerned with scandal or Daimler's dismal failure to reposition itself in the burgeoning middle-class car market than they did other missed opportunities. In fact, over time, the Board had become dismayed with the BSA Group's inability to occupy a central position in the advanced sectors of British engineering, particularly supplying components for the aircraft industry and nuclear power generators. This they blamed on Docker's undue preoccupation with Daimler. Because of his poor leadership during the critical years after the war, a majority of directors believed that BSA had failed to press home its advantages.[139] Docker and the other members of the Board decided that this information must be kept confidential, no doubt because they feared a negative impact on the value of BSA's shares had it become public knowledge.

Although he had not shown much interest in motor cycle production, during March 1954 Docker had set up a permanent Motor Cycle Policy Committee which was charged with examining the activities of the various subsidiaries. There is no evidence that the Committee ever actually met, but after May 1956 Docker was succeeded as Chairman by Jack Sangster, a motor cycle specialist nearly all his working life. The way was now open for a thorough re-evaluation of the BSA Group's direction.[140]

In spite of changes at BSA, the industry faced daunting problems at the end of 1956. Production and exports had dropped to their 1948 levels, and imports had grown from virtually nothing to alarming levels. The 'window of opportunity' that existed in 1951 may not have closed entirely but was certainly not as wide open as it had been before. The high hopes of earlier years were quickly ebbing away. If the industry was going to maintain its position, a new manufacturing strategy was necessary to challenge increased foreign competition and to meet the changing expectations of the market. Failing such positive action, the promise with which the era had opened would very likely remain unfulfilled.

CHAPTER FIVE

The window closes, 1956–1961

THE 1956 SALES RECESSION provided a necessary incentive for manufacturers to enter the expanding light-weight field. However, they remained puzzled by the fact that, while overall sales of motorised two-wheelers had generally declined, imports actually continued to increase. During the period 1956 to 1961, sales did gradually improve overall, and 1959 would in fact become the best year ever for British motor cycle sales. Thereafter, a more severe long-term decline in home market sales commenced, aggravated in part by an increase in negative publicity about motor cyclists but also because of changing consumer preferences. However, poor sales at home had been offset by an increase in exports, particularly to North America. Yet, at the end of this period, the British motor cycle industry faced the prospect of the most dangerous threat it had ever faced from a foreign competitor. For the first time, this did not originate from either the Continent or, as it had before 1919, the United States but, instead, from Japan.

British scooters and mopeds make their debut

The impact of the market changes on the industry's manufacturing programmes, particularly the growing popularity of mopeds, scooters and smaller motor cycles, was evident as early as the 1955 Show, where there was an unprecedented number of light-weight models on display, including over 40 different types of auto-cycles and mopeds, along with as many scooters. Most of these were either imported or the products of smaller British companies, although, most important, they included two light-weight scooters from BSA. Several of the British mopeds originated from bicycle companies, such as the Phillips Gadabout, the Norman Nippy and the Hercules company's incongruously named Grey Wolf (later retitled the Her-cu-Motor). Nearly all these models were either fitted with imported

49 cc power units or used foreign-designed engines built in Britain under licence.[1]

The first all-British designed and manufactured scooters also made their belated debut. These likewise originated from smaller dedicated firms or non-traditional manufacturers. The DKR company, for example, proudly advertised its 150 cc Dove as the 'All British Scooter' and other entries included the DMW 98 cc Bambi and Dayton Cycle's 224 cc Albatross. Two new entries were from BSA. One, the 70 cc Dandy, was promoted as a 'scooterette', although it was really more of a moped but with a modest degree of bodywork. The other, a large size scooter, the so-called Beeza, was by contemporary scooter standards both large and expensive. It had a 200 cc engine (compared to the best-selling Vespa's 145 cc model) along with an electric start. The design reflected the proposed price (it was not yet in production): £204 compared with £188 for the Vespa.[2]

The business press was particularly optimistic about the implications of BSA's entry into the scooter market. The *Financial Times* noted that up until then, with the exception of Douglas's licensing agreement with Vespa, the imports had this market for themselves. In view of developments on the Continent, 'many in Britain have expressed surprise that the UK motor cycle manufacturing industry has not as yet seriously entered the scooter field'. This had now changed because, among all British manufacturers, 'BSA is perhaps in the best position ... to bring out a scooter for the British market at a really competitive price'.[3]

Besides the mopeds and scooters, British manufacturers had already introduced a new range of light-weight motor cycles. These machines were in the 98 cc engine class and again were produced by smaller firms such as Excelsior, James, Norman and Sun. Many catered for commuters, prompting one newspaper to dub them 'Volks Bikes'. One new model, the Ambassador, even came equipped with an electric starter, a highly unusual feature to be found on a British model at this time.[4] Other companies, such as Francis-Barnett, produced two 147 cc models, the Plover roadster and the sportier Falcon 77, and Royal Enfield had the 148 cc Ensign. Among the larger manufacturers, both BSA and Triumph had revamped editions of their existing 150 cc and 250 cc models and even two of the most traditional firms, Norton and Matchless, made changes to their 350 cc models, the smallest machines then manufactured in their factories. The Board of Trade, which had a correspondent at the Show, was much impressed with this new interest in the light-weight class and used its journal to publicise the motor cycle industry's long-awaited 'Counter-attack on Continental Competition'.[5]

Indeed, the trade press took great pride in the sheer diversity of British motor cycle production. The 1955 Show, it was said, demonstrated just how strong they remained, even in the face of burgeoning foreign competition. While the Continentals put their resources into mopeds, scooters and light-weight (under 250 cc engine capacity) motor cycles, British manufacturers continued to offer a range extending from 50 cc auto-cycles to the four-cylinder 1000 cc heavyweights. No other industry came anywhere close to matching the British for variety. One trade journal proudly claimed that the British industry 'today dominates the markets of the world, and has few rivals in the production and marketing of orthodox motor cycles'. Moreover, the Show served warning on foreign competitors that British firms were now 'prepared to challenge the Continent of Europe in these fields in which hitherto our foreign competitors held a virtual monopoly'.[6] The journal was especially enthusiastic about the new British-built 'ultra-lightweights' and scooters, which not only challenged the 'foreign invaders, but far outstripped them in appearance and specification'.[7] (See table 19.)

Table 19   *Comparative prices, British and imported motor cycles*

Scooters:

British		Foreign	
Britax Scooterette (48 cc)*	£99	Vespa (125 cc)	£158
DMW Dolomite (249 cc)	£240	Lambretta (123 cc)	£149
Dayton Albatross (224 cc)	£182	Zundapp 'Bella' (148 cc)	£170

Prices of selected British-built light-weight motor cycles:

BSA Bantam (123 cc)	£81
BSA C10 (250 cc)	£256
Excelsior Consort F4 (98 cc)	£66
Francis-Barnett Falcon (98 cc)	£127
Royal Enfield Ensign (148 cc)	£93
Triumph Tiger Cub (149 cc)	£127
Velocette LE (192 cc)	£163

Source: 'Buyers' Guide', contained in *The Motor Cycle*, 18 November 1954.
* This model used an imported engine unit.

Yet, only several months later, columnist Francis Jones noted the lackadaisical manner in which British manufacturers had marketed their new mopeds and scooters. At the Brussels Show, he observed, the BSA Dandy and Beeza were the only British-made lightweights on display, and Jones was not at all pleased about the failure of other firms to participate: 'The blunt fact of it is that Britain is not, as yet, putting up any strong competition – or, really, any serious competition, in the moped/scooter market.' Britain might still be the major producer of orthodox motor cycles, but in Jones's opinion, that 'does not alter the fact that we were late in grasping the possibilities of the unconventional type of machine'. This criticism was shared by one Sunday paper, which commented on how the new British-made mopeds were a 'belated attempt' to stem the 'invasion by Continental scooters'. It was these types of lightweights which consumers now wanted, not the 'fast and almost exclusively masculine motor cycles so favoured by British manufacturers'.[8]

Sales during the 1956 season did nothing to deflect the critics. These continued to decline, except in the light-weight class. True, British-built mopeds and scooters sold, but in fewer numbers than the imports. Even the two new heavily promoted BSA models failed to make much of a dent in either home or export markets. The Beeza scooter, for example, never even went into production. It was cancelled by the BSA Board of Directors on the grounds of high projected manufacturing costs, price and inappropriate design. The Dandy, on the other hand, did go into production but was plagued with numerous troubles. According to Bert Hopwood, then BSA's Chief Designer, this was the result of it being rushed into production without adequate development work. One particular design flaw was the use of cast iron, instead of light alloy, in the cylinder material, which caused considerable problems for its owners. Ironically, one of BSA's subsidiaries had pioneered a process of coating cylinder bores with a hard chrome surface, which would easily have cured this particular difficulty, but this was unavailable to the motor cycle division, yet another example of the poor internal co-ordination that hobbled this large engineering enterprise.[9]

Blame the government

As sales fell, British manufacturers again blamed government credit policies for their problems in the home market. In a letter to shareholders in mid-1956 AMC Chairman Samuel Hogg attributed the poor performance of their company and its subsidiaries to hire/purchase restrictions imposed in late 1955, which had caused dealers to slow up their factory orders during the winter. This, in turn, meant they held low stocks for the critical spring selling season, which traditionally opened at Easter. The weak state of the economy also played its part. As reports of redundancies and short-time working circulated, Hogg claimed, this 'increased the lack of confidence amongst prospective motor cycle buyers, who are in the main young craftsmen and artisans, who naturally feared that they might themselves be out of work or on short-time, in the comparatively near future'.[10]

Motor cycle manufacturers were furious about the decision of the Chancellor of the Exchequer in February 1956 to push up the minimum deposit for hire/purchase sales by 50 per cent. One trade journal went so far as to accuse the government of diverting British consumers away from the more expensive medium- and heavy-weight motor cycles in favour of cheaper, mostly foreign, lightweights. The implications of this policy, it was maintained, would only aggravate sales difficulties, 'because of the established nature of the British motor cycle industry', and so lead inevitably to the 'dampening down of business in traditional British machines while at the same time encouraging sales of low-capacity imported ... scooter and ultra-lightweights'.[11]

Yet it remained difficult for the manufacturers to explain how these restrictions, which did not distinguish between British or imported motorised two-wheelers, always seemed to have less impact on the latter. As the 1956 season got under way, this point was noted in an article published in the *Financial Times*, which reported that the British motor cycle industry appeared now to be caught in a two-way squeeze. First, exports in 1956 had not recovered to their 1951 levels (58,800 compared to 91,700 units). Second, the British manufacturers' share of the home market had continued to slip. There was little doubt why this was so: 'British styling has failed to keep abreast of fashion.' In contrast, the industry's rivals 'were setting new fashions which have come not only to dominate many European markets but have, it is being said, become the unmistaken beginning of a world fashion'.[12]

Motor cycle design evolves

There were considerable differences in the manner with which the British and Continental manufacturers approached the question of design. For the former, virtually all firms were heavily reliant on in-house factory-trained talent.[13] Some senior managers, such as Triumph's Edward Turner, who took an active interest in matters of design and styling, were essentially self-taught. Others, such as Bert Hopwood, had received a measure of formal training, but were often frustrated by the unwillingness of higher management to listen to their advice. It was also true that, being a smaller industry which was at a disadvantage in terms of pay rates, skilled designers were frequently lured away by more lucrative offers from the aeronautics and motor car industries.[14]

The situation with regard to design work was very different on the Continent, particularly in Germany. In that country, motor cycle and scooter manufacturers placed great emphasis on making their machines as attractive as possible. As a report commissioned by the Manufacturers' Union noted, the larger firms employed 'styling experts, who are the links between the design and sales departments'. While most of these stylists were 'highly qualified engineers', some firms were also using personnel who had been trained as commercial artists. The aim of this concern, British manufacturers were told, was to broaden the appeal of their machines to non-motor cyclists and scooterists, especially women.[15]

Irrespective of their beliefs in the significance of design, the industry was very sensitive to criticism that it had fallen behind the competition. As early as 1952, Triumph Managing Director Edward Turner felt compelled to respond in the pages of an enthusiasts' journal. If, Turner retorted, the industry had failed to produce 'much that is fresh', it was for good reason. The strong demand for their orthodox motor cycles had caused the manufacturers to adopt conservative policies which understandably discouraged what he described as 'excursions into difficult design projects and the accompanying expensive tooling'. Turner noted that the very dedicated nature of the industry was itself an obstacle to new ventures: 'A rapid changeover to the manufacture of an entirely different machine is more difficult nowadays than ever before.' Turner dismissed any notion of abandoning what had been, up until then, very successful orthodox motor cycle production programmes: 'There is no point in radically changing design unless the resulting machine is going to be a marked improvement on the orthodox type evolved after years of painstaking development.'[16]

Another wave of imports arrives

By 1956 Industries' Association Director Hugh Palin was provoked sufficiently by the continuing criticism to respond personally in the business press. He defended the record of the industry and offered an explanation for the gains made by imports on the home market. In Palin's view, the rise of Continental manufacturers was the result of their new factories combined with a favourable geographical position close to large concentrations of consumers. Like Turner, Palin denied that the British industry had been caught unaware by the rapid growth of the moped and scooter markets. On the contrary, he claimed that British manufacturers were fully informed of changing tastes on the Continent. The reason why they had been so slow to react was two-fold. Firstly, the British industry had been entirely committed to their main product, orthodox motor cycles, and were 'working to capacity to meet the world-wide demand'. Under those circumstances, until very recently, the industry was unable to divert factory space for the manufacture of either scooters or mopeds in any number, as they were 'quite separate and distinct from orthodox motor cycles from both the sales and production point of view'.[17]

Secondly, Palin claimed, the industry had suffered from persistent shortages of labour, factory space and raw materials such as steel. These restrictions had also 'made it impractical to lay down new plants for scooter and moped production'. In any case, it would have been 'foolish indeed' for British manufacturers to have shifted their resources towards the lightweights at a time when demand for their traditional products was so high. In fact, Palin added, the supremacy of the British industry had created an opening for its foreign rivals: 'It would not be fanciful to suggest that the domination of the world's markets for orthodox machines [especially in the over 250 cc classes] … has perhaps led at least in part to the concentration of Continental motor cycle manufacturers in the production of machines not hitherto built in Britain.'[18]

Corporate investment

Palin's explanation for the industry's failure to meet growing demand for motorised two-wheelers does leave one unanswered question. Why, after 1955, in the face of the rapid and sustained expansion in the post-war motor cycle market (albeit in the light-weight classes), did the British industry fail to increase capacity in order to meet demand?

In fact, there was some expenditure on new plant and factory expansion on the part of the larger firms during this period. The largest firm, BSA, is a case in point. In late 1953 the BSA Board sanctioned a capital expenditure of £500,000 over the following three years at the Small Heath factory. This was a substantial figure, although it probably also included expenditures on non-motor cycle plant, and still far less than the £1 million alone the company spent on purchasing Carbodies in 1954, in order to guarantee a secure source of components for the Daimler motor car division. There were a series of improvements made to Triumph's Meriden factory, although this was done mainly to increase production of the large displacement twin-cylinder models which were so popular overseas. Moreover, the Small Heath factory always operated at less than 100 per cent capacity. Nor did BSA's motor cycle production ever again reach its peak annual output of 65,000–70,000 machines achieved over 1951/52, at a time moreover when labour and materials shortages were acute.[19]

Instead, the most ambitious expansion programme took place at the industry's number two producer. In contrast to BSA, AMC not only moved into light-weight production by way of its acquisition of James and Francis-Barnett, but also made a large investment at its Woolwich factory. This project was intended both to improve motor cycle production and to reduce the company's reliance on certain components from outside suppliers. The work began in 1954, and by February 1956 company chairman S.R. Hogg estimated that it had already cost nearly £500,000 in new tooling and additional factory space.[20] AMC Managing Director Donald Heather even claimed that this project was the 'largest single investment' in the history of the entire industry.[21]

The heart of AMC's investment programme was an ambitious plan to enlarge and re-equip the Woolwich factory, enabling the company to compete more effectively in both home and export markets. One part of the programme was the development of a new 250 cc two-stroke engine which could be used to power the light-weight models produced by its subsidiaries. Although AMC had previously obtained these engine units from Villiers, a proprietary supplier, friction between it and AMC caused the latter to become more self-sufficient. The second part of the investment was the creation of facilities to manufacture a new gearbox. Like Villiers, the company had become disillusioned with its existing supplier, Burman.[22]

Ariel Leader

When it first appeared, the Leader seemed to have been the realisation of the dream of an 'Everyman' motor cycle that some manufacturers had promoted during the 1920s and 1930s. Designed for Ariel Motors during the mid-1950s by industry veteran Valentine Page, it was the final achievement of his long and distinguished career.

The Leader incorporated a number of unorthodox features that Ariel hoped would appeal to an entirely new market of motor cycle consumers. Unlike most motor cycles of the era, it had a two-stroke rather than a four-stroke parallel twin-cylinder engine. Instead of the usual tubular frame, it was constructed of a pressed-steel rigid 'boxed' beam from which the engine was suspended. Its fuel tank was a dummy (the space there could be used for storage) with the fuel actually kept in a container placed within the frame beam. In response to the increasing popularity of imported scooters, the Leader used pressed steel to enclose the engine. It also came with a windscreen to provide greater weather protection for the rider.

Ariel incurred considerable expense producing this machine, not least because it had to re-tool the Selly Oak factory. However, some manufacturing economies were gained by bringing in a good amount of the pressed steel from another BSA subsidiary, Carbodies. Despite the originality and innovation surrounding the Leader, it was never the commercial success Ariel had expected, although it did stay in production until 1964. It was never a cheap machine, especially in comparison with other two-wheeled competitors. In 1960, for example, a Leader retailed at £199, while an imported 175 cc Lambretta scooter cost £189 and a more 'orthodox' motor cycle, such as a 250 cc BSA C15 sold for £172. True, the recently arrived 250 cc Honda Dream cost £238, but unlike nearly any other British bike including the Leader, this came standard with a superior overhead-cam engine and also had an electric starter.

According to motor cycle historian Steve Wilson, the Leader was 'a bold, often effective concept, indifferently styled, betrayed by inadequate lights, brakes and finish'.

Consequently the Leader fell betwixt and between in terms of finding a market. More traditional motor cyclists thought it something less than a 'real' motor cycle. On the other hand, the non-motor cyclists, who were expected to find the Leader irresistible, never took to it either, at least in any significant number. Indeed, after 1959, when Austin introduced its Mini car, they would have even less reason to look at two wheels for economy motoring.

Valentine Page (1892–1978)

Valentine Page was probably the most widely respected motor cycle designer ever to work in Britain. He spent part of his youth employed as an engineering apprentice at a motor car dealership on the south coast. Later he was taken on as a draughtsman with automaker Talbot. In 1914 he switched from four- to two-wheeled manufacturing when he was hired by proprietary engine-maker JAP.

After war-time service with the aviation industry, Page returned to JAP in 1920 as their chief designer and helped produce a string of successful racing engines. Several years later he was employed at Ariel Motors and designed a new range of motor cycle engines. He and the recently hired Edward Turner also developed the Square Four, an innovative four-cylinder model which, in various configurations, would remain in production until the late 1950s.

In 1932 Page left Ariel to start work at Triumph, where he designed a new range of single-cylinder machines along with a 650 cc parallel vertical twin-cylinder model, the 6/1. Several years later the restless Page moved again, this time to BSA, where he re-designed several single-cylinder models, including the M20, a motor cycle used extensively by the British military during the Second World War.

In 1939 Page returned to Ariel where he designed yet another model for use by the military and, several years later, new machines for the post-war era.

After decades in the industry, in the mid-1950s Page created one of his most famous motor cycle designs, the Ariel Leader. However, Page was most disappointed that another of his creations, a new 50 cc engine, which he believed was desperately needed if Britain was to become a serious force in the light-weight motor cycle class, was rejected by the BSA Group board for being too radical. Several years later the Honda Supercub powered by its 50 cc motor appeared in Britain and proved just how astute Page had actually been.

Valentine Page depicted in a social setting with his sometime colleague Triumph MD Edward Turner.

Both ventures were expensive failures. The two-stroke engine, which was designed by an Italian contractor, there being no available British talent, was disappointing. Nor did the gearbox project fare any better. Although the design was sound, it cost significantly more than the ones supplied previously by Burman. Bert Hopwood, by that time Managing Director of Norton Motors, was greatly dismayed when forced to use the new unit, especially as it added appreciably to the retail cost of his factory's motor cycles. According to him, such a 'costly upheaval of this fundamental change in commercial tactics' neither 'improved the products nor reduced costs'. The stage was set for far more serious problems for the entire AMC Group.[23]

More cars on British roads

During this period a greater threat was coming from a familiar source. As motor cycle sales fluctuated, the gap between motor car and motor cycle sales continued to grow. Although the number of automobiles on British roads had long before exceeded the number of motorised two-wheelers, the differential between the two widened dramatically after 1950, even though, in general, motor cycles were still cheaper to operate than motor cars.[24] The fact that the gap was initially slow to increase after 1945 was, in part, a reflection of the relative scarcity of motor cars on the home market. By 1955, with a burgeoning manufacturing capacity combined with the introduction of cheaper family vehicles, motor car registrations began to pull far ahead of motor cycles. Models such as the Ford Anglia and Popular, along with the Austin A30 and A40, followed up the initial success of the Morris Minor in the economy leagues.

These, and similar models produced by other manufacturers, combined with an expanding pool of second-hand vehicles, opened up motor car ownership to a vastly larger segment of the population. Prices of cars increased at a lesser rate than those for large orthodox motor cycles.[25] For example, over the period 1955 to 1960 the price of a Ford Popular increased from £413 to £494, and an Anglia went from £541 to £589. At the same time, the price of a Norton 500 cc twin-cylinder machine went from £438 to £533, and a BSA 650 cc twin-cylinder machine went from £216 to £345.[26]

The greater attraction of cheaper motors cars over motor cycles was even reflected in popular music. One song, for example, which was played on British jukeboxes during the late 1950s, had a verse purportedly sung by a female motor cycle pillion-rider. It recounted how she was 'tired of looking at the back of your head' and urged her boyfriend to 'trade in your motor cycle and get an automobile'.[27] Judging from the rapid increase of car ownership compared to the much smaller rise in motor cycles during this time, many others shared her sentiments, a point that was reflected in press reports at the time.[28]

Consumers of motorised two-wheelers showed similar buying patterns as motor car owners with respect towards smaller economy models. This trend was represented in the growing levels of moped and scooter sales, which suggested that there were many consumers who wanted more than a bicycle but could not yet afford a motor car. Indeed, bicycle sales began to drop during this time, along with those of heavy-weight orthodox motor cycles, while mopeds and scooters were sold in increasingly larger numbers.

Table 20   *Motor car production and registrations, 1945–1975*

	Production	Registrations
1945	16,938	1,521,581
1946	219,162	1,807,067
1947	287,000	1,983,505
1948	334,815	2,002,201
1949	412,290	2,178,411
1950	522,515	2,307,379
1951	475,919	2,433,172
1952	448,000	2,564,686
1953	594,808	2,824,789
1954	769,165	3,172,869
1955	897,560	3,609,400
1956	707,594	3,980,511
1957	860,842	4,282,438
1958	1,051,551	4,651,021
1959	1,189,943	5,080,510
1960	1,352,728	5,650,461
1961	1,003,967	6,113,764
1962	1,249,426	6,706,159
1963	1,607,939	7,546,650
1964	1,867,640	8,436,193
1965	1,772,045	9,131,075
1966	1,603,679	9,746,887
1967	1,552,013	10,554,193
1968	1,815,936	11,078,000
1969	1,717,073	11,504,300
1970	1,640,966	11,801,780
1971	1,741,940	12,357,870
1972	1,921,311	13,022,760
1973	1,747,321	13,815,000
1974	1,534,119	13,947,934
1975	1,267,695	14,060,973

Source: SMMT, *The Motor Industry of Great Britain*, 1976.

Letting down our side

The fact that a large proportion of the light-weight motorised two-wheelers used on the home market were imported, combined with a continued drop in British exports, reinforced the manufacturers' conviction that poor government representation at trade talks was again the real cause of their difficulties abroad. As before, their accusations did not always take into account all the factors faced by British trade negotiators. Perhaps the most illustrative example of the problems faced by British exporters during the late 1950s was the Italian market. In this instance, the inherent weakness of the British industry's criticism of government trade negotiators was most evident.

Throughout the 1950s, British motor cycle manufacturers had been infuriated by the fact that, while thousands of Italian scooters flooded into their home market, it was extremely difficult for them to export to Italy. In 1955, for example, some 16,200 motorised two-wheelers (mostly scooters) had been exported from Italy to Britain. Yet, over the same period, only 234 British machines had entered Italy. Although the Italians were subject to a British import duty, they were not affected by any quotas. In Italy, on the other hand, high tariffs and quotas kept out all but a token number of British exports, or so the manufacturers claimed.[29]

During the following year, this unequal trading relationship worsened. In the first six months of 1957, the Italians exported a total of 24,299 motorised two-wheelers, nearly all lightweights and most of those scooters. By contrast, over the same period, a grand total of just 29 British machines went to Italy. In light of these statistics, it was about time, the British industry complained to the Board of Trade, to force the Italians to trade more fairly.[30]

Motor cycle manufacturers adamantly believed that the cause of poor exports to Italy, and elsewhere, was not their fault, but the fault of the irresolute government trade negotiators. In late 1957 Industries' Association Director Hugh Palin summed up the situation in a confidential internal memo distributed to manufacturers:

> British negotiators approach these meetings [the bi-lateral trade conferences] in a very different frame of mind to that of the negotiators from competing countries. This is a complaint that has been frequently made over the years and as frequently rebutted, but having recently met some of the negotiators who conducted a particular series of trade talks, I cannot help expressing the personal view that they are not at all the kind of people who would likely drive a hard bargain, or to get 'tough' if necessity arose.[31]

However, upon closer examination, the question of government representation was again far less straightforward than British manufacturers insisted. As with the Dutch and Swiss markets several years before, the fact remained that demand in Italy was oriented towards light-weight scooters and mopeds, not the larger orthodox motor cycles the British industry specialised in making. This point was confirmed in an analysis of the Italian market which was prepared for the Industries' Association that same year. The report stated that the continuing popularity of the light-weight models had affected the manufacturing programmes of the domestic producers. It also noted that 'demand for machines over 200 cc is now so small' as to be almost insignificant and concluded that it was 'doubtful whether Italian firms will devote any further capital to new development of this type of machine other than racing models'. Under these circumstances, with Italian demand so heavily in favour of the kind of models not made in any volume by British factories, it was questionable whether this was even a market worth fighting for at all.[32]

Nevertheless, in 1958 Industries' Association Director Hugh Palin was able to inform members that the Italians had finally liberalised their import regulations to allow in the larger British machines. He claimed that 'great pressure has been put on HMG to secure this concession', which he had to admit 'has only been obtained at a price'. The price paid, Palin continued, was that, in order to facilitate greater motor cycle exports, 'the UK has had to make certain concessions outside our Industry's interests'. Several months later, members of the Motor Cycle Manufacturers' Section had to concede that the successful effort at dismantling the Italian import barriers had been a costly victory. Even though Italy's import regulations were now even more liberal than those of Britain, exports to that country still had not improved. In future, it was predicted, this embarrassing development would make the Industries' Association's position with the Board of Trade regarding other trade matters 'particularly weak'.[33]

Changing consumer tastes

British motor cycle manufacturers were in trouble in other important markets because of changed consumer tastes. In Sweden, for example, AMC Sales Director J.M. West discovered that the market for heavy-weight motor cycles had become so poor that the main Stockholm dealer wanted to get out of the business altogether. After visiting Sweden and other Scandinavian countries, West reported that sales of motor cycles over 250 cc displacement had 'fallen catastrophically' and that 'such models are now rarely seen on the streets. Swedish youths are now to be seen in quantity in early post-war cars that can be purchased for but a fraction of the cost of a 500 cc motor cycle.' What sales could be made were either to the police or armed forces.

George Formby was one of Britain's leading entertainers both before and after the Second World War. Here he is shown doing his bit for Britain's post-war export drive, appearing beside a BSA at an unidentified Toronto motor cycle shop sometime in the late 1940s. Formby was a long-time motor cycle enthusiast who also starred in *No Limit*, a 1930s movie about the Isle of Man TT races.

By contrast, sales of mopeds boomed. However, instead of trading up to motor cycles, he noted that 'moped riders tend to progress to cheap light cars'.[34] (See table 17, page 142.)

Conditions in Australia, formerly Britain's best export market, were not much better. As early as 1952 manufacturers were warned by their Australian dealers about changed public opinion. One report referred to 'violent and abusive propaganda' against motor cycles and motor cyclists circulating in the national press and radio. One Australian government official had gone so far as to call for the banning of motor cycles from public roads. Scooter sales, on the contrary, had increased, a development the dealers attributed to the influx of immigrants from Continental Europe, people who 'had no ties with the Mother Country' and hence, they believed, were less likely to buy the big British motor cycles.[35] The biggest problem, however, was competition from four-wheeled vehicles. A report received in 1955 noted that it 'would appear that many members of the public here prefer to purchase a car rather than a motor cycle'.[36]

The North American market beckons

Although sales in the more traditional export markets had deteriorated, these losses had been largely offset through the development of an entirely new region. North America had been an insignificant market before 1945; in fact, during the 1930s, more British motor cycles were sold to Liberia than to the USA. But it was to become the big export success story of the post-war era.[37] This was largely the result of a combination of liberal import policies and the peculiar nature of this market, especially its predilection towards larger displacement, sports-oriented motor cycles.[38]

The post-war North American market had several obvious attractions to British manufacturers. This area had escaped damage during the war and contained a large numbers of potential consumers, the single most affluent group in the world at this time. Perhaps most importantly, both the USA

As in Britain, many North American retailers had long realised the commercial advantage of sponsoring riders in sporting events. They knew that racetrack success would often translate into higher sales in a market that contained many sports enthusiasts.

COURTESY OF DAN MAHONY

These three motor cyclists are shown at a sporting event near Toronto, Canada, probably sometime during the late 1930s. All of them are mounted on British-made motor cycles, at a time when sales throughout North America were dominated by US-made Harley-Davidsons and Indians.

COURTESY OF ED MOODY

Founded by William Johnson in the late 1930s, Johnson Motors (or 'JoMo' as it was often known) was a much visited port of call for motor cyclists in the greater Los Angeles area. Indeed, Johnson Motors was one of the largest British motor cycle retailers in the USA and did much to promote Triumph's sales on the west coast.

COURTESY OF THE IVOR DAVIES COLLECTION

Racing ace Rod Gould on a Triumph at Daytona, Florida, sometime in the mid-1950s. The Daytona races were one of the most important and prestigious in North America.

and Canada were hard currency markets without significant tariff barriers or other trading impediments. It was not surprising that, during this time, British industry generally had come under heavy government pressure to export there as much as possible.[39] In fact, British motor cycle makers did not need much prompting from the government to commence a North American export drive. This market held enormous sales potential, which was an irresistible attraction to British motor cycle manufacturers.

In 1951, having just returned from the USA, Triumph's Edward Turner gleefully reported to fellow managing directors that there was 'a bottomless pool of American dollars waiting for British motor cycles'. He was especially excited about the sports orientation of many American consumers: 'It is heart-warming to see the enthusiasm for the sport which exists in America today, and in a nation of 142 million people, a large proportion of whom are tough, sporting young men, the potentialities are remarkable.'[40] At about the same time, Norton's Gilbert Smith observed that, unlike his British counterpart, the average young American 'goes almost straight from pram to a car and becomes interested in owning a motor cycle only when he gets bitten by the "sporting bug"'. Indeed, most Nortons were sold to 'young men who regard them as part of their sports kit'.[41]

An entirely new stratum of consumers, mostly sports-oriented riders, had recently discovered the advantages of British machines.[42] These new riders were not disturbed by the social disadvantages of riding a motor cycle and used their machines far more for leisure pursuits than as basic transport. As it had in Britain, sporting success often translated into increased sales.[43] Bill Johnson, Triumph's Los Angeles-based west-coast distributor, observed: 'Motor cycling in America is essentially a sport and this is particularly true with machines of the British type … There are the few who buy motor cycles for transport, but I do believe that even these are only kidding themselves, for actually they enjoy riding the motor cycle.'[44] Johnson's statement was confirmed by AMC's Sales Director J.M. West, who noted that the 'majority of motor cycles sold in the USA are used for competition work and few are used on the road'.[45]

The sporting aspect of the American market was well understood by British motor cycle manufacturers generally. During a meeting with the Manufacturers' Union held in 1949, Alfred Rich Child, BSA's distributor on the American east coast, was quite emphatic on this point. Singling

Light-weight BSA Dandy motor cycles rolling off the assembly line. For decades most motor cycle riders in Britain were male, as were the workers that built the bikes. However, there were exceptions. As this photograph shows, the workers building these machines were almost exclusively women.
© BSA OWNERS CLUB

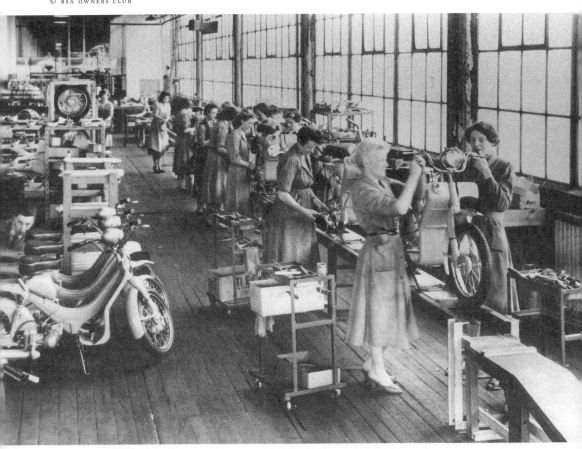

Flat-track rider Bingle Cree, seated on a stripped-down British-made motor cycle and ready to race, Oshawa, Canada, *circa* 1952.

COURTESY OF ED MOODY

out Norton, which had scored a series of recent victories on American racetracks, Child assured the British manufacturers that these had been of 'the greatest value' for the sale of all their motor cycles.[46]

BSA's Export Manager, S.F. Digby, also emphasised the importance of participation in American sporting events, such as the Daytona Florida races. In his opinion, 'prestige in the competitive sphere has a considerable effect on sales', and he advised active participation by British manufacturers in these activities. Digby also remarked on the striking contrast in performance between many of the British and American motor cycle models. He noted how the 'highly developed British machines, with their severely functional design and remarkable power–weight ratios' came as a 'revelation to the American public' when they were first displayed.[47] Although, by American standards, British machines were in the 'middle-weight' category (350 cc to 650 cc engine capacity) they frequently outperformed the heavier and more powerful but less agile 1000 cc to 1250 cc Harley-Davidsons.[48]

British manufacturers realised that, as in the home market, American motor cycle enthusiasts were drawn towards machines that had excelled on the racetrack and which were built to higher performance specifications. In 1959, for example, Triumph introduced one of its best sellers, the Bonneville, a 650 cc (subsequently 750 cc) twin-cylinder model that was one of the first production machines available which, even without after-market modification, could quickly reach 120 miles per hour, virtually from off the showroom floor. Essentially a further development of existing large displacement twin-cylinder models, this machine had been fitted with upgraded components to give it the improved performance levels. And, in a clear nod to American enthusiasts, the bike was named after the famous Bonneville salt flats track in the state of Utah. Later on the company came out with another performance-oriented model, the Daytona, named after the famous Florida track.[49]

Still, however lucrative, British manufacturers discovered that the North American market was not an easy one to develop. The sheer physical size of both the USA and Canada was daunting, and distribution networks had to be created virtually from scratch. In the USA domestic manufacturers began a campaign of harassment against the entry of British machines into American sports activities.[50] They also tried to shut them out of existing distribution networks by forbidding their dealers from handling imported products.[51]

The biggest obstacle to overcome was the fact that despite, or perhaps because of, their affluence, neither Canada nor the USA was a natural motor cycling nation. Not only vast geography but the social stigma that Major Watling had observed during his visit to North America in the late 1920s had lingered on. There remained a widely held conviction that motor cycles were inferior to motor cars, and motor cycle ownership thus reflected poorly on one's social standing. Such attitudes forced retailers to struggle for every sale. This situation was greatly aggravated by a series of incidents in the late 1940s and afterwards between marginal groups of American motor cyclists, self-styled 'outlaws', and the police.

One of the most notorious confrontations occurred during 1947 in Hollister, California, and generated much unwelcome nation-wide publicity for motor cyclists in general.[52] This incident ultimately became the inspiration for the popular and controversial motion picture, *The Wild One*, which featured Marlon Brando as the leader of a motor cycle gang (all mounted on British machines) who terrorised the inhabitants of a small rural California town.[53] Whether accurate or not, the negative depiction of American motor cyclists contained in this film, one of shiftless and violent hooligans rampaging around the American countryside, created a highly emotive image which persisted for long afterwards.[54]

British manufacturers encountered other more mundane problems in their efforts to expand the North American market. The severe climate and the relatively low cost of second-hand cars created serious sales barriers. Such was the experience of F.G.Norman, Managing Director of Norman Cycles, a lower-volume maker of light-weight models, which was trying to break into the Canadian market. He conceded that the long and cold Canadian winters, combined with the availability of cheap cars, 'acted as deterrents to motor cycle ownership'. Another firm, Douglas, also discovered it was not at all easy to sell its lighter weight motor cycles in Canada. The company admitted that it had trouble attracting consumers, since the Douglas models were 'not large enough for the Canadian taste, which is all for the big machines as manufactured in the USA'.[55]

By the mid-1950s, three major conduits brought British motor cycles into the rich American market. The first, and most sophisticated, was organised by Triumph, and originated as a distributorship run by Johnson Motors in Los Angeles, California. Triumph's organisation would grew into two fully owned factory distributorships, one based in Los Angeles, the other in New Jersey, and ultimately serviced hundreds of dealerships around the USA.[56] BSA's presence in America, by contrast, started with an agreement with former Harley-Davidson executive Alfred Child, who operated his New York-based Rich Child Cycle Co. to cover much of the eastern part of the country. The west coast was managed separately through a distribution agreement with former Indian motor cycle dealer Hap Alzina.[57] Following Triumph's example, BSA took over Child's organisation as a fully owned factory distributorship in 1954.[58]

The third conduit was created by Brockhouse Engineering when it bought into the dealer network of the ailing Indian Motor Cycle Co., in 1949.[59] This convenient arrangement not only allowed Brockhouse to market its own very limited range of machines, but also those of a number of other British manufacturers such as AMC, Royal Enfield, Vincent and Douglas, through a ready-made distribution network.[60] Known as the Indian Company, it was later the distribution agent for Royal Enfield (which had been badging its own models as 'Indians' for sale in the USA). Later on it was purchased by AMC, although it never really achieved much commercial success. Finally, some small manufacturers, such as James Cycle, chose to work through export brokers such as Hambros Bank, and Veloce (Velocette), for one, worked out a separate arrangement with a dealer in Los Angeles for limited regional distribution.[61]

Factory production is reorganised

The greater emphasis on sales in the North American market had implications for how the motor cycle factories organised their production schedules back in Britain. Prior to 1939 and into the late 1940s, when southern hemisphere markets such as Australia and Argentina accounted for a higher proportion of export sales, the factories had been geared for an intense four-month production and selling season starting in the spring. However, as has already been described, the significance of these two markets faded away in the late

1940s and early 1950s, so while the trade cycle remained much the same, the sales emphasis changed.

As before, the factories were usually closed during August for staff vacations. By the end of the summer the following year's design prototypes and drawings should have been received and production could begin. Much interest was directed at the reception given to the new models by the technical and enthusiast press as well as the motor cycling public when the new models debuted at the various trade shows, especially the Earl's Court show in London which normally occurred some time during October or November. Assuming all went well, up until Christmas, stock would be built up for the home market as well as for dealers in areas not affected by winter weather conditions.[62]

By the late 1950s, the pattern had changed. After Christmas, production would now begin for the North American market and shipments had to leave the factories by the end of January. It was here that the growing

A motor cycle enthusiast astride a Triumph at Wasaga Beach in Ontario, Canada. After the Second World War growing numbers of American and Canadian motor cyclists started buying British-built bikes. Until then Harley-Davidson, along with Indian, had accounted for the vast majority of North American motor cycle sales.

reliance on these two markets became more apparent. The trade 'pipeline' to North America was lengthy, often requiring up to two months or more for the motor cycles to travel from British seaports to the west- and east-coast distributors. And it was absolutely essential that enough machines were in American and Canadian warehouses by early spring so that sufficient stock was available to be placed on showroom floors. If for any reason the bikes were late, the consequences were likely to be severe. Customers wanted their motor cycles ready for the spring and summer riding season, and if not, they might simply buy from a competitor or perhaps not buy at all.[63] As the manufacturers would later discover to their chagrin, timing was everything, and North American customers would not easily forgive delay.

Harley-Davidson beleaguered

The growing numbers of British motor cycles entering the USA also had consequences for what was left of the American industry. In 1951, its sales severely damaged, the sole remaining American motor cycle manufacturer, Harley-Davidson, launched an application before the US Tariff Commission. This sought the imposition of quotas and higher duties as the remedy for Harley's failure to compete successfully against British imports. The stakes on the outcome of this application were high, with individual British manufacturers as well as the Manufacturers' Union helping to fund the legal costs.[64] At home, the Board of Trade also showed considerable interest in the course of the proceedings. As far as it was concerned, Harley-Davidson's attempt to close off motor cycle imports represented 'the spearhead of the American attack' on British imports generally.[65] Should Harley-Davidson succeed, it was believed there might be serious implications for other British exports, especially motor cars. A dangerous precedent could be set for future applications to the Tariff Commission.[66]

During the hearings, evidence was presented to the Commission which showed that post-war American motor cycle sales had peaked at 54,000 sales in 1948, but had subsequently averaged around 26,000 machines annually. This was a substantially higher total than pre-war figures, which the Commission later attributed to a growth in overall population, a three-fold increase in national income and the growing popularity of motor cycle sport. Significantly, it was noted that British motor cycles, particularly those in the 500 cc to 650 cc engine displacement class, especially benefited from the Americans' devotion to sporting activities.[67] The Commission also heard evidence that numbers of British imports jumped from under 3 per cent of total sales before 1939 to 40 per cent between 1949 and 1951, thanks in part to a 30 per cent devaluation of sterling in 1949.[68] In the event, the Commission turned down Harley-Davidson's application. It reasoned that since, 'to a very considerable extent, middleweight importers' machines have created their own demand', they could not be held responsible for the decline in Harley-Davidson's sales. The Commission referred to evidence put before it which demonstrated that these consumers 'doubtless would not have bought any motor cycle if the middleweight machines had not been available'.[69]

The situation for British importers in Canada was a little different from that of their counterparts south of the border. True, they too faced much the same challenges in terms of climate, comparatively underdeveloped roads and long distances. However, unlike the USA, there was no established domestic producer such as Harley-Davidson or Indian. Consequently, very little opposition rose up against British imports; quite the contrary, thanks to the British (later Commonwealth) Preferential Tariff, British motor cycles could be brought in duty-free, by distributors in Quebec and New Brunswick and elsewhere on a regional basis through individual dealers such as the Nicholson Brothers in Saskatoon, Saskatchewan, and the Deeley operation in Vancouver, B.C.[70] British motor cycle exports to Canada skyrocketed, going from 153 machines in 1945 to 6,449 five years later. The numbers would later rise and fall year by year, but Canada remained one of the strongest markets for British motor cycle manufacturers anywhere, sometimes even better, albeit on a proportional basis, than the USA.[71]

Altogether, the growing importance of North America had a profound effect on British export patterns for the next 20 years. In the face of protectionism and fluctuating or declining demand elsewhere, it became the critical market. During the following years, an increasingly greater proportion of British motor cycle exports would go to North America (see table 16, page 139). In turn, because of the sporting tastes of these consumers, the accent was increasingly put on performance, reinforcing the traditional inclination of British manufacturers to produce mostly larger displacement performance-oriented motor cycles.[72]

The very nature of the North American market was also an important factor in distracting the British from considering the large-scale manufacture of light-weight models. Under the conditions of world trading, they had little choice with so many other markets closed to them. This was a point understood well by Triumph's Edward Turner. America, he declared at the opening of the company's new distribution centre in Maryland, was 'the richest country in the world and a fair amount of its wealth was in the hands of young men who were interested in the larger and more powerful machines, whereas the rest of the world wanted smaller, simpler motor cycles for utility transport'. The problem with the 'rest of the world' was that by then much of it was closed to British exports because of import restrictions.[73]

The resurgence of the German motor cycle industry

Success in North America did not blind British motor cycle manufacturers to competitive threats elsewhere. Their fears of a resurgence by their pre-war trade adversary, the German industry, seemed to have been realised.[74] In 1948 annual German motor cycle production was only 14,000 units, yet only four years later, after the Allied occupation authorities had lifted their controls, this soared to a total of 292,000 motor cycles, scooters and mopeds, most of which had less than 250 cc engine capacity. By 1953 DKW, the major producer during the pre-war era, had already manufactured 100,000 of its 125 cc light-weight models.[75] Nor were British fears soothed by assurances from German producers that they were currently too absorbed with supplying their home market and therefore had no intention of competing in British export markets.[76] Triumph chief Edward Turner was also worried. He too had seen the reports of new German motor cycle factories which greatly impressed him with 'the modernity and excellence of the plants, equipped probably with American lease-lend [sic] money'. There was, he concluded, a distinct danger of the British being 'handicapped right out of the running'.[77]

British manufacturers followed closely the growth of the re-emerging German industry. This interest extended beyond the trade press to the popular enthusiasts' publications, whose reporters visited Germany and prepared stories on the activities of their struggling factories.[78] Furthermore, beginning in May 1953 the Manufacturers' Union received the first of a long series of confidential assessments of developments among their German rivals. These reports detailed production levels, the state of their factories, anticipated changes in design and other important commercial information.[79]

The reports all confirmed the alarming increases in levels of production and exports. In 1953 one such report warned that there were now nearly two million motorised two-wheelers registered on German roads (compared to slightly over one million in Britain), and 'owing to the continuously improving living standards, there was no immediate danger of saturation in the German home market'. The German Society of Cycle and Motor Cycle Manufacturers (VFM) claimed that 70 per cent of all motor cycle registrations were used for 'daily transport by manual and office workers of the low income group'.[80] The following year, the growth of the German industry was such that it was widely reported that NSU alone produced 110,855 machines, as many as the entire British industry, albeit nearly all in the light-weight class, and its products were being described in the business press as the motor cycle equivalent of the Volkswagen motor car.[81] For British manufacturers, it now seemed possible that a revived German industry might again threaten their hard-won hegemony.

The Manufacturers' Union was especially concerned about the role of the German government in promoting exports. In mid-1955 Union Director

Hugh Palin wrote to manufacturers and contrasted the way Britain and Germany represented their respective industries:

> There have been numerous occasions where we have found that arrangements have been made for German machines to be imported into a particular market under much more favourable terms than those accorded to the British. I have felt that German negotiators put German bicycles and motor cycles very high on their list of goods which they desire to export, whereas in the case of our negotiators they are seldom willing to 'push' any particular product. The results for us have already been unfortunate in a number of instances and could be dangerous.[82]

In the event, despite state assistance, the German 'threat' never materialised in the form the British feared it would. Instead, thanks to changes in their home market, by late 1956, German motorised two-wheel manufacturers faced a severe crisis of over-production.[83] Moreover, like their British counterparts, the Germans also suffered from a press campaign that focused on the high rate of motor cycle accidents. As early as 1954, the German government responded by beginning to tighten up regulations covering motor cycle use. A riding test was made compulsory for all machines over 50 cc, and the following year there was public agitation for a riding test for mopeds. Meanwhile there were more and more complaints from the German public about noise emitted by motorised two-wheelers.[84]

The German industry's most serious problem was the public's rapidly rising levels of personal income, which led to greater levels of motor car ownership (particularly the Volkswagen 'Beetle') and caused motor cycle manufacturers to reconsider their future plans.[85] Indeed, the rapid changes in German society forced a fundamental re-alignment in the direction of the German motor cycle industry. During NSU's Annual General Meeting held in early 1957, Managing Director Dr von Heydekampf reported to the shareholders that, such was the state of the domestic motor cycle market, it had become 'an economic necessity' for the company to diversify its product line and commence manufacture of a small motor car. His was a dour commentary on the future of motor cycle use in Germany:

> After careful market research it has become evident that the demand for motor cycles will decline further, while scooters and mopeds will retain their popularity, although in the foreseeable future demand for them will tend to decrease.[86]

Later von Heydekampf described the financial year 1956/57 as 'a catastrophe' for the entire German motor cycle industry. His company alone suffered from a 25 per cent drop in overall turnover, and the severe slump in demand for motor cycles caused nearly 50 per cent of its productive capacity to be diverted to manufacturing small cars.[87]

NSU was not the only German motor cycle firm to commence diversification into four-wheeled vehicles because of the falling demand for motor cycles. Firms such as BMW, Horex and Zundapp soon followed its lead, while other firms such as Adler and Triumph (no relation to the British firm of the same name) were bought up by electrical giant Grundig and ultimately ceased motor cycle production altogether. There was another major consolidation in 1958 when motor car manufacturers Mercedes Benz purchased the Auto-Union combine which included DKW. Finally, in 1959, the two remaining large producers, Victoria and Express, joined DKW to create the so-called 'Zweirad Union'. Like its British counterpart, the German industry had become more and more concentrated.[88]

Trying to enter the Japanese market

Because of their intense pre-occupation with the perceived threat posed by the German industry, British manufacturers were largely oblivious to developments in the Far East. In view of the outstanding success of the Japanese motor cycle industry only ten years later, it is ironic that, for most of the 1950s, the British industry saw Japan nearly exclusively as a potential market, not as a possible rival. Although British motor cycle manufacturers had had a modest export trade with Japan during the 1920s, this had virtually ceased after 1930 when Japan became dominated by militarists, who clamped down on imports of foreign manufactured goods. After the war, the British again looked to Japan, now under American occupation. As Japan rebuilt its devastated economy, there was much demand for cheap personal transport, which British motor cycle manufacturers believed they were well placed to provide. This belief was reinforced by reports from the British embassy in Tokyo which described a strong upsurge in motor cycle usage, albeit virtually all in the light-weight class. It also stressed that there was much interest in imported machines, especially those from Britain.[89]

The Japanese motor cycle industry, insignificant before the war, grew rapidly after 1948, a development that will be examined more closely in a later chapter. As in Germany, this growth was in large part the result of American economic aid. British motor cycle manufacturers were well aware of the heavy emphasis American policy-makers put on a speedy Japanese economic recovery. The US Congress had, the Manufacturers' Union was informed by a reliable source, told the occupation authorities that their top priority was to 'get the Japanese on their feet, solvent and able to pay their way without American aid. This is almost a "religion", and nothing else matters.' Such an attitude did not bode well for future British exports to Japan.[90]

Indeed, Japan's desire to protect its re-emerging industries was not at all conducive to encouraging imports. Despite the continuing demand from consumers for imported motorised two-wheelers, the Japanese government was singularly uncooperative when British manufacturers requested increased import quotas. Instead, imports were restricted to a small trickle.[91] Repeated protests from the Embassy on behalf of British manufacturers to increase import quotas were fruitless. The Japanese claimed the restrictions, which included high tariffs, were necessary because of their low sterling balances, although one Ministry of International Trade and Industry (MITI) official, writing in response to a query from the British Embassy, offered another explanation. The import restrictions, he stated baldly, were protectionist in nature, and those few British motor cycles being allowed in were strictly for inspection by Japanese manufacturers, not for the general use of consumers.[92] Later there were small increases in the British import quota, although the Japanese refused to allow entry of British motor cycles with more than a 250 cc engine displacement size, on the grounds that, other than for police and military forces, there was very little consumer demand for the larger machines.[93]

Protectionism splits the British motor cycle industry

By the mid-1950s British manufacturers had become as concerned about the influx of light-weight machines from the Continent as they were about restricted export markets. However, Industries' Association Director Palin was reluctant to recommend an appeal to the government for increased tariffs. He urged caution on the grounds that, 'in view of our world-wide interests it would not be wise to make any official move for a restriction of imports by quotas, or by an increase in import duties'. Several months later, Palin again wrote to the Council reporting a further deterioration of trade. For the first six months of 1956, production was down nearly 25 per cent on the comparable period in 1955. Imports, however, had continued to rise. As before, these were mainly in the under 49 cc engine capacity category.[94]

The higher levels of imports caused a split in the ranks of British motor cycle manufacturers. While there continued to be consensus about the need to maintain, if not to increase, existing tariffs and import quotas, some manufacturers wanted to petition the Board of Trade to reduce the current duty of 30 per cent on imported moped components. In the absence of a domestic manufacturer providing 49 cc engine units, they claimed a reduction was necessary to allow them 'to compete more favourably with foreign machines both at home and abroad'. The Industries' Association's governing Council, however, turned their motion down.[95]

Tariffs and import duties also created friction among manufacturers and certain retailers. In 1958 the Industries' Association Council debated

Motor cycles at work in public service, in this case police officers on scooters. The good news here was the continuing use of motorised two wheelers by institutional users; the bad news was that all too often they were imports.

a motion that would have restricted its membership only to manufacturers with a total commitment to British products. The motion was not adopted, but the following year the Council did create a membership category for concessionaires and defined a 'British' manufacturer as one whose wages and materials were at least 75 per cent British origin. Another successful motion forbade manufacturing members from exhibiting foreign machines on their pavilions at the annual Show.[96]

Although sales of all motorised two-wheelers declined between 1956 and 1958, light-weight models were affected proportionately far less, and the market share of the under-150 cc machines continued to gain relative to the heavier weight, orthodox motor cycles. The former now held two-thirds of total new sales, compared to one-half in 1955. The trend was vividly illustrated in sales to various governmental and service organisations. While it was disappointing that British consumers were buying more and more foreign machines, the manufacturers were outraged to discover that formerly loyal fleet purchasers had also begun to stray. Not only did police forces begin to buy foreign machines, mainly scooters, but so did high-profile commercial users such as the airline company BOAC. Even the RAC began to use Vespas (albeit British-built models) for its patrol vehicles. Protests were made, phrased as patriotic exhortations, but without success.[97]

Moreover, the motor cycle press, or at least the technical publications, were becoming less obedient than they had been before in toeing the manufacturers' line. For example, in a memo written in 1959, Industries' Association Director Hugh Palin expressed his 'complete frustration' with the editor of the *Motor Cycle and Cycle Trader* who, despite having been warned on several occasions, had given prominent coverage to the expansion of the premises of a leading importer. This editor had subsequently compounded his disloyalty by providing what was described as 'extensive and enthusiastic' coverage of foreign machines. Such reporting, Palin told the miscreant, was simply not acceptable. Industries' Association members were 'extremely annoyed' by this editorial policy, and it was the *Trader*'s duty, 'as a British trade paper [that] the emphasis should always be first and foremost on British products'. If it insisted on carrying stories about overseas rivals, they 'must be included … [in] much less prominent positions towards the back'.[98]

Yet even Palin had to concede that British manufacturers really had only themselves to blame for the fact that press coverage was shifting to the imports. As the editors of the technical press had pointed out to him, they would have provided more coverage of British-made models, but the manufacturers had failed to provide them with test machines. As Hugh Palin noted, neither did the manufacturers 'exert [themselves] very much to provide interesting copy, which they [the press] urgently need'. If they wanted better coverage, there would have to be more co-operation.[99]

By 1958 the light-weight market, particularly that for scooters, finally began to settle down. The manufacturers had still to produce a scooter of their own to challenge the imports successfully. Writing in the *Financial Times* the following year, Edward Turner mounted his own defence of the industry's failure to make an entry into the scooter market. He agreed with the industry's critics that the type of people who bought scooters was quite different from the kind of consumers the industry had catered for in the past:

> The scooter owner is not an ex-motor cyclist, he or she, is a new class of motor vehicle owner who is in many ways parallel to the average car owner who buys his vehicle to tour, to shop, to go to work, and is not technically interested in the vehicle as such. This is in contrast to the motor cyclist who is usually an enthusiast for motor cycles and motor cycling, and is ready to discuss technicalities of design and performance at the drop of a spanner.[100]

True, the Italians may have gained a stronghold in the British scooter market, but Turner claimed this did not have to be permanent. This was now about to change, since both BSA and Triumph were planning to make their first serious incursion into the scooter market since the abortive 1956 Beeza project. Despite the fact that most scooters were powered by engines in the 98 cc to 175 cc displacement class, Turner's firm intended to manufacture what he called a 'super-scooter' in the 250 cc class, although this would be priced competitively against a Vespa. The new model (badged as either the Triumph Tigress or BSA Sunbeam), Turner was convinced, would establish a strong British presence in the domestic scooter market.[101]

Motor cycle manufacturers feel the squeeze

Such confidence notwithstanding, the trading patterns continued to work against British motor cycle manufacturers. During 1957 and 1958 the flow of imports had grown even larger. By the late summer of 1958 they had actually exceeded Britain's motor cycle exports in volume, if not value, an 'unprecedented situation' in the words of Industries' Association Director Hugh Palin.[102] The composition of the imports continued to be overwhelmingly in the under-150 cc category and were mostly Italian in origin. Palin was convinced that this situation, which he said was 'causing us considerable concern', was actually the result of the 'great pressure' being put on British concessionaires by Italian factories. He further noted that Britain had become the Italian scooter industry's 'biggest and most important market'. In a review of domestic sales over the past 12 months which he prepared in mid-1957, Palin reported the good news that, for the first time, over 200,000 new machines had been sold on the home market. Unfortunately, more than 100,000 of these were now foreign-made. The British industry still seemed incapable of winning back the loyalty of its own consumers, no matter how many different types of new light-weight machines they introduced.[103]

Moreover, sales of the traditional large-displacement motor cycles slumped. In 1958 after 200 workers at the AMC Woolwich factory had been made redundant, an official stated that 'home demand had fallen off to such an extent that they could be said to be living on export orders'. He also expressed apprehension about the contents of the upcoming Budget, which was believed to contain further credit restrictions.[104]

Again the industry blamed government policy for its problems. The official briefs dating back to the 1920s and 1930s were dusted off and recycled, as the manufacturers travelled down from Coventry to London to seek concessions again from Ministers in Whitehall. These were necessary, they adamantly maintained, to resuscitate the industry's fortunes, both at home and abroad. The industry insisted that the solution to improving its economic health was simple. They must expand production at home, especially in the lightweights and scooters, in order to lower their costs and so remain competitive in export markets. In time, presumably, this would result in healthier sales of the larger, orthodox motor cycles.[105]

The best way the government could help boost domestic sales was to follow the manufacturers' four-fold policy: it must reduce Purchase Tax, stabilise fluctuating hire purchase terms, lessen regulations (i.e. lower or maintain the riders' age, and not require safety devices such as compulsory helmets or turning indicator lights), and copy their Continental rivals by removing tax and drivers' licences and tests for mopeds.[106] Once more, the industry tried to shift responsibility onto the government to create a more favourable environment for greater motor cycle sales. The lightweights and scooters did not have to be foreign-made; the British industry could supply the home market, if only given the proper incentives. The fact that the legislative concessions sought by the industry would also benefit imported machines equally did not particularly seem to trouble British manufacturers.

Moreover, the industry's arguments still rested on what was essentially an article of faith. Once again, their case failed to contain enough factual information necessary to convince sceptical Ministry of Transportation and Board of Trade officials to change their policies. And the industry's problems were now vastly aggravated because of growing public reaction against its products, reflected in even more sensationalist press coverage of motor cycle accidents.

In April 1957 a delegation from the Industries' Association met with Harold Watkinson, Minister of Transport, in order to press their arguments that, in the interest of stimulating sales of mopeds, the government should drop the minimum riding age from 16 to 15 and waive the requirement for riding tests and licences. During their presentation, the delegation showed some sensitivity towards public disapproval of how motorised two-wheelers had been operated on British roads. Their brief defended the skills of both motor cyclists and scooterists, explaining that 'young men of today handle with competence complex machinery that their fathers ... only dreamed of'. They admitted, however, that there 'will always be so-called reckless young men. Some will ride motor cycles, some drive sports cars ... and in wartime pilot aircraft, command tanks or submarines.' The manufacturers claimed that government regulations were 'strangling output' and maintained that prospective moped buyers were 'put off because they fear the test or regard it as too much of a nuisance'. Yet, they insisted, greater moped sales would ultimately stimulate sales of the larger orthodox models.[107]

Shortly afterwards Director Hugh Palin and another delegation met with Richard Nugent MP, Parliamentary Secretary to the Ministry of Transport and Civil Aviation. During this meeting they were told that there was little likelihood of any change in existing legislation, because of the high motor cycle accident rate. As the minutes of the meeting record, Nugent left the delegation little room for doubt about the government's position. Because of the 'high density of traffic' on British roads, which made motor vehicle operation so demanding, 'he saw little chance of public opinion, or of opinion in Parliament, accepting the idea of abolishing the requirement that young riders of low powered cycles [hold] driving licences and pass a driving test'. Moreover, the 'motor cycle was shown by accident records to be the most dangerous type of vehicle', and Parliament simply would not agree with any measure lowering the age limit for riding one.[108]

Nor were Ministry officials convinced by the industry's arguments that removing the regulatory impediments would help encourage the use of mopeds and so reduce road congestion. Again, privately they remained suspicious of the industry's motives:

> Mr. Palin's arguments about the relative safety of the moped are open to some doubt and his argument that increased use of mopeds would reduce the use of motor cycles and so assist road safety is inconsistent with his point that the manufacturers wished to appeal to a new class of user. It is more likely that increased use of mopeds would, in fact, result in decreased use of pedal cycles and therefore bring additions to the numbers of mechanically propelled vehicles on the roads and so add in some degree to accidents figures unless the moped were safer than the pedal cycle which even Mr. Palin does not claim.[109]

There were also instances when the industry failed to prevent the indiscretions of its own members, which reinforced the prejudices of its critics. In 1960, for example, after a bill which would have liberalised existing moped regulations had died in Parliament, Palin wrote to manufacturers to explain why they had been unable to muster a sufficient number of sympathetic MPs to carry the Bill. The problem, Palin claimed, was that the Association's lobbying effort had been 'sabotaged' from within. The finger of blame was pointed at the 'ill-advised publicity' generated by a certain importer, who had widely advertised that he had mopeds in stock which could easily reach 50 miles per hour. This had occurred at a time when the Association was trying to convince parliamentarians that the moped was essentially a powered bicycle and not capable of speeds in excess of 30 miles per hour![110]

The industry's complaints that legislative burdens hurt their competitive position with Continental rivals fell on equally unsympathetic ears. As one Board of Trade official noted in 1957, the real issue was the fact that the industry was trying to shift the responsibility of its own tardy reaction to market changes on to the government. Noting that there were peculiar circumstances prevailing on the Continent which had created their robust home markets for such machines, he made the following observation:

... I think it would be true to say that in 1949, had the UK Industry been asked then whether the mopeds which were just beginning to be thought about in European production circles would become the popular vehicles they have, the answer would have been to the effect that the demand was bound to be a temporary one, and that the vogue would die away as quickly as it appeared. The UK Industry now accepts that in this assessment of the situation in 1949 manufacturers made an error of judgement. Belatedly, they have tried, and are still trying hard, to catch up with their European competitors, but they are some four years behind, and their efforts must at first be concentrated on the home market for technical and commercial reasons.[111]

Once more the Ministry refused to bail the British motor cycle industry out of a dilemma of its own making.

The industry steps forward

Despite its failure to move either politicians or Whitehall officials, by 1959 the industry seemed to be improving its hold on the home market, at least in orthodox heavy-weight motor cycle sales, and was even believed to have begun to make inroads in the moped and scooter markets. More significantly, two large manufacturers who had hitherto not committed substantial resources to the light-weight machines now entered the marketplace. Raleigh Industries, Britain's largest bicycle producer, came out with a moped in 1958. This was followed by a much anticipated announcement by Villiers Engineering, the country's dominant producer of proprietary engines, declaring that it was finally going to produce a 49 cc unit for mopeds. This would place the smaller independent manufacturers in a far better competitive position relative to overseas rivals.[112]

One event subject to great publicity was the launch of the new BSA/ Triumph scooter, conducted in London at a Park Lane location and attended by, among others, motor car racer Stirling Moss and entertainer Harry Secombe. Managing Director Edward Turner had to admit that, although there were an estimated quarter million scooters on British roads, 'so far, however, only a relatively small proportion' was made in British factories. That, he predicted, would soon change, especially as both AMC and Velocette were also near to introducing their own scooters.[113]

The vitality of the German industry might have flagged, but the British on the other hand, so the trade press claimed, were stronger than ever. The proof was to be found in the new models, mainly in the light-weight category, that continued to be developed by the British firms. Not only did the domestic scooters have good designs and 'contemporary styling', but they were manufactured with 'the traditional quality in workmanship and finish for which British motor cycle factories are renowned'. New models in the 250 cc category included the Ariel Leader, which was heavily influenced by scooter design, including extensive use of fibreglass bodywork. In fact, many of the more traditional models produced by Triumph, Norton and Royal Enfield featured scooter-type styling.[114] The influx of foreign scooters and mopeds continued, but they now had more determined domestic competition. Even the columnist Francis Jones, reviewing the 1958 Show, expressed the belief that the industry had finally got it right and was producing the kind of machines that British consumers really wanted.[115]

Losing on the racetrack

Not all was well, however, on the racetrack. As in the marketplace, British competitive success in sporting events was declining. Yet, for some years after the war, their position had seemed secure. Unlike their football and cricket teams, British motor cycles kept on winning race after race, particularly in road-racing venues such the Isle of Man TT. In contrast with the defeat of the British national football team by the Hungarians in 1953 (the first time a foreign football team had won a major match on a home pitch), British motor cycles stayed on top, at least in the medium- and heavy-weight categories.[116] However, starting in 1947 (the first post-war TT), Italian machines scored victories in the light-weight (under 250 cc) category, although as late as 1954 British machines still maintained a strong presence at the Senior and Junior TTs. As one trade journal commented, such victories demonstrated 'once again that while British manufacturers have been content to leave to the Continental makers the development of the lightweight as a speed machine, in the 350 cc and 500 cc classes British reliability remains unsurpassed'.[117]

British supremacy in the Senior and Junior categories (respectively 500 cc and 350 cc engine displacement) lasted until the mid-1950s, when the Italian Gilera and Moto Guzzi teams started to take the top prizes. The greater technical sophistication of the foreign competition, especially the more advanced multi-cylinder engine designs, gave them an increasing edge in performance. Then, in 1955, a four-cylinder Gilera model won the prestigious Senior TT race (with a British rider, Geoff Duke). Company owner Giuseppe Gilera had no doubt about the significance of this victory: 'We race to win. It brings prestige. That sells motor cycles.'[118]

The big single-cylinder Nortons, once so formidable, were now dated and unable to maintain the pace set by the opposition.[119] The tone of press coverage reflected a sense of dismay that this traditionally British-dominated sport was slipping into foreign hands.[120] Finally, in late 1956, Norton Motors Managing Director Gilbert Smith and AMC Sales Director J.M. West made a 'surprise announcement' that shocked many in the motor cycle racing world. Henceforth AJS and Norton, both AMC subsidiaries, would no longer sponsor an official factory race team.

Smith and West stated that their firms could no longer compete successfully with foreign entries, which, like the Gilera, were now highly developed, special-purpose 'one off' models. The two British managers maintained that, unlike the foreigners, their machines were essentially production models modified for the racetrack. AMC had neither the resources nor the desire to try and match the achievements of the foreign machines. In the words of AMC Managing Director Donald Heather, they would withdraw 'to enable the companies to devote all their technical knowledge and experience to standard products'.[121]

The following year, Hugh Palin responded to criticism that the industry had been lax in allowing foreign motor cycles to wrest away its long-time racetrack supremacy. He stated that the Italian victors at the TT were 'specialised products bearing no relation at all to what the manufacturers concerned normally produce'. The British, by contrast, used 'virtually standard production models'. Palin drew a parallel between the racetrack and the showroom. While it was true that the Italians and Germans had scored successes in both areas, Britain was still the world's major supplier of orthodox motor cycles above 350 cc capacity. Moreover, Palin argued, for all the criticism the industry had suffered, it 'has remained on a sound economic basis, unlike its German rivals'.[122]

Changing the guard

The industry may have been in a stronger position than before, but it was also in a state of transition, at least as far as the character of higher management was concerned. From the mid-1950s and for several years afterwards, a number of senior managers who had come into office during the 1930s or before left the scene. One of the first to go was Charles Collier, who died at the age of 69 while at work in the factory during 1954. Together with his brother Harry (who had died in a motor cycle accident in 1943) and then subsequently Donald Heather, he had managed AMC for many years. His obituary noted that 'throughout a lifetime devoted to the production of motor cycles, he never lost his deep interest in motor cycling'.[123]

The same could not be said of his successors, Alan Sugar and J.F. Kelleher (who was Harry Collier's son-in-law), were more interested in the financial side of the enterprise rather than the technical. Indeed, J.M. West, a fellow Board member, doubted whether either of them could 'tell the difference between a two-stroke and a four-stroke engine'.[124] Gilbert Smith, by contrast, had begun work at Norton Motors as a boy and was appointed Managing Director in 1945. Largely under his direction, the company built up a reputation of manufacturing Britain's finest racing machines. In 1958

Smith had a falling out with the AMC Board, which had bought Norton several years earlier, causing him to tender his resignation. He subsequently became a Director of Raleigh Industries, responsible for its Motor Division. Smith died in 1964.[125]

Also during 1958 Eric Walker, long-time Chairman and Managing Director of the Excelsior Motor Company, died at the age of 74. Walker was described as a 'life-long [motor cycle] enthusiast' who had received an MBE during the war for designing a paratroopers' motor cycle.[126] Several years later Eric Barnett, long-standing Managing Director of Francis-Barnett even after it had been bought up by AMC, was killed in a traffic accident. Son of the company's founder, Barnett was a dedicated enthusiast who enjoyed personally testing his firm's motor cycles whenever possible, on the grounds that he believed in 'manufacturers riding their own machines and knowing their products'.[127] The following year another senior management figure from the inter-war era, Frank Smith, who had been Chairman and Managing Director of Enfield Cycles since 1935 (having succeeded his father), died after a lengthy illness. Smith, another dedicated enthusiast, had also been, among other things, President of the Redditch Motor Cycle Club.[128]

The passing of these men did not necessarily mean a radical change of orientation in their firms. In some cases these did not long outlast their former managers. It was BSA, however, where the changeover was particularly marked. In 1956 James Leek, who had become Managing Director of BSA's Small Heath operations during the war, retired at the age of 64 because of ill-health. It was noted that as late as 1946 he had remained a keen motor cycle enthusiast. One report claimed that there was 'nothing he loves better than "hitting it up" to 80 mph or more in a car or a motor cycle on a road which lends itself to such speed'. It was also true that, at least until shortly after the war, he used to come to the factory riding a motor cycle side-car combination. The following year it was announced that Edward Turner, Managing Director of Triumph Engineering since 1936, would become head of BSA's newly formed Automotive Division, which covered both the motor cycle subsidiaries and the Daimler motor car operation.[129]

Turner should have been an ideal choice to manage BSA's motor transport interests, particularly the motor cycle end. During his long career in the industry, he had been involved in virtually all aspects of design work and factory management while at Ariel Motors and then Triumph Engineering. Often a difficult person to work with (Hopwood recalled him as 'the most egotistical man that I have ever met' although also praised his 'down to earth business common-sense and … his ingenuity'), he nonetheless succeeded in making it a highly profitable company.[130] His subsequent tenure at BSA was less successful. Triumph's operation was small in comparison with

Motor cycle Titan. Undeniably the single most important figure in the British motor cycle industry until its collapse during the mid-1970s, Jack Sangster towered above his contemporaries.

that at BSA, and Turner may well have been overwhelmed by the task of supervising a much larger enterprise.[131]

In fact Turner refused even to move his office from Coventry to Birmingham. On one occasion Neile Shilton, a Triumph sales representative, once saw him move his desk from one side of his Meriden factory office to the other, declaring that he intended to get no closer to the main BSA Small Heath headquarters. Hopwood recalled that he seemed 'to hibernate at Meriden with rare visits indeed to Selly Oak [the Ariel factory] and Small Heath'. Worse yet, Turner, at heart always a Triumph partisan, did little to encourage the smooth coordination of the three motor cycle subsidiaries, and instead 'greatly encouraged the animosity between the three operations'.[132] He also began to suffer from health problems, which may have been the cause of his occasionally eccentric public statements and which would ultimately cause him to retire in several years' time. In practical terms, all this meant that during the period between 1956, when James Leek retired, and 1964, when a new Managing Director was appointed, BSA's motor cycle operations functioned virtually without any central direction or strategic purpose.[133]

After years as the dominating figure of the industry, Sangster himself was now ready to reduce his leadership role. Having taken over the BSA Chairmanship after the turmoil following the removal of Sir Bernard Docker, within several years he had been able to stabilise the firm. BSA underwent a period of retrenchment, selling off various subsidiaries, such as the bicycle and earth-moving equipment divisions, and substantially reduced the debt passed on from the Docker era.[134] Yet, among all this activity, Sangster retained his earlier interest in motor cycling and motor cycle sports. Shilton, for example, recalled an incident during this time when Sangster arrived at the Mallory Park race circuit in his Bentley motor car, but 'within a few minutes [he] had put on his riding kit and was enjoying himself round the circuit on my Tiger'.[135] However, Sangster never made any secret of the fact that he had taken over from Docker only as a short-term measure until a more permanent replacement could be found.[136]

In 1959 he found his successor. Eric Turner (no relation to Edward), an accountant who was Managing Director of Blackburn Aircraft and barely 40 years old, was recruited to join the BSA board. Unlike either Sangster or Leek, Eric Turner was not an enthusiast as well as a manager. When Shilton first met him, his immediate impression was that he 'did not like motor cycles' and was inclined to see them as just another 'consumer durable'. Nonetheless, the new era started off well. Sangster delivered his final Chairman's speech at the 1960 Annual General Meeting, proudly informing shareholders of a profit of £3,418,548, compared to the £1,604,941 declared in 1956. He then retired as chairman and, although still a board member, appeared to play little active role in the running of the company. He is remembered by one senior executive at this time as a 'dapper man' who 'lived in some style in his Park Lane apartments'.[137]

BSA's improved position was reflected throughout the industry. Indeed, 1959 had been the best sales year ever for the British motor cycle industry, with a grand total of some 250,000 machines sold, of which 127,500 were orthodox motor cycles. There was a number of factors responsible for the high sales. For one thing, the weather was exceptionally good that spring and summer. Also, with an eye to an impending general election, the government had relaxed hire/purchase regulations and lowered Purchase Tax.[138] Many managing directors must have thought that this development vindicated their many briefs to Ministers, and at last, they had cleared the hard times and entered a period of increased sales which would be more than temporary (see tables 21 and 22). However, these were deceptive statistics. For example, many of the machines listed as part of British production were actually foreign-designed units, such as the Douglas Vespa scooter that was built under licence in the UK. Of the estimated 500,000 lightweights on British roads, only a small proportion was believed to have been produced domestically.[139]

Table 21 *Number of motor cycles for which licences were current at any time during the quarter ending 30 September, between 1951 and 1955*

Capacity	1951	1952	1953	1954	1955
Solo units:					
up to 60 cc	79,473	120,472	153,919	191,732	227,173
60–150 cc	178,755	205,914	224,856	254,170	287,340
150–250 cc	129,156	138,765	150,774	166,351	191,227
over 250 cc	314,871	326,448	338,935	344,075	354,419
Total solo:	702,255	791,599	868,484	956,328	1,060,159
Combo units:	120,316	130,229	140,671	151,506	160,827
Tricycles and others:	25,192	26,999	28,384	30,786	34,880
Grand total:	847,801	948,860	1,037,362	1,138,629	1,148,310

Source: Ministry of Transport, *Return showing the number of Mechanically Propelled Vehicles.*

Table 22 *Number of motor cycles for which licences were current at any time during the quarter ending 30 September, between 1956 and 1959*

Capacity	1956	1957	1958	1959
Solo units:				
up to 60 cc	246,443	283,608	272,795	347,307
60–150 cc	321,513	404,167	446,944	534,552
150–250 cc	210,703	232,396	256,920	304,697
250–350 cc	168,905	165,662	157,926	152,822
350–500 cc	137,612	135,291	128,063	124,167
over 500 cc	46,271	49,645	54,298	59,787
Total solo:	1,131,447	1,270,769	1,316,946	1,523,332
Combo units:	158,446	160,376	158,142	155,276
Tricycles and others:	36,306	40,238	44,834	54,723
Grand total:	1,326,210	1,471,292	1,519,935	1,733,342

Source: Ministry of Transport, *Return showing the number of Mechanically Propelled Vehicles.*

In fact, it was estimated that British light-weight and scooter producers had a total annual manufacturing capacity of only 75,000 units and that the size of the average company was still small – it was a case of too many firms producing too few machines.[140] This hampered the competitiveness of the industry; as one industry executive noted, the 'principal trouble with the British powered two-wheeled industry is that very largely it is composed of a number of small manufacturing units which tend to be at a disadvantage against the large Continental concerns'.[141]

Nor was the situation in export markets really much improved. In early 1959 Industries' Association Director Hugh Palin prepared a confidential report that showed that Britain's share of world motor cycle sales had been declining steadily. From 60 per cent of all exports in 1935, the British proportion had dropped to 19.3 per cent in 1955 and reached 12.4 per cent in 1957. It was small comfort that Germany's share, 61 per cent in 1938, had been 34 per cent in 1955 but 23 per cent in 1957. The difference had been made up by the Italians and Czechs (34 and 20 per cent respectively in 1957).[142]

'Teddy boys' on wheels

Even if the 1959 season had been exceptionally good, the industry's higher sales were achieved with the backdrop of even greater public hostility, a fact that was reflected by press coverage of young British motor cyclists.[143] During that summer one reporter visited a transport cafe which was frequented by motor cyclists, curious to discover the character of these daredevils who so enjoyed racing on British roads. He interviewed one motor cyclist who commented on the public opprobrium directed at him and his colleagues:

Let's face it. We are regarded as Teddy Boys on wheels. If we hang around street corners we get into trouble. So we buy a pair of wheels to get away from it. But still we are in trouble because we are motor cyclists. You can't please some people.[144]

Later, another reporter visited the 'Busy Bee' cafe in north London and met a group of youthful motor cyclists who complained about their low public standing:

People in cars, even old Blokes on motor bikes, shake their fists at us as we go past. The police try to pull us in for the smallest things. I don't know what they're trying to prove when they do that, but their attitude doesn't help anybody. When people see a teenager on a motor bike, they think he must be mad. They'll believe anything about us, so long as its bad enough.[145]

Such stories were hardly unique. It and the others always seemed to stress the extreme danger of operating high-powered motor cycles on public highways.[146] In fact, the Ministry of Transport, convinced that publicity used by motor cycle companies which focused on its racing successes, was a contributing factor in the higher accident rates, actually asked that they be toned down in the interests of road safety.[147]

Much of this press coverage then, and several years later about the so-called 'Mods and Rockers', may have been a grotesque exaggeration of

British economy motor cycles

Both before and after 1945, few of the larger manufacturers devoted much effort developing light-weight (250 cc and less engine capacity) motor cycles. There were, however, a number of smaller firms that tried to produce their own versions of economy or 'Everyman' machines.

These became even more important during the post-war austerity period when the virtues of a cheap, fuel-efficient and easy-to-maintain motor cycle were very much appreciated. Consequently, starting from the late 1940s and carrying on even into the 1960s, a number of such smaller machines appeared at various times.

True, some of these were orthodox-type motor cycles, such as the 250 cc BSA C10, produced by larger manufacturers. Although these machines were often contemptuously referred to by die-hard motor cycle enthusiasts as 'grey porridge', they still found ready buyers, including commuters, who might otherwise have preferred a car but could not afford either the purchase price or the attendant running costs.

In response to the growing volume of imported Italian Vespas and Lambrettas, a number of British-built scooters, such as the 99 cc BAC Gazelle, 150 cc DKR Dove, and the 250 cc Dayton Albatross, began to arrive in British showrooms. Moreover, there were also

Bantam owners frolic, but this motor cycle, whose design was actually German in origin and made available to BSA through the war Reparations Programme, was already well out of date by the time this advertisement appeared, some time in the early 1960s.

a variety of powered bicycles such as the 45 cc Cyclemaster and mopeds such as the 49 cc Hercules Grey Wolf that experienced fleeting popularity during the early post-war era.

Lacking either the technical or financial resources available to the larger companies, the smaller firms were heavily dependent on proprietary engine-makers such as Wolverhampton-based Villiers Engineering. The availability of these motor units allowed them to produce a wide range of machines that otherwise would have been impracticable. Yet, virtually none of these British companies, large or small alike, ever really seemed to get the sales formula right and were unable to find either a substantial or an enduring market.

In part, this was the result of their persistent failure to break out of a dilemma created by relatively high costs combined with low production. Consequently, not only were their machines frequently higher priced than the imports (in 1958, for example, British-made scooters such as the 150 cc Sun Wasp cost £181, while an Italian Lambretta sold for £174), even worse, they frequently looked stodgy and unattractive, lacking the design flair that so often characterised the offerings of their foreign rivals. And quality control problems remained intractable despite repeated efforts to remedy them. It seemed as if British manufacturers simply could not produce the kind of light-weight economy models that consumers wanted.

There was one significant exception. BSA's Bantam was not only the best light-weight machine to emerge from any British factory, it was also probably the most popular and widely used motor cycle ever made in Britain. This was all the more remarkable because BSA had a generally poor record in the light-weight field, having produced a string of failures starting in the 1950s with such machines as the still-born 200 cc Beeza scooter, the disappointing 70 cc Dandy and, after 1960, the equally ill-fated 75 cc Beagle and 50 cc Ariel Pixie, a dismal record that culminated in 1971 in the Ariel 3 debacle.

Perhaps the Bantam was a success precisely because BSA had not actually designed it, having started out in Germany as the DKW RT125 which was acquired by the company via the post-war German Reparations Programme.

The Bantam was not built at the main Small Heath factory but rather at a plant in nearby Redditch with a workforce that, unlike most other British motor cycle assembly lines, contained a high proportion of female workers. It became one of BSA's regular money-spinners, not least because the company had incurred few substantial development costs putting it into production, other than converting the measurements from metric to imperial and, following British practice of the time, moving the gear shift lever from the left to the right side of the engine.

Further incremental modifications followed during its lengthy production life, including progressively increasing the engine capacity size from the original 124 cc to an ultimate 175 cc.

The Bantam was a rare example of 'Fordism' in the British motor cycle industry, at least insofar as it benefited from a mostly standardised design and a long production run. It was also highly versatile. The Bantam was many younger motor cyclists' 'starter bike', and it was purchased in large numbers for institutional fleets such as those of the Royal Mail and, if company advertisements are to be believed, was also used to herd sheep in the Australian outback.

Still, although a notable British success story, the BSA Bantam was far less impressive by international, especially Japanese, standards. Between 1948 and 1970 a total of approximately 250,000 Bantams were manufactured, more than any other single model produced by the British motor cycle industry. However, that total still pales in comparison with the 50 cc Honda Supercub. According to the Honda Motor Co., from its first introduction in 1958 to the end of 2005, close to 50 million Supercubs had been made. Indeed, it remains in production, making this undeniably the most prolific motor vehicle, either two- or four-wheeled, ever manufactured.

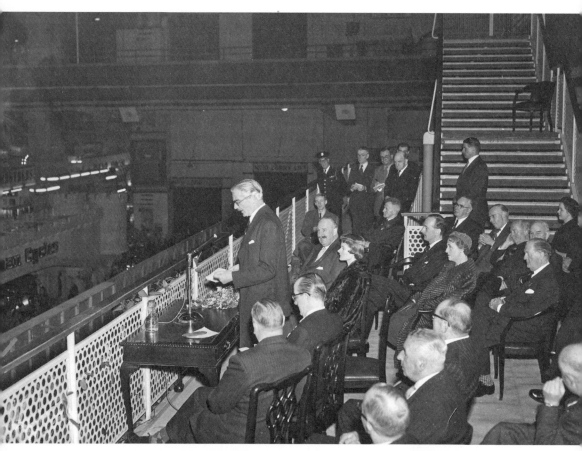

Foreign Secretary Anthony Eden (who would become Prime Minister in 1955) opening the 1953 Motor Cycle Show. Right up through to the end of the 1950s, senior government ministers regularly attended these shows. However, with growing public concern about motor cycle accidents, along with the sometimes outrageous behaviour of riders such as the 'Rockers', senior politicians became increasingly reluctant to be associated publicly with the industry.

what was really happening on Britain's roads, but it obviously tapped into public concern about the behaviour of at least some motor cyclists. That made it the cause of great anxiety on the part of the manufacturers. The negative state of public opinion was symbolised in an incident that Palin unhappily recounted to manufacturers during a Council meeting in 1959. Palin told them he was 'appalled' to hear that a north London magistrate had 'severely criticised' a schoolmaster for running a motor cycling class on the school playing field during his spare time for the benefit of his pupils. The magistrate had gone on to denounce this activity as 'a most undesirable practice' which he insisted should cease forthwith.[148] By 1960, such was the poor reputation of British motor cyclists, that Palin had fallen into a state of near despair. In a confidential memo to manufacturers he conceded that there had been 'much adverse publicity [against motor cycles] and frankly [we] have not been too successful in countering it'.[149]

Cold shoulder for the industry

This further manifested itself in the changed public attitude of politicians towards the industry. Since early in the inter-war period virtually every one of the Manufacturers' Union's annual Motor Cycle Shows had been opened by a senior government representative. As late as 1953, for example, a prominent member of the Cabinet, Foreign Secretary Anthony Eden, was present for the ceremony and gave a speech of welcome. Not only was he fulsome in his praises of the industry's accomplishments, he even confided that he had once been an enthusiast himself, having owned a Douglas motor cycle for a time in his younger days.[150] Increasingly, however, the tone of the opening speeches given by visiting dignitaries had become distinctly cooler, with fewer words of praise. For example, when Minister of Transport Ernest Marples opened the 1960 Show, his speech was not at all well received by the audience. He had followed, one trade journal reported, what was 'becoming the standard formula for elderly official persons addressing riders of two-wheeled vehicles – in other words he began to preach'.[151]

In 1959, when the Industries' Association sought a senior government representative to open their new headquarters building in Coventry, they encountered an open reluctance on the part of senior politicians to be associated with the industry.[152] Although the comparatively junior Minister of State for the Board of Trade, John Rodgers MP, did agree to attend the dedication of the building, privately the manufacturers were keenly disappointed that someone more prominent could not have been present instead. Their disappointment was compounded when, during his speech, Rodgers criticised the industry for their declining exports.[153] In future the shows would be opened more often by sports and racing personalities than by those who frequented the corridors of power in Whitehall.[154]

Most important, there was no indication that the leading executives had really learned anything at all about the changing tastes of consumers either at home or abroad. The views of Edward Turner, now arguably one of the most influential executives in the entire industry, on the continuing primacy of large-displacement models in the manufacturers' production programmes, despite the major shift in consumer demand since 1951, is a case in point. Speaking at a banquet laid on for Triumph's overseas distributors in late 1958, Turner reflected on his firm's accomplishments over the past year:

> Triumph was making more sports motor cycles than ever before and last year was the best year in the history of the company. Deep in

our hearts of hearts we are interested in highly developed sport motor cycles that give so much pleasure to young men all over the world.

Turner concluded with the assurance that, 'Triumph knew the man and the market and would go on pleasing him'.[155]

There seemed no doubt in the minds of those in the top echelons of the industry that they had continued to read their market correctly and that their policies were essentially sound. Not everything, however, was quite as rosy as some may have wished. One trade journal noted how the Show was more and more dominated by foreign machines. In 1953, for example, 33 of 35 motor cycles, 2 of 3 scooters and 6 of 13 cyclemotors (or 80 per cent of the total) were British-built. By 1960, however, only 17 of 32 motor cycles, 11 of 25 scooters and 4 of 25 mopeds (or 39 per cent) came from British factories.[156] While superficially the position of the industry may have seemed secure, in reality it was resting on a shaky foundation.

This foundation would soon come under far heavier pressure than ever before. During mid-1960 trade discussions had commenced with the Japanese government, which some in the industry suspected might result in significant liberalisation of imports into Britain. Two years earlier, responding to rumours of a new treaty, Industries' Association Director Palin had informed the British government 'in no uncertain terms that the Industry would be violently opposed to the unrestricted entry of Japanese products into the UK market'. However, the manufacturers were resigned to the fact they would have to deal with the possibilities of at least quotas being set for Japanese imports.[157] As will be seen, beyond this protest, no other action seems to have been taken. Nor were they appreciably alarmed by the report of a light-weight Honda Dream motor cycle, the first time a Japanese model had appeared in a European motor cycle show. It was a model they would all soon become quite used to seeing in showrooms across Britain. Whether or not its leadership fully appreciated it, the British motor cycle industry was about to face a threat that within just over a decade would precipitate its downfall.[158]

CHAPTER SIX
The firms and their workers, 1960–1973

Τ HE OPTIMISM with which the industry began the new decade dissipated
quickly. By the very next year, 1961, manufacturers were deep into their
worst sales recession since 1945. The recession was slow to lift, and home
market demand for British motor cycles would never return to anything like
its former levels. This made export markets, particularly North America, even
more important, although not all companies could find a substitute abroad
for their lost home market sales. Consequently, by 1970, most remaining
British motor cycle manufacturers were either out of business or in serious
trouble. During this period, another problem emerged. Starting in the early
1960s, labour militancy began to grow to alarming levels, even if only one
company, Triumph, was affected significantly by it. By the end of the decade,
Triumph's Meriden factory seemed to be in perpetual crisis, and by 1973
BSA's Small Heath operation, which had enjoyed mostly good industrial
relations until then, looked to be on the verge of major labour confrontation.

Trade recession

Although throughout the 1950s sales and registrations of motorised
two-wheelers had been growing, albeit gradually, in 1961 they began to drop
off. Total registrations, which had gone from 1,519,935 in 1958, then 1,733,342
in 1959, peaked at 1,795,555 in 1960. The following year, they slipped back
to 1,790,200, a decline which represented the first stage of a long-run trend
that would persist for the next decade. By 1975 registrations had slipped
to 1,282,576, and sales had declined to 50 per cent of their 1959 level. The
most disturbing development of all was the sluggish home market demand
for models of 500 cc and over. Between 1956 and 1960, registrations in this
class had climbed from 46,271 to 67,089 per year, only to fall back to 66,700
the following year. In contrast, sales of light-weight machines in the 150 cc
and under category had been continually improving. While there had been

567,956 of these registered in 1956, by 1961 there were some 986,000 of the smaller machines on the road. This was another trend that would persist for years to come (see tables 23 and 24).

Table 23 *Number of motor cycles for which licences were current at any time during the quarter ending 30 September, between 1960 and 1962*

Capacity	1960	1961	1962
Solo units:			
up to 50 cc	388,050	396,100	397,400
50–150 cc	581,327	590,000	604,100
150–200 cc	176,915	195,400	198,100
200–250 cc	179,190	193,500	193,400
250–350 cc	140,210	113,200	102,900
350–500 cc	117,287	97,800	86,400
over 500 cc	67,098	66,700	63,500
Total solo:	1,650,077	1,652,700	1,645,800
Combo units:	145,464	137,500	133,500
Tricycles and others:	65,692	78,400	86,400
Grand Total:	1,795,555	1,790,200	1,866,000

Source: Ministry of Transport, *Return showing the number of Mechanically Propelled Vehicles.*

Table 24 *Number of motor cycles for which licences were current at any time during quarter ending 30 September, between 1963 and 1966*

Capacity	1963	1964	1965	1966
Solo units:				
up to 50 cc	434,700	497,00	500,300	464,000
50–150 cc	580,600	566,000	515,100	445,000
150–200 cc	196,400	191,000	180,500	161,000
200–250 cc	194,000	180,000	158,600	131,000
250–350 cc	91,200	76,700		54,000
350–500 cc	76,200	66,400	257,200	58,000
over 500 cc	62,400	60,300		93,000
Total solo:	1,635,500	1,637,400	1,611,700 (plus combos)	1,406,000
Combo units:	119,600	103,600	n/a	n/a
Tricycles and others:	91,800	93,900	91,000	86,000
Grand total:	1,896,900	1,834,900	1,702,700	1,492,000

Source: Ministry of Transport, *Highways statistics* (1964–1967).

These figures were deeply troubling to industry leaders, who attributed the sales recession to the increased hire/purchase restrictions that had been introduced in the 1960 Budget. These had been followed by large increases in insurance premiums, some up to 30 per cent. The situation was worsened early in 1961, when the Budget increased the rate of Purchase Tax. Such measures did little to encourage motor cycle sales, although they did not seem to have had the same effect on sales of motor cars.[1]

The recession inevitably affected employment levels. Alarmed by redundancies at the nearby Triumph factory, Coventry Labour MP Maurice Edelman demanded the government help the industry. In response, Keith Joseph, Minister of State for the Board of Trade, expressed his sympathy for the plight of motor cycle manufacturers but cautioned that 'the outcome would depend primarily on the industry'.[2] On 1 December, thanks to Edelman, Parliament experienced a rare, if only brief, exchange on the state of the British motor cycle industry.[3]

During his remarks in the House of Commons, Edelman noted that the 18.5 per cent drop in production and sales from 1960 meant that the manufacturers had been forced to cut back on their labour force. While it was true that the credit restrictions were dampening demand, Edelman believed that the industry's biggest problems were those of its own making. It was a case, he said, of 'too many producers and far, far too many models'. Take, for example, industry leaders BSA and Triumph, who, despite common ownership, each carried a completely separate model line, albeit with a number of similarities; 12 for BSA, ranging between 123 cc to 650 cc and 10 for Triumph, ranging from 199 cc to 650 cc.[4]

Moreover, because of its stubborn dedication towards traditional heavy-weight motor cycles, the industry 'had produced its own nemesis'. They might be 'attractive to young men who want to show their capacity for speed', but had now 'become dead weight in the stock of most of the leading companies'.[5] The motor cycle had, Edelman said, 'come to be regarded as a sort of lethal weapon, and, indeed, it can be so, because the emphasis on high speeds, the fact that these vehicles can be put into the hands of the very young who have not the temperament to control them properly'. The manufacturers must, he concluded, 'bear some blame for neglecting the social implications of their products'.[6]

BSA motor cycles moving down the factory production line sometime in the early 1960s. Smaller models such as these made up a steadily diminishing proportion of the industry's output.

© BSA OWNERS CLUB

The business press also saw room for improvement. One reporter remarked that the 1961 recession demonstrated how the industry had 'been brought to its knees by a combination of social and economic factors'. He then went on to observe that 'constant criticism of the British industry has been that it lives too much in the past in matters of design and building what today's customer wants'. Nor was the poor image that motor cycles and motor cycling had with the general public doing much to help. The reporter noted that 'most people associate them [motor cycles] with accidents, youthful irresponsibility and the esoteric games of "coffee bar cowboys"'.[7]

Another business journal, examining the state of the industry shortly afterwards, stressed that the industry's poor sales were a reflection of its inability to react effectively to changing consumer tastes – witness its tardy entry into the scooter market during the 1950s. The industry was still incapable of producing a truly competitive popular light-weight model. BSA, for example, had needlessly dawdled before introducing the 70 cc Dandy, which in any case 'proved largely abortive'. Furthermore, the industry's manufacturing plant had been allowed to decay. It was out of date and 'too much craft-based and too little acquainted with modern engineering'. If it were to survive, the industry had to rethink its future strategy.[8]

The combined criticism from parliamentarians and the business press generated both interest and resentment from within the industry. The *Motor Cycle and Cycle Trader*, for example, was receptive to Edelman's remarks and only a few days later ran a leading article entitled 'The Motor Cycle Industry should put its House in Order'. In early January 1962 the journal was instrumental in convincing the industry to create a Motor Cycle Design Commission to try and address some of the failings identified by Edelman and others.[9] While the trade press recognised the need for change, the same could not be said of the manufacturers. During a press conference in early 1962, arranged to launch the new line of 500 cc and 650 cc Star twin-cylinder models, BSA Sales Director Bill Rawson took the opportunity to lash out at the critics.

These detractors, he argued, had misunderstood the industry's many accomplishments, most particularly the fact that output had increased vastly since the 1930s and that it was a particularly successful exporter, especially to the USA. As for why fewer motor cycles were being sold in the home market, Rawson blamed the industry's favourite villains. Credit restrictions, high Purchase Tax, 'outrageously high insurance premiums', and the continued bad publicity caused by an 'overemphasis on motor cycle accidents in the daily press' were the main causes for the poor sales, rather than any failing on the part of the manufacturers.[10]

Despite the angry public defiance, in private many in the industry acknowledged that there were problems, and not all of them had been caused by government policies. Nor would they be easy to resolve. In late

1961 a meeting of the Industry Association's Publicity Committee was held to consider the 20 per cent drop in the sales of motor cycles and scooters. During the course of the proceedings, Industry Association Director Hugh Palin noted that 'most people seemed to be of the opinion that the main cause of the present recession was public antipathy to motor cycling'. Committee members pin-pointed 'parental objection' as a major and persistent deterrent to sales to younger consumers.[11]

This was a theme upon which Palin subsequently expanded in a memo that analysed why the British public had turned so decisively against motor cycles and motor cyclists. He insisted that opinion had been 'distorted by adverse, sometimes hostile publicity'. Yet, he admitted, this was aggravated by 'an implication lurking in the public mind that manufacturers are irresponsible in placing high-powered machines in the hands of young boys untrained to manage them'. It was up to the industry itself to correct this impression, a job which could take a long time to achieve.[12]

Material improvements in British society created their own problems for motor cycle manufacturers. There were some, such as BSA's motor cycle chief Edward Turner, who still thought the industry could increase sales by presenting itself as an viable alternative to public transport. During a speech at the 1962 Earl's Court Show, he stressed how regular motor cycle commuting was far better than catching 'winter colds in germ-laden trains and buses'.[13] Others, however, saw matters differently. In July 1962, at a meeting of the Joint Advisory Committee, made up of representatives of both manufacturers and retailers, another lengthy discussion was held to consider the causes of declining sales. Committee members focused far more on changes in British society than on levels of Purchase Tax and credit restrictions. For them, the main problem was the fact that contemporary Britain had become 'an affluent society', with the consequence that 'a large section of the public who, but for this, would otherwise be potential customers, can now afford and in fact are buying cars'.[14]

Sales paradox

No doubt the safety issue was a major factor in the lower motor cycle sales. Yet there was a continuing paradox among the overall figures which puzzled motor cycle makers. True, sales of all motorised two-wheelers were declining, but those of smaller displacement motor cycles were still holding up well. One business journal noted that teenagers and twenty-year-olds had been 'reluctant to spend upwards of £250 on a 500 to 650 cc motor cycle' and had 'turned instead to a lower-powered and cheaper product'.[15] This was not always an economic decision. The Road Traffic (Driving of Motor Cycles) Act, 1960, which had been passed in response to the high accident rates of younger riders, restricted all prospective motor cyclists to machines of no more than 250 cc while they were in their probationary period. This may have promoted safety but did little to help sales of the larger displacement motor cycles.[16]

In fact, for the manufacturers, the biggest threat to motor cycle ownership, one that was very difficult for them to counter, remained four-wheeled competition (see table 18, page 143 and table 20, page 157). This too, one report noted, was the result of improving living standards, as bigger 'wage packets' combined with what was described as 'insidious status seeking'. While advertising copywriters could 'purr that you can "get out of the ordinary" by getting into a particular make of car – no such claim can be made for the humble motor cycle.'[17] Hugh Palin admitted that 'our main problem is that much of the public is antagonistic to the motor cycle', compounded by the fact that 'everybody buys a car if they can afford it'. This was in contrast with the motor car industry, Palin explained, whose 'only problem is to persuade the customer that his is the best buy'; the motor cycle industry 'first [has] to persuade people that [a motor cycle] is a good thing in itself'.[18]

The effect of family pressures on young, would-be motor cyclists was often critical. Hugh Palin remarked this influence was now so intense that 'many parents would rather buy their son a clapped-out second-hand car with no brakes than a motor cycle'.[19] Price was, moreover, a crucial factor. The average 500 cc and larger motor cycle cost between £250 and £350, or about the same price as a second-hand car. Add roughly another £50 per year insurance and the traditional heavy-weight motor cycle was less and less competitive for all but the most dedicated enthusiasts.[20] By late 1965 one long-term dealer decided he had enough of declining sales and closed his business down. His explanation was simple: 'There's no point in going on any longer. Young people are no longer interested in motor cycling – not the way we were. Nowadays they would rather save up and buy a car.'[21]

In light of these problems, what kind of measures did the industry undertake to try and improve its standing with potential consumers? In 1962 the Industries' Association decided to sponsor a publicity campaign designed to improve its image. It funded a number of projects which were financed by a levy of 2s. on each machine sold by members. These projects included a rider training programme at a number of schools across the country, the provision of motor cycles to the ACU/RAC training programme, the donation of spare equipment for the 'engines for schools' initiative and co-operation with the Ministry of Transport on research on motor cycle safety, along with the underwriting of a special research unit at Birmingham University. The Association even sponsored a 'National Essay Contest' for school children (a 'surprising number of girls' had also participated) which was designed to stimulate an interest in motor cycling. The question posed in the 1967 contest, for instance, was 'Does motor cycle racing help to improve road safety?'.[22]

But it was precisely the issue of road safety which again prevented the industry from convincing civil servants and politicians to offer the kind of legislative relief that the industry so badly wanted. This was especially the case in its attempts to convince the Ministry of Transport to relax regulations affecting mopeds. In one instance, an importer claimed that the 'bulk of people who are potential buyers of mopeds will not buy them if there is any degree of paperwork attached', but this too failed to move Ministry officials.[23] As far as they were concerned, the existing regulations should continue to be applied in the public interest. The registration system was necessary for larger enforcement purposes, and abolishing tax would 'involve a considerable sacrifice in revenue'.[24]

The industry's central argument for a change in the regulations – that their removal would stimulate demand of mopeds – was also poorly received by Ministry staff. Their conclusions, after reviewing a brief sent in by Hugh Palin, was that the 'abolition of licences [for mopeds] would certainly involve a risk to someone or other. The question is really whether any additional risk to road safety is justified on what amounts to commercial grounds.'[25] Transport Minister Ernest Marples was more diplomatic in a letter he wrote to P.T. Bolton, an importer of German mopeds. 'I must face the fact,' he stated, 'that these … [safety] statistics show that, for the same distance travelled, the risk of the moped rider being killed is eight times higher than the risk of the car driver and that the risk of the moped rider being seriously injured is nine times higher.'[26]

Industry in the doldrums

How did the various firms react to the downturn in the motor market and the deep-seated shift in consumer demand? In his speech to shareholders during late 1962, Chairman Eric Turner announced that, because of commercial difficulties, the BSA Group Board had decided to shut down the Ariel factory at Selly Oak, Birmingham, and transfer production of its reasonably successful 250 cc model to the main Small Heath factory, which was now operating well below capacity. There were, Turner insisted, still some bright spots in this otherwise gloomy picture. A Triumph had just set another world speed record, and the company had introduced a new lighter weight scooter, a 100 cc machine called the Tina.[27]

In fact the situation was actually much worse than Chairman Eric Turner was willing to inform the shareholders. He admitted as much in a letter written in September 1961 to former Board Deputy Chairman Patrick 'Paddy' Hannon, who had earlier asked permission to arrange for a tour of the Small Heath factory on behalf of a group of visiting Commonwealth prime ministers. Turner declined to provide an invitation, on the grounds that it would have been too embarrassing for the company to have drawn public attention to facilities that were obviously under-used. Turner also offered the following explanation for the poor showing of BSA's Motor Cycle Division:

> The hard facts are that the organisation has not had a sufficiently vigorous development policy which would ensure that new products were constantly coming along to provide expansion or to take the place of products with falling demands.[28]

The state of Ariel, a BSA subsidiary since 1944, was illustrative of the problems of the entire group, as it had tried to respond to changed market conditions. The company had severely pared down its line-up of models in the late 1950s. Gone were the traditional large-capacity single-cylinder models, along with the venerable 1000 cc Square Four, replaced by a new 250 cc model, the Leader. Launched in 1959, the machine was planned as a means of stemming foreign incursions in the light-weight market.[29] Although the Leader was innovative, sales, like those of the Velocette LE, never approached expectations. The problem was that it was unable to find a market, either among established motor cyclists or with non-traditional riders. Consequently production was ended in 1965, with a total of only 17,000 units having been built.[30]

Unrest among AMC shareholders

Despite BSA's many problems, the situation at the number two producer, AMC, was even worse. The company had been especially hard hit by the shift to light-weight models over the past decade, and one manifestation of its declining fortunes were two successive shareholders' revolts. The first, which occurred in 1959, focused on the failure of the AMC Board to anticipate the surge in demand during that year's boom season. In late 1958 the company had predicted a slow year and had reduced production, with the result that it had insufficient machines ready to meet the much higher demand the following spring and summer. The so-called 'rebels' were able to force a postponement of the 1960 Annual General Meeting, when the re-election of two directors, which was expected to be routine, was opposed from the floor.[31]

The following year, a far more dangerous threat to the Board emerged, precipitated by the two-stroke engine fiasco and reports of losses at the Indian Sales Corporation, AMC's American distributor. A shareholders' committee had been formed which sought to remove Managing Director Heather along with two other directors, Alan Sugar and J.F. Kelleher, and replace them with their own nominees.[32] An Extraordinary General Meeting was forced by the Committee in August 1961, and although the rebel shareholders' motions were defeated, Heather's position was greatly weakened, and within months he had retired.[33]

Notwithstanding the defeat of the Shareholders' Committee, the condition of the company remained poor. Between 1954 and 1961 AMC's average share price had declined sharply, from 29/- to 5/-, and profits had slipped alarmingly from £541,461 to £234,772. Two of the company's most effective senior managers, Bert Hopwood and J.M. 'Jock' West, had resigned in April and August 1961 respectively, and left for different firms. Although the new chairman, T.C. Cowell, had a financial background, he too seemed baffled at finding a solution for the company's mounting troubles.[34]

During his speech to the 1962 Annual General Meeting, Cowell had further bad news for shareholders. Thanks to continuing weak sales, the main Woolwich factory had suffered a 20 per cent drop in turnover and had lost £27,000. Moreover, plans to relocate production in a new facility on the nearby Isle of Sheppey had been dropped because of labour shortages. Despite the stronger demand for light-weight motor cycles, the Francis-Barnett and James subsidiaries, which manufactured a line of models in the 98 cc to 250 cc range, including a scooter, continued to do badly. The AMC-built two-stroke engine had been scrapped and the company was forced to return to Villiers for power units used in their light-weight models. Finally, Cowell had to admit that its distributor in the USA, the Indian Sales Corporation, in which AMC had invested £250,000, had turned in a £113,000 loss.[35]

Cowell identified AMC's main weakness as its over-dependence on motor cycle manufacturing, which now constituted 90 per cent of its activities. When their sales went into steep decline, the company had suffered disproportionately. It had also suffered from its rapid expansion between 1947 and 1953, when it grew from its single factory to become four separate manufacturing units.[36] In order to offset losses, the Coventry-based Francis-Barnett factory (along with its subsidiary Clarendon Pressing and Welding Company) were closed down and operations moved to the James factory at Greet, Birmingham. Yet, several months later, newly appointed Chairman Sir Norman Hulbert was forced to report a loss of £350,000, which he attributed to a 'steadily diminishing demand' for the AMC Group's motor cycles. In consequence, the Board decided that it needed no more than two-thirds of its existing motor cycle manufacturing capacity and would shut down further factory and plant.[37]

At the next Annual General Meeting, Hulbert reported a staggering loss of £658,902, which he claimed was the result of the 'continuous severe reduction of motor cycle and scooter demand'. The Board decided to close the Norton factory in Birmingham and transfer operations to Woolwich. The Indian Sales Corporation was judged an irretrievable failure and had been closed down. The Board, however, still maintained hope for larger sales in the USA and had made arrangements for distribution there through the Berliner Motor Corporation. Finally, for the second year in succession, no dividends were paid out. The future looked bleak for this major motor cycle producer.[38]

Other manufacturers stumble and fall

Nor were the other smaller firms in much better condition than the two larger companies. On the surface at least, Royal Enfield had managed reasonably well over the previous years, so well in fact that BSA had considered purchasing it in 1957.[39] It had been helped along by its non-motor cycle activities, including sundry military contracts and the manufacture of diesel engines. The company had also maintained its stake in the Madras, India, factory which manufactured motor cycles under licence and a scooter, the Fantabulus. However, it had been hurt badly by fluctuating credit restrictions and recurrent labour shortages at its Redditch factory, compounded by the overall shrinking of the motor cycle market. In November 1962 Royal Enfield was purchased by E. & H.P. Smith Ltd, a holding company that owned a number of engineering enterprises. After the buyout, the Enfield model line-up, which had ranged from 148 cc to 736 cc machines, was reduced to solely the latter models, many of which were exported to North America. The company was out of business by 1970.[40]

Douglas, which after 1957 had dropped production of orthodox motor cycles, concentrated on its licensing agreement with Vespa, but found itself in trouble as scooter sales flagged in the early 1960s. In 1965 it ceased scooter manufacture as well. Production lingered on at Panther (Phelon & Moore Ltd), whose small factory in West Yorkshire continued to produce modest numbers of large-capacity single-cylinder machines. These were frequently used in conjunction with sidecars, whose numbers were steadily declining on British roads. However, the company did manufacture a small-displacement model, using a bought-in Villiers power unit, and, after 1957, began to import a French-built scooter, which was sold as the Panther Scooterrot. Neither model was very successful. Undeterred by this experience, the company, in partnership with two light-weight manufacturers, Sun and Dayton, developed its own scooter. Using a Villiers power unit, the Panther Princess was also a failure, not least because of what were described as 'costly and delaying teething troubles'. The 1961 recession crippled the company, and the following year a receiver was brought in. Although production continued, it rarely exceeded 1,000 of the big single-cylinder models each year. By 1968 the firm was defunct.[41]

The Veloce (Velocette) company also tried to make a late entrance into the scooter market. Although it continued to build the LE, first introduced in 1948, it remained loyal at heart to the traditional single-cylinder models

During the 1950s and early 1960s this best-selling Italian-designed scooter was made under licence by the venerable Douglas company, which otherwise would have gone out of business much earlier than it did.

which were frequently used by sporting enthusiasts. However, production of the larger models had averaged little more than 3,000 machines per year during the late 1950s. In 1961 Velocette launched the Viceroy scooter, a well-engineered machine but too heavy and expensive when compared to a Vespa. Nor did it help that this machine was introduced just as the scooter boom was ending. Although 5,000 units were scheduled for 1962, only 644 were actually built, of which a mere 130 were sold.[42]

As sales of traditional orthodox motor cycles, which had been Velocette's manufacturing mainstay for decades, continued to decline, the company tried to diversify its operations. The LE motor unit, for example, was adapted to other purposes, for use on ice-cream vans and hovercraft. Production of motor cycles, including the LE and the larger displacement single-cylinder machines, continued but did not exceed 1,500 units per year. Finally, in mid-1970, the company announced it would go into voluntary liquidation. The last motor cycles were produced in early 1971.[43]

A dwindling group of smaller firms, with outputs of no more than a couple of thousand of units each, had managed to survive on the periphery of the industry. Reliant on proprietary engine units and catering to more specialised segments of the market, their condition began to deteriorate badly during the early 1960s. Companies such as Cotton, DMW, Excelsior and Norman, which largely manufactured light-weight models with two-stroke engines and scooter makers such as Ambassador, Dayton, DKR and Bond, suffered from many of the same weaknesses. Low-volume production and lack of product development facilities meant that prices or design could never really be competitive with the imports. Virtually all these firms were out of business by 1965.[44]

Nor did Raleigh, the bicycle manufacturer which branched out into moped manufacture during the late 1950s, have any lasting success. Its RM1 model, introduced in 1958, was evidently 'developed in too much of a hurry' and was dropped in 1960, to be replaced by an imported French moped and an Italian scooter, the Roma.[45] Subsequently, it would again try to break into the moped market with the Wisp, which was introduced with much publicity in 1967. Although it enjoyed good initial sales, especially among women, it was ultimately withdrawn from production only two years later. While Raleigh continued on as a force in the bicycle industry, management blamed its failure with motorised two-wheelers on a general decline in the moped market. However, some could not help noticing that the Austrian Puch company continued to sell its models profitably on the British market without much difficulty.[46]

Labour relations in the motor cycle industry

If the industry's troubles out in the marketplace were not bad enough, during the 1960s a new problem emerged, this time one originating from within their own factories. Labour relations which, for decades, had not been any great matter of concern, were becoming a growing preoccupation, if not across the entire industry, at several firms and at Triumph in particular.

Trade unionism and collective bargaining in the British motor cycle industry, certainly before 1945, is far less well documented and studied than its counterpart in the car industry.[47] No doubt this was because it was a far smaller industry, but it was also a reflection of the lesser importance of organised labour, at least until well after 1945. However, trade unions had roots going back to the beginnings of the industry even if among only a minority of the firms, notably BSA and Triumph. At BSA, for example, there are suggestions of at least some trade union activity during the pre-1914 era. There was, for example, a one-month strike in the autumn of 1911 carried out by the Engineers and Allied Trades Society, which ended with the company agreeing to increase wage rates in line with other firms affiliated to the Engineering Employers' Federation (EEF).[48]

Nonetheless, the evidence suggests that the following decades were a period of industrial peace at BSA. This may have been the result of a conscious policy of paternalism. During the First World War, according to the company-sponsored history, *Munitions of War*, it offered a wide range of benefits to BSA's workers including extensive medical surgeries (provided free of charge), canteens with subsidised food and even a works' choir.[49] By the 1950s and 1960s, these services had been expanded to include further benefits such as a full-time doctor and dentist along with regular on-site eye clinics. The company also sponsored social clubs (including an amateur theatrical society), sporting events and hobby clubs that were co-ordinated by a company recreational officer.[50]

Paternalistic policies notwithstanding, by the mid- to late 1940s, trade unions seemed to have become well established at the Small Heath factory but were not necessarily strong or effective. In fact, indications are that the employer was often able to set piecework and wage levels unilaterally, virtually without negotiation, even though there was a form of consultation carried out with the shop stewards. The picture that emerges at BSA is of a trade union organisation that was either unwilling or unable to challenge the company with respect to more fundamental issues of employment.[51] Yet this happened during a time when the company was experiencing considerable difficulty holding and recruiting labour, a problem that would bedevil the company until almost the end.

Indeed the labour market in the Midlands was then so tight that there was intense competition between firms for certain classes of labour, often forcing BSA to go far afield in order to hire additional workers.[52] Draughtsmen, for example, were leaving the company because of higher pay offers in the aircraft industry, and it was believed that labourers, storesmen and production counters were 'practically unobtainable' to the extent that management was considering selective increases in wages.[53]

Militancy at Triumph

If the trade unions were weak at BSA, the situation at Triumph's factory in Coventry before the Second World War was very different. The trade unions there appeared a more assertive and militant force, at least up to the late 1920s. While owner Siegfried Bettmann seems also to have run his firm along paternalist lines, he had to contend with a more truculent workforce. All through the pre-1914 period, one can find numerous references in the AEU (Amalgamated Engineering Union) records of various conflicts related to setting piecework rates at the Triumph plant.[54]

During the First World War, Triumph was embroiled in a major labour dispute when the Ministry of Munitions introduced a scheme to embargo or control the employment of skilled workers in a number of factories. The Coventry trade unions viewed this order as the beginning of labour conscription and they initiated a city-wide strike that affected some 10,000 toolmakers and other employees. After the war Triumph joined the engineering employers' industry-wide attack on what was considered excessively high piecework rates. In January 1921 factory management unilaterally cut these rates and shortly thereafter followed up with a 12 per cent cut in the daywork rates.[55]

The following month, workers at Triumph responded with a strike conducted by both the AEU and the Workers' Union. However, there was evidently much internal dissension among the ranks, and the strike was called off in March after most of the workers had returned to their jobs.[56] Several years later, there was a report of another strike at Triumph's paint shop, but no information remains to describe its outcome.[57]

Nonetheless, as noted in chapter one, it seems as if some form of trade union organisation persisted at Triumph until well into the 1930s. Future senior manager Bert Hopwood, whom Jack Sangster brought in from Ariel Motors to work in the draughting department of the newly formed Triumph Engineering Co., recalled that there were pockets of union strength in the factory left over in the toolroom and several other parts of the factory.[58] But this rump organisation was not strong enough to resist Sangster's take-it-or-leave-it wage cut that he imposed upon them after his acquisition of the firm. Indeed, one suspects that Sangster probably took advantage of the situation to pare down the workforce and pick and choose only those workers he wanted to keep on.[59]

For years afterwards, labour peace appears to have prevailed at the Triumph factory, both in Coventry and, after the Luftwaffe bombing attack in late 1940, at the new factory in Meriden as well. Although there are no records of any strike action or unrest, after 1945 some evidence exists that the unions had succeeded in establishing better than average terms for themselves. In 1954, for example, the Brass and Metal Mechanics' Union pressed a successful wage claim for polishers at another Coventry firm by citing the example of Triumph, which treated that job as 'skilled' and so eligible for a wage increase.[60]

The situation regarding trade unionism and collective bargaining elsewhere in the industry is less clear. AMC, for example, the industry's other major producer, was probably unionised, at least to some extent, although there do not appear to have been any recorded strikes at the main Woolwich factory either before or after the war. Norton, which became an AMC subsidiary after 1953 and had a mostly unionised workforce at its Birmingham factory, also appears to have enjoyed labour relations peace at least up to the mid-1950s.

Worker militancy re-emerges

Then, in May 1956, a strike was begun by AEU members at Norton's Bracebridge St factory in Birmingham over the issue of redundancies, which was in turn part of a larger wave of labour unrest sweeping through the automotive engineering industry, most prominently at Coventry's Standard Motor Company. The Norton strike ran for over six months and caused much bitterness between the company and its workforce. There was also a political dimension to the Norton strike, through the active participation of a group which was subsequently known as the Socialist Labour League.[61] In late November the dispute was ultimately settled without significant concession on the part of the company, even after an attempt to disrupt that year's Motor Cycle Show, when AMC and its subsidiaries had their stands 'blacked' (or boycotted) by the building staff, acting in support of the AEU.[62] Thereafter, however, no further record of disputes or stoppages exists at Norton.

As for other industry firms, a lack of documentation makes it difficult to assess the state of labour relations. However, beyond BSA, Triumph and Norton, it is unlikely there were strikes elsewhere in the motor cycle industry after 1945, certainly none that was mentioned in either the mainstream or trade press. Some of the smaller firms, such as James or Vincent, probably did not even have any unionised employees in their factories. However, it might also be the case that, from time to time, these companies would have been affected by labour stoppages among some of their component suppliers or the shipping industry or the docks.

However, it is undeniable that the Triumph factory in Coventry had to contend with growing levels of worker militancy that became more intense throughout the 1960s and early 1970s. The first recorded post-war era strike of any consequence occurred there in June 1959 when the company attempted to change a long-standing clocking-in practice which had allowed employees to report to work up to 15 minutes late each day. The company's action was probably a reaction to the more demanding circumstances in export markets as well as to declining home market motor cycle sales figures. Quite possibly this was one among several other cost-saving measures that the company had decided to implement.[63]

Nonetheless, trade union representatives seemed genuinely offended by the employers' more aggressive stance when the dispute was later discussed during a meeting at the Coventry District Engineering Employers' Association (CDEEA) offices. After all, in the words of one of the union officials, 'the industrial relations in this company have been amongst the finest we have been able to achieve in the district and we consider that the attempts to remove small concessions such as this can seriously affect the relationships between the workpeople and management'.[64]

The following year, as described at the beginning of this chapter, labour relations at the larger firms were further strained by a series of redundancies. Throughout the industry employees were laid off as a result of falling sales, particularly on the home market. At BSA production was cut, and the workers at Small Heath placed on short time. At Triumph's Meriden factory, production cuts of up to 30 per cent resulted in a four-day week.[65] Later that year the situation continued to deteriorate. One hundred Meriden workers had been made redundant, although a subsequent agreement with the unions there had allowed the company to institute further short-time arrangements, and the workers were soon re-instated. The factory, however, was now on a three-day week. This time management blamed falling export orders for the factory's slowdown.[66]

The short-time practices at Triumph do not appear to have lasted very much beyond 1962 when the factory resumed full operation. But as the export trade began to play an increasing role in the financial well-being of the company, trade union militancy seems to have risen correspondingly as a result. Indeed, CDEEA records contain some 52 separate files covering the period 1959 to 1973 relating to disputes at the Triumph factory. Many concern informal Works' Conferences that were often settled without further discussion at the higher levels of the disputes procedure. However, 12 document the proceedings of Local Conferences, and another 6 relate to disputes that were referred to the Central Conferences held at York.[67]

The majority of these conferences were called to deal with disputes over piecework rates which seem to have become a continuing source of friction between the company and its shop stewards. Some of these disputes were settled at the Conferences or through being referred back to discussions held at the factory. But a growing number remained unresolved and, one suspects, similar to the earlier clocking-in arrangements dispute, were settled only after industrial action at the factory.

By 1964 two themes began to emerge during labour–management negotiations at the Triumph factory. One factor was that, despite the company's frequent boasts of export success, it had become increasingly worried about the emerging Japanese competition, especially with respect to the relatively higher level of British labour costs, a point that will be examined further in the next chapter. The other theme was how the trade unions countered this argument by trying to draw the employers' attention towards comparisons between Triumph and other firms within the Coventry Engineering District (especially those covered, as was Triumph, by the 1941 Coventry Toolroom Agreement) and the motor car industry.[68]

Those comparisons were rejected just as stubbornly by the company. Any reference to the automobile industry was irrelevant to the present situation, employer representatives would insist, and in any case workers at the Meriden factory were already the 'highest paid in the motor cycle industry in Great Britain and possibly in the world'.[69] For Triumph the real issue remained relative labour costs and the company's ability to compete internationally. During a 1964 Works' Conference, this message was spelt out in detail to the assembled shop stewards who were reminded that it was 'well known' to them that the company was 'experiencing great trading difficulties'; and that its hold on the market was shrinking thanks to Triumph's main competitors, the Japanese, who 'were now achieving a far greater share with the aid of their lower wage costs'. Nonetheless, despite all the rhetoric, Triumph still went ahead and agreed to increase the piecework rates.[70]

Higher rates notwithstanding, for the remainder of the decade and on into the next there were increasing numbers of shopfloor disputes, partic- ularly ones occurring outside the process outlined in the so-called 'Blue Book', the official Confederation of Shipbuilding and Engineering Unions (CSEU) and Engineering Employers' Federation collective agreement, and they actually seemed to be moving beyond the control of the full-time trade union officials.[71] Works meetings were becoming frequently punctuated by management accusations of 'irresponsible, unofficial, unconstitutional action'. Not only had trade union officials failed to prevent this, but, in some cases they claimed, the action had gone on without the knowledge, or perhaps even with the connivance of, local convenors.[72]

Further labour turmoil at the Triumph factory

In early 1966 T.D. Williams, CDEEA Assistant Director and Bill Lapworth, Transport and General Workers' Union (TGWU) Coventry District Secretary, carried out an informal inquiry into the causes of an illegal strike that had recently broken out in the Triumph factory's Lug Section and which had already dragged on for two weeks. John Walford, the General Works Manager, was reported to have called a shopfloor meeting and angrily denounced this dispute, which was apparently the latest in a long line of seemingly endless unconstitutional stoppages plaguing the factory.

Ray Allsopp, Triumph's TGWU Works Convenor, came in for particular criticism from management as a source of the company's labour woes. A hard-line activist, Allsopp could be described as the motor cycle industry's answer to Derek 'Red Robbo' Robinson, the militant trade unionist widely believed to be the inspiration for a series of disputes that swept through British Leyland's Longbridge automobile factory.[73] As one account later put it, Allsopp, a man whose public-speaking style was sometimes compared by his detractors to the late Italian dictator Benito Mussolini, 'could frequently be seen stalking the factory draped with a red hand wipe, the cloth that custom demanded he put over one shoulder when on union business'.[74] Wherever he went, trouble quickly followed.

Although careful never to be heard actively encouraging strikes and work stoppages, Alsopp certainly seemed to be doing all he could to undermine management's authority by calling frequent union meetings wherever and whenever he thought them necessary, and he did so without any reference to supervisors.[75] General Works Manager Walford wanted the CDEEA and the trade union district officials to come to an agreement that would be imposed upon their constituencies so that 'in future the proper procedure should be adhered to by all concerned'. Of course, this assumed that agreements entered into by the full-time officials would be binding on the shop stewards and the rank and file, something which, under the circumstances that now prevailed at Triumph, simply could not be taken for granted.[76]

There are no comprehensive and reliable records available that describe the total number of work stoppages at the Meriden factory. There must have been a fair number. Many of the Works and Local Conferences were precipitated by illegal strikes which were caused in turn by the breakdown of the piecework negotiations. These proceedings contain further references to other stoppages which are not recorded in the remaining files.[77]

For their part, trade union leaders at Triumph defended themselves against accusations of undue militancy by placing the blame for the unrest at the shop floor squarely upon factory management. A. Boyle, District Secretary for the AEU, for example, agreed that the high level of unofficial strikes was 'deplorable' but only to be expected considering the employers' approach to the piecework negotiations. Triumph workers had encountered 'an unwillingness and indeed a refusal' on the part of management to negotiate in 'a proper fashion' over new and improved rates. As far as Triumph's trade unions were concerned, the main problem was that the company had 'misinterpreted' the intent of the Labour government's 'White Paper on Income Standstill',[78] using it as a pretext to avoid any sort of serious bargaining and also to question the integrity of the local convenors. If there were on-going problems at the Meriden factory, then they had been created by the company.[79]

Labour–management peace prevails at BSA

By the mid-1960s, therefore, Triumph was notorious throughout the industry for its labour militancy, but the situation at BSA's main factory at Small Heath in Birmingham, like others elsewhere in the industry, was dramatically different. BSA appears to have suffered little in the way of strikes, either official or unofficial, during the period 1959 to 1969. This does not necessarily imply a passive workforce, however, since there are indications that a trade union structure was gradually becoming consolidated in the years after 1945, and it was one that the employer had to take into account at least from time to time.[80]

In the absence of the same documentation available to describe labour relations at Triumph, it is difficult to assess what were the issues at the Small Heath factory or the character of the relationship between management and labour on the shop floor. At an official level at least, these seem to have been quite cordial for some time. In July 1960, for example, the *BSA Group News* carried a story about the retirement of Frank Tidmarsh after 51 years' service with the company. Tidmarsh had been the Transport and General Workers' long-time Small Heath factory Branch Secretary and Works Convenor, as well as a member of the Union's National Executive. A party was laid on for Tidmarsh which was attended not only by the Works Manager but also Frank Cousins, the General Secretary of the TGWU. A photograph of the event depicts smiles all around and implies a fairly high degree of co-operation between the parties at least at this level.[81] Moreover, the minutes of the West Midlands District Engineering Employers' Association (WMDEEA), in contrast to those of their Coventry counterparts over the same time period, make only two references to BSA, and these relate to pay claims for the smaller unions.[82]

However, one should not necessarily infer that there were no labour problems at the Small Heath factory. Yes, for many years the factory suffered few if any strikes or other industrial action, but there certainly were other forms of discontent present. In 1964, for example, BSA engaged the services of the consulting firm Urwick, Orr and Partners Ltd to conduct a study on wage policy. Their subsequent report focused on an alarming level of labour turnover, which had reached 40 per cent yearly as of 31 July 1964.[83] Over 1963–64, there had been some 817 'leavers' out of a total of 1,650 employees. The rate had been particularly severe in the machines shops, two of which had turnovers of over 100 per cent.[84]

The causes of this problem were easy to find: compared with other Birmingham pay rates, Small Heath simply was not paying enough in order to retain staff. In fact, according to Urwick and Orr's survey, 33 per cent were below, 52 per cent comparable with, and only 15 per above, the district average.[85] The wage situation was also having other negative implications to the smooth operation of the factory.

Those employees who had stayed on were pressing their supervisors to increase the piecework and day rates to the extent that lower- and middle-rank management had become 'preoccupied with wage problems to the detriment of the real job they should be doing'. This pressure was also expressing itself in an upward wage drift as the rates were increasing in a fragmentary fashion, and there was also concern expressed over the erosion of labour flexibility because of the piecework system.[86]

The consultants made a series of recommendations which included a revision of the wage structure by way of a job evaluation system, a gradual changeover from individual piecework to group incentive schemes and more training of management personnel right down to the foreman level.[87] It is unclear just how many of these recommendations were ever implemented. However, there was most certainly change in the method of calculating the piecework rates that began about this time. Evidently, the factory switched over a 'value' to 'time' based piecework system which was, for all intents and purposes, a measured day work (MDW) scheme.[88]

Even with the new piecework rates the company continued to have trouble holding on to experienced labour. In his speeches to the BSA Group's Annual General Meetings at several times during the 1960s, Chairman Eric Turner might proudly recount the latest record-breaking export figures but would always seem to qualify his remarks by adding that the results would have been just that much better but for the on-going labour shortage.[89] What Turner would not say was that other employers – especially in the motor car and metal casting industries – paid more. Put simply, because BSA's Small Heath factory wages did not keep pace with the district averages, there was a detrimental impact on manufacturing operations as workers left to seek better pay elsewhere.[90]

BSA's labour troubles gained some national attention, but not everyone was sympathetic to its plight. The *Guardian*, for example, quoted A. Bottomly, the AEU's West Midlands' Regional Officer as saying, 'labour shortage? The British Motor Corporation have no difficulty getting labour – they pay the wages. I know there is a vicious circle and in the end the employers get hurt but there it is.' Bottomly went on to note that his union's members received a net weekly pay of between £24 and £26 at the British Motor Corporation but only £18 to £20 at BSA. Little wonder, then, that there should be labour shortages at this motor cycle factory.[91]

At Triumph labour militancy continues to spiral upwards

If BSA was spared industrial disruption, at Triumph's Meriden factory, during the mid- to late 1960s, labour relations deteriorated even further. BSA's new Motor Cycle Division Managing Director, Harry Sturgeon, a former senior executive from the aviation industry who had replaced the recently retired Edward Turner (although Turner remained as a non-executive member of the BSA Group Board of Directors), laid heavy pressure on the staff there to keep on increasing production in order to meet the burgeoning demand, especially from North America. He left absolutely no doubt about his determination to press ahead. In one instance, for example, while walking about the factory floor with fellow manager Bert Hopwood, he emphatically stated, within earshot of a group of workers, 'if I want to double the output, I don't care what it costs'. Sturgeon subsequently told Hopwood, when the latter expressed concern about higher labour costs, that the profits generated by the increased levels of production would more than amply cover those costs. But the costs turned out to be much greater than Sturgeon anticipated. Yes, production did go up, but realising management's increased vulnerability to stoppages, constitutional or otherwise, the shop stewards had pushed their case for all it was worth.[92]

One incident illustrates just how aggressive the unions had become at the Triumph factory. In the spring of 1967, during the course of an informal Works' Conference called to discuss the parties' differences in the application of the company's bonus scheme, the shop stewards enraged employer representatives by tabling a demand that certain employees be allowed a special *ex gratia* payment to compensate them for lost earnings caused by a series of illegal stoppages that had rocked the factory. These had so disrupted production that, in consequence, the bonus scheme, which was calculated on the basis of the number of motor cycles coming off the assembly lines each month, had ceased to yield sufficient benefit to its intended recipients. In February, for example, there had been 785 motor cycles built weekly on average, but by March, because of disputes over piecework and other issues, this total had dropped to only 175 units. Production did recover later on, but all the disruptions had so diminished the bonuses that the shop stewards wanted some sort of extra payment made to their affected membership in order to offset their losses.[93]

The company indignantly refused these employees relief. For them to do so, the shop stewards were informed, would in effect amount to the company subsidising the recent wave of unconstitutional strike activity. As the Director of the CDEEA pointedly reminded the assembled trade union representatives, from the company's point of view that record had been 'unsatisfactory, to put it mildly'.[94]

The problems facing management at Meriden as it tried to set piece and day work rates, as well as to administer the bonus schemes, were truly formidable. Nor were matters made any easier when negotiations often went round and round in circles. For example, the company was constantly faced with union claims to adjust wages on the basis of internal comparisons.[95] Nor would the shop stewards ever let up pressure over the company's position on the 'White Paper' on Prices and Wages Standstill. They defined the issue as being the 'inability of the company to regulate their wages' owing to its misunderstandings of government policy which the shop stewards said had created an 'anomalous situation'.[96] However, the employer representatives would always respond by pointing out that, even if the unions' claims had merit, the workers at Triumph's Meriden factory were still paid well above others in the Coventry Engineering District. That might also be true, the shop stewards would reply, but the real point was that the day rates had slipped well behind those of the production workers and that problem must be resolved first.[97] Then there was always the on-going matter of the 1941 Coventry Toolroom Agreement which continued to cover Triumph workers during this time. Every time wages and rates slipped below the district average, the shop stewards were sure to draw this to the company's attention. And so it went on, for meeting after meeting, year after year.

One could argue that these factors would have arisen no matter who owned and managed the Meriden factory. Its geographic location within the Coventry Engineering District meant that wage rates, by definition, would be higher than those elsewhere. However, during the latter half of the 1960s the BSA Group had become so committed to supplying the insatiable demand of North Americans for its products that it was forced to follow a high-production programme, which in turn crippled the ability of local management to run the factory effectively. Indeed, such was their determination to service the export trade that BSA Group Chairman Eric Turner and Motor Cycle Divisional chief Harry Sturgeon simply refused to accept any interruption of production, no matter what the cause. In practical terms, it meant that, should there be any strikes or other labour stoppages, they must be settled without delay.

This would have serious ramifications on the ability of local management to assert its authority. In 1968, for example, an employee was discharged from the Service Department for unsatisfactory performance. The other employees in that section thereupon walked out in protest, and the dispute quickly spread and became a factory-wide stoppage. General Works Manager John Walford was prepared to uphold the decision of the department head and wait out the inevitable strike. Two days later, Walford received a telephone call from BSA Chairman Eric Turner enquiring why production had been held up. Once Walford had explained the situation, he was informed, in no uncertain terms, to resolve the matter forthwith. The BSA Group could not afford to have Triumph motor cycle shipments delayed for even a day longer.[98] Consequently, negotiations began with the shop stewards, which resulted in the worker being re-instated, albeit to another department.

This was apparently not an isolated incident. Time and time again, Walford discovered that the Group Board would be extremely reluctant to back him up in any labour dispute if that meant any time being lost in production. Instead, he was expected to sort out differences as expeditiously as possible and keep the assembly lines moving. In this manner, stoppages were nearly always settled quickly, but, as Walford later explained, under those circumstances, 'never on our terms'.[99] The result of all this was that, to no one's real surprise, Triumph workers continued on as some of the highest-paid engineering workers in the Coventry area. By undercutting the authority of their factory management, the BSA Group board also, intentionally or not, encouraged a continuing round of militancy and work stoppages that would carry on until an unsuccessful attempt was made to shut the factory down in 1973.

The labour relations climate changes at BSA

At BSA's Small Heath factory management suffered a quite different set of problems. Costs there increased but productivity declined. The reasons were easy to understand. As the BSA board kept on pushing up production goals to satisfy the demands of export markets, more employees had to be hired. However, because of the lag between market upswing (a reflection of the inherent seasonal nature of the motor cycle trade) and the time required to recruit and train the additional labour, there always seemed to be too many workers present long after they were needed.

For example, over the period 1964 to 1971, the total labour force increased from 1,949 to 3,292, but in between the numbers fluctuated as demand for motor cycles rose and fell. The company's best year was 1968/69 when the labour force, now 42 per cent larger than three years before, produced 59 per cent more motor cycles. But thereafter, production kept on dropping at the same time as the labour force actually grew. By 1971 the ratio between the 31,045 motor cycles built to the over 3,000 employees was obviously unsustainable, and major cuts to the workforce were inevitable, a situation that was compounded by a disastrous new model line-up, a development that will be examined more closely in the next chapter.[100]

It was at roughly this time that the workers at Small Heath started to become far more militant than before. Possibly this was an indication of demoralisation among the workforce as they saw the BSA Group slip further and further into financial distress and their markets steadily being eroded by foreign competitors. It might also have been caused by a growing jealousy or resentment towards their counterparts at the Triumph factory in Meriden who always seemed to enjoy better pay than they did. Whatever the cause, the trade unions' reaction to the redundancies that took place in 1971 was unprecedented. True, there had been at least one strike during the spring of 1969 after the company announced it would contract out case-making and motor cycle packing.[101] Now, as BSA's predicament became more acute, plans to cut back the workforce started to be implemented.

In October 1971, the news that BSA would soon make a number of Small Heath factory workers redundant was broken to the local trade union leadership by the Group Chairman Eric Turner himself. According to Turner, the shop stewards were 'a bit taken aback' by his advice that they were about to lose up to two-thirds of their membership before Christmas.[102] In fact, a fair amount of preparation at the highest levels of the company had gone into planning these severe cuts to the workforce. The BSA Group board was especially conscious of the current 'work-in' being conducted by employees of the Upper Clyde Shipyards (UCS) and feared similar industrial action at BSA.[103] Indeed, BSA went as far as to engage the services of a personnel consultant to devise strategies to ensure that a similar work-in would not occur in their factory.[104]

Within a few days of the announcement of the redundancies, it did appear as if the BSA shop stewards might organise some form of resistance to the job cuts. George Wright, West Midlands District Secretary for the TGWU, organised a mass meeting of the shop stewards which was addressed by Moss Evans, the TGWU's General Secretary. Plans were made to create joint liaison committees with the Birmingham Trades Council and with regional committees of the TUC and the CSEU. The stewards also enlisted the assistance of Birmingham area Labour MPs Denis Howell (Small Heath), Roy Hattersley (Sparkbrook) and the Shadow Chancellor Roy Jenkins (Stechford) to help with lobbying on their behalf at Parliament and in Whitehall.[105]

Stories began to appear in the local press highlighting the plight of the about-to-be redundant BSA workers. A protest rally, attended by nearly all 5,000 BSA employees who had booked off work three hours before the end of their shifts, was staged in a nearby park. At the rally, a union official told the assembled workers that a UCS type work-in might possibly be the best answer to the threat facing the factory. However, most of the focus of action was placed on continuing discussions with the EEF, at a set of labour–management conferences being then conducted in York and by working through political channels.[106]

A few days later, calls for a work-in became increasingly insistent as it appeared more and more obvious that BSA was in serious trouble and that the first redundancy notices were imminent. At another mass rally held on 21 October, the Chairman of the Joint Shop Stewards Committee openly called for workers to reject their redundancy notices, the first 1,000 of which were due to be issued any day, and instead to occupy the Small Heath factory. TGWU General Secretary Moss Evans, who also attended the meeting, later declared that 'the lads have decided that they reject these redundancies and there is going to be a scrap'. It looked as if a major labour–management confrontation could happen at any time.

Yet all the talk of fighting on came to an abrupt end just two weeks later. A special trade union meeting held to discuss an action plan degenerated into chaos, and the BSA workers failed to support their local leadership by either occupying the factory or launching a full-scale strike. Instead, they voted by a margin of nine to one to accept the employers' redundancy payments and walk away from their jobs at the factory.[107] Why this happened remains unclear. The TGWU convenor later claimed that the employer cleverly played off different classes of workers by age group and job category and that the unions were unable to maintain solidarity.[108]

It may be true that the internal dissension and the long-established moderation of the BSA workers were the main reasons for the collapse of the nascent militancy. However, one cannot discount the tough, uncompromising message that came from the new Group Chairman Lord Hartley Shawcross who had only just replaced his predecessor Eric Turner. 'The situation is looking very grave,' he advised the workers; either they must co-operate with the company 'or we go into liquidation'. Shawcross claimed that he would soon be approaching Sir John Eden, the Minister of Trade and Industry, as well as the Barclays Bank in order secure further funding, but should there any strike or work-in, these negotiations would be scuttled. If that happened, he warned, then not just Small Heath but the entire BSA Group would go under. Better that 3,000 jobs be phased out now than all 9,000 later on.[109]

Labour peace may have been re-established at BSA, and indeed the factory would remain open, albeit with a drastically reduced workforce, for a while longer. Yet, as the following chapter will explain, the company's problems were very definitely not resolved and its future was highly uncertain.

CHAPTER SEVEN
The collapse of the British motor cycle industry, 1960–1975

T HE PROBLEM of labour militancy might only have been an on-going preoccupation for one firm in the industry – Triumph – but all of the British motor cycle manufacturers would soon feel a much more fundamental threat in the form of a new flood of imports. This began at the end of 1962, when a trade agreement was signed between Britain and Japan which threw open the home market to foreign competition of unprecedented intensity. By 1971, even with increased exports to North America, the BSA/Triumph combine remained unsteadily on its feet, standing along side Norton-Villiers, a newer company that incorporated what remained of the now-defunct AMC concern. However, instead of trying to consolidate its tenuous position in the home and export markets, BSA launched a risky counter-attack designed to regain market share, especially in the light-weight model category. The programme was both badly misjudged and executed, and ultimately resulted in disaster for BSA.

Whirlwind out of Japan

In the early 1960s, while the British motor cycle industry struggled with the trade recession, the danger from the Far East was about to strike. It actually took some time before British motor cycle producers became aware of developments in Japan, although one British enthusiasts' journal had published a review of a Japanese motor cycle as early as 1946.[1] Indeed, for many years Japan lagged far behind Britain in both motor cycle production and usage. In the early 1920s, for example, when there were already over 250,000 motor cycles in use on British roads, there were barely 3,000 in Japan.[2] And, before 1939, Japan's tiny handful of motor cycle producers was barely known elsewhere and, moreover, highly dependent on foreign designs and manufacturing technology. In fact, for years after 1932, the leading producer, Rikuo, built American designed Harley-Davidson models under licence at its Tokyo factory. Overall national output during the inter-war period rarely exceeded 2,000 units per year; imports dominated the home market for much of the time; and virtually no Japanese motor cycles were exported.[3] Indeed, the industry was so marginal that it was not even mentioned in the post-war US Strategic Bombing Survey.[4]

However, within several years after 1945, the Japanese motor cycle industry had expanded dramatically to consist of nearly 200 firms, albeit mostly small volume manufacturers, some barely more than backyard or garage-based assembly operations with monthly outputs of fewer than 100 units.[5] By 1950 the industry had essentially split into three segments. The largest was composed of these numerous small manufacturers. A smaller portion of the industry was made up of surviving pre-war dedicated manufacturers such as Rikuo and Meguro and also some new entries such as the Lilac company. These firms built larger, more orthodox motor cycles which, if not always direct copies, were still strongly influenced by foreign, particularly European, designs.[6]

The third part of the industry was composed of aircraft companies such as Mitsubishi and Fuji Industries (formerly Nakajima Aircraft Co. and later Subaru Motors), which had been pushed out of the aviation field by the American occupation authorities and subsequently switched over to scooter manufacturing. These companies would ultimately drop motorised two-wheelers and move on to 'mini' car production during the late 1950s and early 1960s.[7]

A large proportion of the post-war Japanese industry was based in the Nagoya City–Hamamatsu area, the Japanese equivalent of Britain's Midlands, where skilled labour and a supplier network were available largely because of the presence of the Toyota Motor Company. However, as the post-war motor cycle industry expanded far more quickly than its automobile counterpart, new suppliers had to be developed independently. Once established, these ultimately benefited the automobile industry when it entered a period of rapid growth after the mid-1960s.[8]

During the early 1950s, as demand for motor cycles steadily grew, other firms, backed by greater financial and engineering resources, entered the industry. Suzuki (textile looms) Yamaha (musical instruments) and Tohatsu (small engines) created motor cycle subsidiaries and soon became leading producers. Then there were firms such as Meihatsu (a subsidiary of Kawasaki Aircraft) which built proprietary engines used by the scores of small companies who lacked the resources to make their own motor units. Later on Kawasaki would go into full motor cycle manufacturing for itself.

There was also a marked influence exercised by former Japanese aircraft companies in the post-war motor cycle industry. Not only did some of them take up making two-wheelers, but the influx of highly gifted war-time aviation engineers such as Yoshio Nakamura, who later became a vice-president of Honda Motor, was very important for motor cycle and scooter producers.[9] As noted earlier, a similar phenomenon also occurred in post-war Germany and Italy.

The rapid growth of the Japanese motor cycle industry would clearly not have been possible without the strong and continually expanding home market demand for motor cycles, mopeds and scooters, a point which distinguishes the Japanese motor cycle industry from its future international competitors, particularly Britain. While total industry output was only 7,500 units in 1950, five years later it had grown to more than a quarter million and then reached nearly 1.5 million in 1960, this at a time when both British motor cycle production and usage were stagnating.

This demand was generated by a combination of factors including relatively scarce and expensive automobiles, high-priced petrol, narrow urban streets and restricted space for parking motor vehicles, as well as low, albeit steadily increasing, consumer income levels. Government policy also encouraged the increased use of motorised two-wheelers through loose licensing regulations and low tax rates. In response, motor cycle, scooter and moped use exploded in Japan, particularly between 1955 and 1960, when it soared from one million to three million road registrations.[10]

However, despite such favourable regulations, for the most part and in distinct contrast to their automotive counterparts, motor cycle producers were treated with what amounted to benign neglect by the Japanese government. They were not, for example, covered by policy initiatives such as the 1955 Ministry of International Trade and Industry 'People's Car' White Paper which had tried to encourage automobile companies to build smaller-sized cars.

Nor was there any effort made by the government to rationalise this disorganised, highly competitive industry or encourage it to seek technical tie-ups with foreign firms. Instead, motor cycle producers were for the most part left alone to follow their own paths, although they did benefit directly from the many protective measures which the Japanese government implemented after 1952 in order to create a more self-sufficient economic base. These included tight currency exchange controls as well as steep tariff rates and restrictive import quotas, much, as noted in chapter five, to the great chagrin and loud protest of British motor cycle companies who tried, repeatedly and unsuccessfully, to gain entry to the Japanese market.

Motor cycle makers such as Honda and Suzuki also gained significant advantage by way of access to foreign designs and manufacturing technology which was facilitated and encouraged by agencies such as the US Technical Assistance Programme and the Japan Productivity Centre.[11] Mr Honda, for example, went to Europe not only to study advances in the German motor cycle industry but also to visit the Volkswagen automobile plant, one of the leading innovators in mass production technologies. Mr Suzuki himself led a tour sponsored by the Japan Management Association to the USA and Europe during 1955, and Honda Motor Co. conducted several other independent overseas visits of its own.[12]

In another instance of motor cycle technology transfer, Yamaha, like firms in Britain, the USA and the USSR, made free use of successful pre-war German designs. There is no question that a number of firms in the Japanese motor cycle industry acquired at least some design and manufacturing know-how from abroad. What is harder to determine is the significance of these acquisitions for their subsequent rapid development. The case of Yamaha Motor Company highlights the issues involved with technology transfer.

Yamaha was a comparatively late entrant to the industry and only began building motor cycles in a former war-time aircraft propeller factory during 1955. The company's first motor cycle, the YA-1 (the so-called Red Dragonfly), was more or less a direct copy of the German DKW RT-125 which the company had received under somewhat murky circumstances. However, as noted in chapter three, BSA also used this design, as did the American firm Harley-Davidson which they had both received from the Germans via the official post-war Reparations Programme.[13]

However, in this case the point is less how the design was acquired but rather what the three companies did with it. BSA and Harley-Davidson used theirs as the two companies' standard light-weight models from 1948 onwards, although very few substantial improvements were ever incorporated during either of their lengthy production lives. Indeed, it was actually BSA's single best-selling model (sold under the name Bantam; Harley-Davidson called their version the Hummer), and the British company was still cranking them out, fundamentally unchanged, some 20 years later.

Yamaha, on the other hand, only produced the YA-1 for a fairly brief period of time and then quickly moved on to manufacture more advanced models. By 1957 it had introduced the YD1, a motor cycle with a larger, more powerful engine as well as other features which made it a significant improvement over the original YA-1. In essence, Yamaha used foreign technology more as a starting point or springboard for further development rather than, as had BSA and Harley-Davidson, a cheap substitute for serious motor cycle research and development and, for all intents and purposes, an end in itself.

Yamaha also bought up more established Japanese motor cycle companies in order to acquire their skilled labour and design staff and thereby strengthen its position in the highly competitive Japanese market. By the late 1950s, for example, it had absorbed several other firms including Showa and Queen Rocket and had become, along with Honda Motor, one of Japan's leading motor cycle manufacturers.[14]

Yamaha needed all the help it could get in order to keep up with the rapid pace of its competitors. By 1960 the structure of the industry had been radically altered. In the face of fierce domestic competition, there had been such severe attrition and consolidation that fewer than a dozen firms of any consequence remained. Ten years later only four firms, Honda, Kawasaki, Suzuki and Yamaha had survived, a situation that prevails to the present day.[15]

Honda Motor, by far the most successful of these small firms, had started up specifically to build motor cycles and other motorised two-wheelers, and soon became the industry's leading firm. It was founded in 1948 by Soichiro Honda, a self-educated engineer and former piston-ring maker who, before and during the war, had supplied Toyota as well as the aviation industry. Like the other smaller operations, his first machines were essentially just bicycles powered by tiny 'clip-on' engines. Unlike the rest of the competition, Honda soon began work on other models of far greater technical sophistication.[16]

In 1949 Honda introduced the 98 cc Dream, and progress thereafter was rapid, although the company did not produce any model with an engine capacity greater than 250 cc until 1955.[17] The company also enjoyed the advantage of particularly effective senior management. The unique combination of Soichiro Honda's engineering brilliance and his business partner Takeo Fujisawa's remarkably astute financial and marketing skills made them, after a fashion, the Japanese motor cycle industry's answer to American automobile industry leaders Henry Ford and Alfred Sloan.

Although Honda, a former automobile racer, was fascinated with motor sports, because of the state of the Japanese economy the company focused production on a limited range of light-weight models (for many years their largest machine had a 305 cc capacity engine) used mostly for utilitarian purposes. In 1958 Honda took a huge step forward and introduced the 50 cc Supercub, which came equipped as standard with advanced features such as an automatic clutch that could not be found on any British motor cycle. Although, strictly speaking, a motor cycle, this model had a 'step-through' design which made it look more like a motorised bicycle and was especially appealing to female customers. The Supercub was hugely successful, at home and abroad, helping Honda to consolidate its position as Japan's leading motor cycle manufacturer. Out of the 285,000 machines built by Honda during 1959, 168,000 were Supercubs.[18]

This progress being made in Japan did not go entirely unnoticed in Britain. As early as 1952, columnist Francis Jones warned of the threat posed by the rapidly developing Japanese motor cycle industry. Jones approved of the manufacturing strategy that was being followed by Japanese firms. In contrast to the British, they had avoided production of the 'high-performance motor cycle' in favour of light-weight models, a policy which he labelled 'sound business'. Yet Jones, as usual, was exceptional in his views. Many more observers were dismissive of Japanese competition. At around the same time, Bill Johnson, Triumph's distributor in California, acknowledged that, while some Japanese motor cycles had already appeared in American showrooms, they should not be taken 'too seriously'. His views were mirrored in Britain. Indeed, in contrast with their intense curiosity about German motor cycle manufacturing during the 1950s, the Industries' Association did not commission even a single report about the state of the Japanese industry.[19]

In 1957 columnist Francis Jones had become concerned enough by subsequent developments to issue another warning to British manufacturers. Not only were Japanese motor cycle companies well established, they were now 'even beginning to show originality, and the products are no longer copies of European models'. Furthermore, he declared, it was time to discard outmoded cultural stereotypes: 'British makers can no longer treat Japanese competition as a joke, in the way they used to do. It has got past that stage and must now be taken seriously.'[20] Once again his warnings were ignored.

Because home demand was so strong, the Japanese presence overseas built up gradually. During 1958 the Japanese industry was already capable of producing approximately 400,000 mostly light-weight motor cycles per year, and in 1960 Honda built a new factory with a capacity of 30,000 units per month.[21] That same year, the Japanese created the foundation for their subsequent dominance abroad. As the Boston Consulting Group report observed years later, having 'developed huge production volumes in small motor cycles in their domestic market', the resulting economies of scale led to cost reductions which put them in a highly advantageous position, one which they would soon exploit to the full.[22]

Then, in 1959, the Honda factory team, following a string of successes on Japanese racetracks, made its first appearance at the Isle of Man TT, competing in the light-weight 125 cc class. Greeted at first with what was termed 'polite derision', the Honda machines finished in comparatively poor positions. The following year they returned and won all positions between first and tenth place.[23] Shortly afterwards, an unnamed British company reportedly procured a light-weight Honda for examination. According to its Managing Director, the results of the investigation were highly disturbing:

When we stripped the machine it was so good it frightened us. It was made like a watch and was not a copy of anything. It was the product of original thinking, and it was very good thinking.[24]

British motor cycle manufacturers were now aware of the impending danger but still took no action. However, whether or not they were ready to face it, a new threat had emerged, this one created by their own government.

The 1962 Anglo-Japanese Treaty

What particularly worried the British manufacturers were rumours of upcoming changes to trading relations between Britain and Japan. In fact, negotiations between the two governments had been in progress since 1955 with the aim of liberalising their import restrictions/regulations. In late 1959, the Industries' Association was informed by the Board of Trade that it would shortly commence discussions with the Japanese government for the purpose of concluding a bilateral trade agreement.[25] Several months later, BSA's motor cycle chief Edward Turner informed members of an Industries' Association Council meeting that he had heard news of a concessionaire canvassing dealers around Britain to discover whether or not they would carry Japanese motor cycles. This unwelcome information was worsened by the fact that the Industries' Association was unable to prevent dealers from selling imported products, thanks to the recent dissolution of long-standing trading agreements, implemented because of advice that they were now illegal under the Restrictive Practices Act.[26]

In July 1960 Palin sent out a report to inform members that an interim trade agreement between Britain and Japan had just been concluded which was designed to promote greater trade between the two countries. He admitted that it contained a provision liberalising motor cycle and bicycle imports which had come as a 'bombshell'. A 'strongly worded' letter had already been sent to the President of the Board of Trade about the lack of prior consultation.[27] Subsequently, Palin discovered that the new agreement, which also contained a £100,000 quota clause for imports of scooters and mopeds, failed to provide a definition of either vehicle. It was now feared the Japanese might take advantage of this omission to increase their exports. At a Council meeting held in July 1960, members discussed the agreement and condemned the government's failure to consult with them beforehand. Palin was instructed to arrange for a meeting with President of the Board of Trade Reginald Maudling as quickly as possible.[28]

Maudling subsequently acknowledged the 'dissatisfaction' expressed by several British industries about the increased import liberalisation. He agreed that 'some industries would face increased competition' but added that he was 'confident that there would be no risk of a flood of imports from Japan'. True, it would be easier for the Japanese to export to Britain, but the agreement would give British exports 'new opportunities' which, he claimed, 'on balance, would be of substantial advantage to the UK'.[29] Palin met with Maudling shortly afterwards, in the company of representatives from the photographic, toy and sewing machine industries, who were equally enraged about the interim trade agreement. At the end of that meeting, Maudling was forced to concede that 'consultation with various Industries had not taken place and it would perhaps have been better if it had'. In future, he promised, the government would be more co-operative.[30] Palin for one was not reassured. In a report sent out to members in November 1960, he stated that the trade agreement was a 'major blunder'.[31]

Why had the British government not consulted with the industry before concluding the interim agreement with the Japanese? Having met with 'many senior Board of Trade officials', Palin concluded that, unlike British manufacturers, 'they really had no conception of the size or importance of the Japan [sic] Motor Cycle Industry, and could not believe they could constitute a serious threat to us'.[32] In the meantime, however, the Industries' Association would try and press the government to impose a quota on motor cycle imports in place of the current loosening of import restrictions.[33]

Was the British motor cycle industry, however, justified in being so critical of the British government's alleged failure to represent its interests? The fact was that the industry itself had not done much to prepare for Japanese competition, despite warnings in the trade press. In mid-1960, concerned by the increasing activity of the Japanese in various export markets, BSA had dispatched Edward Turner, then still a Group Board member and Managing Director of the Automotive (soon to be retitled the Motor Cycle Division), to Japan to conduct an on-the-spot investigation.

His report, dated 26 September 1960, must have caused some disquiet among his fellow directors. Turner, who toured the Honda, Suzuki and Yamaha factories, was much impressed with what he saw, both in terms of yearly output (now over a million units in total) and the quality of their products. Indeed, he noted that the very scale of the Honda factory alone, which by then produced approximately a quarter million units per year (compared to 140,000 for the entire British industry) was far ahead of anything he had ever previously encountered, with plant and equipment considerably more automated than its BSA counterpart at Small Heath. Having reviewed their operations, Turner qualified what he had seen by stating that it must 'borne in mind that we have not now nor ever have had, the quantities of any one product which would justify these highly desirable methods being used'.[34]

However, while still in Japan, Turner was also quoted in the Japanese press as claiming that he thought the situation there, particularly its burgeoning motor cycle market, was unique. In Turner's opinion, that was why there was little likelihood companies such as Honda would be able to sell their products abroad in any appreciable quantities. Yet, within a very short time the Japanese motor cycle industry generally, and Honda Motor in particular, would confound Turner's assessment by launching a stunningly successful export drive, starting in North America and then quickly moving on to Britain itself.[35]

Turner's brief for his visit had been to gather information on the Japanese industry, in order to enable BSA and Triumph 'to plan counter measures to try and preserve our own share in the motor cycle world markets'. It is unclear, however, just how his report, which made no concrete suggestions for action, was received by the BSA Group Board. Presumably, as a senior Group Board member and long-time motor cycle expert, any recommendations from Edward Turner on how to respond to developments in Japan would have been given the most serious consideration by his colleagues. Yet no action would be initiated for another several years, a critical period when the Japanese began to consolidate their hold on markets previously dominated by British manufacturers.[36]

For its part, during the trade negotiations with the Japanese, the British government had its own priorities which did not always take into account the interests of the industries potentially affected. The perspectives of ministers and civil servants were coloured by the consideration that Anglo-Japanese trade 'had begun to assume much more importance … in view of the remarkable progress of the Japanese economy'.[37] When, for example, the President of the Board of Trade visited Japan in April 1962, he was informed by his own advisors that there was 'little doubt that scope exists for a substantial increase in trade between the UK and Japan in future'. Specifically, there were 'considerable opportunities for the sale of machinery of all kinds' such as machine tools, office machinery, chemicals and radar. The problem was that an increase in Anglo-Japanese trade might not benefit everyone.[38]

Indeed, motor cycle manufacturers might have felt a bit alarmed had they been aware of certain remarks the President of the Board of Trade had made before a meeting of the Japan-British Society in Osaka in May 1962. The speech, which referred generally to the desirability of increasing trade between the two countries, included the following statement:

> It is certainly not our policy to preserve uncompetitive industries as monuments to Britain's industrial past. We recognise that with constant technological changes, rising labour costs and the growth of production in other countries, some branches of industry are bound to decline because they are no longer competitive. Our future lies in developing new industries, particularly those which call for high technological skill, and not in seeking to protect those which are out of date or no longer economic.[39]

The goal of increased trade in general with Japan was also shared by Federation of British Industries Director-General Norman Kipping, who had made his own visit there only several months earlier. Before he left Britain, he had been informed by the Board of Trade that the price of liberalising trade with Japan might be 'materially affected by the treatment of Japanese imports in this country'.[40] Once in Japan, Kipping visited a number of enterprises, including Honda Motor and, like Edward Turner before him, was greatly impressed by the advanced state of its factory and equipment. He was also struck by the potential market for British exports but was equally concerned about the implications of Japan's sizeable trade deficit with Britain.[41] As a direct result of Kipping's tour, the FBI commissioned an in-depth report on Japan by the Economist Intelligence Unit, which was published in April 1962. Among other things, the report examined the Japanese motor cycle industry and confirmed both Kipping and Turner's assessments about its output and quality. It also singled out Japanese motor cycle models for special praise, noting that they incorporated 'original design features ... [which] are showing competitive strength internationally'.[42]

The formal trade agreement was officially signed in London during mid-November 1962, in the presence of both Prime Ministers Harold Macmillan and Hayato Ikeda. Government officials discounted fears of undue Japanese competition on the home market as 'exaggerated'.[43] The treaty did provide two safeguards against what was termed 'disruptive competition'. One allowed either signatory party to re-impose restrictions should it be shown that imports had arrived 'in such increased quantities and under such conditions as to cause or threaten serious injury to producers of like or competitive products'. The other was a list of so-called 'sensitive items' which needed continuing protection against open competition for a period of three years after the treaty came into force. The items on this list included certain yarns and fabrics, radio and television components and pottery goods. Inexplicably, it did not include motor cycles, scooters and mopeds.[44] The FBI released a statement on the day of signing which welcomed the treaty, on the grounds that it contained 'many good features'. However, it also cautioned that there were 'some [clauses] which caused misgivings'. For its part, the National Union of Manufacturers expressed certain 'reservations' about the treaty.[45]

Japanese imports arrive in Britain

The results of gradual liberalisation of Anglo-Japanese trade after 1960 were soon apparent. In September 1960, during a meeting of manufacturers and retailers' representatives, concern was already being expressed about a 'considerable number of Japanese machines' entering the home market, even though the first Honda Supercub was only sold that November.[46] Later the following year, Hugh Palin informed members of the Industries' Association that, while 464 Japanese motor cycle imports had arrived during 1960, between January and August 1961 alone they had more than doubled to 1,274. Palin noted that the increase was 'particularly remarkable as it occurred at a time when the home trade was very depressed, and when total imports of motor cycles, mopeds and scooters were down by as much as 60 per cent on 1960'.[47]

The threat was now recognised even at the most senior levels of the industry. During his address to the 1961 BSA Group Annual General Meeting, Chairman Eric Turner acknowledged that foreign competition, particularly from the Japanese, 'is growing and the effect is now being felt more than at any other time since the war', although he did not say anything about what BSA was going to do about it.[48] Despite the sales recession, a Honda company representative claimed in late 1961 that Western Europe was 'still the world's largest market for mopeds, motor cycles and scooters'. Afterwards the company announced that it was setting up an assembly plant in Belgium capable of producing 10,000 light-weight machines per month – or nearly the equivalent output of the entire British motor cycle industry.[49]

Honda's sales effort in Britain was put under the direction of J.E. Harrisson, who had been hired away from Raleigh Industries, where he had been a senior manager responsible for moped sales. By June 1963, Harrisson and his marketing team claimed that the Honda Supercub was selling so well that it now represented 40 per cent of sales in the light-weight category. Indeed, in only a few months, overall turnover of the Supercub had increased by nearly 100 per cent, a virtually unprecedented achievement and one that did 'not go unnoticed' by retailers around the country. So successful was Honda's sales campaign that one business journal remarked that it proved the prolonged motor cycle recession was less the result of Purchase Tax and hire/purchase restrictions rather than what it termed 'producer inaction'. Honda, by contrast, 'has clearly discovered an unexploited market where at the moment there are few competitors'.[50]

The Industries' Association's first response to the arrival of Japanese motor cycles was to try and prevent would-be retailers from carrying the imports. In April 1961, for example, a Coventry department store, Owen and Owen, displayed a Honda motor cycle in its front window. An irate Hugh Palin thereupon phoned and successfully convinced store management to remove the offending imported machine.[51] However, many more dealers refused to be intimidated by pressure from British manufacturers. One, for example, wrote a letter to the *Motor Cycle and Cycle Trader* full of praise for Honda's British sales operation. 'Honda has hit,' he maintained, 'the high spots in every direction and from the dealers' point of view has created a new stimulus to the whole two-wheeled business which has been lacking for so long.' His enthusiasm was not an isolated instance.[52]

Actress Charlotte Rampling appears delighted with her 1965 vintage light-weight Honda motor cycle. While few, if any, women bought the larger more powerful British-built motor cycles that were the industry's bread and butter, many more could be seen riding the smaller Japanese models such as this one.

© MOTOR CYCLE INDUSTRY ASSOCIATION OF GREAT BRITAIN

Early in 1963 the FBI created a Working Party on the Anglo-Japanese Commercial Treaty in order to monitor Japanese imports and collect evidence for a possible application to activate the Safeguard Clause. It was chaired by R.F.K. Belchem, who had been hired in 1959 to work directly with then BSA chairman Jack Sangster and was still a senior executive with the company. Upon questioning by other committee members present, including Hugh Palin, Belchem admitted that the FBI had not been consulted by the Board of Trade about how the Safeguard Clause would operate.[53] Shortly afterwards, Palin expressed his concern about the clause's future effectiveness. It was true that repeated assurances had been issued by the Board of Trade, pledging that vulnerable British industries would be protected against 'disruptive' Japanese competition. However, as Palin later wrote to motor cycle manufacturers, it was 'far from clear how the Government defines the degree of injury that must be suffered before action can be taken' nor did he know 'precisely what is meant by "disruptive"'.[5]

During the spring of 1963, the industry watched with growing dismay as more Japanese light-weight motor cycles, mostly Honda 50 cc Supercubs, flooded into the home market. Some 4,270 had arrived in 1962, but by July 1963, with full liberalisation now in force, this number had swollen to some 28,454 (see table 25). That autumn Palin informed Industries' Association members that, despite the large numbers of imports, it might not be possible to lodge a formal protest with the Board of Trade. The industry must first, Palin explained, 'establish injury or threat of injury, and this is the rub'.[55]

Table 25   *British imports of two-wheeled motorised vehicles, 1955–1966*

	Mopeds	Scooters	Motor cycles	Total
1955	38,000	20,000	2,000	60,000
1956	23,000	25,000	1,000	49,000
1957	38,500	69,000	2,300	109,800
1958	17,500	55,000	1,200	73,700
1959	62,300	109,200	1,536	173,036
1960	48,400	85,800	1,961	136,161
1961	42,411	34,923	4,789	82,123
1962	27,225	33,316	7,402	67,943
1963	70,541	21,197	54,993	146,731
1964	55,809	28,536	102,340	186,685
1965	19,830	23,514	37,952	81,296
1966	7,654	20,879	30,141	58,674

Source: MSS 204/3/1/86 (Modern Records Centre).

Shortly afterwards, during an Industries' Association Council meeting, members heard Association President Edward Turner inform them that he 'doubted whether the Industry could currently make out a very good case so far as Japanese competition was concerned'.[56] He expanded on this pessimistic statement at a subsequent meeting. According to Turner, 'it was perhaps true that the bulk of Japanese imports were of a type of machine which the industry had not hitherto marketed'. Furthermore, he was unable to recommend, as some had evidently urged him to do, that a formal protest be made to the Board of Trade, accusing the Japanese of 'dumping' their machines on to the British market at unrealistically low prices. Again, Turner had to admit that such a protest 'might be difficult to establish as the prices were not altogether unreasonable when one considers the vast volume of production'.[57]

Even with diminishing likelihood of success, Palin kept on hammering away at the Board of Trade to invoke the Safeguard Clause. In December 1963 he arranged to meet with Edward Heath, the newly appointed President of the Board of Trade (and future Prime Minister), to press the industry's case further. However, as Palin advised Industry Association members, he held few hopes for a favourable reception. He had, in fact, already been informed off-the-record by Board officials that 'it will be difficult for us to *prove* injury, or to establish that the decline in British motor cycle production and home sales is due directly to Japanese competition' (emphasis in the original).[58] He then wrote to Belchem to inform him of another meeting with an unnamed Board official, whom he described as 'not very sympathetic'. Palin subsequently wrote once more to Belchem and quoted from a letter he had just received from 'Phillips', another official at the Board, rejecting his arguments for invoking the Safeguard Clause:

> Our general conclusion ... is that the fall in home deliveries of motor cycles this year, during which period Japanese imports have become significant, continues to an established trend and that the Japanese are building up a market which would not otherwise have been exploited by the British industry.[59]

Palin angrily refuted this statement in a further letter to Belchem. He denied that the Japanese had created a new market; rather, what they had done was to encroach on the one already serviced by domestic manufacturers: 'We are quite satisfied that the Japanese machines are not being sold to an entirely new public but to precisely the same people who might otherwise have bought British.' Yet, Palin had to agree that the light-weight Japanese models did attract many British consumers: 'They are attractive and sell at rather a lower price than the cheapest light-weight British motor cycle.'[60]

British consumers desert the industry

Despite repeated rebuffs from the government over import restrictions, the Industries' Association continued to agitate for a relaxation of Purchase Tax.

Cutting this tax, manufacturers stated, would reverse declining sales on the home market and, by implication, make the industry more competitive abroad. This argument continued to be met with scepticism by officials at the Board of Trade. In December 1963, having reviewed a recent Industries' Association brief, one official remarked that while 'many statistics can be adduced to show that exports go up as the home market expands, and decline as it contracts', there were 'obvious limitations' to this line of argument. Cutting Purchase Tax, he continued, 'may not wholly offset a secular [sic] decline in which other factors are at work'.[61]

Shortly afterwards, another Board official expressed his own scepticism about the industry's case. He doubted whether any reduction in Purchase Tax would help improve the sales of motor cycles, the heavy-weight models in particular. As he observed, 'some will doubtless continue to buy these of choice and a reduction in Purchase Tax might stimulate some slight revival in demand. One cannot, however, help feeling that people will tend increasingly to prefer a car as they come to be able to afford one.' On the other hand, the Japanese 'seem to have created something of a new market', and cutting the Purchase Tax would not necessarily help British producers compete with them.[62] Indeed, the Board of Trade was simply not willing to accept the central theme of the industry's submissions, the allegation that the inexpensive Japanese imports somehow represented unfair trading. As another Board official concluded: 'Given the strength of the Japanese and Italian industries, … and the initiative which the Japanese have succeeded in taking in the ultra light weight [50 cc engine capacity class] … it is difficult to accept the industry's case without reservations.' The industry could not expect any help from this quarter.[63]

At least one British motor cycle retailer shared the conclusions reached by civil servants. Writing in to a trade journal, a dealer from Wigan, Lancashire, explained why he thought British consumers had been buying the imports in such quantities. The fact was, he wrote, that 'British designers have little idea of how to combat the Honda and Suzuki machines'. Citing the BSA 75 cc Beagle, this dealer insisted that the specifications of domestically produced machines were simply not good enough to match the foreign competition. The latter came standard with, among other things, better suspension, a speedometer, legshields, and more attractive chrome styling. The dealer held little hope for the future of British machines: 'I have given the Beagle prominence in our window display but Wiganers are just not interested.'[64] Shortly afterwards, another BSA light-weight model proved equally unsuccessful. This time the company actually tried to compete directly with the Honda Supercub when it introduced the Ariel-badged 50 cc Pixie. Sales of the small Ariel were so poor that it only appeared between 1964 and 1965 before being permanently withdrawn from the market.[65]

The relative merits of British and Japanese motor cycles were fiercely

BSA Beagles hot off the production line being readied for despatch to retailers sometime during the early 1960s. Market response for these light-weight models was poor. The Beagle came out a distant second best in comparison to Japanese bikes such as the Honda Supercub.
© BSA OWNERS CLUB

debated among enthusiasts around Britain. In one instance, the newsletter of a motor cycle club in Kent reported an exchange between supporters of both national producers. Partisans of Japanese machines seemed to be in the majority. Not only could they point to successes on the racetrack, but in comparisons of performance and design the British motor cycles lost out time and again. The Hondas had better brakes, an electric starter was standard, and they were far more reliable. As one enthusiast described it: 'Until one has ridden a Japanese bike, one doesn't know how wonderfully superb they are.'[66]

Industry solidarity is shattered

Then, in July 1963, a major British manufacturer joined the stampede to buy Japanese motor cycles. AMC, which had been conducting secret negotiations with Suzuki, succeeded in gaining the distribution rights for their light-weight models throughout Britain. The news of the agreement, which came as a complete surprise to Palin and virtually everyone else in the industry, created great consternation, being the first time a significant British manufacturer had co-operated with a foreign rival on the home market. Such a split among manufacturers now ensured the impossibility of a united position on imports.[67]

For its part, AMC argued that such an arrangement with a Japanese producer was inevitable and necessary for its continuing survival. In his address at the subsequent shareholders' meeting, Chairman Hulbert stated that the distribution agreement was 'reached only after the most careful consideration of the many problems involved'. It was the expanding light-weight motor cycle market which showed real potential, not the traditional heavyweights which AMC had specialised in manufacturing over the years. As Hulbert informed the shareholders:

> The products [Suzuki imports] are of a type which have not been developed or promoted to any extent by the British industry for the very good reason that the total demand in this country could never warrant the heavy investment required to produce a comparably priced product. Once accepting the fact that the vast Japanese home market confers such immense benefits in product costs that it is impossible for British manufacturers to compete, it is then a logical step to develop the type of distribution undertaken by your company in support of its traditional British motor cycle products which are sold in Home and export markets.[68]

The implications of the AMC–Suzuki deal were soon felt at the Industries' Association. During the October Council meeting, the AMC representative present made it very clear that his company would oppose any further move to convince the Board of Trade to impose import restrictions. Not only did the Industries' Association fail to make such an application, but thereafter the entire issue became a closed subject. Several months later, when the managing director of a small all-British light-weight motor cycle manufacturer inquired about what was being done about increasing numbers of imports, Palin admitted that the Industries' Association was powerless. Now that AMC was involved in retailing and promoting Japanese motor cycles in the home market, the Association ceased to refer to the matter in order to avoid aggravating any further internal splits.[69] Nor would the Board of Trade help. 'We are doing all we can,' Palin declared, '[but] ... making no headway at all and it seems pretty clear that the present Government is committed to a liberal trade policy and only a severe bout of unemployment would, I believe, shift them.'[70]

The industry regains respectability

Although their domestic sales had not revived, industry leaders believed that there was a marked improvement in the image of motor cycling in Britain, irrespective of the origin of the machines. In mid-1964, Hugh Palin reported to Industry Association members that, thanks to their publicity work, the so-called 'Mods and Rockers' phenomenon, which 'could so easily have developed into an anti-motor cycle and anti-scooter campaign', had not done so, a fact he attributed to 'a reflection of the much better public relations which now exist in relation to two-wheelers'.[71] Shortly afterwards, Hugh Palin was invited to a school in Shrewsbury, to witness the presentation of a motor cycle to the headmaster as part of an initiative to instigate a motor cycle and scooter training scheme. As Palin later informed industry leaders, he had been 'tremendously impressed' by the 'significance of this occasion for the future of the industry'. Recalling how, 'only a few years ago', motor cycling had been looked upon 'by many as an undesirable activity, you can perhaps imagine my feelings sitting on the platform of this modern school, before an assembly of all 700 pupils, and listening to the Chairman of the School Governors extolling the virtues of the motor cycle and the value of training on two wheels'. If this was the trend of public opinion, then the industry's publicity campaign was finally showing results. The problem was that, although motor cycling enjoyed an improved image, the public had largely stopped buying British-produced motor cycles.[72]

Japan's export drive reaches North America

The one place British motor cycles did continue to sell in substantial numbers was North America, but there too the Japanese had made their mark. Japanese machines first appeared on the west coast in the late 1950s, several years before they entered the British market.[73] Subsequently, Japanese exports to the USA and Canada grew rapidly. A report prepared in 1961 noted that, during 1958, 2,000 motor cycles had left Japan for the US, and this total had jumped to 8,000 in 1960, a development which was termed 'particularly menacing' for British importers. This was simply the beginning. In 1962, 25,000 machines, mainly Honda 50 cc Supercubs, arrived at American destinations and the following year this number soared to 100,000.[74] Ironically, the Japanese did not have to worry about import restrictions, thanks to the successful case made by British manufacturers to the US Tariff Commission nearly ten years before.

By 1962, one American enthusiasts' journal observed that a 'cold draft of Japanese competition has sent a shiver through the ranks of the [British] industry with both home and export sales in the decline'. While the British blamed much of their poor sales at home on restrictive legislation, from the perspective of American consumers, the problems were more to do with the kind of models the British were selling. Not only were there 'too many machines to choose from', but if they wanted to hold on to their share of the market, they 'must redesign models that will appeal to the general public in neatness, efficiency and above all quietness'. In the absence of such changes, their hold on the loyalty of American motor cyclists might not last as long as British manufacturers expected.[75]

Honda, in particular, exploited its initial advantage by launching an advertising campaign more extensive and better funded than any that had ever been attempted before by either the British or American industries. In 1962 Honda hired a professional advertising company expressly to devise a change in the image of the motor cycle as 'a plaything for juvenile delinquents'. The campaign, which cost an unprecedented US$2,000,000, was headlined by the slogan, 'You meet the nicest people on a Honda' and, in another break with orthodoxy, appeared in a number of popular magazines such as *Life*, *The Saturday Evening Post* and *Playboy*. As Honda's 1963 Annual Report put it, their intention was to follow a 'policy of selling, not primarily to confirmed motor cyclists but rather to members of the public who had never before given a second thought to a motor cycle'.[76]

As in Britain, the boom in the North American light-weight motor cycle market was led by the Honda Supercub. During 1963, for example, out of

C-100 Honda Supercub. In the early years Japanese motor cycle companies often copied British and other foreign manufacturers, but by the late 1950s this had changed dramatically. The Supercub was uniquely Japanese, brilliantly designed as well as technologically advanced.

© HONDA

a total of 149,147 imports, 50,252 were less than 50 cc displacement, 15,573 larger than 250 cc and 83,322 between 50 and 250 cc.[77] Whether or not by design, even sales of the far larger British machines were pulled along by the momentum developed by the Japanese sales campaign. The result was increased popularity for the heavyweights, and as one British newspaper reported: 'novices who probably never would have become customers for British machines' moved up to the larger more powerful BSAs, Triumphs and Nortons once they tired of the smaller Hondas.[78] (See table 26.)

Table 26   *US total motor cycle registrations, 1945–1980*

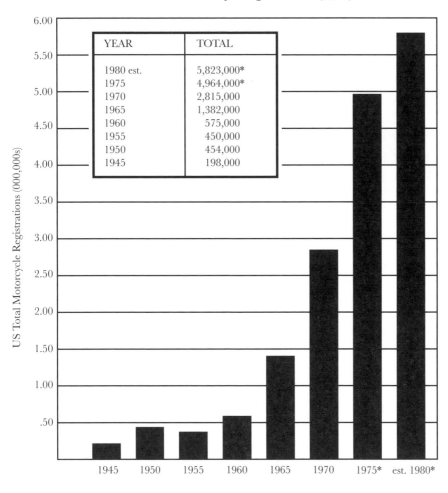

YEAR	TOTAL
1980 est.	5,823,000*
1975	4,964,000*
1970	2,815,000
1965	1,382,000
1960	575,000
1955	450,000
1950	454,000
1945	198,000

* Total US and several state registration figures for recent years may be inflated due to the implementation of staggered registration renewal systems and off-highway vehicle registration reporting systems, and the reporting of dual registration and titling transactions. No accurate revisions are available at this time.
Source: *1981 Motorcycle Statistics Annual*, Irvine, California, USA: Motor Cycle Industry Council, 1981.

Luciana Paluzzi on the fabulous rocket firing British Motor Cycle made famous in the James Bond thriller – Thunderball.

American film star Steve McQueen frequently represents his country in International motorcycling events – using his powerful British Motor Cycle.

Famous golfer Peter Thompson taking delivery of his new small wheel bicycle.

Riding a rocket-firing BSA: a publicity photograph from the 1965 Bond movie *Thunderball* – the woman pictured is Italian actress Luciana Paluzzi. Thanks in part to this and other films including *The Wild One* and *Easy Rider*, motor cycles became an important part of popular culture during the 1950s and 1960s.

© MOTOR CYCLE INDUSTRY ASSOCIATION OF GREAT BRITAIN

This phenomenon was well appreciated by British motor cycle manufacturers. In 1966 a delegation of industry executives visited North America and observed developments there first-hand. They were deeply impressed by the explosive growth of Japanese imports to the USA in particular, which had increased from 300 in 1959 to 313,200 in 1965. While they found it disturbing that Britain's overall share of the US motor cycle market had declined from 33 per cent (by value) in 1958 to 12 per cent in 1965, 'we did not find any feeling of alarm in the British importers' camp, and indeed business has never been so good'. Certainly, sales had jumped by 25 per cent between 1964 and 1965. The fact was that 'the great bulk' of Japanese sales were in the 'small utility machines' which sold for approximately $215, 'whilst almost all British sales are in the retail bracket between $1,000 and $1,500'. In the event, and contrary to their earlier fears, the British were not 'losing sales to the Japanese to any appreciable extent'; instead, 'we are each operating at opposite ends of the market'.[79]

The delegation also noted that, 'in the opinion of many well informed observers', the Japanese advertising campaign had 'done a great deal of good to the motor cycle trade as a whole'. The vast sums spent on advertising, 'much of it in the high-class magazines', had helped 'make motor cycling more "respectable" and [wiped] out the unfortunate "leather jacket" image'. The overall result was that the Japanese 'have put tens of thousands of ordinary folks on two-wheels, folks with two and three cars very often, and quite a few of these become "sold" on motor cycling and graduate to larger machines'. The report, however, ended on a note of caution. The light-weight market, currently dominated by the Japanese, 'is not one which the British Industry is particularly well equipped to attack at present', and it would do well to try and develop. Moreover, there was no guarantee that in future the Japanese might not decide to move into the heavy-weight market.[80]

British motor cycle manufacturers retrench

It was debatable whether or not the British industry ever had the resources to take full advantage of the growing demand for motor cycles in North America during the 1960s. AMC, for example, remained in poor condition. Although its motor cycle sales had been assisted by the business generated through the Suzuki link-up, this alone was not sufficient to prevent financial distress. In order to counter continual losses, the company tried to diversify into general engineering work while also increasing motor cycle exports. The export drive was fairly successful (in late 1964 Chairman Hulbert claimed that between 70 and 90 per cent of its output was sent abroad, mainly to the USA), but the company's efforts to increase production were repeatedly frustrated by labour shortages. Moreover, financial losses kept on mounting and by 1965 had reached a total of £1.5 million.[81] AMC managed to stagger on for another year but finally went into receivership in July 1966 with debts totalling £2.2 million. At the time, the business press remarked that the company had been brought down by its concentration on large-displacement motor cycles, 'the static market for really powerful machines bought by racing and rallying enthusiasts'.[82]

AMC's motor cycle operations were thereupon bought up by Villiers Engineering, which had in turn earlier been purchased by Manganese Bronze Holdings, a diversified engineering concern. The assets, comprising five separate motor cycle marques, subsequently became known as Norton-Villiers. Severe rationalisation followed. By 1969 the Woolwich factory had been closed down, with production being moved to the existing Villiers factory in Wolverhampton and a new facility at Andover. The model line-up was narrowed down to a 750 cc (later 850 cc) twin-cylinder model dubbed the Commando – essentially an improved modification of an older Norton design – and described in the press as the 'Aston-Martin of motor cycles'. A light-weight 250 cc machine, marketed under the old AJS name, was also produced in small numbers. Virtually all Norton-Villiers' output went abroad, 85 per cent alone to the USA.[83]

Buy the bike and get the girl too? This Norton motor cycle advertisement from 1974 carries a less than subtle message. Still, for all the pretty girls and glamour, advertising such as this did little to disguise the fact that British motor cycles were now burdened with increasingly outdated design and technology.

Further change at BSA

As the remnants of AMC struggled along under new management, BSA (together with its Triumph subsidiary) was now the industry's overwhelmingly predominant firm, accounting for approximately 80 per cent of total output. In 1960, after selling off the Daimler motor car subsidiary to Jaguar for a reported £3.5 million, it appeared as if it might sideline motor cycles in favour of more lucrative pursuits. However, instead of investing the proceeds of the Daimler sale into existing operations, the BSA Group Board of Directors decided to purchase the Churchill Grinding Machine Company for £6 million. Chairman Eric Turner justified the expenditure on the grounds that there had been a 'remarkable upsurge in the demand of machine tools', thanks to the requirements of the expanding motor, electrical and domestic appliance industries. This was the kind of growth sector in which BSA wanted to participate. Motor cycles, by contrast, were declining to the extent that it was 'causing some concern' to the Board.[84]

The move to diminish the significance of motor cycles in the BSA Group's overall production strategy did not last long. By 1964 Chairman Turner informed shareholders that they were again becoming the Group's most important product, thanks to rapidly expanding North American sales. Turner later claimed that recent marketing research had shown that, as the result of the stimulus provided by Honda's advertising, there was rich sales potential in North America for the large and powerful motor cycles that the BSA Group specialised in making.[85] Shortly afterwards, BSA's newly appointed Motor Cycle Division Managing Director, Harry Sturgeon, expanded upon this strategy. True, Honda had vastly broadened the North American market through their successful advertising campaign and by doing so had also created significant opportunities for BSA. Sturgeon claimed that sales there could be much increased, based as they were, 'on the national acceptability of our machines which in turn would largely depend upon their performance in sporting events'.[86]

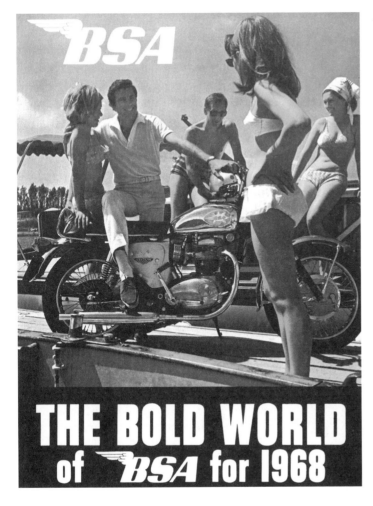

Although the male model in this advertisement looks well pleased with himself, by 1968 BSA and the British motor cycle industry in general were already in serious trouble.

COURTESY OF DAN MAHONY

This intensified export drive was to be facilitated by a series of plant improvements at the Small Heath factory, beginning with a £750,000 investment over 1964–65. Soon afterwards, the company began to install a new computer-assisted assembly-line system, modelled on the one already in place at Austin's motor car works at nearby Longbridge.[87] This was expected to increase production substantially at the main Small Heath factory, a large, old (parts of it dated from before the First World War) rambling and multi-storeyed structure that had defied earlier efforts to improve efficiency. The cumbersome process of having to shift around parts and components and then assemble them was further complicated by having to move partly completed units up and down lifts and then transfer them by truck between buildings scattered around the sprawling enterprise. The new assembly lines were expected to solve these shortcomings.[88]

Another facet of the programme to increase production was the creation of a centralised motor cycle design centre. In a move intended to inject new blood into the existing design establishment, the centre was located at Umberslade Hall, a country house near Birmingham, and staffed primarily by personnel brought in from the aircraft industry, not from long-time BSA or Triumph factory-trained experts. While the newcomers may have been talented, they did not know the intricacies of motor cycle design and production and had, therefore, trouble getting started. The ensuing delays caused many at the Meriden and Small Heath factories to deride the new design centre as 'Slumberglade'.[89]

At first, BSA's decision to move in on the growing opportunities in North America created by the Japanese export drive there and so to offset the weak home market seemed to have paid off. In 1966, Chairman Eric Turner claimed that motor cycle output was up by 50 per cent on the previous year and that 75 per cent of output was going abroad. Indeed, the level of exports was now so high that BSA/Triumph won the Queen's Award for Industry in both 1966 and 1967. Profits were up as well, to a

Harry Sturgeon, Managing Director of the BSA and Triumph motor cycle subsidiaries during the mid-1960s. His premature death in 1967 was a setback for the BSA Group's plans to counter Japanese incursions in the critical North American market.

COURTESY OF THE IVOR DAVIES COLLECTION

An aerial view of the BSA Small Heath factory at Birmingham. Large and sprawling, this factory complex, which had some buildings dating back to the nineteenth century, proved difficult to modernise during the late 1960s.

healthy £3.6 million in 1966. In 1967 Turner remained breezily optimistic, despite the fact that profits had slipped back to £3.2 million, on account of factors beyond the company's control in the American market, such as poor spring weather, a credit squeeze and uncertainty caused by the escalating war in Vietnam.[90] The latter factor was particularly worrying, since it was young men in the main who bought the larger, high-powered motor cycles produced by BSA's factories.[91]

Nonetheless, Turner thought these problems were merely transitory. North America held boundless opportunities, not least because of its demography. Marketing research, he informed shareholders, had indicated that there were now so many Americans under the age of 25 – those most likely to buy motor cycles – that they actually numbered nearly twice the entire population of Britain. Most of these were 'young people [who] have far greater purchasing power than anything we are accustomed to in this country'. BSA, as the major supplier of heavy-weight motor cycles in the North American market, was ideally placed to exploit this sales boom, which had been developed 'very largely for leisure and sporting purposes'.[92]

Japanese sales strategy changes gear

All this good news, however, was based on the assumption that the British would continue to dominate the heavy-weight market. Even in 1965 it was already quite evident that the Japanese were capable of building bigger motor cycles than they had until then. That year Honda introduced a 450 cc twin-cylinder model which, like the established lightweights, was far more sophisticated than the British competition, coming standard with, among other things, an overhead cam engine and an electric starter. The significance of its debut was not lost on the business press, which observed that Honda now had 'its sights obviously fixed on the fast-expanding market in the US for heavy weight cycles'. Having virtually abandoned sales of motor cycles under 250 cc, and with most of their output now exported to the North American market, British manufacturers viewed this as a very ominous development.[93]

Honda CB 450 cc. When this motor cycle was introduced in the mid-1960s it was a clear signal that the Japanese were serious about breaking into Britain's 'big bike' stronghold.
© HONDA

Starting in the 1940s, William Johnson, Triumph's long-time retailer in the Los Angeles area, made a special point of cultivating a clientele of Hollywood personalities as a way of popularising motor cycling. In this instance, Swedish-American actress Ann-Margret, shown here seated on a Triumph, demonstrates that this successful sales strategy carried on into the 1960s.

COURTESY OF DAN MAHONY

However, the appearance of larger Japanese motor cycles did not provoke the British to any sense of urgency. Their strategy, larger Japanese models or not, remained based on the firm belief that, while they were unable to compete effectively in categories under 250 cc, BSA and the other British manufacturers still held a secure position in what they saw as their traditional stronghold of heavy-weight sports-oriented machines. More particularly, they believed that British motor cycles would continue to retain a dedicated and expanding market. In late 1966, a press feature on the future of the motor cycle industry described this optimistic outlook:

> British manufacturers are confident that they will continue to hold the market for bigger machines, despite the attempts from Japan to break into this market. The British reasoning is that by keeping the big machines from here simple in design, they appeal to the enthusiast who wants to do his own tuning and generally fiddle with the bike ... The big Japanese machines, although impressive on paper, have been too complex for the enthusiast amateur the British manufacturers argue.[94]

The Honda CB 750 appeared in 1969 and was conclusive proof, as if anyone still needed it, that the Japanese could build competitive large-capacity motor cycles as well or better than anything comparable coming from British factories. This Honda was more mechanically sophisticated than its British rivals such as the Triumph Trident and Norton Commando.

© HONDA

This was not an isolated view and it continued to be shared by the most senior managers in the industry.[95]

Despite the likelihood that the Japanese would soon produce larger displacement motor cycles, BSA had failed to take measures to meet the threat of future competition. Even though Triumph had actually developed the Trident, a new 750 cc triple-cylinder model, which evidently could have been put into production several years earlier, no action was taken. When BSA's senior management heard rumours that Honda was working on a four-cylinder 750 cc machine of its own, far beyond anything they could offer, the Trident was quickly adapted and a crash production programme initiated. Although the new Triumph 750 cc model (which was also sold as the nearly identical BSA Rocket 3) still arrived in the American market in 1968 ahead of the big Honda, it was not at first a success. Development had been too rushed and it was consequently 'a flop'. The problems were ultimately sorted out, but valuable time had been lost.[96]

By contrast, when the Honda CB750 arrived in the US market during 1969, the reception was highly favourable.[97] Not only did this machine look good, it was well engineered and its 750 cc parallel four-cylinder motor had overhead cams (unlike the more traditional overhead valve Triumph) and was capable of speeds up to 120 miles per hour. Furthermore, it came standard with such features as an electric starter and a disc brake, and did not – like most British motor cycles – leak an embarrassing amount of oil. It was also carefully priced at US$1,500 to undercut the Triumph Trident and was backed by a 'major advertising campaign'.[98] Yet, BSA Motor Cycle Division Managing Director Lionel Jofeh (who had previously been at Sperry Gyroscopes and was hired by BSA in 1967 to replace the recently deceased Harry Sturgeon) professed not to be perturbed about this new Japanese onslaught. True, Honda had an edge on research and development because of its greater production volume, but this advantage, he insisted, would be 'counter-balanced by the British genius for technical innovation'.[99]

The higher specifications and greater mechanical reliability of the new heavy-weight Japanese motor cycles allowed them to appeal to a different type of American consumer, one largely separate from that traditionally serviced by the British. As an internal report prepared for BSA noted, the decline of sales for British motor cycles in North America did not reflect weaker demand overall but, instead, the introduction of the new Japanese models. North Americans bought them because of their advanced engineering and also their design features such as extra chrome finish and gadgets. The latter was particularly significant:

> This is an increasingly important point because the mechanically enthusiastic type of customer is accounting for a smaller proportion of the market as growth in market penetration is coming from a different type of person.[100]

British manufacturers suffer in comparison to their Japanese competition

The fact was that, even by the mid-1960s, BSA and the British motor cycle industry in general began to suffer from their inability or unwillingness to update their increasingly outdated and sometimes even antiquated designs. While the big twin-cylinder BSA Golden Flash, Norton Dominator and Triumph Bonneville models might have been ground-breaking years earlier, they and their successors had remained essentially unchanged and were now beginning to look a bit long in the tooth. The only major upgrades in the interim had been with their engine capacity, which in many instances had increased from 500 cc to 650 cc and then 750 cc, mostly in response to the demands of North American customers for more power and performance. This would cause problems later on in terms of quality control and reliability: the enlarged engine capacity not only meant increased vibration, much to the considerable discomfort of many riders, but also additional power,

'Are you man enough for Triumph?' The company's slogan may have answered its own question. From the very beginning motor cycle advertisements often stressed the inherent masculinity associated with riding a motor cycle.
© MOTOR CYCLE INDUSTRY ASSOCIATION OF GREAT BRITAIN

which was not always allowed for by the corresponding redesign of other components such as gearboxes, resulting in further mechanical defects.[101]

Instead, in terms of real technical advancement, the British manufacturers chose to do very little. Since 1945, British motor cycle engine technology had not advanced in any significant way, the producers preferring to stay with their familiar but now dated push-rod-driven overhead-valve designs. True, front forks were no longer girder construction, largely having been changed over to hydraulic damping systems by the 1940s. However, it is also true that none of the British manufacturers ever really did switch over to electric starters and instead remained loyal to the traditional manual kick-starter.[102]

Moreover, British motor cycle owners became increasingly frustrated with their machines' persistent unreliability, particularly of components such as the brakes and electrical systems (the leading supplier, Joseph Lucas, was widely known among enthusiasts both in Britain and abroad as 'The Prince of Darkness').[103] Another of the many annoying shortcomings were the seemingly perpetual oil leaks. This was partly a result of building engines with vertical rather than horizontally split crankcases or even because of oil 'sweating' through the sometimes porous metal castings. However, far more often than not, it was simply a reflection of ageing motor cycle designs and factory production equipment. Although the leaks were irrelevant in terms of performance, they were indicative of the old-fashioned approach the British industry seemed either unable or unwilling to leave behind. Such deficiencies were to be later frequently and unfavourably contrasted to the more technologically sophisticated Japanese machines.

Breakdown at BSA and Triumph

If quality control had become a pressing concern, maintaining success in the North American market was also dependent on improving productivity levels. These were now seriously jeopardised by the inability of either the Small Heath or Meriden factories to manufacture sufficient numbers of motor cycles. This problem was not always easy to rectify. In part, as noted in the previous chapter, BSA was subject to continual shortages of skilled labour, particularly at its Birmingham factory. Production levels, especially after 1965, were also hampered by growing labour unrest, if only at the Meriden factory. Triumph suffered from late deliveries of crucial components and found it increasingly difficult to meet output targets. In 1965, for example, 18,000 motor cycles were scheduled for export to the USA. In the event, because of various setbacks, only 16,000 were actually sent.[104]

Throughout 1969, BSA encountered mounting difficulties at the Small Heath factory. Once again, this was partially due to the inability of its suppliers to deliver on time, resulting in 'persistent failures to reach production schedules'. One press report described the factory as 'cluttered with machines unfinished for lack of one or more components – perhaps even the final stick-on transfer'. Such a breakdown of relations between the

Too little, too late. This Triumph T150 Trident (and its nearly identical sister, the BSA Rocket 3) was a well-designed triple-cylinder motor cycle that, but for boardroom dithering, could have been in production years before it finally appeared in 1968.

factory and its suppliers can only be seen as further proof of the very serious management failings at the upper levels of the BSA organisation.[105]

The factory's biggest problem, however, lay with the new assembly system, which was mostly but not completely installed, and had plainly failed to live up to expectations. At the beginning, the company was immensely proud of their new automated production technology, describing it in the mid-1960s as 'the most modern motor cycle assembly plant in Europe', a specious claim since the entire system was still not fully in place as late as 1970 and in any case comparisons with competitors other than the Japanese were irrelevant.[106] But the production system's primary flaw was that all it really did was move parts and components around in a manner that purported to be more efficient than the one that prevailed before.

What it did not even begin to address was the problem of the outdated motor cycle designs as well as the ageing production apparatus. In fact, many of the machine tools and related equipment that this shiny new delivery system serviced were themselves largely old and worn out. Moreover, even with what BSA called 'new flow line production', the motor cycle assembly process remained, as it did at Triumph's Meriden factory, highly labour-intensive. Only in 1967, for example, did BSA even begin to introduce compressed air and hydraulic tools to replace many of the workers' hand tools.[107]

In the meantime, sales also began to flag in the US market, as dealers there waited to see how BSA would react to the appearance of the Honda CB750, a situation aggravated when Kawasaki introduced its own heavy-weight model, a triple-cylinder 500 cc machine which was some 30 per cent cheaper than either the Triumph Trident or BSA Rocket 3. Moreover, BSA's competitive position was further undercut by its continual point-blank refusal to incorporate technical improvements despite repeated appeals, especially from North American dealers, to do so. For its part, BSA management insisted that features such as electric starters and five-speed gearboxes, now virtually standard on Japanese machines, were still unnecessary.[108]

BSA's big gamble

Throughout the 1960s, the BSA Group had become more and more dependent on its motor cycle division as the other subsidiaries were sold off. Daimler was already long gone, and had been followed by the machine tool subsidiary in 1966 when it was merged with Alfred Herbert Ltd (although BSA retained a ⅛th equity). The next year, the steel-making division was sold to Firth Brown and its specialised titanium business to Imperial Metal Industries. Finally, in 1970, the central-heating section was merged with Shell-Mex and BP to create Harford-Unical.[109] All this meant that any slowdown in motor cycle production or sales would now have a disproportionately stronger impact on the entire group, far more than would have been the case previously, a point well appreciated by BSA's leadership.

During his speech at the BSA Group's Annual General Meeting later in 1969, Chairman Eric Turner attributed his company's misfortune to a number of factors. He conceded that the Japanese had begun to undercut the company's position in the vital North American market through the introduction of their own heavy-weight models. With 90 per cent of the group's motor cycle output now going abroad, a large number of them to the USA, this was a matter of some concern. Although BSA and Triumph still held 90 per cent of the 650 cc and 60 per cent of the 750 cc engine capacity classes in the American market, it now held only 50 per cent of the 500 cc and a mere 14 per cent of the 250 cc segments. Worse yet, overall motor cycle turnover had declined 6 per cent on the 1968 levels and 11 per cent in the USA. In response to the lower profits, the BSA Board had commenced a policy of retrenchment and closed down the Redditch factory (at a saving of £250,000).[110]

Not only were production levels disappointing, but the chronic quality control problems had become even worse. The cost of the emphasis on increased output as the overriding priority began to show in the greater number of defects appearing, and this had an overall detrimental effect on the reputation of British machines throughout North America.[111] During the latter part of the 1960s, for example, motor cycles had arrived in the USA missing important components, and even when they had been installed, the parts were badly corroded. North American consumers began to lose patience.

In 1970, for example, a BSA 650 cc twin-cylinder Lightning received a poor review in the American enthusiasts' journal *Cycle World*. The test machine, the account noted, suffered from a 'quite annoying' level of vibration, which the tester attributed to loose engine mounts. Although the general design was praised, he concluded that overall it was 'frustrated by poor execution and inattention to certain detail'.[112] Nor were these types of problems restricted to export models. At a meeting held between manufacturers and home market retailers during 1970, one dealer 'pleaded for the introduction of quality control on all British machines'. Another was just as critical of the factories' inability to supply him with sufficient supplies of spare parts, nor was he able to 'get the answers to their service problems'.[113]

Despite these persistent internal problems and, in the face of increasing competition from the Japanese, the BSA Group Board of Directors decided to adopt a more aggressive manufacturing strategy. By doing so, they rejected one plausible alternative left open to them. The Board could have adapted a more conservative approach, given up manufacturing all but the large, comparatively high-priced models (which, in fact, it had already been doing for all intents and purposes) thus following the example of BMW, one of the few remaining survivors of the once huge German motor cycle industry. Indeed, as late as September 1969, Chairman Turner had described the future of the British motor cycle industry as 'selling at a premium price for widely recognised quality, rather as Jaguar does for cars'. Shortly afterwards, however, the company inexplicably shifted its emphasis back to the light- and medium-weight market segments.[114]

Rather than concentrating its efforts either on improving the existing heavy-weight models, or, as Bert Hopwood had been vainly urging for years, to redesign a fundamentally new range of machines based on a 'modular' concept, the Board decided to make what would turn out to be a reckless gamble. A redesigned line of 13 separate models was prepared for the 1971 season. At the 1970 Annual General Meeting, Chairman Turner grandiosely claimed that they represented 'the largest number of new machines ever introduced at one time by any motor cycle manufacturer anywhere'.[115]

In fact, the majority of these 'new' models was essentially the same as the ones which preceded them, barring some cosmetic changes.[116] The two exceptions were an entirely new 350 cc machine, the Fury, which was powered by an overhead cam engine, and the so-called 'revolutionary' 50 cc Ariel 3, a three-wheeled moped. Backed by a £250,000 development programme, the light-weight Ariel, a machine the company specifically targeted at 'beginners' and commuters, was designed to win back ground lost to the Japanese in both home and export markets. Despite the Small Heath factory's unresolved production problems, it was still believed that the Ariel 3 would sell up to 40,000 units, including 20,000 in Britain alone. BSA was so optimistic about the potential of the new models that, during the course of a sales meeting held during September 1970 between dealers and manufacturers, a company representative actually claimed that it would produce 160,000 of all models during the 1971/72 season.[117]

In the event, the 1971 season was an unmitigated disaster for BSA. Existing problems at both the Small Heath and Meriden factories, compounded by frequent changes in specification emanating from the Umberslade Hall design centre, reduced their production schedules to a shambles. At Small Heath, in particular, the effort of producing the new models, even with (or perhaps because of) the new assembly equipment, was, in the words of a later analysis, 'probably too great an organisational strain'.[118]

Consequently, few motor cycles had arrived when the crucial North American selling season opened the following spring, something that disappointed a good number of potential consumers, many of whom simply went off and purchased Japanese motor cycles that were available. When the new BSAs and Triumphs finally did appear, the much vaunted 'new line-up' turned out to be a major letdown. For example, the seat height on some models had been increased so that only the very tallest riders could

Bert Hopwood (*left*), photographed in his natural habitat, out on the shop floor, personally overseeing production, in this case at the Triumph factory at Meriden, although earlier he also managed the Norton factory in Birmingham.

comfortably place their feet on the ground when at rest. Because of all the manufacturing problems in the factory, the 350 cc model never materialised at all. As for the Ariel 3 moped, which was supposed to challenge Japanese hegemony in the light-weight market, it was a complete flop. Sloppy design work seems to have been the chief culprit. It could not, for example, be sold abroad because it failed to meet legal requirements for all but two countries. Even in Britain, where it was available, consumers greeted it with overpowering indifference. Only 2,000–3,000 units were actually sold, and a 'Mark 2' version, with the many defects corrected, was never even attempted.[119]

Lionel Jofeh left BSA in disgrace during July 1971, and Eric Turner followed him later in the year.[120] A new Board was assembled under the chairmanship of Lord Hartley Shawcross, which also included long-time motor cycle designer and factory manager Bert Hopwood. Their challenge was daunting. The company had run up a massive debit balance of £8.5 million along with an overdraft with British and American banks totalling another £10 million. Nonetheless, BSA was still able to muddle along for over another year, and indeed during 1972 there were even some signs of improvement. However, by the following year, hopes of continued government funding, which was critical for the survival of BSA, was not forthcoming in sufficient amounts. The company seemed ready to slide into bankruptcy.

Then, as part of a last-ditch rescue operation, the Heath Government brokered a sale of BSA to Manganese Bronze Holdings (MBH), owner of Norton-Villiers, even though BSA was by far the larger firm. The sale was ratified in July 1973, effectively leaving Britain with one remaining motor cycle manufacturer, with ownership of three factories: the Triumph works at Meriden, BSA's Small Heath operation and the former Villiers engine plant in Wolverhampton. As subsequent events would soon demonstrate, the new firm, which became known as Norton-Villiers-Triumph (NVT), would not be any more successful than the company it replaced.[121]

The British motor cycle industry since 1973

D ENNIS POORE, the Chairman of the newly formed NVT, soon concluded that his company could no longer afford to carry on a three-factory operation. One of them would have to go. Speculation abounded throughout what was left of the industry as to which it would be. The guessing ended on 19 September 1973 when Poore arrived at the Meriden factory and personally delivered the bad news. Yes, it was true the Triumph operation was no longer economical and would have to come to an end, with production being gradually wound down over the autumn and winter and final closure scheduled for February 1974.

However, unlike the BSA's Small Heath factory only a year and a half before, the workers at Meriden were not divided against each other and resolved to fight for their jobs. Poore had badly underestimated their determination and resources. Subsequent meetings held between NVT management and the Meriden trade unions were fruitless. The shop stewards simply refused even to discuss the timetable for the factory run-down. Instead, within a short period of time the workers occupied the factory, blockaded the existing inventory of completed and partially completed motor cycles as well as all the tools and other equipment. They also put the entire premises off-limits to management personnel in order to prevent any interference with their plans. Then they prepared to wait out their employer.[1]

The Meriden factory occupation derailed Poore's plans to rationalise the remainder of the industry. Subsequent events have been covered at greater length and detail elsewhere.[2] In brief, by 1975, NVT had been brought to its knees by a combination of continuing poor sales and the bitter labour dispute that had dragged on at Meriden. Although the government had poured money into the industry in order to prevent bankruptcy, the losses still exceeded a crushing £20 million. In August 1975, having reviewed the findings of the Boston Consulting Group's *Strategy Alternatives for the British Motor Cycle Industry*, Harold Wilson's Labour government decided enough

All dressed up with nowhere to go. NVT supremo Dennis Poore (*left*) and local MP Denis Howell saddle up for a ride. Poore's plans to revitalise the British motor cycle industry through his Norton-Villiers-Triumph combination failed after government subsidies were cut off because of continued financial losses.

COURTESY OF THE IVOR DAVIES COLLECTION

A defiant message posted outside the Meriden factory. In 1973 the workers there, supported by fellow trade unionists from around the Midlands, successfully took over their factory and shut out the management. With the support of Harold Wilson's Labour government, they went on to re-open the factory in 1975 as a workers' cooperative which continued production until 1983.

COURTESY OF THE IVOR DAVIES COLLECTION

Triumph's Meriden factory, 1942–83

When it first opened in 1942, the Triumph factory in Meriden, a village located just outside Coventry, was very likely the most modern and best equipped motor cycle manufacturing facility in the world.

By July 1979, however, when the author was given a tour of the premises by its workers' cooperative owners, this factory really amounted to little more than a working museum.

It was badly run-down, the result of years of underinvestment by BSA, who had been its owner since 1951. Not only were much of the plant and tooling antiquated but the motor cycles themselves, mainly the big 750cc twin-cylinder Bonnevilles, were, aside from the enlarged motors and various improvements in the electrics, frame and suspension, not significantly different from the Speed Twins which Triumph had begun manufacturing in 1937.

Consequently, working at the Meriden factory in 1979 was essentially much the same as it had been in 1959 or perhaps even 1949. The bikes moving on the assembly track were still pushed along manually and many manufacturing functions remained highly labour-intensive right up until the end. Motor cycle production carried on at the Meriden factory for several years afterwards but the buildings were torn down in 1983 after the cooperative went out of business. The site has now become a housing estate.

Most of the workforce at the Triumph factory had been, and continued to be, male. However, as the woman shown in this photograph demonstrates, there were exceptions in specific areas such as wheel-building.

PHOTOGRAPH: AUTHOR

Although the 1979 era factory did have a semi-automated paint shop, features such as the gold stripe on the petrol tanks were added manually. In this instance a veteran worker carefully applies the striping with a brush in a manner that was probably little different from how it had been performed decades before.

PHOTOGRAPH: AUTHOR

Engine sub-assembly work in progress. While much of the factory employed old-fashioned production methods, certainly in comparison with its Japanese rivals, powered hand tools, such as those shown in this photograph, had been installed during the 1960s.

PHOTOGRAPH: AUTHOR

Here the completed motors come off the sub-assembly line. They would then be loaded on to dollies and manually transported to another location in the factory where they would be fitted into the frames.

PHOTOGRAPH: AUTHOR

Motor cycles moving down the assembly line with the headlamps just about to be fitted.

PHOTOGRAPH: AUTHOR

A motor cycle nearing complete assembly comes to the end of one of the tracks.

Another motor cycle at the start of the final assembly track. The motors and other items have already been fitted, and the bike will soon be moved further along the track so that items such as its seat and petrol tank can be added.

A completed Bonneville reaches the end of the assembly line. It will now be moved to the packing department and readied for shipment to a retailer either in Britain or, more likely, overseas.

PHOTOGRAPH: AUTHOR

This automatic rolling test equipment was one of the more advanced pieces of equipment in the factory. Installed in the mid-1960s, it replaced the practice of having motor cycles taken out on public roads by test riders.

PHOTOGRAPH: AUTHOR

The Hesketh motor cycle represented an abortive effort to revive British motor cycle manufacturing during the early 1980s. However, while it had some innovative design features, this premium-priced bike suffered from technical flaws which led to the company's demise soon after its introduction.

BY COURTESY OF GRAHAM FISHER

was enough and ended the subsidies.[3] This was the end of NVT's hopes for the future. The BSA Small Heath factory had been barely operating since 1973 and was finally closed. Ultimately the buildings were torn down and the site cleared. The old Villiers factory in Wolverhampton continued to manufacture engines for the big Norton Commandos until the late 1970s, when it too ended production.

British motor cycle manufacturing had not yet entirely ceased, however. The workers at the Meriden, who defied NVT's efforts to close down their factory, refused to end their occupation until its future was assured. They stayed there for nearly two years and went on to negotiate the creation of a workers' co-operative, with the crucial assistance of Tony Benn, then Secretary of State for Trade and Industry. The result was something of a compromise. The co-operative received a £5 million loan from the government but had to allow NVT to hold the rights to the Triumph name and to handle all sales and marketing of their motor cycles.[4]

In 1975 the factory was started up again under the name Meriden Motorcycle Co-operative and enjoyed some success over the following years, producing a small annual output of the traditional heavy-weight twin-cylinder models. This was a remarkable achievement under the circumstances, in light of the antiquated plant and motor cycle design and the persistent and chronic lack of capital and investment. Nonetheless, the co-operative stubbornly carried on for as long as it could, until August 1983, when the worker-owners finally voted it out of business.[5]

There would be subsequent efforts to revive motor cycle manufacturing in Britain. Soon after the co-operative ended, some of the old Meriden plant and equipment was purchased by businessman Les Harris and moved down to a small factory at Newton Abbot in Devon. There they were used to produce a few of the famous old Triumph machines under a licensing scheme for several more years. Nor were the Triumphs the only motor cycles being built in Britain after 1975. On several occasions, entrepreneurs attempted to resuscitate Norton, each one with varying credibility and none enjoying any lasting success.

There was also the abortive Hesketh enterprise, launched by Lord Hesketh, on his Easton Neston estate near Daventry. For a short time, he produced a small number of premium-priced large-capacity, albeit technically flawed, machines. Finally, there has been a steady trickle of Enfield motor cycles sent to Britain from a factory in Madras India (using essentially unchanged 1950s vintage designs), the result of the licensing agreement that the Royal Enfield company had made decades before. Although Royal Enfield had gone out of business in the late 1960s, motor cycles modelled on its classic 350 cc and 500 cc single-cylinder Bullets have continued to be manufactured at Madras right to the present day.

However, the main development in the post-1975 period was the revival of British motor cycle manufacturing using the Triumph name.

Tearing it all down at Meriden. A sad end to what was once one of the most renowned motor cycle factories in the world.
COURTESY OF THE IVOR DAVIES COLLECTION

Triumph's old government-built wartime vintage factory at Meriden was demolished shortly after the co-operative came to an end and the 22-acre site became a housing estate. However, the rights to the name and some key assets, including all the remaining research and development projects, were purchased in December 1983 by John Bloor, a former plasterer become wealthy property developer with no previous experience in motor cycle manufacturing. He may have been partly inspired by the recent success of the nearly bankrupted Harley-Davidson company, which had been rescued by a management buyout in 1981. Although under heavy pressure from its Japanese competitors, Harley had subsequently made a surprising comeback thanks to a combination of temporary tariff protection from the US government and, more crucially, with an appealing line-up of their traditionally styled but mechanically re-engineered motor cycles.[6]

Unlike Harley-Davidson, Bloor decided on a clear break with the past. He created a privately owned company, Triumph Motorcycles Ltd, and built a new factory, not at its long-time base at Meriden or even at its birthplace in nearby Coventry, but instead at a greenfield site in Hinckley, about 15 miles to the east in Leicestershire.[7] Bloor and his team recruited a younger workforce that contained only a few veterans from the old Meriden factory and also acquired new machine tools, mostly from Germany and Japan. Furthermore, he decided against following up on any of the designs inherited from the Meriden Motorcycle Co-operative and chose instead to create a new model line more in tune with contemporary production, particularly those from Japan. Bloor soon sent out a design team which visited the Kawasaki, Suzuki and Yamaha factories and closely studied their products. Upon their return to Hinckley, the factory reviewed the team's recommendations and decided to go ahead with a range of more modern machines. These were, like the Triumph motor cycles of the past, large sport-oriented models but now powered by three- and four-cylinder liquid-cooled engines displaying more than a little inspiration from the Kawasaki GPx series.[8]

Indeed, while Triumph motor cycles may have been entirely designed and assembled in Britain, the styling was, and remains, far more along contemporary Japanese lines instead of being simply 'retro' versions of the machines that used to be produced at the old factory at Meriden. This was an obvious result of the fact that Japanese manufacturers, with far greater production and sales levels, now dominated the motor cycle trade in much the same way the British had done decades before. However, this fact also created opportunities for producers such as Triumph to create their own low-volume, specialist niche in the world motor cycle market.[9]

For the next several years, Triumph quietly proceeded to prepare to manufacture the motor cycles and officially launched the new line-up at the 1990 Cologne Motorcycle Show. While the engines (which were designed on a 'modular' basis, much as Bert Hopwood had unsuccessfully urged

BSA and Triumph to do years before) and chassis work were the product of in-house development and manufacturing, other components, such as electrics and suspension were imported, especially from Japan. This was no surprise considering that most previous British suppliers were now either out of business or no longer willing to service the motor cycle industry.[10]

Press reaction to the new bikes both in Britain and elsewhere was positive and sales encouraging. Annual factory output increased from 5,000 units in 1992 and reached 12,000 by 1995. In response, factory capacity was doubled in order to meet consumer demand. As with the old Triumph company, exports became particularly strong, amounting to some 80 per cent of production, but also geographically dispersed. Within a few years, Triumph re-entered most of its former overseas markets, including continental Europe (making up nearly 60 per cent off all sales), Australia and Canada. However, the USA, which had been such a key sales region for the company in the 1950s and 1960s, was only re-entered during 1994 and, subsequently accounting for roughly 30 per cent of sales, was far less important to the company than previously when that market had taken a lion's share of production.

By the later 1990s, the company was producing between 25,000 and 30,000 units per year, or roughly the same as the old Triumph company had done at its Meriden factory during its best years. Production has stayed more or less at these levels up to the present.[11] By 2011 Triumph was reporting annual sales of 48,684 machine and a pre-tax profit of £22.3 million.

While the post-1983 Triumph has been careful to distance itself from the labour troubles and the persistent quality-control problems of the past, it has followed the Edward Turner era management strategy of continuing to emphasise the mostly higher priced, larger sports-oriented performance machines, and has even revived some of the famous names from the past such as Bonneville and Daytona. The company does not build any motor cycles with a smaller than 600 cc engine capacity and so far has shown no interest in entering the light-weight, never mind utilitarian, commuter market.

Ironically, today Triumph, with its all-British ownership and management, has thrived at a time when domestic automobile production, after the collapse of Austin-Rover in 2005, is now almost (with the exception of very marginal specialist producers such as Morgan) entirely dominated by foreign branch plant operations that are either American- or Japanese-owned. While Triumph's overall output is miniscule on a worldwide basis compared to its Japanese (and, in growing numbers, Chinese) counterparts, by European standards it still has some significance.

Although the revival of British motor cycle manufacturing is likely to continue in the foreseeable future, nothing fundamental about its process has changed. True, British motor cycles continue to be sold by retailers in Europe and elsewhere, but the industry, as the global manufacturing force it once was, has perished.

CONCLUSION
The strange death of the British motor cycle industry

T HE HISTORY of the British motor cycle industry between 1935 and 1975 presents a rather peculiar case of decline. It did not take the form of a consistent downwards trajectory, but instead occurred gradually and irregularly over time. Nor is it possible to advance any single explanation for the industry's ultimate destruction. Instead, there were several factors of relative importance that underlay the course of events culminating in the collapse of 1975. As described in the previous chapters, these are highlighted in the three major phases through which the industry passed.

The first occurred as the industry adapted to the abrupt collapse of demand, both at home and abroad, after 1930. Manufacturers took a highly conservative approach to this crisis, concentrating on a loyal but limited market of essentially dedicated enthusiasts. Ironically, at the same time as the industry found security building motor cycles primarily in the medium- to heavy-weight classes, the motor car industry surged ahead, partly at the expense of its two-wheeled rivals, producing economy vehicles in the lower horsepower ranges. Although motor cycle manufacturers had already been subject to much criticism from various quarters for their loyalty to the larger displacement motor cycles and their orientation to sports competition, none of the larger firms made any real effort to try and break out of the impasse presented by a contraction in the market.

If the solution was, as some urged, to try and discover a new type of consumer and so enlarge the market, for the most part the industry was unwilling to find out whether or not he or, more significantly, she existed. As this book has described, it was usually left to the smaller-scale producers to experiment with the light-weight models along the lines of the so-called 'Everyman's' machines. Nevertheless, by largely following

A 1949 Vincent Rapide engine, one of the high points of British design.
PHOTOGRAPH BY COURTESY OF JOHN OLSEN

265

a conservative strategy even if it did mean passing up opportunities for growth, manufacturers survived a very difficult period but, in doing so, had done little to prepare the industry for success in the future.

The second phase occurred during the years immediately after 1945, within the context of an artificially favourable commercial environment. Pre-war competitors had been put out of action, at least temporarily, leaving British motor cycle manufacturers with an unparalleled opportunity to consolidate their renewed international supremacy. They failed for the most part, with the notable exception of the BSA Bantam, to exploit the opportunities presented by the post-war Reparations Programme and gain access to superior design and technology as well as factory plant and equipment.[1] Moreover, when the industry came under pressure from the Attlee government to review and possibly modernise its operations or, more modestly, at least to standardise components, the leadership indignantly rejected any suggestion that manufacturing programmes needed to be changed or that the industry might be insufficiently prepared to meet revived foreign competition.

Once again the industry was a prisoner of its own preconceptions of what the market was and could see no reason why it should not continue as it had before; so, once again, the industry let such opportunities slip away. Indeed, for a few more years at least, sales of its products, especially the larger displacement, twin-cylinder models, seemed to remain strong, with little sign of slackening. Even though imported scooters and mopeds took over and vastly expanded the light-weight market by the mid-1950s, the British industry in general survived because these imports did not actually directly threaten its core market of the medium- to heavy-weight models. Of equal importance was the development of the North American market which provided a substitute outlet for that portion of their production either shut out of other export markets by tariffs and import quotas or which could not be sold in the numbers they once had in Britain. Export sales ensured the continuation of its 'Big Bike' production strategy.

The third and final phase occurred in the face of Japanese competition during the 1960s and early 1970s. Limited by their well-entrenched, self-imposed structural constraints, motor cycle manufacturers were unable to react effectively to the appearance of these new foreign lightweights. Even after they had lost what was left of the home market with the implementation of the 1962 Anglo-Japanese trade agreement, British manufacturers again found a substitute in the form of increased exports to North America. As the British industry's last stronghold came under pressure from Japanese producers, BSA decided to veer away from its long-time strategy of manufacturing mostly comparatively small numbers of premium-priced large powerful motor cycles. Instead, in 1970, the company launched its ineptly managed bid to try and re-enter the middle- and light-weight market.

These three phases underscore several important factors which explain the decline of the British motor cycle industry. However, several factors should first be removed as significant causes of the industry's collapse. Firstly, government policy was never as detrimental as the industry so frequently claimed. Time and again, manufacturers failed to convince either the Board of Trade or the Ministry of Transport to grant the concessions they sought, particularly the removal of tax and regulations from light-weight motor cycles. This, the industry continually insisted, was the reason it failed to produce a successful light-weight model. But, on the evidence, the industry consistently failed to provide the hard facts to substantiate its case.

Instead, their arguments were always advanced as a virtual matter of faith, amounting to the proposition that, if the lesser regulations and lower taxes worked on the Continent, then they must also work in Britain. This point ignored the internal circumstances which prevailed in these countries, specifically the matter of relative income levels. Moreover, even if the government had granted the concessions the industry wanted, it is highly problematic whether or not this would have actually worked to the benefit of domestic producers. Quite likely, and certainly after the early 1950s, had the concessions been granted, the main beneficiaries would have been the distributors of imported mopeds, scooters and light-weight motor cycles.

Nor can the government be held entirely responsible for the many export markets that were closed to the industry over the years because of tariffs, import quotas and various sterling crises. First, many of these markets had only a limited sales potential for the large sports-oriented motor cycles that were the mainstay of the manufacturers. Second, and most important, the leadership of the British motor cycle industry did not seem to appreciate fully the fact that only so much could be done in terms of representation by trade negotiators, especially in the face of foreign governments who were determined to protect their own vital interests. This was equally true with respect to the Argentines in 1936, to the Japanese after 1950 in fostering their own domestic industry, and to the Australians from time to time, determined as they were to preserve dwindling sterling reserves.

Was it also true that, thanks to government indifference, the industry was put at an unfair disadvantage to its foreign competitors, as the manufacturers often maintained was the case? The hard fact is, however, that these foreign machines– whether they were the German bikes that began appearing in British export markets during the 1930s, or the Italian scooters of the earlier post-war era and then, finally and most fatally, the Japanese motor cycles which stormed into Britain and North America during the 1960s – met market demand while frequently the British ones did not.

The Honda Supercub is an especially relevant example. Far from stealing British market share, at least at the beginning, the Japanese, like the Germans and Italians before them, simply responded to a latent consumer demand neglected by the domestic producers and created a market which had not previously existed. Even afterwards, during the late 1960s and early 1970s, when the Japanese began to move 'up-market' and compete more directly against the British for the lucrative larger sized motor cycles, they did so by offering a combination of generally cheaper prices, greater technical sophistication and, most critically, higher levels of mechanical reliability. This was a point well appreciated by both Whitehall civil servants and their ministers and it simply reinforced their reluctance to continue to protect British motor cycle manufacturers with tariffs and import quotas. In any case, one could argue it was equally the internal divisions suffered by the industry, especially once AMC decided to sell Suzuki motor cycles through its retail network, as much as it was the government's trade liberalisation policy, that kept the British market open to the flood of Japanese imports.

Worker militancy and trade union activity must also be discounted as having any substantially detrimental effect on the industry. During most of the time covered by this book, there is very little evidence of strike activity or other labour unrest at least for most of the inter-war period. Indeed, for some time after 1945, other than a brief labour stoppage at Ariel Motors in 1944 and the six-month strike at Norton Motors during 1956, there is virtually no record of significant disturbance elsewhere. Moreover, coming as it did during the middle of a severe sales recession, the Norton strike may not have been an entirely unwelcome development for the company management.

BSA enjoyed fairly good labour relations until the late 1960s, although also, mostly because of its comparatively low wages, it suffered from considerable labour turnover. True, starting in the early 1960s, its leading subsidiary Triumph was subject to fairly constant disruption because of numerous, albeit generally very brief, work stoppages. However, the company had other, equally troublesome but unrelated difficulties during this time. Additionally – TGWU militant Ray Allsopp and his provocative red hand-wipe notwithstanding – strike activity at the Meriden factory more accurately reflected the labour militancy which typified the Coventry engineering district during the 1960s, rather than industrial relations in the motor cycle industry more generally.

Moreover, as management at the Meriden factory was often painfully aware, the BSA Group Board was quite prepared, in the interests of 'production at any cost', to appease trade union demands for years on end, as long as Triumph continued to churn out motor cycles for the North American export market. Yet it must also be noted there were persistent problems with the tardy deliveries of component supplies (which were, in turn, sometimes the result of strikes in that sector) which also affected Triumph and the other firms as well.

Overall, no matter how harmful the labour militancy, on balance it does not seem to have disproportionately weighed down the industry any more than the other difficulties they were facing. In particular, BSA's abortive attempt to modernise its assembly line during the later 1960s and the design fiasco of the 1970/71 season almost certainly inflicted far more damage on both the Meriden and Small Heath factories than any strike or even any series of strikes.

Finally, it has been suggested that lack of technical skill or education on the part of British management generally has been a serious handicap to industry.[2] Yet, on evidence, this was not the situation in the motor cycle industry. Although managers rarely had formal university educations, they were scarcely without technical knowledge. AMC Managing Director Donald Heather may have been singular insofar as he was a university-trained engineer, but many of his colleagues were still highly respected for their technical knowledge, irrespective of whether they had acquired it through experience in the factories or through attending night school. For example, several industry executives presented papers at meetings of the Institution of Automotive Engineers and later at the Automotive Division of the Institution of Mechanical Engineers. Indeed, one of them became president of the latter organisation during the late 1950s.[3] They may have had a very conservative attitude to design and marketing, but that did not necessarily make them uneducated. Indeed, the motor cycle industry, like its automotive counterpart, is far more representative of the 'Practical Man' thesis, than it is of a version of industry declining thanks to the inattention of languid would-be aristocrats.[4] The real management problem was rather different, as indicated below.

Instead, this book has identified a number of other factors which are of greater significance in explaining the decline of the industry. The often poor state of co-ordination within BSA, the predominant firm, prevented it from taking the leading role its size and diversity warranted. Because of sometimes sloppy management at the group level, the company was unable to pull together the separate but still potentially mutually supporting subsidiaries. Under the direction of a more effective senior management, the ingredients were there for the company to have evolved into a powerful industrial combination. Instead, internal problems plagued the company throughout the period in question, and that must have badly hurt the efficiency of the motor cycle operations. The period between 1928 and 1932 when the company went through three chairmen in nearly as many years is indicative of this weakness. While the company did well during the 1939–1945 war, it later suffered under the disastrous tenure of Chairman and Managing Director Sir Bernard Docker. His pre-occupation with the Daimler motor car subsidiary excluded any coherent forward planning. Nor was there effective co-ordination between the subsidiaries. And the chronic

Get astride the exciting life

BSA

The excitement begins on Stand 6

THE BEST SELLING RANGE OF MOTOR CYCLE SCOOTER AND MOPED ACCESSORIES. See us on Stand 4

MOTOPLAS

She may have looked keen, but the chances of seeing a woman, such as the one shown here in this late 1960s vintage advertisement, riding a large motor cycle would have would have been poor, both then or during the previous decades.

© MOTOR CYCLE INDUSTRY ASSOCIATION OF GREAT BRITAIN

financial losses that resulted from Daimler's abortive effort to enter the middle-class motor car market worked to the great disadvantage of the entire group. Although Sir Bernard was finally toppled by his fellow directors, who had tolerated his mismanagement for far too long, the company never really recovered.

Nor did it help that, between the retirement of James Leek in 1956 and the appointment of Harry Sturgeon in 1964, there was no effective leadership at BSA's motor cycle operations, which were allowed to drift aimlessly. Several years afterwards, a series of badly considered decisions made by Chairman Eric Turner, his fellow board directors and Motor Cycle Divisional chief Jofeh pushed the entire group into bankruptcy. While the lack of effective direction at BSA did not necessarily infect the other firms, except the Triumph and Ariel subsidiaries, the industry leadership which one could reasonably have expected from the company was seriously compromised. Furthermore, the kind of management exercised by Bernard Docker, Eric Turner and Lionel Jofeh raises questions about the amount of discretion granted to senior company executives. It may legitimately be asked why so little was done over such a long period of time by other Board members or by the shareholders to correct this sort of activity.

Another critical factor is the concept of their market which was held by senior management in general. With the exception of those noted above, these men were, as a rule, competent managers, albeit ones with a very narrow view of what they conceived as the typical consumer. It could be argued that their manufacturing strategy, especially during the 1930s, was very conservative but had at least kept the industry afloat through some very difficult times. Yet it could also be argued with equal force that they had failed through their reluctance at least to explore seriously the sales potential offered by the economy ('Everyman') motor cycle. Even more telling was their ambivalence over the strategy of creating greater numbers of female customers during the pre-war era. Their inability (or unwillingness) to broaden the market by discovering new consumers, such as women, is striking. A new market, with or without women, may not have existed in the 1930s, but it was this kind of mentality which was to result in their inability to either grasp the other opportunities open to the motor cycle industry after the war or react effectively to the challenges posed by Italian scooters, French mopeds and then Japanese light-weight machines.

A further illustration of this weakness is the industry's intense involvement with motor cycle sport. In isolation, this was not an entirely bad or harmful commitment, as Honda's experience would demonstrate. Nor did the high profile accorded to the sport entirely match the reality, at least in terms of the way it was portrayed to the public. As the columnist Francis Jones noted:

> One is apt to think of the TT as a sporting event that the trade happens to find worth while to patronise. But it is more accurate to consider it as a trade event that happens to be of a sporting character … The ultimate purpose of the [race] meetings is to sell motor cycles.[5]

In fact, as motor cycle manufacturers understood well, the sporting events had two very practical functions. First, they provided commercial opportunities in their own right, providing fodder for advertising campaigns and also raising the prestige of British motor cycles in foreign markets.[6] Second, the sporting events offered a cheaper alternative for more systematic research and development, the extreme conditions prevailing on the racetrack being thought an ideal way to improve and refine both design and mechanical reliability, the benefits of which were thought to 'trickle down' to standard production models. Whether or not those racetracks really did provide a proper substitute for adequate funding of research facilities is a more difficult proposition to sustain. Nonetheless, many throughout the industry believed it was essential that, from the shopfloor up to the boardroom, all should share a strong commitment to motor cycling and motor cycle sport, and this even influenced their factory hiring policies. As AMC's Donald Heather observed, this was an industry which very much believed that 'as motor cycles are sold to enthusiasts they can only be built successfully by enthusiasts'.[7]

Unfortunately, the pre-occupation with sports events also came with an expensive price tag. Once more, virtually by definition, it meant that the industry placed another self-imposed limitation upon its market. It created an engrained perception throughout the industry of the 'typical' consumer, which was continually reinforced every time the managers attended a sports event. Even so, many in senior positions in the industry thought that this was an ideal way for them to keep in touch with the market. This outlook was manifested in other ways as well. J.M. West, AMC Sales Director, believed that an important aspect of his job was to attend owners' club meetings regularly in order to maintain close contact with his firm's core market. No doubt these types of encounters strengthened loyalty to the marque and resulted in frequent exchanges of very helpful information about the strengths and weaknesses of particular models, but this may not have been the best way to learn about how to sell motor cycles to non-enthusiasts or to explore ways to expand the existing market.[8]

In the final analysis, racing was largely enjoyed by those who were already convinced enthusiasts, but it had little or no attraction to those who simply wanted cheap transport and nothing else. It may well have been the case that, as one advertising slogan went, 'racing improves the breed', but it also created a very specialised breed, with a limited commercial application. It is far from certain whether experience on the racetrack provided any significant help in the development of a better commuter machine, whose virtues needed to be simplicity, ease of maintenance and economy.

Moreover, the commitment to sport also inhibited flexibility on the part of the manufacturers. The Velocette LE, for instance, was a good example of what an economical commuting model looked like when produced by a company that was owned and managed by enthusiasts. Undoubtedly a piece of exceptionally sound engineering (or perhaps over-engineering), it was, however, a machine which simply did not appeal to a wider group of consumers, not least because of its comparatively high price. Indeed, unlike its foreign competitors, the history of the British motor cycle industry is littered with various failed attempts to create an attractive light-weight machine. Starting with the abortive scooter experiments of the 1920s, continuing with the BSA Dandy, Beagle and Ariel Pixie of the 1950s and 1960s and ending with the Ariel 3 fiasco, the industry was unable to get the formula right and lacked the persistence to keep on trying until it did.

The BSA Bantam superficially contradicts this argument, but the design was German rather than British. And, in contrast to Yamaha's experience with its equivalent model, the YA-1 Red Dragonfly, BSA saw the Bantam as virtually an end in itself and was reluctant to develop it substantially or to replace this light-weight machine. Instead, the company kept on producing the Bantam year in and year out with only comparatively minor changes. In fact, the British motor cycle industry is best remembered for its larger, sports-oriented machines, such as the Royal Enfield Interceptor, the Triumph Speed Twin (and subsequent derivatives such as the Bonneville), the Norton Dominator and Commando, the BSA Gold Star and the Vincent Black Shadow. There is very little room in the industry's pantheon of fame for the humble economy models.[9]

There were other drawbacks stemming from the industry's infatuation with the racetrack. The orientation to the larger sports machines meant that the industry kept on manufacturing precisely the kind of motor cycle which most antagonised the public and government officials. As one technical

The Triumph Speed Twin

Few British motor cycles have been as influential as the Triumph Speed Twin. Conceived by Edward Turner after Jack Sangster had put him in charge of Triumph in 1936, the Speed Twin had its origins in designer Valentine Page's 6/1, a 650 cc parallel twin-cylinder machine which never actually went into production.

The Speed Twin was a sharp break from established practice. Until then, most British motor cyclists had used single-cylinder machines. These were relatively cheap to manufacture and maintain and well suited to the roads of the day. Triumph now offered something better.

In 1937, Turner was able to fit two vertical parallel cylinders into one finned casting, along with overhead valves and a single carburettor. His goal, to create a compact but powerful engine, easy to start and smooth running, was achieved spectacularly. Soon afterwards the Speed Twin was joined by the Tiger 100 (the '100' referred to its top speed), its performance-tuned sister. Together they set a new standard which other companies would take years to match with their own equivalent models, and single-cylinder motor cycles would never regain their previous popularity.

Post-war versions of the Speed Twin were essentially the same as the original although a few years later, responding to power-hungry North American motor cyclists, a 650 cc parallel twin-cylinder variant, the Thunderbird, appeared. Then, in 1959, the Speed Twin concept reached a new level of development when Triumph introduced the 650 cc Bonneville. This high-performance machine also had the now familiar parallel twin-cylinder engine but also a redesigned crankshaft, twin carburettors and later on a duplex frame and unit-construction engine. To the delight of motor cyclists around the world, it was capable of 120 mph without any significant after-market modifications.

Triumph continued to manufacture the Speed Twin, in much the same form as it first appeared in 1937, until 1966. The Bonneville, which later had its engine increased to 750 cc, carried on even longer and was still coming off the Meriden factory assembly lines, also fundamentally unchanged, as late as 1982.

Sectioned Triumph Speed Twin motor. Launched in 1937, this was a significant breakthrough which would set the pace in motor cycle engine design for years to come.

journal observed as early as the 1930s: 'Every credit must be given to those responsible for the advanced stage of development that the racing motor cycle engine has attained. Nevertheless, to put relatively expensive, heavy, noisy engines, difficult to start, and sometimes critically stressed, into commercial production and available to the general public is not in the best interests of the Industry.'[10]

Yet, it was precisely these high-performance machines that were most likely to involve their operators in accidents. All this brought the entire industry into disrepute and created an image of motor cycles and motor cyclists which relentlessly dogged the industry from the 'Promenade Percys' of the inter-war era, the 'Teddy Boys on Wheels' and 'Rockers' of the late 1950s and early 1960s straight through to its final days. There may have been some short-term gain in this respect. It did, over the years, give motor cycling an image of danger and risk which doubtless helped sales among a certain type of consumer. However, this advantage must be balanced against the damage that was done to the industry's relations with government ministers and civil servants during its attempts to have tax and regulations changed.

Several additional points should also be stressed. The failure of the industry to master consistent quality control, starting as early as the 1930s, was an important problem which continued to damage manufacturers. In part, this was the price paid for insufficient investment in modern plant, which burdened the industry with another deep-seated weakness. As Barbara Smith noted, one of the chief characteristics of British motor cycle factories was the fact that their products were 'hand assembled and fitted'.[11] This, in turn, reflected the importance that the industry assigned to the concept of 'craftsmanship', a virtue considered central to British motor cycle manufacturing. The end result was a continuing reluctance to convert the industry to larger scale production and not only because they refused to believe market demand would match the higher output. Managers had a lingering aversion to building motor cycles in any way other than by their traditional crafts-based methods. Norton's reluctance before 1939 to build motor cycles on a track assembly line is a case in point. There were also those who believed, even well after 1945, that motor cycles, unlike motor cars, were inherently unsuited for assembly line production.[12]

This stubborn resistance to larger scale assembly technology is highlighted in the case of the Power-Pak (a small clip-on engine unit made for use on bicycles and popular in early 1950s). This machine would seem to have been a particularly ideal candidate for larger scale production. Significantly, when it was advertised the manufacturer chose to stress the fact that it was built using decidedly old-fashioned techniques. As the advertisement text read: 'The Power-Pak is not mass-produced. It is the only bicycle motor that is handbuilt. Every motor is individually tuned and tested.'[13]

No doubt one must be wary of how British motor cycle manufacturers defined concepts such as 'handbuilt'. It does not, for example, necessarily mean the same thing as 'craftsmanship'. In view of the industry's long-standing quality control problems, it could just as easily be an excuse for shifting attention away from its mostly under-capitalised, antiquated factory plant and work practices.[14] The essential point, however, is that these manufacturers did not place any great emphasis on developing a trouble-free machine. Nor did this seem to cause them much concern. After all, even if their motor cycles required close and regular maintenance, that was scarcely a drawback for the kind of consumer who was thought cheerfully to take up spanner and screwdriver without a moment's hesitation and happily spend a Sunday afternoon repairing their machine.

The matter of design and the lack of professional designers is yet another problem for the industry. Frequently, this work was performed by senior managers, more particularly by executives such as the Collier brothers who had come into the industry at the beginning. On occasion, this practice

Triumph Managing Director Edward Turner (*right*) personally testing one of his company's products during the so-called 1953 'Gaffers' Gallop'.
COURTESY OF THE IVOR DAVIES COLLECTION

was used as a form of advertising. In 1953, for example, when Triumph launched its new Terrier light-weight motor cycle, the company arranged for Managing Director Edward Turner, accompanied by the factory Works and Service Directors, to ride three of these machines from Land's End to John O'Groats, in a publicity stunt that became known as 'The Gaffers' Gallop'. An advert was designed around this event, with potential owners assured that this motor cycle had been field-tested by 'The man who designed it, the man who made it and the man who will service it'.[15]

Many benefits probably resulted from the close association of senior management with design work. However, one industry commentator noted that there were also shortcomings implicit in this relationship:

> The industry had been built up by gaffers who designed, made, developed and rode. Inevitably, the gaffers are a dying race and, perhaps, because they had largely kept matters in their own hands, there was today a shortage on the design and development sides.[16]

Finally, it was the unwillingness or inability of British motor cycle manufacturers to develop skills in larger scale production engineering which caused a common weakness throughout the industry or at least among its larger companies. During the 1950s, the industry reached an annual production plateau of between 150,000 and 200,000 units, a level at which the various firms could comfortably manufacture using their existing facilities. Manufacturers appeared willing to trade off their ability to increase production for lower investment in plant capacity. Alternatively, since the manufacturers made their profits more from the higher prices they were able to charge for the larger capacity motor cycles, there was no pressing incentive to improve productivity.[17]

Ultimately, the failure to enter larger volume production cost the industry dear. BSA, for example, which had nearly always used less than 100 per cent of its manufacturing capacity, floundered after the mid-1960s when it tried to overhaul its Small Heath factory in order to increase output substantially. The concept may have been sound, based on experience in the motor car industry, but it went seriously adrift in the execution. Shortly afterwards, the company compounded its weaknesses by bungling the critical 1971 'new' range of motor cycle models and so virtually guaranteed the slide into bankruptcy. These disappointing results seem to have been caused mainly by shortcomings among top management, particularly on the part of BSA Group Chairman Eric Turner and the Motor Cycle Division's Managing Director Lionel Jofeh, but such was the extent of failure that this must have extended beyond just these two individuals.

It has been the central thesis of this book that the British motor cycle industry collapsed primarily because of the implications arising from its failure to develop a successful light-weight 'economy' model. Because of the nature of the home market, it was, virtually from birth, a comparatively small-scale producer of larger displacement models and showed little inclination to change. Unlike its counterparts on the Continent or Japan, there was a much weaker tradition of building light-weight machines. Thus, British motor cycle manufacturers were never able – nor did they ever seriously try – to develop a two-wheeled equivalent of the Austin Seven, Morris Minor or the Mini. This failure did much to determine their long-term future.

The foregoing provides an historical explanation for what the Boston Consulting Group has identified as 'segment retreat' which led to the destruction of the industry and also presents a case study of British de-industrialisation, even if only on a small scale. It has been the intention of this book to show that the decline and collapse of the industry was the manifestation of a series of constraints largely created by the manufacturers themselves, which had been in existence long before the appearance of their Japanese competitors. It may well be that the 'segment retreat' was not inevitable. Nor was it unique to motor cycle manufacturing.[18] However, over time, it was the accumulation of these self-inflicted wounds that brought about the 'Strange Death' of the British motor cycle industry.

Notes and references

Notes to Introduction

1. From 1910 to 1956 the industry was represented by the British Cycle and Motor Cycle Manufacturers' and Traders' Union. Thereafter the name was changed to the British Cycle and Motor Cycle Industries Association and then, in 1973, again to its present title, the Motor Cycle Industry Association. References throughout the text will use the title in effect at that particular point in the historical chronology.

2. See untitled brief, prepared for a meeting held on 11 December 1969, contained in the Industries' Association Guardbook on deposit at the Modern Record Centre (MRC), MSS 204/3/1/116.

3. *Ibid.*

4. *Ibid.*

5. See Boston Consulting Group, *Strategy Alternatives for the British Motor Cycle Industry*, London: HMSO, 1975, p. x.

6. *Ibid.*, p. xv.

7. See remarks of Eric Varley, Secretary of State for Industry, in *Hansard*, [896] 1974–75, 31 July 1975, cols 2059–62.

8. See, for example, 'Who's left holding the motor-bicycle baby?', *The Economist*, 9 August 1975, pp. 75–6, and 'How British motorbikes went backing down the wrong road' by Terry Dodsworth, *Financial Times*, 2 August 1975, contained in MRC MSS 123, Temp 3. See also leading articles, 'An Industry Outclassed', *The Times*, 1 August 1975, p. 15, and 'A short ride to disaster', *The Guardian*, 1 August 1975, p. 12.

9. See Richard T. Pascale, 'Perspectives on Strategy: The Real Story behind Honda's Success', *California Management Review*, Spring 1984, pp. 49–50 and Robin Wensley, 'Marketing Strategy', contained in M.J. Baker (ed.), *The Marketing Book*, London: Heinemann, 1987, p. 37. The Boston Consulting Group report is explicitly noted in Karel Williams, John Williams and Denis Thomas, *Why are the British Bad at Manufacturing?*, London: Routledge

and Kegan Paul, 1983, pp. 27–8, pp. 48–9, and D.O. Ughanwa and M.J. Baker, *The Role of Design in International Competitiveness*, London: Routledge, 1989, pp. 16–17 and pp. 78–9.

10. See Tom Lester, 'How the British Bikes Crashed', *Management Today*, May 1976, pp. 44–53.

11. Nor are there are any real two-wheeled equivalents to the numerous studies of the British automobile industry. See, for example, George Maxcy and Aubrey Silberston, *The Motor Industry*, London: George Allen & Unwin Ltd, 1959, D.G. Rhys *The Motor Industry: An Economic Survey*, London: Butterworths, 1972 or, more recently, Roy Church, *The Rise and Decline of the British Motor Industry*, London: Macmillan, 1994, James Foreman-Peck, Sue Bowden and Alan McKinlay, *The British Motor Industry*, Manchester: Manchester University Press, 1995 and Timothy R. Whisler, *The British Motor Industry, 1945–1994*, Oxford: Oxford University Press, 1999. And one looks in vain for a motor cycle counterpart to popular but substantive automotive histories like Jonathan Wood, *Wheels of Misfortune: The Rise and Fall of the British Motor Industry*, London: Sidgwick & Jackson, 1988 and Martin Adeney, *The Motor Makers*, London: Fontana, 1989.

12. See Barbara Smith, *The History of the British Motor Cycle Industry, 1945–1975*, Birmingham: The Centre for Urban and Regional Studies, University of Birmingham, 1981, p. v. and p. 25.

13. See Michael Miller, 'The British Motor Cycle Industry before 1939' n.d. (a copy of this paper was kindly provided by its author) and Steve Koerner, 'The British Motor Cycle Industry during the 1930s', *The Journal of Transport History*, March 1995, pp. 55–76.

14. See Nick Rogers, *The British Motor Cycle Industry, 1945–75, Programme Notes for an Epic still to be Written*, Birmingham: The Centre for Urban and Regional Studies, University of Birmingham, 1979,

M. Cenzatti, 'Restructuring in the motorcycle industry in Great Britain and Italy until 1980', *Environment and Planning*, vol. 8, 1990, pp. 339–55 and Filippo Carlo Wezel, 'Location Dependence and Industry Evolution: Founding rates in the United Kingdom Motorcycle Industry, 1895–1993', *Organisation Studies*, 26(5) 2005, pp. 729–54.

15. See John Kelly, 'History of Veloce Ltd. – Motorcycle Manufacturers, Hall Green, Birmingham' (Ph.D. dissertation, Bradford University, 1978), John Tomlinson, 'The Meriden Co-operative' (MA dissertation, Warwick University, 1980), Martin Fairclough, 'The Political Economy of Producer Co-operatives: A Study of Triumph Motorcycles (Meriden) Ltd and Britain's Industrial Decline' (Ph.D. dissertation, Bristol University, 1986) and Steve Koerner, 'Trade Unionism and Collective Bargaining at Two British Motor Cycle Factories: A Study of BSA/Small Heath and Triumph/ Meriden, 1951–1973' (MA dissertation, Warwick University, 1990).

16. See Jock Bruce-Gardyne, *Meriden – Odyssey of a Lame Duck*, London: Centre for Policy Studies, 1973. The rescue attempt and the subsequent workers' occupation of Triumph's Meriden factory are covered from the perspective of the company itself in *Meriden – Historical Summary, 1972–1974*, London: Norton-Villiers-Triumph Ltd, 1974 (no author indicated).

17. See, above all, Bert Hopwood, *Whatever Happened to the British Motorcycle Industry?*, Sparkford: Haynes Publishing Group, 1981. Others in the same genre include Ivor Davies, *It's a Triumph*, Sparkford: Haynes Publishing Group, 1980 and Neale Shilton, *A Million Miles Ago*, Sparkford: Haynes Publishing Group, 1982.

18. See Smith, *op. cit.*, p. 3.

19. See, for example, among many others, company histories such as Barry Ryerson, *Giants of Small Heath – The History of BSA*, Sparkford: Haynes Publishing Group, 1980, Harry Louis and Bob Currie, *The Story of Triumph Motor Cycles*, Cambridge: Patrick Stephens, 1975, Gregor Grant, *AJS – the History of a Great Motor Cycle*, Cambridge: Patrick Stephens Ltd, 1969, Peter Hartley, *Matchless – Once the Largest British Motor Cycle Manufacturer*, London: Osprey Publishing Company, 1981 and Mick Woollett, *Norton*, London: Osprey Publishing Ltd, 1992.

20. See Steve Wilson, *British Motor Cycles* (in six volumes), Cambridge: Patrick Stephens Ltd, 1992. Another, now dated, history of the industry is 'Ixion' (the Rev. B.H. Davies), *Motor Cycle Cavalcade*, London: Iliffe & Sons, 1951. For more general histories, see, among others, Richard Hough and L.J.K. Setright, *A History of the World's Motor Cycles*, London: George Allen & Unwin Ltd, 1966, Phil Shilling, *The Motorcycle World*, New York: Random House, 1974, Massimo Clarke (ed.), *100 Years of Motorcycles – A Century of History of Development*, New York: Portland House, 1988 and Gary Johnstone, *Classic Motorcycles*, London: Boxtree Ltd, 1993.

21. See *The Art of the Motorcycle*, New York: Guggenheim Museum Publications, 1998. See also Steven L. Thompson, 'The Arts of the Motorcycle: Biology, Culture and Aesthetics in Technological Choice', *Technology and Culture*, January 2000, vol. 41, no. 1, pp. 99–115.

22. For the academic literature, see Ian 'Maz' Harris, 'Myth and Reality in the Motorcycle Subculture' (unpublished Ph.D. dissertation, Warwick University, 1986). An abridged version of this dissertation was earlier published as *Bikers. Birth of a Modern Day Outlaw*, London: Faber and Faber, 1985. See also C. Hopper and J. Moore, 'Hell on Wheels: The Outlaw Motorcycle Gangs', *Journal of American Culture*, 6(2), pp. 58–64, 1990 and Daniel R. Wolf, *The Rebels. A Brotherhood of Outlaw Bikers*, Toronto: University of Toronto Press, 1991.

23. For the fiction genre, see among many others, Steve Wilson, *13*, London: Panther Books, 1985 and, for more factual accounts, see Yves Lavigne, *Hells Angels: Into the Abyss*, Toronto: HarperCollins, 1996.

24. George Dangerfield, *The Strange Death of Liberal England*, Stanford, USA: Stanford University Press, 1997. This is the latest edition of a book originally published in 1935.

25. It has also been noted that little has been done to place the role of motor cycles and motor cycling (especially sports activities) into a social context. This is particularly true of the period before 1939: 'The social history of the motor cycle between the wars, to which a side-car could be added to transport a small family, has been obscured by the more sensational antics of the next generation of motor cyclists, whose leather jackets and long hair spread moral panic in the 1950s.' See Richard Holt, *Sport and the British*, Oxford: Oxford University Press, 1990, pp. 198–9. The same generalisation might also, to a more limited extent, be applied to North America.

26. This literature is considerable but include, among the more recent examples, Jim Tomlinson 'Inventing "Decline": the falling behind of the British economy in the postwar years', *Economic History Review*, XLIX, 4 (1996), pp. 731–57, David Edgerton 'The Decline of Declinism', *Business History Review* 71 (Summer 1997), pp. 200–6 and

Geoffrey Owen, *From Empire to Europe*, London: Harper Collins, 1999.

27. See Michael Dintenfass, *The Decline of Industrial*

Britain, 1870–1980, London: Routledge, 1992, p. 71.

Notes to Chapter 1: British supremacy, 1935–1939

1. One particular manifestation of the advanced state of the British motor cycle industry, at least during the 1920s, as the fact that its designers were evidently much in demand with Continental manufacturers. See 'English designers on the Continent', by Erwin Tragatsch, *Classic Bike*, January 1982, pp. 46–51.

2. The Isle of Man TT (Tourist Trophy) race results are listed in detail, along with the nationality of the participants, in Nick Harris, *Motorcourse History of the Isle of Man TT Races, 1907–1989*, Richmond, Surrey: Hazelton Publications, 1990.

3. For details on the formative years of the industry, see Eric Walford, *Early Days in the British Motor Cycle Industry*. Coventry: British Cycle and Motor Cycle Manufacturers and Traders' Union (no date but probably 1934), W.F. Grew, *The Cycle Industry: Its Origin, History and Latest Developments*, London: Pitman and Sons, 1921, pp. 105–12 and 'The Evolution of the Motor Cycle', by Lieut-Col. E.W.C. Sandes, *The Royal Engineers' Journal*, vol. LIX, 1945. See also Cyril Ayton, Bob Holliday, Cyril Posthumus and Mike Winfields, *The History of Motor Cycling*. Norwich: Orbis Publishing Ltd, 1979, especially pp. 109–10.

4. A photo of British built motor cycles in use at an Italian Fascist rally was published in *The Motor Cycle*, 14 November 1929 and again on 6 June 1935. The *Midland Bank Monthly Review* also commented on the popularity of British motor cycles among Italians in its March/April issue of 1933 at p. 5.

5. The motor cycle and automobile output figures are derived from the 1930 *Census of Production, Part 2*. London: HMSO 1931, p. 334. By way of comparison, that same year the British bicycle industry produced 878,966 units, worth a total of £3,410,000.

6. See various Board of Trade memos, including one authored by C.E. House entitled 'Motor Cars', regarding British automobile and motor cycle sales dated 13 September 1938 on deposit at the National Archives (hereafter NA) at London as BT 59/24/489/20 and BT 59/24/589.

7. See the *Daily Telegraph*, 22 August 1927, contained in newspaper clipping book MSS 204/10/1/2, on deposit at the Modern Record Centre (MRC), University of Warwick.

8. These figures are drawn from *A Survey of the*

Trade in Motor Vehicles. Report of the Imperial Economic Committee, Thirtieth Report. London: HMSO 1936, pp. 7–9, 101. The relative difference between the two industries has also been noted in G.C. Allen, *British Industries and Their Organisation*, London: Longmans, 1959, p. 181.

9. For a comprehensive guide to the various models produced during this period, see Roy Bacon, *British Motorcycles of the 1930s, the A–Z of Pre-war Marques*. London: Osprey Publishing Company, 1986.

10. The boast was made by Manufacturers' Union Director Major H.R. Watling as quoted in *The Motor Cycle Overseas Annual and Buyers' Guide 1925*, published by the popular journal *The Motor Cycle*, London: Illiffe and Sons, 1925, p. 12.

11. For information about model ranges during the years referenced, see the 'Buyers' Guide' contained in *The Motor Cycle*, 20 November 1913, 'buyers' Guide', contained in *ibid.*, 17 March 1921 and 'Price Classifications of 1925 Machines', *ibid.*, 27 November 1924. Car prices are derived from the 'Buyers' Guide' contained in *The Motor*, 5 November 1920. Motor cycle side-car combination prices come from the 'Buyers' Guide' in *The Motor Cycle*, 17 March 1921.

12. See 'A Survey of Current Motor Cycle Design' by D.S. Heather, *Proceedings of the Institute of Automobile Engineers*, 1918/1919, vol. XII, p. 56.

13. See 'Ixion', *op. cit.*, pp. 66–97.

14. The membership of the 'Big Six' was, in alphabetical order, Ariel Motors, Associated Motor Cycles (formally Matchless Motor Cycles), BSA, Enfield Cycle Co. (Royal Enfield), Norton Motors and Triumph.

15. See Alfred Plummer, *New British Industries in the 20th Century*, London: Sir Isaac Pitman and Sons Ltd, 1937, p. 95. A thorough description of the wide range of the services that the Triumph factory in Coventry was capable of can be found on Jack Wick's audio tape of reminisces which is on deposit at the Coventry Records Office. Wicks was a staff designer who began work with the company in the late 1930s.

16. See Michael Miller, 'The British Motor Cycle Industry Before 1939', *op. cit.* According to one post-war survey these two unnamed firms produced 63 per cent of all output, see H. Leak and A. Maizels, *The Structure of British Industry*

(1945), p. 52. Lack of sufficient documentation related to the output of individual firms prevents a more precise calculation of market share.

17. BSA's best pre-war year was 1926 when it manufactured a total of 29,099 motor cycles. In 1933 production had dropped to a low of 10,979 units and thereafter it fluctuated from year to year with a high of 18,563 in 1937. See BSA's 'Report on Accounts, 12 Months ended July 1938', contained in the BSA Collection, MRC MSS 19A/2/37, p. 4.

18. This observation is based on a communication between J.M. West, who was BMW's British Sales Manager during the latter half of the 1930s, and the author, June 1991.

19. See Hartley, *op. cit.*, pp. 10–64.

20. See *ibid.*, p. 117, Gregor Grant, *AJS – The History of a Great Motor Cycle*, London: Patrick Stephens, 1969, p. 13 and Bacon, *op. cit.*, pp. 13–19, 102–7. In 1932 Matchless bought Wolverhampton based Sunbeam motor cycle company from ICI although it did little to develop the marque afterwards.

21. See *Stock Exchange Gazette*, 25 April and 27 September 1935.

22. See Peter Hartley, *The Ariel Story*, Watford: Argus Books, 1980, pp. 11–71.

23. *Ibid.*, pp. 100–6, 118–31. See also the entry on Jack Sangster written by Barbara Smith contained in the *Dictionary of Business Biography*, vol. 5, pp. 55–9.

24. For detailed biographical information on Bettmann, see Steven Morewood, *Pioneers and Inheritors: Top Management in the Coventry Motor Industry, 1896–1972*, Coventry: Coventry Polytechnic, 1990, pp. 104–17 and Ivor Davies, *op. cit.*, pp. 11–36. The information on Triumph's financial situation is drawn from *The Economist*, 15 December 1934. See also Siegfried Bettmann's own unpublished memoirs, the three volume 'Struggles: A Man of No Importance", that outline Triumph's history from its foundation to the mid-1930s and which are on deposit at the Coventry City Records Office.

25. See Peter Hartley, *The Story of Royal Enfield Motor Cycles*, Cambridge: Patrick Stephens, 1981.

26. See Mick Woollet, *op. cit.*, pp. 11–74. C.A. Vandervell and Company later became known as CAV and was subsequently purchased by Joseph Lucas in 1925. The purchase gave Lucas a 'virtual monopoly' over the supply of lighting and ignition equipment for both the British motor cycle and automobile industries. See Harold Nockold, *Lucas: The First Hundred Years. Volume I: The King of the Road*. London: David & Charles, 1976, pp. 204–5.

27. See Bacon, *op. cit.*, pp. 124–7.

28. In two notable years, 1935 and 1937, Norton motor cycles placed in five of the six top slots. See Matthew Freundenberg, *The Isle of Man TT*, Bourne End: Aston Publications Ltd, 1990, pp. 162–4.

29. See 'Motor Cycles', *The Automobile Engineer*, August 1928, p. 273 and 'Motor Cycle Sport', *The Export Trader*, July 1937, p. 231. *The Export Trader* was published between 1924 and 1952 when its title was changed to *The Motor Cycle and Cycle Export Trader*. Publication under that name continued until 1968.

30. A writer in a popular journal noted that the value of the TT races 'cannot be over-stressed.' Not only was it simply sport, but the 'machines are subjected to a grueling more severe than could be imposed by any other test.' See 'The future of motor cycle sport', by T.W. Loughborough, *The Motor Cyclist Review*, July 1927, p. 14.

31. See 'The Influence of Racing on Motor Cycle Design', by 'G.E.T.', *The Export Trader*, July 1934, pp. 245–6, 'The Super-Sports Motor Cycle' by John Wallace, *Proceedings of the Institution of Automobile Engineers*, 1929/1930 session, vol. XXIV, pp. 161. 'Motor Cycle Progress', by H.D. Teage, *ibid.*, 1931/1932 session, vol. XXVI, p. 385.

32. See photo feature about James Norton's sales tour of South Africa, *The Motor Cycle*, 22 December 1921, p. 865.

33. The Managing Directors present at the 1939 Donnington event included Jack Whitlock (Rudge-Whitworth), Ernest Humphries (OK Supreme), Edward Turner (Triumph), Jack Sangster (Ariel and Triumph) and Gilbert Smith (Norton). See untitled feature, *The Export Trader*, June 1939, p. 250.

34. In his speech to the 1922 Annual General Meeting, BSA's Chairman specifically noted that the recent acquisition of Jessops and Sons, a steel manufacturer, was motivated in part to give the parent company a greater degree of control over raw materials. See Chairman's speech, delivered on 25 April 1922. Copy contained in the BSA papers on deposit at the Birmingham Central Reference Library, MS 321/A (Reports and Accounts).

35. Rogers was Unionist MP for the Moseley riding in Birmingham between 1918 and 1921. Manville had been President of the Society of Motor Manufacturers and Traders (SMMT) during 1911/1912, a founding Vice-President and long-time Council member of the Federation of British Industries (FBI) and a Conservative MP for Coventry. While in Parliament, Manville was Chairman of the Common Industrial Group. Before becoming appointed Chairman, Arthur Pollen had been on the BSA Board during

the 1920s and was also a Vice-President of the FBI. Alexander Roger was a Director of the Commercial Bank and the Midland bank and was also a Vice-President of the FBI. See the various entries for the above in the *Dictionary of Business Biography*.

36. Hannon was also a founder of the British Commonwealth Union, founder and President of the National Union of Manufacturers and the Vice-President of the FBI. See Hannon's obituary in *The Times*, 11 January 1963. A collection of his correspondence with Chamberlain, among others, can be found in Box 17 of the Hannon Papers on deposit at the Parliamentary Archives.

37. See R.P.T. Davenport-Hines, *Dudley Docker. The Life and Times of a Trade Warrior*. London: Cambridge University Press, 1984, especially pp. 214–33.

38. See Ryerson, *op. cit.*, p. 46 and BSA Chairman's speech, delivered on 29 April 1924, contained in the BSA Collection, MS 321/A, Birmingham Central Reference Library.

39. In 1931 BSA suffered a loss of £204,194 and another loss of £797,928 the following year.

40. See correspondence, Hannon-A.W. Wood (a future BSA Board director), dated 1 October and 4 October 1932, both contained in the Box 31, File 1 of the Hannon Papers, Parliamentary Archives.

41. See memorandum prepared by Hannon, dated 13 December 1933 and entitled 'Administration of Birmingham Small Arms Company', contained in *ibid*.

42. See memo, 'BSA: Notes on BSA Organisation by the Chairman', dated 29 June 1937, contained in MRC MSS 19A/1/2/54. Roger's confidential assessment of the company had already been echoed in an article that appeared in the 1 February 1935 issue of *The Stock Market Gazette*. It stated that BSA was 'far more a holding concern than a direct owner and operator of plant.'

43. One rare example of internal sharing of technology was the use of the Daimler automotive pre-selector gearbox and fluid flywheel which was adapted to a BSA motor cycle. See untitled news item, *The Times*, 23 November 1933. The experiment could not have been a great success since it was never repeated.

44. See biographical piece on Barnett, prepared by R.H. Thomas, *The Export Trader*, June 1946, p. 332; and Humphries obituary, *The Motor Cycle and Cycle Trader*, 13 December 1963, p. 90. Details on the Goodman family are from Wilson, *op. cit.*, vol. 6, pp. 190–208.

45. The Union had been founded in 1910, as a continuation of an existing organisation

representing bicycle manufacturers. It kept its name until 1956, when it became known as the British Cycle and Motor Cycle Industries' Association. See the Union's *Annual Report* for 1956, p. 2.

46. A very brief outline of these activities is also contained in 'The Cycle and Motor Cycle Industry' by H.R. Watling, contained in H.J. Schonfield (ed.), *The Book of British Industries*, Edinburgh: Denis Archer, 1933.

47. Major Watling did not appear to have been a motor cycle enthusiast, at least in the same way as other senior industry executives. He did, however, share something else in common with several others of them, being membership in the Masonic Order. Indeed, Watling later rose within the Order to become a Master and presided over meetings attended by industry leaders such as Sir Harold Bowden of the Raleigh bicycle company, Frank Smith of Royal Enfield, BSA's James Leek and Donald Heather of AMC. See 'Master of Ceremonies of Masons', *Motor Cycle and Cycle Trader*, 29 July 1949, p. 170 and untitled news item, *ibid.*, 7 April 1950, p. 36.

48. The Guardbooks of the CTU contain numerous case files relating to various miscreants who had broken Union rules and had suffered the appropriate punishment. See MRC MSS 204/CT/3/1/1–5.

49. See, for example, the 1935 'Bond', on deposit with the Union papers in the MRC at MSS 204/4/1. The agreements were renewed annually.

50. See document entitled 'Pricing Agreement between: BSA, Raleigh, Enfield, A.J. Stevens, H. Collier and Son and Rudge-Whitworth', dated 1 September 1927, listed as item #134, at the BSA Collection, Solihull Public Library.

51. A point that was repeatedly made by Major Watling, when he testified on behalf of the Union before the Committee on Resale Price Maintenance during July 1948. A verbatim transcript of the proceedings is contained in PRO BT 64/540, file 376/1949.

52. See the *Annual Report and Balance Sheet* for 1934 and 1939, contained in the Union's paper at MRC MSS 204/4/3/2.

53. In 1934 the respective circulation of the three journals was estimated as follow: *The Motor Cycle*, 126,004, *Motor Cycling*, 39,160 and the *Motor Cycle and Cycle Trader* as 8,550. The figures are contained in the minutes of the Union's Management Committee meeting of 12 March 1935, MRC MSS 204/1/1/12. Another popular journal, *The Motor Cyclist Review*, went out of business in 1930.

54. Graham Walker, for example, was an executive with the Rudge-Whitworth motor cycle company before going on to become editor of *Motor Cycling*.

55. According to statistics maintained by the Union, in 1934 there were 95,643 machines registered on American roads although there had been 210,000 machines registered in 1923. See *Review of the British Cycle and Motor Cycle Industry* (third edition). Coventry: British Cycle and Motor Cycle Manufacturers and Traders' Union Ltd, 1935.

56. See Watling's report, *Notes on the Cycle & Motor Cycle Trade in Canada and USA*, published by the Manufacturers' Union, Coventry: June 1928, p. 70. This report, prepared as a 99 page booklet, is contained separately in MSS 204/3/1/18B.

57. See 'Motor cycles in the USA. Reasons for Decline', contained in the Union's *Quarterly Journal*, October 1927, p. 389, MRC MSS 204/4/2/4 and 'Report on the USA', *The Motor Cycle*, 24 December 1924.

58. The proportion of motor cycles in Germany under 200 cc had grown to 60.5 per cent of all registrations by 1936 and had jumped to 72 per cent in 1938. See Fritz Blaich 'Why Did the Pioneer Fall Behind?' contained in Theo Barker (ed.) *The Economic and Social Effects of the Spread of Motor Vehicles*, London: Macmillan, 1987, p. 151. See also 'Germany adopts the motor cycle', *The New York Times*, 6 January 1929 and 'German Motor Cycles – Bid for Supremacy in Production', *The Times*, 5 August 1929.

59. For a general review of German motorisation policies during the 1930s, see R.J. Overy, 'Cars, Roads and Economic Recovery in Germany', *Economic History Review*, 2nd Series, vol. XXVIII (1975), pp. 466–83.

60. See Michael Worthington-Williams, *From Cyclecar to Microcar. The Story of the Cyclecar Movement*, London: Dalton Watson Ltd, 1981, pp. 15 and 101.

61. See Donald Heather, 'A Survey of Current Motor Cycle Design', *Proceedings of the Institution of Automobile Engineers*, vol. XVII (1918/1919), p. 56.

62. See 'The Passenger Motor Cycle', *The Motor Cycle*, 23 October 1942, pp. 578–83.

63. A point not lost on automaker Herbert Austin when he gave private instructions for the model 'Seven' to his design assistant Stanley Edge. Austin was explicit about the dimensions of this vehicle, which were not to exceed those of a side-car combination and to so fit easily into the same garage space. See Roy Church, *Herbert Austin. The British Motor Car Industry to 1941*, London: Europa Publications, 1979, p. 77.

64. See remarks of L.J. Shorter reported in 'The Light Car and Motor Cycle and Side-car' contained in the *Proceedings of the Institution of Automobile Engineers* (1921/22), xvii,ii, p. 25 and 'The Garage Problem and Suburban Motor Cyclists' by Richard Twelvetrees, *Motor Cyclist Review*, March 1926.

See also 'About Motoring. Are motor-cyclists insane?' by R.E. Davidson, *The New Statesman and Nation*, 1 July 1939, pp. 30–1.

65. See 'Sympathetic Tinkering: Motorist and Motor Cyclists Compared', *The Motor Cycle*, 6 March 1924, p. 308.

66. According to figures calculated by the Society of Motor Manufacturers and Traders (SMMT), using a benchmark of 100 in 1924, prices had dropped to 49.8 by 1935. See SMMT, *The Motor Industry of Great Britain 1939*, p. 47. The question of automobile prices during the interwar period is addressed in Roy Church and Michael Miller, 'The Big Three: Competition, Management, and Marketing in the British Motor Industry, 1922–1939', contained in Barry Supple (ed.), *Essays in British Business History*, Oxford: Clarenden Press, 1977.

67. For details on the advances in automobile technology, see T.P. Newcombe and R.T. Spurr, *A Technical History of the Motor Car*, Bristol: Adam Hilger, 1979, especially pp. 42–3, 48.

68. These were points well recognised by the motor cycle press. See, for example, 'Finality of Design. Has the motor cycle field stagnated?' by H.V. Taylor, *Motor Cyclist Review*, November 1929, p. 229 and 'An Engineer Discusses Design' by 'OS', *The Motor Cycle*, 28 January 1937, pp. 96–7.

69. See 'Motor Cycle or Car?' by Richard Twelvetrees, *ibid.*, 8 August 1929. The issue of the diminished social prestige of motor cycling is also directly addressed in Christopher T. Brunner, *The Problem of Motor Transport*, London: Ernest Benn Ltd, 1928, pp. 33–4.

70. See, for example, 'Side-car combos for business and pleasure', *The Motor Cyclist Review*, August 1925, 'Where does the side-car stand?', *ibid.*, October 1928 and *Carry on by Side-car*, Coventry: British Cycle and Motor Cycle Manufacturers and Traders' Union, 1927. The latter is contained as an insert within *British Industries*, 15 September 1927, MRC MSS 200/F/4/24/13.

71. See *Road Traffic Census, 1936 Report*, London: HMSO, 1937, p. 10. Over the same period of time, the number of motor cycles registered for road use dropped from 731,298 to 505,779 or a decrease of 31 per cent.

72. A point discussed more generally in 'The Second-Hand Car', *The Economist*, 17 September 1938, pp. 531–3.

73. Miller attributes the 'long-run extermination of combinations and tri-cycles' to the fact that they 'served as cheap substitutes for light cars and vans.' With 'their discomfort, exposure to the elements, and limited loads, they were poor substitutes,

and only cheapness to run could allow them to compete.' All prices quoted are derived from this source. See Miller, *op. cit.*, p. 6.

74. See memo entitled 'Trade in Australia', dated 5 November 1925, contained in Guardbook MRC MSS 204/3/1/12.

75. See memo entitled 'Trade in East Africa', dated February 1927, contained in Guardbook MRC MSS 204/3/1/15. Reports from Japan indicated that motor cycle sales there had also been threatened by increasing numbers of light automobiles along with an improved public transport system. See memo entitled '60/35: Japan – Use of British motor cycles', dated 21 March 1935, contained in Guardbook MRC MSS 204/3/1/37a.

76. According to the Ministry of Transport's *1936 Road Traffic Census*, bicycle use had increased by 94.98 per cent from 1931 to 1935. See *op. cit.*, p. 6.

77. The average price for bicycles is found in the *Census of Production* for 1935 at p. 377; see also Miller, *op. cit.* for details of other perceived barriers that prevented bicycle owners from upgrading to a motor cycle.

78. Some of the complaints made to various public officials can be found in NA HO 45, particularly sub-files 17413, 17414 and 456309. There was evidently a widespread belief among motor cyclists that they were subject to considerable bias and discrimination from the courts and police forces. See, for example, 'Those Anti-Magistrates" contained in *The Motor Cyclists' Review*, March 1929.

79. See House of Lords Sessional Papers, 1937–1938/4, *Report by the Select Committee of the House of Lords on the Prevention of Road Accidents together with the Proceedings of the Committee, Minutes of Evidence and Index* (1938). Tripp's evidence is found at pp. 49–50. Mention of Watling's approach to the Lord Chancellor with respect to the coroners is contained within the Union's *Annual Report* for 1934, p. 3. MRC MSS 204/4/3/2. Evidently, he kept up the pressure during 1935 and 1936 as well. It is unknown whether or not the Lord Chancellor was ever receptive to the Union's lobbying.

80. There was considerable discussion in the motor cycle press during the 1920s and 1930s about what kind of machines should be built by the manufacturers. See, for example, 'An 'Everyman' Prophecy' by 'Ixion', *The Motor Cycle*, 31 January 1929, p. 158 and 'Making Motor Cycle Sales', *The Motor Cycle and Cycle Trader*, 29 January 1937.

81. See Bart H. Vanderveen, *Motor Cycles to 1945*, London: Frederick Warne and Co. 1975, p. 33.

82. In fact so-called 'Ladies Motor Bicycles' had appeared before the First World War albeit in only very limited numbers. See, for example, the 'Buyers' Guide' contained in the 20 November 1913 edition of the enthusiasts' journal *The Motor Cycle*.

83. See Betty and Nancy Debenham, *Motor Cycling for Women. A Book for the Lady Driver, Side Car Passenger and Pillion Rider*, London: Pitman & Sons Ltd, 1928.

84. *Ibid.*, p. ix.

85. See Clare Sheridan, *Across Europe with Satanella*, London: Duckworth, 1925.

86. See, for example, 'Through Feminine Goggles' in *The Motor Cycle*, 15 December 1921, pp. 816–17 and 15 February 1932, pp. 212–14. For 'Cylinda', see 'Entirely for Eve', *The Motor Cyclist Review*, January 1929, p. 348.

87. See 'Motor Cycling for Health', by Betty and Nancy Debenham, *Daily News*, 16 March 1926, contained in BCMCMTU press clipping volume one, MRC MSS 204/10/1/1.

88. See 'Motor Cycling for Health and Beauty' by Betty and Nancy Debenham, *The Star*, 16 November 1927, contained in *ibid.*, volume two.

89. See 'From Berlin to Birmingham' by Suzanne Koerner, *The Motor Cycle*, 19 May 1927, pp. 810–12.

90. See 'The Appeal to the Feminine' by L.F. Jones, *Garage and Motor Agent*, 17 July 1926, p. 532. Thanks to Sean O'Connell for drawing this article to the author's attention.

91. See untitled memos dated 21 September and 26 October 1926 contained in MRC MSS Guardbook 204/3/1/16.

92. See 'The Woman Rider' *Sunderland Echo*, 5 October 1926, contained in press clipping volume two, *op. cit.* See also, 'My Lady Comes to Town' by 'Hildegarde', *The Motor Cycle*, 14 October 1926, pp. 694–7.

93. See Major H.R. Watling, 'The Utility Motor Cycle' *The Motor Cyclist Review*, September 1929, pp. 129–30. Failing reliable statistics for this era, it is impossible to judge the validity of Watling's estimate, although one suspects that it may have been on the optimistic side.

94. See Marjorie Cottle, 'Motor Cycling for Beauty', *Evening* Standard, 25 September 1938, contained in press clipping volume two, *op. cit.* The final sentence of the quote probably alludes to the wide spread belief at the time that certain types of strenuous physical activities might damage a woman's reproductive organs. The author would like to thank Barbara Joans and Jeanne Zasadie, who raised this point during the 16 February 'Motorcycle Culture and Myth' session of the 2002 SW/TX Popular Culture Association conference held in Albuquerque New Mexico, USA.

95. See 'The Modern Girl and the Motor Cycle. A Defence of the Motor Cycling Sporting Girl' by Mabel Lockwood-Tatum, *The Motor Cycle*, 5 October 1922, pp. 472–3.

96. See 'Random Jottings' by 'Wayfarer', *Motor Cyclist Review*, July 1927, p. 12.

97. See 'My Lady Comes to Town' *op. cit.*, p. 694.

98. A leading article in the *Motor Cyclists Review* entitled 'Motor Cycling for Ladies' made references to other female riders had had been kept out of motor cycle sports activities. The leading article is contained in the August 1927 issue of the magazine at page 75. For details on Wallach and Blenkiron, see Theresa Wallach's posthumous memoir, *The Rugged Road*, High Wycombe: Panther Publishing Ltd, 2001 especially Barry Jones' introduction, pp. 1–12. However, for her part, Cottle did continue to participate in sporting events especially on the Continent. See 'Having the time of my life', by Rebekka Smith, *Classic Bike*, December 1983, pp. 18–22, 61.

99. For three recent studies of female motor cyclists in the USA, see Ann Ferrar, *Hear Me Roar: Women, Motorcycles, and the Rapture of the Road*, New York: Crown Publications, 1996, Susie Hollern, *Women and Motorcycling. The Early Years*, Cortland: Cortland Press, 1999 and Barbara Joans, *Bike Lust. Harleys, Women, & American Society*, Madison: University of Wisconsin Press, 2001.

100. The reasons for the original expulsion remain obscure. See 'The MCC Decides', *The Motor Cycle*, 31 January 1946, p. 87.

101. See 'Performance in the Making', *The Export Trader*, May 1938, pp. 192–3.

102. See minutes of the Motor Cycle Manufacturers' Section meeting of 9 July 1935, contained in MRC MSS 204/1/1/12.

103. Sean O'Connell, *The Car in British Society. Class, Gender, and Motoring, 1896–1939*, Manchester: Manchester University Press, 1998, p. 95. Much the same has been observed about women motorists in the USA, see Virginia Scharff, *Taking the Wheel. Women and the Coming of the Motor Age*, Albuquerque: University of New Mexico, 1992.

104. See 'Record Buying in the Home Market', *The Times*, 25 June 1925, in press clipping volume one, *op. cit.*

105. *Ibid.*

106. See untitled feature, *The Motor Cyclist Review*, February 1927.

107. See 'A plea for 'Everyman' motor cycles', *The Motor Cycle*, 3 January 1929. There is no record of any manufacturer having claimed the prize.

108. See 'The 'Utility' motor cycle', By Major H.R. Watling, *The Motor Cyclist Review*, September 1929. See also memo entitled '87/26 – Silencing of Motor Cycles', dated 12 August 1926, contained in Guardbook MRC MSS 2/4/3/1/14.

109. From what evidence survives, it seems there was no systematic marketing survey being conducted for the British industry during this time. As one industry-based commentator remarked: 'Who uses motor cycles and why? Is a simple question, and the answer should not be too difficult to find if some attempts were made to discover it. And yet today there is no one in the country who can with accuracy provide that answer, because the job of finding it out has never been properly tackled.' See 'Who rides motor cycles – and why?' *The Motor Cycle and Cycle Trader*, 4 March 1938.

110. This at least was the opinion of BSA's Chairman, who in a speech to shareholders, identified 'the wage earning classes' as 'the backbone of the motor cycle market on which the prospects of your Birmingham factory depends.' See Chairman's *Speech* of 15 November 1932. Copy on deposit in the BSA papers, MS 321/A (Reports and Accounts) at the Birmingham Central Reference Library. His words were later echoed by the Chairman of AMC during his speech to shareholders at the company's Annual General Meeting of 28 December 1939 when he described the motor cycle market as being 'principally comprised of young men.' See *AMC Annual Report for 1938/39*, on deposit at the Guildhall Library, London.

111. Harrow is an exclusive fee-paying boys' school located near London and the Borstal is a type of reform school for juvenile delinquents. See 'Hampered by the DU [Dealer/Union] Agreement' by 'Peeping Tom', *Cycle and Motor Cycle Trader*, 17 June 1938.

112. A point convincingly made in Christopher T. Potter's 'Motorcycle Clubs in Britain During the Interwar Period, 1919–1939: Their Social and Cultural Importance', *International Journal of Motorcycle Studies*, March 2005, posted on www.ijms.nova.edu/.

113. See 'Motor Cyclists in the Making', *The Motor Cycle*, 12 September 1923 and 'Schools in Competition', *ibid.*, 11 January 1923. The same journal also produced a special volume entitled *The Motor Cycle Book for Boys*, London: Iliffe and Sons Ltd, 1928. If its illustrations are to be believed, this book seems to have been directed mainly at the male offspring of middle-class parents.

114. After Lawrence died in a motor cycle accident, he received an admiring obituary in *The Motor Cycle* issue of 23 May 1935. Lawrence regularly rode, indeed was killed on, a Brough Superior, undoubtedly the most expensive motor cycle

available in Britain, or perhaps anywhere else, at the time. A Brough Superior could cost as much as a new higher grade economy automobile, or about £140 to £150.

115. See 'About Motoring', *New Statesman*, 12 June 1926.

116. 'See 'What's wrong with the motor cycle trade?' by 'A Rider', *The Garage and Motor Agent*, 11 February 1933, and 'Making Motor Cycle Sales' by 'A Well-Known Dealer', *Motor Cycle and Cycle Trader*, 29 January 1937.

117. See memo entitled 'TT Races 1931', dated 26 February 1931 contained in MRC MSS 204/3/1/26. These views were shared by *The Automobile Engineer* several years later, when it stated that the industry had been held back by a 'continued emphasis of the sporting and racing aspects.' See 'The Motor Cycle Industry', *op. cit.*

118. See 'Shall we Scrap the TT?' by 'Exporter', *The Motor Cycle and Cycle Trader*, 26 April 1935. Earlier this same journal had attributed the decline of the market to the industry's devotion to what it called 'sporty-boy' enthusiasts, who, 'in the past few years [was] the mainstay of the motor cycle market, and for him alone have the manufacturers catered, with the result that practically every machine today is noisier and more ferocious than it should be.' See editorial entitled 'No more uncertainty', *ibid.*, 4 January 1935.

119. See 'Two foreign wins', *Motor Cycle and Cycle Trader*, 28 June 1935.

120. A copy of Barnett's memo, dated 9 July 1935 and entitled 'Review of the Situation in the British Motor Cycle Industry' is contained in Guardbook MRC MSS 204/3/1/38. Barnett, was director of Francis-Barnett, a leading manufacturer of smaller displacement motor cycles.

121. See article entitled 'Showmanship', *The Motor Cycle and Cycle Trader*, 10 September 1937.

122. A copy of the Union's brief to the government on the subject of motor cycle taxation is contained in PRO BT 59/24/589.

123. See the BSA Chairman's *Speech* of 11 October 1934, which specifically mentions the launch of the 'Empire Star' model. According to the annual 'Buyers' Guide' published by *The Motor Cycle*, the 150 cc model was not available in 1939, although there were more 250 cc models for consumers to choose from. The company also continued to offer its larger 500 cc and 1000 cc motor cycles.

124. Sangster only bought the motor cycle operations of the company, the bicycle and automobile segments went to other buyers. See 'The Triumph Rejuvenation', *The Motor Cycle and Cycle Trader*, 31 January 1936, p. 73. Profit figures are derived from

the 1949 Accounts, contained in the Triumph Engineering papers, MRC MSS 123/2/1/1.

125. See 'Bridging a Gap' by Peter Watson, *Classic Bike*, February 1985 and 'Comfort with Cleanliness' by Jonathon Jones, *The Classic Motor Cycle*, July 1991. Thanks to Mr. Watson for drawing the author's attention to these two articles.

126. At the 1939 Motor Cycle Show there were nine companies (none from the 'Big Six') which had auto-cycles on display compared to half that number several years before. See G.S. Davidson (ed.), *The Motor Cyclists' Annual, 1939–1940*, London: H.E.W. Publications Ltd, 1939 and an untitled feature in *The Export Trader*, December 1938. See also 'Cheaper than taking the bus' by Brian Woolley, *The Classic Motor Cycle*, February 1989.

127. See 'Fewer motor cycles in use', 1 January 1937 and 'False Figures', 7 May 1937 both contained in *The Motor Cycle and Cycle Trader*.

128. See memo 'Denmark: Imports of motor cycles', dated 7 February 1936, contained in Guardbook MRC MSS 204/3/139, 'Spain: Imports of cycle and motor cycle goods', dated 15 April 1936, contained in Guardbook MRC MSS 204/3/1/40 and 'Secondary Industries – Treaty Negotiations', dated 15 January 1937, contained in Guardbook MRC MSS 204/3/141.

129. See memo '211/35: Review of the British Cycle and Motor Cycle Industry', dated 3 December 1935, contained in Guardbook MRC MSS 204/3/1/39. There were also problems with tariffs in Empire and Dominion markets as well, thanks to the 1931 Ottawa Agreement. See, for example, memo '85/36: Australia: Import Restrictions', dated 18 June 1936, contained in Guardbook MRC MSS 204/3/1/40.

130. See memo, 'Argentina: Customs Tariff', dated 30 May 1936, contained in *ibid*.

131. One correspondent informed the Union that the Germans were 'penetrating with the characteristic Teutonic thoroughness every country East of Suez.' See memo entitled '16/37. India: German Motor Cycle Competition', dated 1 February 1937, contained in Guardbook MRC MSS 204/3/1/41.

132. See editorial entitled 'Motor Cycles and the Politicians', *The Motor Cycle*, 20 February 1935.

133. See, for example, memo '58/38 – British East Africa: Use of Lightweight Motor Cycles', dated 3 May 1937, contained in MRC MSS 204/3/1/42, 'Motor Cycle Exports: German Competition', dated 18 August 1937, contained in MRC MSSS 204/3/1/43 and '159/37: Germany: Developments in the Bicycle and Motor Cycle Industry', dated 25 November 1937, *ibid*.

134. See memo entitled 'Department of Overseas Trade, discussion with UK Trade Organisations, no. 25. Motor Cycles, dated 26 October 1938' contained in NA BT 59/24/589.

135. See 'Shall we scrap the TT?', *op. cit.* There was also a wide-spread perception that the Germans had moved ahead of the British in terms of technical improvements and 'there was more originality of design from German manufacturers in the late 1930s than from any other source.' See Hough and Setright, *op. cit.*, p.142.

136. A copy of the agreement negotiated by the two motor cycle industries, entitled 'Protocoll [sic] of the Result of Discussions of Expert Delegations of the British and German Motor Cycle Industry on March 16th 1939', is attached to the minutes of the Management Committee meeting of 14 February 1939, contained in Minute book MRC MSS 204/1/15. For an overview of the Anglo-German commercial talks, see C.A. MacDonald, *The United States, Britain and Appeasement, 1936–1939*, London: Macmillan, 1981 and Scott Newton, *Profits of Peace: The Political Economy of Anglo-German Appeasement*, Oxford: Clarendon Press, 1996.

137. See 'Why not a Scooter revival?' by 'Nitor', *The Motor Cycle*, 7 November 1935 and 'Can the Scooter make a comeback? By Francis Jones, *Motor Cycle and Cycle Trader*, 1 May 1936. This question was also raised during a discussion which followed Triumph Engineering Managing Director Edward Turner's paper entitled 'Post-War Motor Cycle Development' which was delivered to a meeting of the Institution of Automobile Engineers. See *Proceedings of the Institution of Automobile Engineers*, vol. XXXVII, 1942–1943 Session, pp.320–1.

138. For example, according to BSA's own financial records, the company made a profit margin of 27 per cent on the 150 cc size machines but made a 45 per cent profit on their biggest model, the G–9 1000 cc V-Twins. The 500 cc 'Blue Star' models earned a 39 per cent profit margin. This information is drawn from data contained in BSA's *Reports on Accounts*, MRC MSS 19A/2/35, p. 16.

139. AMC's manufacturing and marketing policy ran directly contrary to this strategy. After it had acquired the Sunbeam company in 1932, the Chairman assured shareholders that AMC was now able to offer consumers, along with its existing Matchless and AJS line-ups, three separate and competing sets of motor cycle models. This was considered a positive development in terms of consumer choice. See Matchless/AMC *Annual Report* for 1933, on deposit at the Guildhall Library, London.

140. A record of Watling's testimony is contained in the *Minutes of Evidence*, Committee on Industry and Trade (1924–27), 12 March 1925, pp.451–2. Scepticism about the suitability of mass production technology was common elsewhere in British industry, at least through the 1920s. See, for example, the remarks of attendees of the fourth annual dinner of the Institution of Production Engineers held in London on 21 October 1927. These remarks were reported in *The Proceedings of the Institution of Production Engineers*, vol. VII, Session 1927–1928, no. 1, at pp.1–5.

141. See the 1920s era photographs of the Triumph plant on pp. 30–5 contained in Ivor Davies, *It's a Triumph*, Sparkford: Hayes Publishing Company, 1982; for a further description of the workings of the factory, refer to a cassette audio tape of Jack Wickes (a former member of Triumph's design staff) on deposit in the Audio Records section of the Coventry City Records Office, tape 1, side 1.

142. See 'The Works of the BSA Co. Ltd. – Methods in the Manufacture of Motor Cycle Engines' (no author indicated), *Automobile Engineer*, November 1938, pp. 434–9.

143. According to the minutes of the factory management committee, the assembly line conveyor was put into operation sometime during December 1936. See the minutes dated 30 December 1936, agenda item no. 1491, contained in MRC MSS 19C, File 16.

144. See 'The Final Inspection', *The Motor Cycle and Cycle Trader*, 7 February 1936.

145. See 'Performance in the Making', *The Export Trader*, May 1938.

146. See memo entitled '46/36 Motor Cycles: Criticisms by Users', dated 18 March 1936 and contained in Guardbook MRC MSS 204/3/1/39 (this criticism was echoed by disgruntled dealer E.P. Huxham in a letter published in the 1 April 1938 issue of the *Motor Cycle and Cycle Trader)* and memo entitled '99/39. Motor Cycle Sales Investigation Committee', dated 16 June 1939, contained in Guardbook MRC MSS 204/3/1/47. According to one technical journal, another problem was the poor quality of the materials used in motor cycle frames. These were, it was claimed, 'as a rule rather crudely designed structures in which strength and rigidity have been obtained by the use of heavy gauge tubing and clumsy malleable iron lugs.' See 'The Motor Cycle Show', *The Automobile Engineer*, December 1938, pp.466–73.

147. See 'Motor Cycle Progress: Past, Present and Future', by H.D. Teage, *op. cit.*

148. The history of trade unionism and collective bargaining is examined in more detail in chapter six.

149. Information about dividends come from *Annual Reports* of the companies concerned during the latter half of the 1930s.

150. The fact that BSA received considerable benefit from the rearmament programme, primarily through its small arms division and from Daimler (notably aero engine production), was reported in the business press as well. See untitled feature in the *Statist*, 19 June 1937, p. 965. Other motor cycle firms also picked up similar work. Enfield Cycles, for one, report military contracts as did Matchless Motor Cycles. See *Stock Market Gazette*, 19 November 1938 and *Directors' Report, Matchless Motor Company*, 10th Annual General Meeting, 16 December 1938, copy on deposit at the Guildhall Library, London.

151. Indeed, the British government had entertained the notion of further relaxing the regulations and taxes on the small motor cycles (under 100 cc) but had decided not to proceed because the industry had failed to produce sufficiently strong arguments to justify why further concessions would increase sales. Instead most of its arguments seemed to be based upon negative comparisons with the situation enjoyed by their continental counterparts. Thus, the British manufacturers would assert, if deregulation worked in France or Germany, it would also work in Britain. However, as a minute written by a Mr. Jones, dated 20 December 1938, retorted, in the absence of more hard information from the Union, 'We cannot offer an opinion on how far these regulations are an impediment to the use of the light-weight motor cycle in the United Kingdom.' To which the Department's Comptroller-General had minuted, 'I agree. We have nothing to work on.' See minute from 'Jones' dated 5 December 1938 contained in NA BT 59/24, sub-file 589, *op. cit.*

152. See memo entitled '112/38: Motor Cycle Propaganda', contained in Guardbook MRC MSS 204/3/1/45 as well as 'Motor Show Musing', by 'F.J.' (Francis Jones), *Motor Cycle and Cycle Trader*, 22 October 1937.

153. See, for example, a report received from the company involved, Editorial Services Ltd, summarising its activities during October 1929. Its is attached to a memo from Union Director Major Watling to members of the Management Committee, dated 20 November 1929 and contained in Guardbook MRC MSS 204/3/1/22. The Union appears to have terminated its contract with this company sometime between 1930 and 1931.

154. After the death of James L. Norton, funds were raised by other manufacturers to create a scholarship in his memory at Birmingham University's engineering school. A copy of the Trust Deed for the Fund is attached to memo 'James L. Norton Memorial Fund', dated 18 August 1926, contained in Guardbook MRC MSS 204/3/1/14. Little, however, is known about the activities of this scholarship after its establishment. See also 'James L. Norton Memorial Fund', *The Motor Cycle*, 14 May 1925, p. 713.

155. All the relevant papers read before meetings of the Institute of Automobile Engineers concerned larger displacement motor cycles. See, for example, 'The Light Car and the Motor Cycle Compared' by W. Halcot Hingston, *Proceedings of the Institution of Automobile Engineers*, vol. XVII (1922–1922), pp. 23–59 and 'The Super-Sports Motor Cycle' by John Wallace, *ibid.*, vol. XXIV (1929–1930), pp. 11–231. One study noted that the ill-fated Motor Cycle Research Association was 'not successful in obtaining wide support from the industry.' See H. Frank Heath and A.L. Heatherington, *Industrial Research and Development in the UK. A Survey*, London: Faber & Faber Ltd, 1946, p. 13.

156. This section draws, in part, on the argument contained in S.M. Bowden, 'Demand and Supply Constraints in the Inter-War UK Car Industry: Did the Manufacturers get it Right?' *Business History*, April 1991, pp. 241–67.

157. See 'Building for World Competition', *The Export Trader*, May 1939.

Notes to Chapter 2: The war years, 1939–1945

1. Started up in 1942, the Licence to Acquire restricted the purchase of motor cycles (mainly machines with an engine capacity under 250 cc) for 'essential' civilian use only. For a background of the Licence to Acquire, see document, prepared by the Secretary to the Interdepartmental Committee for the Post-War Resettlement of the Motor Industry, entitled 'Licences to Acquire Motor Cycles', dated 15 June 1945, contained in NA WO 185/224.

2. See G.C. Allen 'The Concentration of Production

Policy' in D.N. Chester (ed.) *Lessons of the British War Economy*, Cambridge: Cambridge University Press, 1951, p. 167. See also W.K. Hancock and M.M. Gowing, *The British War Economy*, London: HMSO, 1949. For a more recent history of Britain's industrial effort during the Second World War, see Alan Milward, *War, Economy and Society, 1939–1945*, London: Pelican Books, 1987.

3. For a detailed account of BSA's contributions to the British war effort, see Donovan M. Ward, *The*

Other Battle (printed privately by BSA in 1946). Barry Ryerson's history of the firm, *The Giants of Small Heath*, contains a section on the war years although it is largely based upon Ward's account. References to BSA's activities are also included in David Thoms, *War, Industry and Society, The Midlands, 1939–1945*. London: Routledge, 1989. Copies of the various contracts between BSA and government ministries such as Aircraft Production and Supply can be found in the BSA collection at the Solihull Public library, mainly within the series 127–262.

4. The war-time activities of Triumph Engineering is covered in Ivor Davies, *op. cit.*, pp. 69–70. Information about Enfield Cycle's non-motor cycle manufacturing activities is contained in NA AVIA 55/130.

5. See memo dated 24 July, 1940, entitled 'EG 24/40: Rationing of Materials: Motor Cycles' contained in Guardbook MRC MSS 204/3/1/49a. Major Watling thought it might be a good idea that the smaller companies might 'co-operate with a view to keeping alive UK export trade in motor cycles in the face of American competition and with a view to ensuring the continuance of 'goodwill' in UK motor cycles so as to enable rapid development of motor cycle export trade after the war'. See memo dated 28 December, 1940 and entitled 'Motor Cycle Exports: Suggested Standardisation', contained in Guardbook MRC MSS 204/3/1/50.

6. See memo entitled 'Bicycle and Motor Cycle Export Groups', dated 30 April, 1940 contained in Guardbook MRC MSS 204/3/1/49a. The Export Groups were charged with keeping statistics, upon which would be calculated the allocations of materials. In 1940 the industry had negotiated an agreement with the Board of Trade that allowed approximately 40 per cent of materials, which Watling thought reasonable since during 1938 the industry had exported between 20 and 40 per cent of output. However, even in the spring of 1940 the industry was already concerned about the loss of the Baltic and Scandinavian markets (which had accounted for 10 per cent of exports in 1938). The loss was especially acute in terms of motor cycle engine exports. Some 70 per cent of the export total went to Sweden and Poland alone, along with 20 per cent of all other component parts. See memo dated 23 April, 1940 entitled 'Union Export Groups' contained in *ibid*.

7. For a more critical account of the Chamberlain government's management of the war economy, see Paul Addison, *The Road to 1945*, London: Quartet Books, 1975, pp. 63–70. According to the unpublished paper entitled 'Historical Narrative:

Wheeled Vehicle Motor Transport, 1935–1943' the numbers of motor cycles ordered by the War Office had grown from 483 in 1935, to 1,176 in 1936, 2,170 in 1937, 2,015 in 1938, and then jumped dramatically to 9,447 in 1939. Apparently pre-war estimates foresaw a need for a total of 22,295 motor cycles. The paper is contained in NA AVIA 46/192; see in particular pp. 20–2.

8. The subject of the use of motor cycles during the Second World War has been addressed by several authors. Among them are, David Ansell, *Military Motorcycles*, London: B.T. Batsford, 1985, Steven Shaker and Alan Wise, 'Motorcycles' in *National Defense*, September 1984, pp. 30–4, and Captain Robert Sigl, 'The Military Motorcycle', in *Armor*, September–October 1982, pp. 26–8.

9. According to the Manufacturers' Union records, in 1940 the War Office ordered 18,000 350 cc machines, which were to be supplied by Enfield, Triumph and Matchless (AMC). Another 36,000 500 cc machines were ordered, to be supplied by BSA and Norton. There was also to be a large order for the bigger motor cycles from the French government, which would also be supplemented by production from the Ariel and Velocette factories. See memo dated 12 January, 1940, entitled 'France; Purchase of Military Motor Cycles', contained in Guardbook, *op. cit.* The Norton side-car outfit did go into a limited production, however, this was halted after the introduction of the four wheel drive Jeep. See Derek Magrath, *op. cit.*, p. 68.

10. Public perceptions of these motor cycle units seems to have been particularly enduring. For example, as recently as the mid-1990s, the 'Blitzkrieg' display at the Imperial War Museum contained a large displacement motor cycle-side-car combination which provides a general impression of what many still believed was an accurate representation of the German armed forces during that phase of the war.

11. See memo dated 24 June, 1940 entitled 'Motor Cycle Propaganda', contained in Guardbook MRC MSS 204/3/1/49a. The article referred to was evidently in a June issue of the *Evening Standard*. It is noted in a memo dated 7 July 1940, entitled 'Motor Cycle Regulation', contained in *ibid*.

12. The details of the meeting are contained in 'Motor Cycle Propaganda', contained in *ibid*. There is little written about the use of two wheeled transport during the war, however, a description of the use of German motor cycle units in France is contained in Alistair Horne, *To Lose a Battle – France 1940*, London: Macmillan, 1969, pp. 220–1 and Len Deighton, *Blitzkrieg*, London: Jonathon Cape, 1979, pp. 169–70.

13. Because of the blackout, motor vehicle accident rates increased 100 per cent after only a few months after the outbreak of war. See Angus Calder, *The People's War*, London: Pimlico, 1992, p. 63. See also memo entitled 'Motor Cycle Regulation', *op. cit.* Watling also blamed the government's pre-war attitude towards the industry for this situation. It was, he claimed, the Road Traffic Act of 1930, which raised the minimum age for a motor cycle licence to 16 years and 'whereas there was a greater discipline imposed from Order to Order upon motor cyclists – either by the 'Construction and Use Regulations' or by taxation'. By contrast Germany and Italy had encouraged use of motor cycling. In Watling's words: 'The responsibility, therefore, for our military disaster must to some extent be placed upon the shoulders of the authorities in Whitehall who had initiated and pursued a repressive policy against motor cycling.' Watling's remarks are contained in *ibid.*

14. One study estimates that the British Expeditionary Force (BEF) left behind 700 tanks, 54,000 motor cars and trucks and 20,000 motor cycles. See M.M. Postan's *British War Production*, London: HMSO, 1952, p. 117.

15. According to Bert Hopwood, who was a designer with the company at the time, by destroying the new military motor cycles that were stored in the factory, the Luftwaffe may have unintentionally done the British army a big favour. He thought it was a poor design and would have not lived up to expectations had it been deployed in the field. See Hopwood, *op. cit.*, p. 39. The book also contains a detailed account of the factory bombing as well as its aftermath, at pp. 39–42. Further descriptions of the Coventry Blitz can be found in the Home Office files at the National Archives, particularly HO 199/442.

16. According to one company history, owner Jack Sangster initially wanted to rebuild on the original factory site on Priory St., Coventry. The War Damage Commission apparently thought otherwise, deciding that Coventry centre was too vulnerable to any future bombing attacks and required the company to relocate to Meriden. See Louis and Currie, *op. cit.*, pp. 27–8. Surviving records from the Ministry of Supply do raise some interesting but unresolved points about the decision making process that surrounded the construction of the Meriden factory. See, in particular, the minutes of a meeting of the Ministry's Executive Committee held on 21 November 1941, which are contained in NA AVIA 22/2491. Further correspondence about Triumph's war damage claim is also contained in NA AVIA 15/1041.

17. Details of the Small Heath bombing are found in Thoms, *op. cit.*, pp. 112–13.

18. At the time BSA Board Director (and future Chairman and Managing Director) Bernard Docker criticised the Small Heath workforce for leaving their jobs without permission although it is unclear whether or not he had stayed in the factory during the bombing or had removed himself to a safer location. According to a confidential Home Office report, the disorder at the BSA works brought it to a 'complete standstill' and workers who had come in to collect wages 'took over and controlled the entrance of the factory'. Management called their attitude 'both ugly and menacing'. See undated report contained in NA HO 192/1178. Another confidential report expressed the opinion that BSA management had been less than thorough about its air raid preparations because the company felt itself hard done by for the poor armaments contracts it received during the 1930s. The report repeats accounts of workers, especially on the night shift, refusing to enter the factory and commence work. Report dated November 1940 is contained in NA HO 192/1232.

19. See untitled feature about the industry during the war contained in the *Export Trader*, April 1946, pp. 278–80 and the Manufacturers' Union 1941 *Annual Report*, p. 4., contained in MRC MSS 204/4/3/2.

20. See Jim Reynolds, *op. cit.*, p. 52. According to a press report in late 1938, Norton may have had all the military orders it could have wished but 'all this has thrown a considerable strain upon the production facilities of the factory, excellent as they are'. The company had placed many of its workforce on regular overtime and had added a night shift in order to keep up with the contracts. See 'No Norton Racing Programme', *Motor Cycle and Cycle Trader*, 9 December 1938, p. 199.

21. See Calder, *op. cit.*, pp. 64, 318. The shortages badly affected the anticipated supplies of motor cycles earmarked for domestic use. In December 1940 Watling had to inform Union members that, although there had been plans to produce 15,000 machines for the home market and 10,000 for export, these totals would have to be reduced. See memo dated 21 December 1940, entitled 'Notes of Interview. Bicycle & Motor Cycle War Export Groups: Statistics and Estimates', contained in Guardbook MRC MSS 204/3/1/50.

22. See 'Notes of Interview', prepared by Major Watling and dated 31 July 1941, being a conference with Major-General Hawksworth, Director of Military Training, War Office (Horse Guards).

Hawksworth noted that the big problem with the motor cycle, either solo or with a side-car, was that by its very nature it 'must always be vulnerable'. Watling had trouble disputing this point and was forced to concede to the Union Management Committee that 'I must admit that to a certain extent I appreciate and accept their arguments'. The memo is contained in the Guardbook MRC MSS 204/3/1/51. No doubt another cause for a reduced use of military motor cycles was improved wireless communications which reduced the need for dispatch riders.

23. See *ibid.* Hawksworth explicitly noted the advantages of the Bren carrier in comparison to the motor cycle. In Germany motor cycles increasingly were replaced with four-wheel vehicles such as Volkswagen's 'Kubelwagen', although far fewer numbers of them were supplied to the Wehrmacht than Jeeps to the Allies – never mind the numbers of horses used by the Germans. See Robin Fry, *The VW Beetle*, London: David & Charles, 1980, pp. 83–9.

24. In fact, by 1942 the manufacturers, even if they could get hold of sufficient materials, were forbidden by the Ministry of Supply from exporting machines of larger than 250 cc capacity. Overall it was noted that 'the output of motor cycles has been severely limited'. See Manufacturers' Union *Annual Report* for 1942, p. 2 contained in MRC MSS 204/4/3/2.

25. See Memo from Watling to all members of the Motor Cycle Manufacturers' Section, dated 19 April 1940 and entitled '69/40: Holland: Development of British Trade' contained Guardbook MRC MSS 204/3/1/49a. In August 1938 the *Motor Cycle and Cycle Trader* noted that the Germans had captured the Dutch market from the British manufacturers although no explanations were provided. See 'Holland's Imports, Germany Controls the Dutch Motor cycle Trade', 26 August 1938, p. 146.

26. See memo '69/40', *ibid.*

27. Apparently in the spring of 1944, under circumstances the Union's Management Committee termed 'very obscure' although hardly an unwelcome development, the Canadian army decided to switch from American Harley-Davidsons to British-built Nortons. See memo dated 22 April 1944 entitled 'S.M. Disposals: Harley-Davidson Motor Cycles', contained in Guardbook MRC MSS 204/3/1/55. The information about the self-sufficiency of British motor cycle supply in relation to that of other forms of wheeled transport is from 'Historical Narrative: Wheeled Vehicle Motor Transport', *op. cit.*, p. 82.

28. See letter from Brigadier K. Hedges to AMC,

BSA, Norton and Triumph, dated 18 January 1944, contained in NA WO 185/124, file entitled 'Standardised Motor Cycle Design'.

29. As one War Office representative wrote: 'The reasons for the existing unsatisfactory state of affairs whereby the Army is equipped with multifarious makes and types of vehicles resulting in the consequential spares and maintenance problems are so well known that they need not be ventilated in this paper.' See document entitled 'Organisation and weapons policy Committee – post war design of vehicles other than armoured fighting vehicles', dated January 1945, contained in NA WO 185/96, 'Policy in connection with post-war standardised military vehicles'.

30. See minutes of meeting held between the Ministry of Supply and the motor cycle industry, dated 10 March 1944, contained in NA WO 185/124.

31. See memo dated 13 March 1944 and entitled 'W.D. Motor Cycles: Design' contained in Guardbook MRC MSS 204/3/1/54. Evidently the industry's reluctance to put their minds to the task of meeting war time requirements caused a great deal of frustration at the Ministry of Supply. In a letter to an official at the War Office, Brigadier Hedges noted that the motor cycle manufacturers 'as a whole are showing considerable resistance to the idea of producing a new standardised W.D. motor cycle'. He thought that it might become necessary for the Ministry to 'invoke the use of its legal powers if their attitude did not improve'. See Hedges to Major-General Murison, [no date but most certainly sometime during 1943–44] contained in NA WO 185/124.

32. See minutes of a meeting at the Ministry of Supply (TT2), 4 September 1941, contained in Guardbook MRC MSS 204/3/1/41.

33. At Norton, for example, matters were chronic, with machine tools there reported to be idle 'for want of labour'. Major Watling was very critical of the way the government had allocated this equipment. The Ministry of Aircraft Production (MAP) he charged, 'had the first choice and [he] had evidence that they were extravagant in their use'. Watling insisted that it was up to the Ministry of Supply to ensure that sufficient amounts of machine tools were earmarked for the motor cycle industry if it were to keep to its assigned production targets. See *ibid.*

34. Ministry of Supply representatives at the meeting suggested that the labour situation might be eased through dispersal to places like Lancashire. In the event, however, the crisis eased and there was no necessity to relocate motor cycle production. See *ibid.*

35. See memo dated 31 December 1943 and entitled '26/43: Mexico: Development of Post-War Trade'. In another two memos, one dated 27 August 1940, entitled 'E.G. 48/40. Development of Overseas Trade: Market Reports' and another dated 16 September 1940 entitled 'Development of Overseas Trade: Market Reports Central and South America', the Union provided members of the War Export Group a survey of promising sales prospects. Many of them had previously been taken over by German manufacturers but were now open to the British again. All memos contained in Guardbook MSS MRC 204/3/1/54.

36. The Department of Overseas market survey is contained in a memo dated 23 August 1940, entitled 'E.G. 40/40. Development of Overseas Trade: Market Reports: USA', contained in Guardbook MRC MSS 204/3/1/50. Copies of correspondence between Edward Turner and Triumph's Los Angeles distributor Bill Johnson are reproduced in chapter eight of Ivor Davies' *Triumph – The Complete Story*, Swindon: The Crowood Press, 1991.

37. See memo dated 30 January 1942 entitled 'Export Policy' (being a report on a conference of export groups the day before), contained in Guardbook MSS MRC 204/3/1/52.

38. *Ibid.*

39. Se letter from Watling to the members of the Motor Cycle and Bicycle export groups, dated 27 March 1942 and entitled 'Union Membership' and contained in Guardbook *op. cit.*

40. See memo entitled 'Export Policy', contained in *ibid.*

41. See the memorandum, dated 12 April 1943, entitled 'Export Trade and Lend Lease Agreement', which is contained in Guardbook MRC MSS 204/3/1/53. Sir Samuel Beale, then Chairman of the Industrial and Export Council, advised delegates at the meeting of the delicate political situation in the USA at that time. In particular, he warned them about 'the position of President Roosevelt vis a vis the US Industrialists – the hostility of the Republican Party to British Industrialists and to the British Empire generally'. Subsequently, Watling told Union members that he personally wanted to see greater assertiveness from the British government with the Americans, but the facts of the matter were such that 'we must always bear in mind that at the present time we were bound to the US for at least 2½ days' food per week and that fact alone – ignoring any question of supplies of munitions and material – must ever be present in our mind in existing circumstances'. See *ibid.*

42. See memo dated 25 September 1942 entitled 'Post-War Export Trade', contained in Guardbook MRC MSS 204/3/1/43.

43. *Ibid.*

44. *Ibid..*

45. . See *ibid.* Presumably the 'definitely friendly' relations mentioned were an allusion to the Dusseldorf Agreement (March 1939) described in the previous chapter.

46. See 'Post-War Motor Cycle Development', by Edward Turner, contained in the *Proceedings of the Institution of Automobile Engineers*, 1942–43, vol. XXXVII, pp. 135–54. A verbatim record of the discussions held at meetings in London, Coventry, and Luton as well as written comments were included in the same issue at pp. 313–52.

47. *Ibid.*, p. 137.

48. *Ibid.*

49. *Ibid.*, p. 317.

50. *Ibid.*, p. 327.

51. *Ibid.*, pp. 332, 336, 348.

52. See volume containing material entitled 'Research and Design Committee Minutes-Motor Cycle Section', particularly the meeting of 29 September 1944, contained in MSS 19C.

53. See the section on Douglas motor cycles contained in Wilson's *op. cit.*, vol. 2, pp. 179–80, Peter Hartley, *Matchless* pp. 132, 137, Magrath, *op. cit.*, p. 69 and Reynolds, *op. cit.*, p. 60.

54. See Roy Bacon's *British Motor Cycles of the 1940s and 1950s*, London: Osprey Publishers, 1989, p. 117.

55. The minutes of the Joint Committee have been preserved by the Motor Cycle Retailers' Association in their London headquarters. The file is marked 'The Motor Cycle Advisory Committee, 4815'. The writer wishes to thank the Association for providing access to this material. A number of years later, member Donald Heather would recall the purpose of the Committee was 'to plan post-war conditions of trading, to avoid chaotic trading conditions and to build a prosperous retail side of the industry'. See *ibid.*, meeting of 24 July 24 1957.

56. See *ibid.*, particularly the meetings of 17 September and 11 November 1943.

57. Both AMC's Donald Heather and Jack Sangster were in favour of a flat discount rate; to have it otherwise 'would be undesirable as it would inevitably lead to abuses, to price-cutting and the like'. The retailers favoured a rate of between 20–25 per cent, provided that there was adequate price control. They were, however, 'emphatically' opposed to the rebate system (in that they had the sympathy of most manufacturers). The

manufacturers were also insistent on their right to have what they called 'casual traders' being dealers most in rural areas who might also carry other lines of goods unrelated to motor cycles. See meetings of 9 December 1943 and 9 March 1944, *op. cit.*

58. See committee meeting of 27 January 1944, *ibid.*

59. A copy of the memorandum, entitled 'Problems of Post-War Reconstruction and Development', is contained in NA BT 60/81/6.

60. It was estimated that up to 50 per cent of machine tools, especially the high speed automatic machines, currently deployed in the motor cycle industry would need an overhaul. *Ibid.*

61. *Ibid.*

62. *Ibid.*

63. By 1944 Union officials noted that, thanks to the Lend-Lease Agreement, they had been shut out of the Canadian and South American markets. See memo dated 24 February 1944 entitled 'Post War Reconstruction', contained in Guardbook MRC MSS 204/3/1/54.

64. See memorandum entitled 'Post-war ...', contained in NA BT 60/81/6.

65. When the Commercial Counsellor at the British Embassy in Washington D.C. interviewed a visiting Triumph Chairman Jack Sangster in June 1946, he was told that very little had been done to organise co-operative marketing arrangements. In Sangster's words, 'most manufacturers seemed to wish to plough a lone furrow, so far as export was concerned, although a considerable element of co-operation and uniform practice existed in connection with the domestic trade'. See notes of the interview, prepared by J.B. Greaves, dated 5 June 1946, contained in *ibid.*

66. See memo, Watling to member of the Manufacturers' Union President's Advisory Committee, dated 6 March 1944 and entitled 'Post-war Reconstruction', contained in Guardbook *ibid.* See also memo dated 24 February 1944 entitled 'Post-War Reconstruction', contained in *ibid.*

67. Before working with Lockheed, British born Child had been, among other things, Harley-Davidson's representative in Japan where the company had sponsored the establishment of a factory to build motor cycles under licence. See Harry Sucher's *Harley-Davidson – The Milwaukee Marvel.* Sparkford: Haynes Publishing Group, 1990, pp. 69–70.

68. See memo entitled 'USA – Motor Cycle Exports', dated 6 May 1944 and contained in Guardbook MRC MSS 204/3/1/54. Among other things, the memo reports information received from the British Consul-General of Chicago, who had recently conducted an interview with Child.

69. *Ibid.*

70. Evidently Major Watling had met with a staff member of the SMMT in late 1944 who wanted the Union to join with them to create a network of overseas representatives 'who will be mainly employed for the purpose of market research, through contacts with trade associations and government departments'. The overall cost was projected to be around £20,000 per year and the subscription rate for the Motor Cycle Manufacturers' Union would have been £1,000. See letter, Watling to G. Smith (Norton) dated 4 November 1944 and entitled 'Overseas Representation', contained in the Guardbook MRC MSS 204/3/1/55. The Union seemingly passed the offer up after only 19 of 120 of its members expressed interest in a questionnaire. See minutes of the meeting of the Motor Cycle Manufacturers' Section, dated 8 January 1945, contained in *ibid.*

71. See minutes of meetings between the Bicycle and Motor Cycle Industrial and Export Groups, held on 20 July and 17 August 1944, contained in the Union Minute Book MRC MSS 204/1/1/18.

72. *Ibid.*

73. See letter from Watling to Gilbert Smith (President of the Manufacturers' Union) dated 4 November 1944 and entitled '1945 Motor Cycle Programme'. The letter described an interview Watling had had the day before with Sir William Palmer, who was chairman of an unnamed Board of Trade committee. The letter is contained in Guardbook MRC MSS 204/3/1/55.

74. See memo dated 22 November 1944 and entitled 'Notes of interview between H.R. Watling and Colonel R. Grantham Ministry of Supply (TT2)', contained in Guardbook MRC MSS 204/3/1/56.

75. See note of a meeting held at the Board of Trade, dated 14 December 1944 contained in *ibid.*

76. See document marked as File 257/Veh/839, dated 12 January 1945 and entitled 'Report of a meeting held at Euston House on Wednesday, January 10th, 1945 to Discuss arrangements to be made for the production of motor cycles for Export' and contained in NA WO 185/224. The Union kept its own records of this meeting in an untitled note dated 12 January 1945, contained in Guardbook MRC MSS 204/3/1/56.

77. The Manufacturers' Union estimated that the firms had the following monthly military commitments, Ariel, 450; Matchless (AMC), 750; BSA, 1,400; Enfield, 520; Norton, 635; Triumph, 1,000. The balance available for civilian production after 1

July was, in the same order, 180, 310, 375, 210, 251 and 410. Grantham had assured industry representatives that the Ministry would not be imposing any quotas, the firms could produce all they were capable of and materials would be forthcoming. See Guardbook *op. cit.*

78. The actual breakdown was as follows:

up to 125 cc machines: 5,000 units.
up to 250 cc machines: 10,000 units.
350 cc and over: 20,000 units.

See memo dated 30 January 1945 entitled '22/45. 1945 Motor Cycle Production Programme', contained in Guardbook MRC MSS 204/3/1/56.

79. The Ministry's estimates were as follows:

Firm	Monthly output	Workers
AMC	800	1,000
Ariel	565	400
BSA	1,300	1,600
Enfield	600	600
Norton	675	900
Triumph	900	600

See memo dated 2 March 1945, signed by J. Zinkin (Ministry of Supply) and entitled 'Interdepartmental Committee on the Post-War Resettlement of the Motor Industry'. Attached is a report entitled 'Production Programme for Motor Cycles. Note by Ministry of Supply'. The statistics are drawn from the attachment. All contained in NA WO 185/224.

80. Privately, civil servants admitted that, with sanction having been given to a limited volume of civilian production and with the re-introduction of the basic petrol ration, the industry had made a valid point about abolition of the Licence to Acquire. See letter from G.D. Frazer (Ministry of War Transport) to R.L. Bryant (Board of Trade) dated 15 May 1945 and contained in *ibid*.

81. See telegram from Watling to the Secretary, Ministry of Fuel and Power, dated 25 April 1945 entitled '1945 Motor Cycle Production Programme' contained in *ibid*. Watling's telegram ended on this rather confrontational note: 'I want to make it perfectly plain that if unnecessary obstruction on the manufacture, sale and use is continued there will be – as the result of the present restrictions – considerable unemployment in the motor cycle industry at the beginning of July 1945 and the industry will have to make this situation perfectly clear to the public at large.'

82. See memo dated 11 May 1945 entitled '1945 Motor Cycle Production Programme' contained in Guardbook MRC MSS 204/3/1/56. A copy of the Ministry's own minutes of the same meeting are contained in NA WO 185/224.

83. A Board of Trade representative noted that in the case of New Zealand, such restrictions were the result of pre-war regulations designed to preserve Sterling balances. See minutes of a meeting held at the Board of Trade's London office on 11 May 1945, contained in NA WO 185/224.

84. Corbett went on to say that his company would not go ahead with their projected production programme (he mentioned the figure of 200 machines a week), unless they had 'a free home market'. Gilbert Smith of Norton said that the industry was not so much worried about a labour scarcity as it was about unemployment caused by the Government restrictions which were holding up their production plans. He noted that the 1945–46 production programme was dependent on the manufacturers' estimates of the division of their output between Home and export markets. Watling could not say what exactly those proportions were, since they varied between firms. However, he did note that in the time before the Germans began to launch their government subsidised export drive it approached 50 per cent of the total value of production. *Ibid.*

85. *Ibid.*

86. *Ibid.* In his report back to the Manufacturers' Union Management Committee, Major Watling noted that he had heard reference made about the government's Interdepartmental Committee for the Post-war Reconstruction of the Motor Industry. He had subsequently made enquiries and was able to inform them that 'it appeared that this rather grandiose sounding committee was really nothing more or less than an occasional meeting of various Government Departments'. See memo entitled '1945 Motor Cycle Production Programme', *op. cit.*

87. See minutes of the General Meeting of the Manufacturers' Union dated 1 February 1944 contained in Guardbook MRC MSS 204/1/1/18.

88. Another problem holding back sales were the fact that many of the surplus motor cycles were obsolete and compared poorly to machines built originally for the civilian market. See document entitled 'Communication no. M.T. 16 – Mechanical Transport Disposal Panel – Motor Cycles', dated 28 March 1945, contained in NA BT 69/171.

89. See Minutes of the General Meeting of the Manufacturers' Union, 1 February 1944, *op. cit.*

90. *Ibid.*

91. See minutes of the meetings of the Mechanical Transport Disposal Board for 28 March and 11 April 1945, *op. cit.*

92. According to government figures, the British motor cycle produced 382,715 machines by the end of 1944. Exact estimates of production from January 1945 until the end of hostilities are not available, but may have amounted to anything between 20,000 to 50,000 machines. The 1939–44 estimate is contained in NA AVIA 46/192. Davies, *op. cit.*, contains an undated photograph of Triumph Engineering handing over the 400,000th British war-time motor cycle to a government representative. The photograph, located on p. 79, is undated but most likely from early 1945.

93. The German figures are based on production throughout the so-called 'Greater German Reich' which included motor cycle plants in the former Austria and part of what had been Czechoslovakia. It is unclear just what the breakdown was between the large twin cylinder and the much smaller single cylinder models, but if pre-war trends continued the latter probably outnumbered the former. By 1944, the last full year of production, only one firm, Auto-Union (based in Zschopau in what would soon become the Soviet zone) continued building motor cycles and then only in the 250 cc and 350 cc range. See US Strategic Bombing Survey, *Report on the German Motor Vehicle Industry*, Washington: Munitions Division, 1947, pp. 7, 13 and 19.

94. Indian's production was 43,044 machines and Harley-Davidson made 88,000 during the period in question. See Harry Sucher's *The Iron Redskin*, Sparkford: Haynes Publishing Group, 1990, p. 283 and his *Harley-Davidson*, p. 183.

95. The story about Triumph's announcement is contained in an article entitled 'Triumph Post-War Motor Cycles' in the *Motor Cycle and Cycle Trader*, 2 March 1945, p. 598. The AMC story, entitled 'AMC War Effort and Prospects', is covered in *ibid.*, 13 April 1945, p. 16. The Institution of Automobile Engineers had circulated a memo that contained information about a BMW 750 cc side-car combination unit brought back from North Africa. See memo dated 9 December 1943 entitled '23/43: Research' contained in Guardbook MRC MSS 204/3/1/54.

96. The opinion piece was carried in the 13 April 1945 issue at p. 33. The correspondent, identified as 'Marcus', condemned the 'racing and reliability trials mentality of manufacturers' and so long as 'that mentality persists we can never hope to see the motor cycle develop as it should – as the cheapest form of powered transport for the man and woman of modest means'. He concluded by stating that if the industry was to survive and expand, 'the appeal of speed must be subordinated, and in its place must be emphasised the handiness and economy of the motor cycle as the everyday transport of the man in the street'.

Notes to Chapter 3: Revival and complacency, 1945–1951

1. Manufacturers' Union President George Wilson thought that, in terms of exports, there were three courses of action open to the industry. One was to continue trading in traditional overseas markets such as Australia. Second, to move into those markets in, for example, South America and Asia, formerly dominated by the Germans, but now open to the British. Third, he saw particularly good prospects in North America, a market where neither the British or Germans had much success before 1939. See 'Better than Ever', *The Export Trader*, August 1945, pp. 12–13.

2. See meetings of 20 July, 14 August and 16 May 1945, all contained in Minute Book MRC MSS 204/1/1/18.

3. Not everyone associated with the British motor cycle industry subscribed to this critical view of German industry. E.A. Mellors, for example, a well known racer (who had been 'Champion of Europe' over 1938/1939) had a more sympathetic attitude towards the Germans, who he thought were far better at marketing than their British counterparts. Their success, in his opinion, had less to do with government subsidies, but was more the result of the fact that they 'were wise enough to supply their customers with what they wanted, and not what we would have like to sell them'. See 'The motor cycles Europe needs' by E.A. Mellors, *Motor Cycle and Cycle Trader*, 27 April 1945, p. 84.

4. During a meeting of the BSA Small Heath factory Management Committee, members were informed that 'manufacturers will be permitted to recommence the production of civilian machines for *export purposes only*'. [Emphasis in the original]. See Management Committee meeting of 20 January 1945, contained in MRC MSS 19A/1/5.

5. See minutes of the Motor Cycle Manufacturers' Section meeting of 26 September 1947, contained in Minute Book MRC MSS 204/1/1/20.

6. See minutes of the Motor Cycle Manufacturers' section of 26 September 1947, contained in Guardbook MRC MSS 204/3/1/61. The Ministry of Supply's 1948 programme is outlined in a Union memo dated 20 October 1947 and entitled '210/47. Motor Cycle Exports'. The author of the Ministry of Supply memo made his estimate of 150,000

machines on the basis of the Union's memo to the Board of Trade in July 1944. However, this memo had actually said the industry could produce 500,000 machines after the war. All material contained in Guardbook MRC MSS 204/3/1/61.

7. See the minutes of the meeting of the Group Export Management Committee, held on 21 October 1947. Members had been informed by the Ministry of Labour that 'there was no priority whatsoever for labour for the Cycle and Motor Cycle Industries'. Complaints were also voiced about the poor quality of steel which had arrived. During that time exports had been increased to 60 per cent of total output. The minutes are contained Minute Book MRC MSS 204/1/1/20.

8. See editorial entitled 'Another Reason the Purchase Tax must Go', *Motor Cycling*, 5 July 1947, p. 163.

9. Nonetheless, some suspected there was every possibility that the Americans might yet launch an export drive of their own and rumours abounded of new designs nearing completion on drawing boards at the Harley-Davidson and Indian companies. See memo 'USA: Motor Cycle Exports', dated 3 February 1947, contained in Guardbook MSS MRC 204/3/1/59a. For details of Harley-Davidson's post-war production programme, see Harry Sucher, *op. cit.*, pp. 185–212.

10. BSA bought Ariel from Sangster in late 1944 for £310,000 cash, along with the rights to the name of Imperial Motor Cycle Co, which was another Sangster asset. Sangster must have been a tough bargainer. Docker was initially mandated by the Board of Directors to offer £80,000, yet a month later this total had more than tripled, albeit with the New Imperial company thrown in as a sweetener. See meetings of September 19, October 17 and November 19, 1944, contained in the BSA Board of Directors' Minute Books, no. 14, MRC MSS 19C/18.

11. See 'Ariel Motor Cycles acquired by BSA', *Motor Cycle and Cycle Trader*, 5 January 1945, p. 352.

12. The New Hudson purchase, which cost £90,000, was approved at a Board of Directors' meeting on June 22, 1943. The Sunbeam purchase, which cost £50,000, was approved at the September 21, 1943 meeting. See Directors' Minute Book, *op. cit.*

13. See Peter Hartley, *The Story of Rudge Motor Cycles*, Wellingborough: Patrick Stephens Ltd, 1985, pp. 118–20 and Ronald Clark, *Brough Superior – The Rolls Royce of Motor Cycles*. Norwich: Goose & Son, 1964, p. 92.

14. For details of the models produced in the post-war years, see Roy Bacon, *British Motor Cycles of the 1940s and 1950s*, London: Osprey Publishing, 1989.

15. The Standard Vanguard motor car was introduced in 1947 as a 'World Beating' export model although, unlike the Triumph Speed Twin motor cycle, it failed to live up to the company's high expectations. See Nick Tiratsoo, 'The Motor Car Industry', contained in H. Mercer, W. Rollings and J.D. Tomlinson (eds), *The Labour Government and Private Industry. The Experience of 1945–1951*, Edinburgh: Edinburgh University Press, especially pp. 172–5. See also, 'Price, size scuttled Vanguard' by Bill Vance, *Times-Colonist* (Victoria BC, Canada), 18 July 1997.

16. See Davies, *op. cit.*, pp. 95–112 and Hopwood, *op. cit.*, pp. 39–68.

17. Turner wrote a glowing account of sales prospects in the western US after one of his American business trips, see his 'From Coventry to California', *Motor Cycling*, 18 October 1945, pp. 436–7. Triumph owner and chairman Jack Sangster also made a point of personally visiting the USA to investigate sales opportunities, albeit not as frequently as Turner. See 'Memorandum of an Interview with Mr. J.Y. Sangster, Chairman, Triumph Engineering Co. Ltd. Coventry', dated 5 June 1946, contained in NA BT 60/81/6, *op. cit.* For a broader overview of Triumph's entry into the American market, see Lindsay Brooke and David Gaylin, *Triumph Motorcycles in America*, Osceola, USA: Motorbooks International, 1993, pp. 14–25.

18. See Hopwood, *op. cit.*, p. 32 and p. 60 and Davies, *op. cit.*, pp. 113–34. In 1947, for example, Triumph built 6,343 500 cc and 3,630 350 cc machines. In 1950, it built 7,427 650 cc, 4,879 500 cc and 1,773 350 cc machines. Information contained in MRC MSS 123/2/3/6/15 and MSS 123/2/1/2.

19. Financial data drawn from materials within MRC MSS 123/2/3/6/15.

20. Norton Motors' building application, dated 14 March 1946, is contained in NA BT 208/17. It is, however, unclear whether or not Norton completed the expansion as planned. See also 'British Industry gets down to it', by G.E. Thomas, *Export Trader*, August 1948, pp. 401–5.

21. A photo of Formby and his new Norton, posed outside the Birmingham factory, is contained in the *Motor Cycle and Cycle Trader*, 18, July 1947, p. 480.

22. See Peter Hartley, *op. cit.*, pp. 80–2.

23. Details of the various models are contained in Roy Bacon, *British Motorcycles of the 1940s and 1950s*.

24. See BSA Small Heath factory Management Committee meeting minutes, entitled 'Motor cycles and pedal cycles, immediate post-war models' held on 28 August 1944, contained in MRC MSS 19A/1/5. For details on investigations

conducted on German and American motor cycles, see memo dated 27 August 1945 entitled 'Research – Captured Enemy Motor Cycles', contained in Guardbook MRC MSS 204/3/1/57.

25. See Ryerson, *op. cit.*, pp. 87–110 and Bacon, *op. cit.*, pp. 32–41, 52–64, 125.

26. See BSA Small Heath factory Management Committee meeting of 10 September 1945, contained in *op. cit.* and Ryerson, *op. cit.*, p. 93 and p. 105.

27. See BSA Chairman's Speech, delivered 31 December 1946, contained in the BSA Collection, Birmingham Central Library, MS 321/A and Robert Cordon Champ, *Sunbeam S7 and S8*, Sparkford: Haynes Publishing Group, 1983, pp. 5–8.

28. See BSA Board of Directors' meeting of 20 March, agenda item 9949, and 17 July 1947, agenda item 9979. BSA paid the Ministry of Supply £55,000 for what was called 'No. 4 Shop' in Redditch The minutes are in Minute Book 15, MRC MSS 19C/19.

29. The Board voted to purchase Interchrome on 19 September 1944 (agenda item 9744) for £14,000 and decided to purchase Monochrome on 19 February 1946 (agenda item 9866) for £26,000. Meetings contained in Minute book no. 14, MRC MSS 19C/18.

30. See BSA Small Heath factory Management Meeting of 20 January 1945, which discussed using a Villiers engine in an Auto-cycle. These minutes are contained in MRC MSS 19A/1/5.

31. See article entitled 'New factory allocated to Coventry Eagle', *Export Trader*, December 1945, p. 146. See also reference to Francis-Barnett's potential Kenilworth factory site (undated memo), contained in NA BT 177/1519.

32. See Roy Harper, *Vincent Vee-Twins*. London: Osprey Publishing Company, 1982, pp. 18–19 and 'Building the world's fastest motor cycle', *Export Trader*, June 1946, pp. 230–3.

33. See article entitled 'Government factory', contained in *The Motor Cycle and Cycle Trader*, 15 March 1946, p. 722. See also the section on the new Vincent factory, contained in NA BT 177/304.

34. See article entitled 'The New Velocette', contained in *The Motor Cycle and Cycle Trader*, 5 November 1948, pp. 172–3. In the opinion of one company historian, the aim of the LE was to 'appeal to the general public, to the pedal cyclist who wanted power transport, to the pedestrian who could not afford a car'. See Kelly, *op. cit.*, p. 139.

35. For information on the James see untitled news item in *The Motor Cycle and Cycle Trader*, 23 November 1945, p. 204. The American order

amounted to 5,000 machines. The Gadabout was covered in another untitled story in the *Export Trader* of February 1947, pp. 58–9. For information on the Gorgi, see article entitled "Paratroopers' motor cycle improved for civilian use': *ibid.*, p. 46.

36. See George Maxcy and Aubrey Silberston, *The Motor Industry*. George Allen and Unwin, 1959, p. 18 and 'What future for the motor industry?', *Labour Research Bulletin*, April 1946, p. 52.

37. See minutes of Council meeting of 13 May 1947 and the Motor Cycle Manufacturers' Section meeting of 15 July 1947, contained in Minute Book MRC MSS 204/1/1/19.

38. See Letter from W.V. Gibson and A.W. Phillips (Joint Secretaries) of the Standing Joint Committee to Hugh Dalton, Chancellor of the Exchequer, dated 27 June 1947 and entitled 'Motor Cycle Taxation' as well as Jack Sangster's letter to Dalton of the same date, entitled 'Motor Cycle Taxation', both contained in NA T228/420.

39. See unsigned reply from the Treasury, dated 17 July 1947, to Gibson and Phillips as well as Sangster, contained in *ibid*.

40. Internal correspondence contained within NA T228/420 backs up the industry's complaint with respect to disruption of cross-industry relationships.

41. See NA CAB 87/15, 'Post War Resettlement of the Motor Industry' dated 21 March 1945; Lord Woolton joined the BSA Board of Directors several months later, see Board meeting of 18 September 1945 (agenda item 9821) contained in Minute Book 14, MRC MSS 19C/18.

42. See, in particular, a minute prepared by 'Hunt', dated 16 January 1946, contained in NA BT 60/81/6.

43. Alarmed civil servants noted how motor cycle fatalities had jumped from 741 to 956 between 1950 and 1951 (they had totalled 959 in 1939) while injuries went from 21,466 to 30,039 during the same period of time. See undated memo, 'Road casualties during 12 months of unrationed petrol, June 1950-May 1951' (no author indicated) contained in NA MT 108/8.

44. See leading article entitled, 'Lightweights for utility', *Motor Cycle and Cycle Trader*, 2 July 1948, p. 399.

45. The Union had already expressed interest in examining captured German motor cycles during the war, see *Union Annual Report* for 1944, MRC MSS 204/4/3/2 and memo 'Research: Captured enemy motor cycles', dated 27 August 1945, contained in Guardbook MRC MSS 204/3/1/57. This interest was shared by the popular press as well. See 'Captured, examined and tested', *The Motor Cycle*, 12 April 1945 and 'A day among

captured motor cycles' by 'Torrens', *ibid.*, 19 April 1945, pp. 272–3. Information concerning the availability of German motor cycle plant was also widely circulated throughout the trade press, see, for example, 'BMW on Reparations List', *Motor Cycle and Cycle Trader*, 16 August 1946, p. 590. The matter of captured German equipment was also discussed among various British industries, see, for example, 'Meeting of Committee on German Reparations', dated 25 April 1946, contained in MRC MSS 200/F/3/S1/21/46 (minutes of the FBI German Reparations Committee).

46. See 'Notes dated 18 June 1945, of a Conference held at Foreign Office (Economic Division) on 14 June 1945 prepared by Major Watling and contained in Guardbook MRC MSS 204/3/1/57.

47. After the aforementioned meeting at the Foreign Office, nominees were initially from BSA, Villiers Engineering and Burman, a gear box manufacturer. However, the team consisted of A.E. Wood, a BSA Executive, Joe Craig, chief development engineer at Associated Motor Cycle Company (previously in the same position at Norton Motors) and C.R.B. Smith of Amal, a leading carburettor manufacturer was selected. Team leader was Captain L.W. Farrer, a senior executive with Villiers Engineering.

48. See 'Notes dated 18 June 1945 …' *op. cit.* Further details on the industry's expectations of the Reparations Programme are outlined in memo '1/46. Germany: Economic Control', dated 1 January 1946 contained in Guardbook MRC MSS 204/3/1/58.

49. The British experience regarding post-war reparations is described in Tom Bower, *The Paperclip Conspiracy*, London: Paladin Grafton Books, 1987. See also I. Turner, 'British Occupation Policy and Volkswagen' (unpublished Ph.D., University of Manchester, 1984).

50. See, in particular, memo entitled 'Review of BIOS activities', dated 17 April 1947 (no author indicated), contained in NA AVIA 46/410.

51. Not all of the managers of German firms were available to meet with the BIOS teams. NSU's principal Director Von Falkenhayn, for example, who had led the German motor cycle delegation at the March 1939 Dusseldorf Anglo-German trade talks, was incarcerated in a Heidelberg prison camp on suspicion of war crimes. There is no evidence that he was ever interviewed by BIOS team members and his ultimate fate is unclear. See *The German Motor Cycle Industry (in the British and USA Zones of Occupation*, BIOS Final Report no. 620. London: BIOS, 1946, p. 30.

52. See minutes of a meeting, entitled 'Germany: Economic Control', held in Birmingham of 28 February 1945 between members of the Reparations panel and the BIOS teams, contained in Minute Book MRC MSS 204/1/1/19.

53. See memo dated 9 December 1946 entitled 'Germany: Acquisition of Prototype Motor Cycles'. Attached to the memo is a letter dated 20 November 1946 to Watling from Colonel R.H. Bright of the Ministry of Supply which detailed instances of American obstructionism. Correspondence contained in Guardbook MRC MSS 204/3/1/60. Notwithstanding the interference from the Americans, several German motor cycles did arrive in Britain. See memo '84/47: Germany: Investigation of Germany Motor Cycles', dated 17 April 1947, contained in *ibid.* and memo dated 26 August 1947 entitled 'Germany: Economic Control: Motor Cycle Components', contained in Guardbook MRC MSS 204/3/1/61.

54. See 'Review of the Exploitation of German Industrial Technical Developments' by E.R. Wood, dated 17 April 1947, contained in NA AVIA 46/410. The reports ultimately also became public, indeed copies are were still on open shelves at the Coventry City Public Library as recently as the mid-1990s. See also 'Supercharged BMW on Show', *Motor Cycle and Cycle Trader*, 20 December 1946, p. 344. The tour visited Birmingham, Manchester and Leeds.

55. See BIOS Final Report no. 654., *The German Motor Cycle Industry Since 1938* by S. du Pont. March 1946. pp. 1–2. Although this report was published by the BIOS, du Pont was identified as a member of FIAT.

56. *Ibid.*

57. *Ibid.* The various reports were reviewed in some detail by the popular, enthusiasts' press. See, for example, 'Experts Examine and Analyse German Industry', *The Motor Cycle*, 7 November 1956, pp. 356–9, 'German Manufacturing Methods', *ibid.*, 17 July 1947, pp. 50–1 and 'US Investigation of the German Industry', *ibid.*, 30 January 1947, pp. 88–90.

58. See BIOS Final Report no. 654, *op. cit.*

59. In contrast, as noted above in chapter one, the only formal link created between the motor cycle industry and British academic institutions, for the purposes of promoting general research, was a scholarship in motor cycle engineering which had been created in 1925 at the University of Birmingham in memory of the recently deceased James Norton, founder of Norton Motors.

60. See BIOS Final Report no. 620, *op. cit.* However, a dissenting view of the German industry was prepared by R.B. Douglas, a Canadian on

secondment to the BIOS. He thought that German manufacturing techniques were between five and eight years behind those practised in Canada or the US. See BIOS Final Report no. 1318. Item no. 19. *Manufacturing Methods in the German Motor Cycle Industry*. London: BIOS, 1946. Douglas' analysis is backed up by J.M. West, a member of BMW's British sales staff, who had visited the company's factory before the war. West found some German motor cycle engineering practices 'primitive' compared to the British. He considered the factory to be highly labour intensive, with work conducted at a leisurely pace: 'no one seemed to hurry'. See J.M. West interview, 23 November 1994.

61. See Watling's memo of 11 April 1946 entitled '82/46: Germany – Economic Control', contained in Guardbook MRC MSS 204/3/1/58.

62. See 'Summary of Ministry of Supply approaches to Trade Association regarding Reparations', [no date but probably late 1946], contained in NA BT 211/504. According to J.M. West, who was AMC's Sales Manager at the time, his company did not place any reparation bids on the grounds that the Board of Directors believed there was simply nothing of interest worth obtaining from Germany. See J.M. West interview, 23 November 1994.

63. See Watling's memo of 24 April 1946 entitled 'Germany: Economic Control' contained in Guardbook MRC MSS 204/3/1/58. See also 'Report for the Directorate' (nd), contained in MRC MSS 200/F/3/S1/21/46.

64. See Ryerson, *op. cit.*, pp. 93–4 and Jeff Clew, *BSA Bantam*, Sparkford: Haynes Publishing Group, 1983, pp. 5–9. According to John Balder, then in BSA's Service Department, the company only used the DKW engine. Balder interview, 18 November 1994.

65. By contrast, there is mention made of BSA's purchase of the plant and equipment of the German machine tool maker Index-Werke, procured through the Ministry of Supply in March 1947. See agenda item 9953, Board of Directors meeting of 20 march 1947, contained in Directors' Minute Book no. 14, contained in MRC MSS 19C/19. The Index-Werke acquisition is also mentioned several times in correspondence contained in the surviving papers of Patrick 'Paddy' Hannon, then BSA's Deputy Chairman. See, for example, Hannon-Docker, 10 December 1948 (Box 32, Folder 1) and Hannon-Docker, 20 August 1947, MacLaren-Hannon, 5 September 1947, and MacLaren-Lord Woolton, 31 January 1947 (Box 32, Folder 2), all contained in Hannon Papers on deposit at the Parliamentary Archives.

66. Harley-Davidson also used the same design for its so-called lightweight 'Hummer', similar in many respects to the Bantam. See Sucher, *op. cit.*, p. 194 and 'Harley-Davidson 125 cc' *The Motor Cycle*, 8 January 1948, pp. 32–3.

67. See letter, Watling to Sangster, dated 19 February 1946 entitled 'Bicycle and Motor Cycle Industry: Government Control', contained in Guardbook MRC MSS 204/3/1/58.

68. See memo from Brotherton, distributed to all members of the Bicycle and Motor Cycle Industrial and Export Groups, dated 4 March 1946, contained in *ibid.*

69. See memo from Watling dated 5 April 1946, entitled 'Development of Overseas Trade', contained in *ibid.*

70. See agenda for the Council meeting of 18 December 1946, contained in Guardbook MRC MSS 204/3/1/60.

71. See memo entitled 'E.G. 2/47: Rationing of Material – Period 11/1947', dated 1 January 1947, contained in *ibid.*

72. There was a great deal of interest in how the industry was faring under the crisis conditions caused by the fuel shortages. See for example, 'The Industry Restarts', 14 February 1947, *The Motor Cycle and Cycle Trader*, pp. 662–3 and 'At the Factories' *The Motor Cycle*, 6 March 1947, p. 151.

73. See minutes of Council meeting of 21 October 1947, contained in Guardbook MRC MSS 204/3/1/60.

74. *Ibid.*

75. *Ibid.* It was remarked that most of the 'no' votes came mainly from motor cycle makers, although Gilbert Smith (Norton) and Frank Smith (Royal Enfield) did vote 'yes'.

76. See 'No show this year', *Export Trader*, February 1947, p. 11.

77. See memo from Watling to members of the Group Management Committee, dated 12 February 1947, attached to which is a second memo entitled '1947 Production Programme – Case against a Steel Cut for the Bicycle and Motor Cycle Industries', contained in Guardbook MRC MSS 204/3/1/59a.

78. Although not stated, presumably this would only apply to production totals after 1930. See *ibid.*

79. Minutes of the Motor Cycle Manufacturers' Section meeting of 26 September 1947, contained in Guardbook MRC MSS 204/3/1/61. See also editorial entitled 'Petrol cut may increase export prices', *The Motor Cycle and Cycle Trader*, 12 September 1947, p. 722 and 'Manufacturers condemn petrol cut', *The Motor Cycle*, 4 September 1947, pp. 178–9.

80. See 'Petrol cut may last for nine months', *The Motor*

Cycle and Cycle Trader, 26 September 1947, p. 788.

81. See *ibid.* The petrol ration was partially resumed in April 1948, see 'Petrol ration restored' *ibid.*, 23 April 1948, p. 84.

82. See 'The Motor Cycling Outlook' by Francis Jones, *ibid.*, 2 January 1948, pp. 382–3.

83. See Watling's letter to the Parliamentary Private Secretary, dated 22 December 1947, entitled 'Donington Park', contained in Guardbook MRC MSS 204/3/1/62.

84. *Ibid.* The letter was also copied to the editors of *The Motor Cycle* and *Motor Cycling* as well as to the RAC and the MAA.

85. See brief entitled 'Donnington: The Motor Cycle Industry's Case', dated 11 February 1947, contained in Guardbook MRC MSS 204/3/1/62.

86. Mention of Hannon's intervention on behalf of the industry with the Ministry of Supply is mentioned in the minutes of the Motor Cycle Manufacturers' Section meeting of 9 April 1948, contained in *ibid.*

87. In fact Stanford Cripps had been invited by the Manufacturers' Union to open the 1948 Show, although he declined the opportunity and was replaced by Field Marshall Bernard Montgomery. See minutes of the Show Catalogue Committee of 23 July 1948, contained Union Minute Book MRC MSS 204/1/1/2. The Union Council subsequently invited Minister of Supply G.R. Strauss, President of the Board of Trade Harold Wilson, Minister of Transport T. Barnes and, no doubt to ensure the appearance of political evenhandedness, former Foreign Minister Anthony Eden. However, only Eden seems to have actually attended the Show. See minutes of the Council meeting of 28 September 1948, contained in *ibid.*

88. The issue is touched upon by Helen Mercer, 'The Monopolies and Restrictive Practices Commission, 1949–1956: a study in regulatory failure', contained in G. Jones and M. Kirby (eds), *Competitiveness and the State*, Manchester: Manchester University Press, 1991.

89. See Council meeting minutes for 20 January 1948, contained in Guardbook MRC MSS 204/3/1/62. The Greene Report, officially entitled *Restraint of Trade, Report of the Committee appointed by the Lord Chancellor and the President of the Board of Trade to answer certain Trade Questions*, London: HMSO, 1931 (Chairman, Wilfred A. Greene, KC) mentions price maintenance schemes in practice in the motor cycle industry on p. 7. and p. 9.

90. See Council meeting minutes of 20 January 1948, *op. cit.*

91. A copy of the full verbatim transcript of this hearing, entitled 'Minutes of evidence taken before the Committee on Resale Price Maintenance, July 1948', is contained in NA BT 64/540, file 376/1949.

92. *Ibid.*, pp. 5–6.

93. *Ibid.*, p. 6.

94. *Ibid.*, pp. 8–9.

95. *Ibid.*, p. 9.

96. A copy of the Jacob Committee's report was published in the *Motor Cycle and Cycle Trader*, see 'Price Maintenance Criticised', 17 June 1949, pp. 446–9.

97. See memo, dated 4 March 1948 and entitled '68/48: Prices and Profits', contained in Guardbook MRC MSS 204/3/1/62.

98. *Ibid.*

99. As late as September 1947 Watling had reported to the Union's Motor Cycle Manufacturing Section that, although he was aware of negotiations between the government and the motor car industry with respect to a programme to standardise automobile models, he did not think there would be any plans 'to interfere with the production plans of the motor cycle industry'. See minutes of the Motor Cycle Manufacturing Section of 26 September 1947, contained in Minute Book MRC MSS 204/1/1/20.

100. Memo from Watling to manufacturing members, dated 2 October 1948, entitled '320/48: Production Efficiency', contained in Guardbook MRC MSS 204/3/164. Some time earlier, Sir Godfrey Ince, Permanent Secretary to the Minister of Labour, had given a speech to the Institute of the Motor Industry. There he had called for higher productivity, despite the general labour shortage. The trade journal which reported the speech, drew its own conclusions for the motor cycle industry: 'in order to ensure maximum production … manufacturers must use every possible aid to production in the direction of equipping their factories with the latest in machine tools, brazing and welding apparatus and plant'. The journal was certain that what it termed as the 'wiser executives' were already aware of this fact and would act accordingly. See editorial entitled 'Modernising the Industry', *Motor Cycle and Cycle Trader* 17 January 1947, p. 469.

101. See *ibid.* Evidently, there were still war-time type Joint Production Councils functioning in at least one motor cycle factory. In late 1948 G.R. Strauss, Minister of Supply, went to AMC's Woolwich factory and met with members of its Council. See 'Minister of Supply at AMC', *Motor Cycle and Cycle Trader*, 8 October 1948, p. 21.

102. See minutes of the Motor Cycle Technical Committee meeting of 8 December 1948, contained in the Minute Book MRC MSS 204/1/1/21.

103. See minutes of the Council meeting of 28 October 1948, contained in Guardbook MRC MSS 204/3/1/64. The larger question of the Labour Government's efforts to reform British industry during the late 1940s is covered Nick Tiratsoo and Jim Tomlinson, *Industrial Efficiency and State Intervention. Labour, 1939–1951*, London: Routledge, 1993, pp. 144–5, 167–8 and Jim Tomlinson, 'A missed opportunity? Labour and the productivity problem, 1945–51' contained in G. Jones and M. Kirby (eds), *Competitiveness and the State*, Manchester University Press, 1991. See also Scott Newton and Dilwyn Porter, *Modernisation Frustrated*, London: Unwin Hyman, 1988, pp. 101–19.

104. See minutes of the Council meeting of 14 December 1948, contained in Guardbook MRC MSS 204/3/1/64.

105. *Ibid.*

106. *Ibid.*

107. See memo authored by Union Assistant Director Hugh Palin, dated 20 January 1949, entitled 'Production Efficiency' contained in Guardbook MRC MSS 204/3/1/64.

108. *Ibid.*

109. See Minutes of the Council Meeting of 18 January 1949, contained in *ibid.*

110. *Ibid.*

111. *Ibid.*

112. See memo prepared by Hugh Palin to the members of the Production Efficiency Committee, dated 26 January 1949, contained in Guardbook MRC MSS 204/3/1/64. The minutes of the Production Efficiency Committee are contained in Minute Book, MRC MSS 204/1/1/21. For a short general history of the Anglo-American Productivity Council, see Jim Tomlinson, 'The Failure of the Anglo-American Council on Productivity', *Business History*, no. 1, 1991, pp. 82–92.

113. See minutes of Council meeting of 18 January 1949, *Op cit.*

114. *Ibid.*

115. *Ibid.*

116. *Ibid.*

117. See minutes of the Union Council meeting of 28 March 1950, contained in Guardbook MRC MSS 204/3/1/68. See also memo, Watling to all

manufactures, dated 15 February 1949, entitled '160/49: Production Efficiency', contained in Guardbook MRC MSS 204/3/1/65. The aversion to standardisation or rationalisation of components was also shared by British sports car companies. See Timothy R. Whistler, 'Niche Products in the British Motor Industry: A History of MG and Triumph Sports Cars', unpublished Ph.D. dissertation (LSE 1991), p. 151.

118. See 'Lightweights for Utility', *Motor Cycle and Cycle Trader* 2 July 1948, p. 399.

119. For a general history of the scooter in Britain, see 'Object as Image: the Italian Scooter Cycle', contained in Dick Hebdige, *Hiding in the Light*, London: Routledge, 1988, pp. 77–115 and 'Scooter Mania', in Gary Johnson, *op. cit.*, pp. 73–85. In the spring of 1949, London dealer Pride and Clark were reported as bringing in a ship of French Motobecane autocycles. See minutes of the Motor Cycle Manufacturers Section meeting of 11 April 1949, contained in Minute book MRC MSS 204/1/1/21.

120. Sangster's forebodings were premature. He was to live on until 1977. See his entry in the *Dictionary of Business Biography*.

121. The sale was approved at a BSA Board of Directors meeting held in January 1951. Evidently the negotiations were carried out between Sangster and Board member Lord Woolton and the decision to buy was based on the belief, according to the Board minutes, that Triumph was 'a desirable asset to acquire'. The money was paid to Sangster in the form of a lump sum, payable by 31 March. See minutes of the Board meeting held on 11 January 1951, agenda item 10246, contained in Minute Book no. 15, MRC MSS 19C/19. The figure for Sangster's original purchase of Triumph comes from Wilson, *op. cit.*, vol. 5, p. 15.

122. After 1955, following the merger of Austin and Morris in 1952 to create BMC, the so-called 'Big Five' motor car manufacturers accounted for 95 per cent of industry output. In 1946, the so-called 'Big Six' had manufactured 90 per cent of output. See Maxcy and Silberston, *op. cit.*, p. 19 and p. 22. See also Rhys, *op. cit.*, pp. 21–2 and Church, *The Rise and Decline of the British Motor Industry*, p. 78.

Notes to Chapter 4: The window of opportunity, 1951–1956

1. For shortages caused by the Korean War and rearmament, especially chrome and steel, see a series of minutes and memorandum from the Minute Books and Guardbooks contained in the Guardbooks from MRC MSS 204/31/69 to MSS

204/3/1/72. In its 1953 Report, the Manufacturers' Union claimed that the materials shortages had ended. See 1953 *Annual Report*, p. 4, contained in MRC MSS 204/4/3/2.

2. Churchill's quote comes from William Plowden's

The Motor Car and Politics, London: The Bodely Head, 1971, p. 318.

3. A point also made by Barbara Smith, *The British Motorcycle Industry, 1945–1975*, pp. 21, 25.

4. See Chairman's speech for the 1951 Annual General Meeting, p. 2, contained in the BSA Collection, Birmingham Central Library, MS 321/A.

5. The figure of 20,000 employees is cited in Docker's speech to the shareholders of 1954, pp. 3–5, see MS 321/A. Details about the South African and Canadian factories are provided in the BSA Directors' Minute Book no. 16, meeting of 27 September 1951, agenda items 10292 and 10293 respectively, contained in MRC MSS 19C/19.

6. BSA dropped manufacture of its light car during the war and did not resume production after 1945. There is a report that the company, along with much of the British motor industry, turned down the Volkswagen 'Beetle', offered via the Reparations Programme. See Owen Wright, *BSA – The Complete Story*, Ramsbury: The Crowood Press, 1992, p. 40. Wright's statement about the VW is made without substantiation and there is no mention in the surviving BSA archives of the company ever showing any interest in the VW design. For the market share estimate, see the *Economist*, 'More Power to the Pedal', 30 April 1955, pp. 399–401.

7. See Roy Bacon, *British Motorcycles of the 1940s and 1950s*, pp. 32–41, 52–64, 125 for details of this range.

8. Barry Ryerson, *op. cit.* See chapter nine for a review of the post-war range, pp. 87–110.

9. See BSA Directors' Minute Book, meeting of 30 April 1953, item 10455, Minute Book 15, contained in MRC MSS 19C/19. See also 'Separation of Motor Cycle and Bicycle Interests. New Company formed', *BSA News*, August 1953, p. 3.

10. According to John Balder, BSA's Service Manager at the time, the Small Heath plant ran three assembly lines simultaneously, one for the Bantam, one for the 'B' series of single cylinder models and another for the twin cylinder machines. See Balder interview of 18 November 1994. The Sunbeam had been the star of the first post-war Show in 1948, one being presented to Field Marshall Montgomery who had been invited by the Union as its special guest and who had opened the proceedings. See *Show Catalogue* for 1948, MRC MSS 204/4/1/29. There was a follow up on how the Field Marshall was enjoying his motor cycle in *BSA News* for Autumn 1952, p. 31.

11. The so-called 'Winged Wheel' was a single cylinder 35 cc engine, which was fitted on to the rear wheel of a bicycle. It cost £25 and could return 200 miles per gallon. See 'The Winged Wheel' in the August 1953 issue of *BSA News*, p. 5.

12. See Hopwood, *op. cit.*, pp. 127–8.

13. See Ivor Davies, *op. cit.*, p. 111. See also an untitled feature article on Triumph lightweight range, contained in *The Motor Cycle and Cycle Export Trader*, November 1952, p. 177.

14. The figure of 65,000 motor cycles produced is drawn from the BSA Management Minutes, meeting of 23 February 1951, agenda item 9258. This total probably includes all motor cycles and New Hudson autocycles made at the Small Heath factory, along with the Sunbeams made at Redditch. According to John Balder, then BSA's service manager, because of market limitations, the Small Heath factory never ran at 100 per cent capacity. See Balder interview, 18 November 1994. No archive material at all remains for Ariel Motors, and it is extremely difficult to estimate its yearly output for virtually any period of time, although after 1945 it probably fluctuated between 5,000 and 10,000 units.

15. See the series of correspondence between BSA Deputy Chairman Patrick 'Paddy' Hannon and various personnel, in particular James Leek and Sir Bernard Docker, during 1947–51, in the Hannon Papers, Box 31/Folders 1–3 and Box 36/Folder 4, on deposit at the Parliamentary Archives.

16. See Davenport-Hines, *op. cit.*, pp. 231–2. At one point, Docker claimed that 90 per cent of the jet engines built in Britain used BSA turbine discs. See *Chairman's Speech*, 9 December 1948, p. 6, MS 321/A, Birmingham Central Reference Library. The cover of the *BSA News* issue for Summer 1956 had a photo of a de Havilland Comet 3 jet airliner, which used jet turbine discs made by BSA's Special Steel Group.

17. A point remarked upon by Ministry of Supply officials in their private correspondence, see, for example, NA SUPP 14/328, specifically a memorandum entitled 'Note of Meeting at the Daimler Company on 12th October 1949' and NA SUPP 14/331, in particular Minute Sheet, dated 16 February 1951, prepared by H. Bailey. See also the minute of 3 September 1951, contained in NA SUPP 14/332.

18. See *Chairman's Speech* delivered on 9 December 1948, contained in MS 321/A.

19. In the opinion of Board members, this strategy was the 'only one likely to enable the company to establish itself in the motor car field'. See Board meeting for 28 March 1950, item 10187, *op. cit.*

20. In June 1950 BSA spent £1,000,000 on re-equipping the Daimler factory and subsequently another

£1,000,000 on purchasing Carbodies, in order to gain a secure source of this vital component. See agenda item 10202, Board meeting of 22 June 1950, contained in Minute Book M15, MRC MSS 19C/19 and agenda item 10552, Board meeting of 20 May 1954, contained in Minute Book 16, MRC MSS 19C/20.

21. Troubles with the Sunbeam had begun even before it went into production, a point indicative of serious design flaws. See, for example, BSA Small Heath factory Management Minutes, meeting of 10 September 1945, agenda item 7821, MRC MSS 19A/1/5. A technical description of this model is contained in Robert Corden Champ, *op. cit.*, pp. 9–10 and his *The Sunbeam Motor Cycle*, Sparkford: Haynes Publications, 1980, pp. 157–65. Designer Bert Hopwood's assessment of the Sunbeam is highly critical: 'The early reputation of difficult maintenance and unreliability stuck with the bike and hampered its sales.' See Hopwood, *op. cit.*, pp. 90–1.

22. See Peter Watson, 'Rise and Fall of the Square Fours', *Classic Bike*, Autumn, 1978, pp. 10–13, Steve Wilson, *op. cit.*, volume 1, pp. 97–102 and Peter Hartley, *The Ariel Story*, Watford, Herts: Argus Books, 1980, pp. 194–209.

23. Owen Wright notes that this motor unit was introduced too late to really capitalise on the boom years of the 'clip-on'. Nor did it appear to have captured the affections of its owners, evidently it was known widely as the 'Stink Wheel'. It faded away after BSA sold its bicycle interests to Raleigh Industries in 1957. See Wright, *op. cit.*, p. 155.

24. See Richard Evely and I.M.D. Little, *Concentration in British Industry*, Cambridge: Cambridge University Press, 1960, p. 52 and p. 123. *The Economist* estimated that AMC, including its subsidiaries, accounted for about 30 per cent of total British output. See 'More power to the Pedal', *op. cit.*

25. For a general overview of AMC's activities during this time, see Gregor Grant, *op. cit.*, pp. 80–3 and Peter Hartley, *Matchless – Once the Largest British Motor Cycle Manufacturer*, pp. 139–70.

26. The Francis-Barnett acquisition was described in an untitled feature in the *Export Trader*, June 1947, p. 213. This purchase also included a subsidiary, Clarendon Pressings and Welding, a company which produced a variety of accessory items for both the motor cycle and motor car industry. Chairman Hogg's quote comes from a letter to AMC Shareholders, dated 4 July 1947, on file at the Guildhall Library. The James' purchase was covered in a news item entitled 'Attention to Detail' contained in *British Cycles and Motor Cycles Overseas*, August/September 1950, p. 369. The James company also manufactured bicycles, although that part of the business was later sold off to Tube Investments, see 'James Pedal Cycle Interests sold', *Times* 21 August 1954, contained in File 12913, Trade Union Congress news clipping collection, MRC. According to J.M. West, AMC Sales Manager at the time, James and Francis-Barnett were purchased very cheaply, for even less than the estimated cost of their assets. See J.M. West interview, 23 November 1994.

27. Donald Heather's view of motor cyclists is described in Hopwood, *op. cit.*, p. 143. This viewpoint was criticised at the time by columnist Francis Jones: 'Extraordinary as it may seem, the belief is still current that a motor cyclist must be something of an engineer if he is to get satisfactory service out of his machine.' See 'Motor Cycle Matters', *Motor Cycle and Cycle Trader*, 20 April 1951, pp. 50–1.

28. AMC's output was discussed in 'Greater Attendance, more Publicity, and Improved Display Standards', 28 November 1952, pp. 176–9. For details of AMC's financial performance at this time, see Barbara Smith, *op. cit.*, p. 31.

29. See the 'Chairman's Speech' to the Annual General Meeting, delivered on 25 February 1953, on deposit at the Guildhall Library, London. Chairman Hogg's remarks were also given detailed coverage in an article entitled 'Norton Acquisition', 7 March 1953, p. 366, *Motor Cycle and Cycle Trader*. AMC's purchase of Norton Motors included its subsidiary, R.T. Shelley, a manufacturer of motor cycle and motor car accessories.

30. For an outline of Royal Enfield's post-war range, See Steve Wilson, *op. cit.*, vol. 4, pp. 53–81 and Peter Hartley, *The Story of Royal Enfield Motor Cycles*, Cambridge: Patrick Stephens, 1981, pp. 92–110. The motorised bicycle engine was an Italian design, the 'Cucciolo', which Enfield built under licence for the Britax company. See 'Britax Bicycle available for Cucciolo Engine unit', in the *Motor Cycle and Cycle Trader* 22 August, 1953, p. 287. The Madras India factory assembled its first 350 cc single cylinder model in 1957 and continues to produce much the same machines up to the present day. See photo story in *The Motor Cycle and Cycle Export Trader*, January/February 1957, p. 13. In 1948 Norton announced its intention to build an assembly plant in Canada but no action was ever taken. See 'Post-war sales of motor cycles in Canada', 19 November 1948, *Motor Cycle and Cycle Trader*, p. 289.

31. See Jeff Clew, *The Douglas Motorcycle*, Sparkford: Haynes Publishing Group, 1981, especially pp. 153–72. For more detail on the scooter licensing

scheme, see 'First British Vespa on March 15', *Motor Cycle and Cycle Trader*, 9 March 1951, p. 492.

32. Vincent was also involved in Britain's rearmament programme, which may have disrupted its regular production programmes after 1950. See 'Fewer Vincent Motor Cycles', 12 January 1951, p. 387., *Motor Cycle and Cycle Trader*. The price for the 'Rapide' is derived from the 'Buyers' Guide', contained in *The Motor Cycle*, 18 March 1954. That same year, the price of a Ford Anglia and Popular motor car was, respectively, £541 and £413, see 'Buyers' Guide', *The Autocar*, 11 November 1955.

33. So determined was the company to develop the Argentine market, that in 1946 one of its 1000 cc models was actually air-freighted to Buenos Aires in order to be displayed in a trade exhibition. See untitled news item, *The Motor Cycle*, 26 September 1946, p. 241. According to owner Philip Vincent himself, the loss of the Argentine market badly damaged the company and was a major factor in its demise. Vincent's remarks are contained in his preface to Roy Harper, *op. cit.*, pp. 8–10. A later history of the company claims that poorly focused and ineffective management was another significant factor in its decline. See Duncan Wherrett, *Vincent*, London: Osprey, 1994, pp. 103–5.

34. See Peter Carick, *Vincent-HRD*, Cambridge: Patrick Stephens Ltd, 1982, p. 21, pp. 35–6, 72. Owner Philip Vincent was also quoted as saying that his company had closed because of 'intense competition from small cars … There is no longer the same demand for our high quality models.' He went on to elaborate that, 'prices have reached a ceiling. With small cars available at such cheap low cost, people are turning away from motor cycles.' See *Evening Standard* (no date but probably September 1955), story entitled 'Motor Cycle Firm is to Stop Production' contained in the Manufacturers' Union press clippings book, MRC MSS 204/10/1/3.

35. See Phil Irving, *An Autobiography*, Wahroongo, Australia: Turton and Armstrong, 1992, p. 292 (thanks to Dennis Frost for drawing this reference to the author's attention). The LE was, however, subject to a test evaluation in the *Daily Herald*. See also Wilson, *op. cit.*, vol. 6, pp. 191–200.

36. See John Kelly, *op. cit.*, pp. 223, 512, 518.

37. For a comprehensive listing of these models, see Roy Bacon, *Villiers Singles and Twins, the Post-War British Two-Stroke Light Weight Motor Cycles*. London: Osprey Publishing Co., 1983. Most of the smaller scale British producers, such as Excelsior, AJW, Bond, Cotton and Sun, continued to use proprietary engines, virtually all originating from the Villiers Engineering Co. As no reliable statistical information is available it is difficult to estimate what their output was although it was unlikely to have been more than 10 per cent to 15 per cent of total British production.

38. At least one firm, Walsall based Helliwell Ltd (which had been building aircraft components along with sidecars and sports cars), entered the utility market soon after the war with its so-called Swallow 'Gadabout'. See feature on the 'Gadabout' in the *Export Trader*, February 1947, pp. 58–9 and also 'New British Two Wheeler for Mr. and Mrs. Everyman', *The Motor Cycle*, 28 November 1946, pp. 412–14. Another entry to this market was the General Steel and Iron Company, which introduced two small motor cycles (122 cc and 98 cc respectively) along with an autocycle (98 cc) in 1952. All these models used proprietary engines supplied by Villiers. See 'Revolutionary Lightweights' *Motor Cycle and Cycle Export Trader*, November 1952, p. 175.

39. Columnist Francis Jones had warned the industry of the dangers of mounting public hostility about motor cycle accidents soon after the war. See 'Red Light Showing for the Motor Cycle Trade', *Motor Cycle and Cycle Trader*, 30 August 1946, pp. 667–8.

40. In the 'Undergraduate Page' of a leading journal, motor cyclist John W. Crawford admitted that public opinion was mounting against higher levels of motor cycle accidents. Rider behaviour was a problem, he agreed, and 'who can resist the temptation to show that attractive girl on the pillion what the bike, and incidentally yourself, are capable of doing?' See 'As to Motor-Cycles' *The Spectator*, 6 June 1952, p. 741.

41. For example, when *The Times* published a collection of letters to the editor in 1951 on the topic of road accidents, only two of the entries related to motor cycles. See *Accidents on the Road*, London: The Times Publishing Company, 1951. Bear in mind too that it is also very likely that many, if not the vast majority, of pedestrian and cyclist fatalities were killed by motor cars. As for motor cyclists, they nearly always came out far worse in an encounter with a motor car than would the driver of the car.

42. As one popular motor cycle journalist put it: 'For surely sport is very near the heart of most of us. Although tens of thousands use their motor cycles solely for pleasure and transport, there is scarcely a rider whose thoughts do not turn towards the Isle of Man TT when June comes round.' See *Motor Cycling Year Book 1951*, compiled by Peter Chamberlain and the staff of *Motor Cycling*. London: Temple Press Ltd, 1953, p. vii. J.M. West

noted that many motor cycles could be used for commuting purposes during the week and then easily modified for sports use on the weekends. See J.M. West interview, 23 November 1994.

43. See Francis Jones, 'Motor Cycle Matters', *Motor Cycle and Cycle Trader*, 27 July 1951, pp. 273–4; the Manufacturers' Union was not blind to the threat either. During the summer of 1951, some of the leading executives discussed what improvements could be made on their machines to make them safer to use, although they were reluctant to adopt any which were too costly or might impair the speed or performance of their motor cycles. See memo prepared by Major Watling, dated 10 August 1951, entitled 297/51: Committee on Road Safety: Investigation of Motor Cycle Accidents, contained in Guardbook MRC MSS 204/3/1/71.

44. For critical press coverage, see the Manufacturers' Union Newspaper Clipping book, MRC MSS 204/10/1/3, particularly a story from *The Sketch* (no date but almost certainly June 1954) entitled 'This TT is Madness. Death and Fear end Island Race' by Len Smith.

45. Watling had retired as Director of the Manufacturers' Union in January 1953. His comments about racing fatalities were reported in the *Motor Cycle and Cycle Trader*, 13 June 1953, p. 153.

46. For details of Managing Directors and other senior executives who attended the Isle of Man races, see for example, 'Norton's TT Double', 15 June 1951, p. 146, 'TT Coverage', 25 June 1955, pp. 154–5, and 'Personalities seen on 'TT' Island', 23 June 1956, p. 149, all from *ibid*.

47. See *The Motor Cycle*, 13 May 1948, untitled story on p. 384. The employees, however, had to pay their own expenses. Heather's quote on AMC hiring practices is from a biographical feature about him, contained in the *Export Trader*, June 1948, pp. 243–5.

48. See AMC Chairman's speech of 4 February 1955, on deposit at the Guildhall Library. Racing successes were also mentioned by BSA Chairman Sir Bernard Docker in his speeches to the shareholders in 1953. He also praised the Triumph subsidiary for winning the world speed record in 1955. See the Chairman's Speech delivered on 5 December 1955, contained in MS 321/A.

49. Smith went on to declare that the Norton racing team 'really embraced everyone in the factory, for all the workers were "back-room boys"'. His remarks were reported in 'Concern at low-priced exports from Europe', *Motor Cycle and Cycle Trader*, 29 June 1951, p. 173.

50. See 'Sport and Speed', *British Cycles and Motor Cycles Overseas*, June/July 1950, pp. 234–47. See also *ibid.*, 'Improving the Breed' June/July 1952, pp. 70–4. In an article published in BSA's house journal, Competitions Manager Dennis Hardwicke endorsed Norton Motors Managing Director Gilbert Smith's earlier remarks, declaring that the 'competition machine has been proved invaluable as a mobile laboratory.' See 'Improving the Breed', *BSA News*, Spring 1954–55, pp. 8–11.

51. The series on the TT races was produced annually by BP and contained biographical sketches of the racers along with a brief historical background and racing statistics dating from 1907. The Shell Guide and the BSA review are on deposit at the BP Archives at the University of Warwick. Other books published during this period catering to motor cycle sports enthusiasts included A.St.J. Masters, *Motor Cycle Sport*, London: C. Arthus Pearson Ltd, 1958, G.S. Davidson, *Racing Through the Century*, Coventry: W.W. Curtis, 1951, Ted Mellors, *Continental Circus*, Coventry: W.W. Curtis, 1949 and Phil Drackett, *Speedway*, London: W. & G. Foyle Ltd, 1951.

52. News of the films was reported in the *Motor Cycle and Cycle Trader*, 2 April 1955, p. 5, 11 January 1952, p. 258, 30 May 1953, p. 135, 21 September 1951, p. 344. The story about the COI film appeared in the 20 August 1955 issue at p. 276.

53. *Ibid.*, 'Cambridge Film Show', 6 April 1951, p. 8.

54. *Ibid.*, 'Motor Cycle Matters', 18 April 1952, p. 65.

55. See 'The Motor Cycle Show' by 'Spero', *Post Magazine and Insurance Monitor*, 1 December 1951, pp. 1279–81, contained in NA MT 108/8. The emphasis is contained in the original.

56. The results of the Gallop Poll were published in the *Motor Cycle and Cycle Trader*, see 'Cycles and motor cycles for business and pleasure', 9 January 1954, pp. 276–8. No details of the methodology followed by the Poll takers, including the size of the sample or the geographic location of respondents, were provided.

57. The low interest expressed by some of the respondents in buying another moped suggests that many current owners were first time buyers. This poll seems to have been unusual for its time, since shortly afterwards, columnist Francis Jones urged the Manufacturers' Union to commission market research on behalf of the entire industry. See 'Motor Cycle Matters', *ibid*, 23 January 1956, pp. 320–1.

58. See R.F.F. Dawson, 'Ownership of cars and certain durable household goods', *Bulletin of the Oxford University Institute of Statistics*, May 1953, p. 181, pp. 185–7, 191. According to figures published several years later, only 12 per cent of working

class homes had a motor car, compared to 41 per cent of middle class homes. For motor cycles, 7 per cent of working class homes had one compared to 6 per cent of their middle class counterparts, leading one to suspect that many working class persons commuted either by foot, bicycle or public transport. See 'Service without a smile', *The Economist*, 14 December 1957, pp. 934–5. Thanks to Hideo Ichihashi for providing these two references.

59. See minutes of the Motor Cycle Manufacturers' Section, 23 November 1951, contained in Guardbook MRC MSS 204/3/1/72.

60. See document entitled 'Committee on Road Safety, meeting at BSH on 19 July 1951. Matters arising out of previous minutes', contained in NA MT 108/8. Presumably, although it was not explicitly stated, the same vulnerability would apply to bicyclists as well.

61. Among other things, the Prime Minister was told: 'The increase of accidents to motor cyclists is especially serious. If you ride a motor cycle, your chance of being killed is 40 times, and your chance of being injured 20 times, higher than if you are in a car.' See document signed by the Minister of Transport and Civil Aviation', dated 6 March 1956 and entitled 'Road Safety', p. 4, point 16, contained in NA PREM 11/1047.

62. Watling's remarks are recorded in the Committee minutes of the meeting of 29 October 1951. During the meeting, Watling argued against a proposed requirement for manufacturers to provide instructions along with their motor cycles on the grounds that it was 'unreasonable'. He also opposed the compulsory use of direction indicators on the grounds that while they might be helpful they were too unreliable for regular use. He went on to criticise the possible requirement of rear view mirrors as being 'more of a danger than an aid to safety'. See 'Minutes of meeting of 29 October 1951', contained in MT 108/8. Watling's remarks were subsequently supported by Graham Walker, editor of *Motor Cycling*, who was invited to appear at the Sub-Committee meeting of 20 November 1951. *Ibid.*

63. See Minutes of Council meeting of 4 October 1955, contained in Manufacturers' Union Guardbook, MRC MSS 204/3/1/81. The Ministry's opinion is found in document no. 23, entitled 'Crash Helmets', contained in NA MT 108/11, 'Committee on Road Safety. Sub-Committee for the Prevention of Accidents to Motor Cyclists, 1951–1954'.

64. Hewitt noted that the mechanical condition of the vehicles concerned would have some effect on accident rates. He added: 'The Committee, however, takes the view that the real trouble is that

machines capable of very high performance are, for the most part, placed in the hands of youths whose main idea is speed and who do not realise the dangers involved. Broadly speaking, it seems to them that it is not so much the machine but the circumstances surrounding its use at a particular moment which matter. In other words, the power to produce speed is there, but not always the ability to control it.' See C.B. Hewitt to S.G. Griffin, Secretary of the Committee on Road Safety, 1 November 1951, contained in *ibid.*

65. W.H. Glanville, an official with the Department of Scientific and Industrial Research, called for all motor cycles to be fitted with compulsory sidecars, supplied free of charge. He claimed that recent accident statistics demonstrated that motor cycle/side-car combinations were one of the safest types of motor vehicles on the road. Glanville did, however, concede that as many motor cyclists considered top mechanical performance a major priority and they might not want the sidecars, free of not. See untitled clipping from the *News Chronicle*, 3 July 1953, contained in NA T228/42, entitled 'Motor cycle taxation'.

66. See *Report to the Minister of Transport on Motor Cycle Accidents*, London: HMSO, 1952, p. 4.

67. *Ibid.*, pp. 4–5.

68. *Ibid.*, p. 5. It was estimated that 50 per cent of the motor cyclists injured were under 27 years of age and that 75 per cent were under 35. See also 'A Review of Information on Motor Cycle Accidents', dated December 1951, prepared by H.J.H. Starks, contained in NA MT 108/8.

69. See 'Motor cycle accidents to male teenagers: A contemporary epidemic' by J.A.H. Lee, *Proceedings of the Royal Society of Medicine*, May 1963, pp. 365–7.

70. The dealer in question, John Hall, of Clarks (Oxford), wrote in to the industry's trade journal, declaring that for him 'the last straw' in all the anti-motor cycling sentiment he had heard happened while listening to the 'Archers' when one of the principal characters, Phillip Archer, mentioned to his family that he was about to exchange his motor cycle for a car, 'because his mother says "she gets a funny feeling every time he puts his leg across the saddle … they are pretty dangerous things aren't they? … they are awful in bad weather", and several other remarks, all in the same strain.' See letter to the editor, 'Unfavourable motor cycle propaganda', *Motor Cycle and Cycle Trader*, 14 November 1952, pp. 133–4; see 'Motor cycles becoming a "perfect pest"', *Bournemouth Daily Echo*, 15 September 1955, contained in the Manufacturers' Union press clipping book, MRC MSS 204/10/1/3.

71. See Publicity Committee minutes, 31 August 1955, contained in the Manufacturers' Union Guardbooks, MRC MSS 204/3/1/81.

72. See minutes of the Motor Cycle Manufacturers' Section meeting of 12 March 1953, contained in Manufacturers' Union Guardbook MRC MSS 204/3/1/75. The Union provided, free of charge, a number of motor cycles for the use of the RAC/ACU Training Scheme.

73. Heavily influenced by Cold War politics, the movie depicted a group of motor cyclists who foil the plans of foreign agents to steal Britain's atomic secrets. According to the Manufacturers' Union Publicity Committee, the object of the *Black Rider* was to show motor cyclists 'in the most favourable light, providing entertainment and, at the same time, valuable propaganda for the motor cycling movement'. See minutes of the Publicity Committee, 26 June 1957, contained in the Industry Association Guardbooks, MSS 204/3/1/86. The film enjoyed modest financial success as well, and by 1955 had already recovered £5,000 of its costs. See Industry Association Council meeting of 24 May 1955, contained in Guardbook MRC MSS 204/3/1/80. Two years later, the Association was informed that 'millions of people had now seen it'. See Minutes of the Motor Cycle Manufacturers' Section, meeting of 9 May 1957, contained in Guardbook MRC MSS 204/3/1/85.

74. See Minutes of the Publicity Committee, 14 May 1956, and memo entitled '342/57 Boy Scouts' Jubilee Jamboree', dated 23 July 1957, contained in Guardbooks MRC MSS 204/3/1/83 and MSS 204/3/1/86 respectively.

75. Unlike motor cars, motor cycles were not covered by the so-called 'Covenant Scheme' which in the interests of holding down the price of used cars in a sellers' market, prevented motor car owners from re-selling their machines for a stated period of time. The subject came up for discussion during the course of a meeting of the Motor Cycle Manufacturers' Section, in the general context of black market selling of motor cycles. The Section opposed the extension of the Covenant Scheme to their trade. See Section Minutes for 23 November 1951, contained in the Guardbook MRC MSS 204/3/1/72.

76. For an overview of these 'ultra-lightweight' machines, see Peter Watson, 'Permanent Attachment', *Classic Bike*, August 1984, pp. 22–6. The trade journal was *British Cycles and Motor Cycles Overseas*, which also noted that these attachments were distinct from the old autocycles and that they had been available on the Continent much earlier

than in Britain. See the December 1951 issue, feature entitled 'Auxiliary Power Units', pp. 190–1. For a contemporaneous article, see 'Why not a cyclemotor?' by 'Nitor', *The Motor Cycle*, 16 April 1953, pp. 460–1.

77. At first the 'Cyclemaster' was sold not through cycle or motor cycle retailers but through the motor car trade. See untitled news item contained in *British Cycles and Motor Cycles Overseas*, August/September 1950, p. 357. A 'Cyclemaster' company brochure outlining the various features of the unit is contained in FBI archives, MRC MSS 200/DEC/3/3/C149.

78. The *Motor Cycle and Cycle Trader* ran a series of articles on these 'clip ons', such as 'The Cyclemaster is here' 16 June 1950, p. 418 and 'Auxiliary motor units' 15 December 1950, p. 290. These units ranged in price from £18 to £40. Most of the companies were small, such as Bantomoto, Cyclaid, Montgomite, Mosquito and Power Pak. However, Tube Investments subsequently joined EMI with its 40 cc rotary engine unit called the 'Power Wheel'.

79. The *Motor Cycle and Cycle Trader* remarked: 'Two or three years ago, it was perhaps permissible to regard the growing popularity of the cyclemotor as being possibly no more than a flash in the pan. We had seen these things come before – and go. History might repeat, or so it was argued.' See 'The Cyclemotor Situation', 30 May 1953, pp. 134–5. See also, for example, the leading article 'Is British Cyclemotor design now lagging?', *ibid.*, 16 April 1955, p. 43. Information of British production and Italian usage contained in 17 October 1952 and 2 May 1953 issues of *ibid.*

80. See 'Bicycles face the future', *Financial Times*, 28 January 1956, contained in newspaper clipping volume MRC MSS 204/10/1/3.

81. The scooter is particularly distinguished from the orthodox motor cycle by, among other things, the rearward position of its engine, its small wheels, seating arrangement and extensive bodywork. See C.F. Caunter, *Motor Cycles, A Technical History*. London: HMSO, 1982, pp. 81–2. For a brief, general history, see Michael Webster, *Motor Scooters*, Aylesbury, Bucks: Shire Publications Ltd, 1986. Significantly, as noted earlier, many British scooter manufacturers during the 1920s, such as ABC and Sopwith, had built aircraft during World War One. After 1945, the first attempts by British firms to again build scooter-like machines originated from aeronautics firms such as Bond Aircraft and Engineering (which made the 'Minibyke') and Swallow (producer of the "Gadabout").

82. Vespa's chief designer, Corradino d'Ascanio, was a man who had little previous contact with motor cycles and had worked in the aeronautics industry during the war. See 'Italy – Where the Scooters come from', *Scooter and Three Wheeler Yearbook, 1957*, pp. 14–18.

83. Vespa scooter production was only 2,484 in 1946 but had grown to 10,000 units during 1948. By 1955 this total had shot to 250,000 units (including machines built outside of Italy under licence). Figures are from *ibid.*

84. See 'Italy being changed by scooters', *Motor Cycle and Cycle Trader*, 19 September 1952, p. 361 and also 'Object as Image: the Italian Scooter Cycle' contained in Dick Hebdige, *op. cit.*, pp. 77–115 and Gary Johnson, *op. cit.* For a more contemporaneous analysis, see 'Scooters for the Millions', *Financial Times* (no date, but probably late 1954) contained in the Manufacturers' Union's newspaper clipping book, MRC MSS 204/10/1/3.

85. According to a report commissioned by the Manufacturers' Union, the NSU company maintained an Adriatic camping site, which was open to all riders using their scooters at either minimal or no charge at all. The report termed this a 'publicity coup' which had been widely covered by the European press. See Confidential Bulletin no. 22, dated May 1955 and entitled 'Developments in the German Cycle, Motor Cycle and Accessories Industry', contained in Guardbook MRC MSS 204/3/1/80. One British newspaper, *The Daily Sketch*, carried a story dated 2 July 1955 about an unnamed (but almost certainly NSU) scooter company's holiday camp, entitled 'They camp for 14 pence a day – if they arrive on a scooter'. The clipping is contained in the newspaper clipping book MRC MSS 204/10/1/3.

86. Several years later, Hugh Palin, Director of the Industries' Association, noted that there was 'no doubt that there is a great future in this market [scooters]. But most people feel that it has introduced an entirely new class of rider to motor cycling and has not in fact taken away from the motor cycle industry.' See memo dated 7 August 1958, entitled '300/58. Director's Personal Report, contained in Guardbook MRC MSS 204/3/1/88.

87. See Hebdige, *op. cit.* See also 'Scooters in Britain', *Financial Times*, 2 July 1955 and 'The Motor Cycle Export Battle', published on 28 May 1956. The latter noted that 'the scooter, with its enclosed motor and quite high degree of weather protection, is both replacing the motor cycle and attracting a new class of motoring public'. Both articles are contained in Guardbook MRC MSS 204/10/1/3.

88. One popular motor journal had actually reviewed a Vespa scooter years before it appeared on the British market. The article applauded its 'many novel and interesting features' with an overall design that made it 'especially attractive for town and short distance work'. See 'The Italian Vespa', *The Motor Cycle*, 31 October 1946, p. 343. Ironically, BSA had a scooter design prepared as early as 1944 but never acted upon it. There is a copy of this scooter patent in the BSA Collection at Solihull Public Library, item 245.

89. See '6/- shock swells the scooter boom', *Daily Mail*, 6 December 1956, contained in newspaper clipping volume MRC MSS 204/10/1/3.

90. For example, Peter Agg, British Lambretta concessionaire, criticised the 'poor standard of service generally obtaining in the motor cycle industry' during a Manufacturers and Concessionaires conference on 25 February 1959. At the same meeting Vespa maker Claude McCormack observed that as a rule most scooter buyers are 'largely newcomers with no mechanical knowledge'. Minutes of this conference are contained in Guardbook MRC MSS 204/3/1/90.

91. Criticism on the tardiness of British motor cycle manufacturers to enter the scooter market were evidently wide-spread enough to prompt Edward Turner, by then Managing Director of BSA's Automotive Division, to reply via an article published in the *Financial Times*. Turner implicitly criticised the past complacency of the industry's leadership (presumably including himself) when he wrote, 'we must disabuse ourselves from the thought that the scooter has only a limited period of marketability. It is here to stay and I cannot conceive of it ever dying out.' See 'Scooters: A British Challenge to the Continentals', *Financial Times*, 20 October 1958, contained in the newspaper clippings book MRC MSS 204/10/1/3.

92. See Francis Jones, 'Room for new ideas', 13 June 1953, *Motor Cycle and Cycle Trader*, pp. 162–3 and 'Is design in the doldrums?', *The Motor Cycle*, 25 February 1954, pp. 242–3. See also 'Are our designs too conservative?' by 'Dominator', *ibid.*, 11 December 1952, p. 738.

93. For critical commentary in the business press, see 'Expansion in UK cycle exports' *Financial Times*, 28 August 1954, 'UK Scooters enter fight for markets' *Observer*, 13 November, 1955 and 'Now Cycle firms are Worried', *Manchester Guardian*, 7 March 1956 all contained in the Trade Union Congress news clipping collection, file 12913. See also 'Scooters in Britain' *Financial Times*, 2 July 1955, contained in the Manufacturers' Union newspaper clipping volume, MRC MSS 204/10/1/3.

94. See 'Motorcycle Trends and Tendencies' by R.B. Holliday. Contained in *The Motor Cycling Year Book 1953*, compiled by Peter Chamberlain and the Staff of *Motor Cycling*. London: Temple Press Ltd, 1953. pp. 3–4.

95. *Ibid.*

96. A leading article in the 3 August 1957 issue of the *Motor Cycle and Cycle Trader*, written in the context of the introduction of the British built DKR 'Dove' scooter, noted defensively that '[t]oo often – and sometimes quite unfairly – the makers of conventional British motor cycles have been challenged for their alleged backwardness in not acquiring quickly the Continental tastes that have developed since the end of the war, and have been exemplified in the scooter.' See 'Eggs in several baskets' at p. 227. The estimate of foreign scooters comes from 'Burdens on an industry', *ibid.*, 31 August 1957, p. 277.

97. For an overview of the Commission's activities, see Helen Mercer, 'The Monopolies and Restrictive Practices Commission, 1949–56: a study in regulatory failure', contained in G. Jones and M. Kirby (eds), *Competitiveness and the State*, Manchester: Manchester University Press, 1991; see leading article, "Free-for-all' Price scramble', *Motor Cycle and Cycle Trader*, 29 June 1951, p. 169.

98. See letter, A.C. Hill to Watling dated 25 July 1951, contained in NA SUPP 14/351, emphasis in the original. See also memo dated 12 July 1951, entitled '258/51 – Retail Price Maintenance', contained in Guardbook MRC MSS 204/3/1/71.

99. *Ibid.*

100. See memo dated 10 August 1951, '299/51: Retail Price Maintenance', contained in *ibid.*

101. *Ibid.*; Watling's draft letter was subsequently approved by the Council during its meeting of 2 October 1951.

102. See memo to the Union Council, dated 27 May 1953, entitled '195/53: The Monopolies and Restrictive Practices Commission', contained in Guardbook MRC MSS 204/3/1/75; memo dated 15 July 1955, entitled '317/55: Monopolies and Retail Price Commission', contained in Guardbook MRC MSS 204/3/1/81; memo dated 23 March 1956 to the Proprietary Articles Manufacturers Committee, entitled '128/56. Restrictive Trade Practices Bill', contained in Union Guardbook MRC MSS 204/3/1/82; memo dated 22 October 1956, entitled 'Restrictive Trade Practices Act – Proposed Line of Action to be Followed by the Association and (where appropriate Individual Members)', contained in Guardbook MRC MSS 204/3/1/84.

103. See, for example, 'Advance of the British Motor Cycle Industry', 12 August 1952, *Financial Times*. Written by BSA's Export Manager, S.F. Digby, who claimed the 'phenomenal growth' of the industry 'could well be maintained steadily for many years, given free markets and a steady flow of raw materials'.

104. The Manufacturers' Union *Annual Report* for 1952 noted 'severe cuts' in their steel allocations along with those for nickel and other non-ferrous materials. See p. 4. of the *Report*, contained in MRC MSS 204/4/3/2.

105. A lengthy report, based on information forwarded from the British Commercial Secretariat in both countries, was circulated by the Manufacturers' Union to a number of members. See memo dated 8 June 1948, entitled '172/48. USA and Argentina: Motor Cycle Exports', contained in Guardbook MRC MSS 204/3/1/63. As far as significance of British motor vehicle exports were concerned, it was noted that the Argentines still drove on the left side of the road until 1945. See news item in *The Motor Cycle*, 12 April 1945, p. 261.

106. See 'Brief no. 3. Bicycles and motor cycles' contained in NA SUPP 14/393. The British government negotiated import licences for 10,000 motor cycles worth £800,000 along with £50,000 worth of spare parts.

107. According to Ministry of Supply officials, the problem was that the Argentines had 'spent wildly, over a billion dollars having been expended in the United States and apart from a few cars, they had little to show for it'. Moreover, the Argentines were 'desperately short of sterling and so it was more than likely that we would commence to purchase from them first, thus putting them in possession of sterling with which they could begin to trade'. See 'Notes on informal meeting held at the Ministry of Supply, Room 736, Shell-Mex House, Strand, London, WC2 on Tuesday, 26th July, 1948, at 3 PM' contained in *ibid*. For the Union's reaction to the situation, see memo dated 13 December 1949, entitled '442/49: Argentina: Bicycle and Motor Cycle Exports' contained in Guardbook MRC MSS 204/3/1/67.

108. See memo dated 13 December 1949, entitled 442/49. Argentina: Bicycle and Motor Cycle Exports, contained in Guardbook MRC MSS 204/3/1/67 and draft memo dated 25 November 1957, entitled 'Bicycle and Motor Cycle Export Trade', contained in Guardbook MSS 204/3/1/87. The memo also resentfully noted that in 1956 Germany had sent 1,000 motor cycles to Argentina.

109. See memo dated 26 September 1952 entitled '285/52. Egypt – Exports' contained in Guardbook MRC MSS 204/3/1/74, memo dated 13 October

1955 entitled '426/55. Finland – Exports' contained in Guardbook MRC MSS 204/3/1/81, memo dated 5 October 1950 entitled '339/50: Brazil: Export of Cycles and Motor Cycle Goods', contained in Guardbook MRC MSS 204/3/1/69 and memo dated 28 December 1955, entitled '507/55. Denmark – Exports', contained in Guardbook MRC MSS 204/3/1/82.

110. Between 1945 and 1950 Britain exported a total of 105,000 machines worth £9,500,000 to Australia, making it the best single overseas market for British motor cycles at the time. See 'Australia Reduces Exports', *British Cycles and Motor Cycles Overseas*, April/May 1952, p. 41.

111. During a meeting of the Motor Cycle Manufacturers' Section meeting of 21 March 1952, the Australian restrictions were called a 'very serious blow' to the British motor cycle industry. The minutes are contained in the Manufacturers' Union Guardbook MSS 204/3/1/73. In his speech to AMC shareholders on 25 February 1953, Chairman Hogg noted that the closing of the Australian market, which had been the company's largest single export outlet, had 'seriously embarrassed the industry'. See AMC *Annual Report* for 1952. See also memo dated 13 March 1952, entitled '88/52: Australia – Import Restrictions', contained in Manufacturers' Union Guardbook MRC MSS 204/3/1/72 and the Manufacturers' Union 1952 and 1953 *Annual Reports*, page 4 and 3 respectively, contained in MRC MSS 204/4/3/2.

112. Smith was quoted in a story entitled 'Greater attendance, more publicity, and improved display standards' contained in the *Motor Cycle and Cycle Trader*, 28 November 1952, pp. 176–9. AMC Chairman Hogg noted that 'our industry swung with great rapidity from a sellers' market to a buyers' market'. See Chairman's speech to the shareholders, contained in the 1953 AMC *Annual Report*. Hogg's remarks were echoed by those of Enfield Cycle (Royal Enfield) Chairman Frank W. Smith in his speech to shareholders on 30 January 1953, contained in the company's 1953 *Annual Report*. Smith reported that motor cycle sales had become seasonal as they had been before 1939 and that the closing of export markets meant having to sell more machines on the home market.

113. The editorial in *The Motor Cycle and Cycle Export Trader*, appeared in the March 1953 issue, pp. 35–6. See also BSA Managing Director James Leek's remarks about export problems, noted in the BSA Management Minutes, meeting of 20 June 1952, agenda item 9305 and 'Maintaining the Lead', *BSA News*, Spring 1952, pp. 6–7.

114. In his speech to the shareholders made on 24 February 1949, Chairman Frank W. Smith of Enfield Cycles criticised the British government's handling of these bilateral trade negotiations, which he thought had resulted in higher tariffs and low quotas. His speech is contained in the Enfield Cycle *Annual Report* for 1948. During the meeting of the Manufacturers' Union Council held on 3 July 1951, mention was made of the 'deplorable results of recent trade negotiations, particularly in the case of Holland'. Other markets noted were Denmark and Belgium. See minutes of meeting contained in Guardbook MRC MSS 204/3/1/71.

115. During a meeting with the Minister of Overseas Trade at the 1951 Motor Cycle Show Manufacturers' Union President Kimberley and Director Watling took the opportunity to explain the situation in export markets. Kimberley expressed the industry's concern 'at the way in which their traditional markets in Western European countries were being closed one after the other; he felt this was mainly due to barter agreements being signed by these foreign governments which present the trade to others'. He also suggested that British trade negotiators 'had not realised the importance of getting import quotas for bicycles and motor cycles and their parts or had not taken a stiff enough attitude on this question'. Kimberley also complained that the industry had not been consulted before the conclusion of trade agreements. See Document #38, entitled 'Export of bicycles and motor cycles, prepared by D. Simpson, dated 14 November 1951 and contained in NA BT 11/4452, entitled 'Japan/UK – Japanese Export Competition in relation to UK Cycle and Motor Cycle Industry'.

116. See memo dated 27 May 1950, entitled '191/50: Dollar Export Board', contained in Guardbook MRC MSS 204/3/1/68.

117. See Minutes of the Motor Cycle Manufacturers' Section meeting of 26 August 1952, contained in Guardbook MRC MSS 204/3/1/73.

118. The Watling-Wilson letter is contained in NA BT 11/3996.

119. See, for example, a memo from S.S. Holmes to various Board of Trade personnel, dated 16 August 1948 and a minute prepared by E.J. Halford-Strevens, dated 6 September 1949, both contained in *Ibid.*

120. See minutes of the Motor Cycle Manufacturers' Section meeting of 26 August 1952, contained in Manufacturers' Union Guardbook MRC MSS 204/3/1/73. In his speech to the Shareholders at the Annual General Meeting held on 20 January 1954, Enfield Cycle Chairman Frank W. Smith specifically singled out foreign competition from

Germany, Italy and Czechoslovakia as being of particular concern to his company. The speech is contained in the Enfield Cycle Company *Annual Report* for 1953, on deposit at the Guildhall Library.

121. See minutes of the Motor Cycle Manufacturers' Section, dated 4 June 1949, contained in Guardbook MSS 204/3/1/66.

122. See leading article, 'British Cinderellas. Machines at Salons imperfectly displayed'. *The Motor Cycle*, 5 February 1953, p. 163.

123. See, for example, memo '157/50: Canada: Motor Cycle Exports', dated 28 April 1950, and '192/50: Visit to USA and Canada', dated 29 May 1950, wherein Major Watling, during a sales tour noted reported he was 'distressed' to discover that dealers were 'grievously short' of both motor cycles and spares. The memos are contained in Guardbooks MRC MSS 204/3/1/67 and MSS 204/3/1/68 respectively. The problem existed elsewhere too, see 'Germany: motor cycle exports', dated 2 December 1952, contained in Guardbook MRC MSS 204/3/1/74. For criticism about English only service manuals, see '3/53 – Belgium – motor cycle exports', dated 1 January 1953, contained in *ibid.* and '23/55. Germany', dated 20 January 1955, contained in Guardbook MRC MSS 204/3/1/79.

124. The article was referred to in a memo dated 7 December 1953, entitled '377/53: Motor Cycles – Propaganda', contained in Guardbook MRC MSS 204/3/1/76.

125. See 'Special Report on the Amsterdam Cycle and Motor Cycle Show', no date or author indicated but it was probably prepared by Director Hugh Palin in early 1957. Contained in Industry Association Guardbook series, MRC MSS 204/3/1/85.

126. A letter from the President of the Swiss Motor Cycle Importers' Association to the Manufacturers' Union warned that British machines, particularly in the 350 cc to 500 cc classes, were losing out in popularity to Italian scooters, thanks to a combination of higher prices and conservative designs. See memo dated 26 November 1952, entitled '341/52: Switzerland – Motor Cycle Exports', contained in Guardbook MRC MSS 204/3/1/74.

127. The importance of the Swiss market was well recognised in the British trade press: see for example a story on the Geneva cycle and motor cycle show, contained in *British Cycles and Motor Cycles Overseas*, April 1949, pp. 160–1. Switzerland was an open market until early 1951 when quotas were instituted. See memo dated 6 March 1951, entitled 'Switzerland: Export of Bicycle and Motor Cycle Goods', contained in Guardbook

MRC MSS 204/3/1/70. An earlier report noted that British motor cycles were well established in Switzerland, having 'an excellent reputation and considerable popularity'. The same report also noted the ominous growth in sales of the Czech and Austrian machines. These models had design features such as chrome plating and a foot gear changer which came as standard equipment and were much appreciated by Swiss consumers. Evidently, British machines suffered badly in comparison. See memo dated 10 November 1948, entitled '356/48. Switzerland: Motor Cycle Market Report', contained in Guardbook MRC MSS 204/3/1/64.

128. See news item, *Motor Cycle and Cycle Trader*, 16 November 1951, p. 137. Triumph was not the only British company so criticised. In 1949 BSA had received a number of complaints from Switzerland about their A7 500 cc models, which had developed a disconcerting tendency of catching fire. Moreover, Swiss motor cyclists found the electrical equipment on the lightweight Bantams to be notoriously unreliable. See *BSA Management Minutes*, meeting of 9 September 1949, agenda item 9146, MRC MSS 19A/1/5.

129. See 'Switzerland: A Brief Market Report and Summary of Impressions of the Geneva Cycle and Motor Cycle Show, 1958', no date, prepared by Industry Association Director Hugh Palin. It is contained in Industry Association Guardbook, MRC MSS 204/3/1/88. See also 'Swiss motor cycle market drops in favour of small cars', *Motor Cycle and Cycle Trader*, 31 March 1956, p. 436.

130. By place of origin, 37,994 of the imports were West German, 16,200 Italian and 2,608 French. See memo dated 26 April 1956, entitled '173/56: Director's Personal Report', contained in Union Guardbook MRC MSS 204/3/1/83.

131. The figures for 1955/56 are quoted in an undated memo [but probably spring of 1957] entitled '164/57. Director's Personal Report', contained in Guardbook MRC MSS 204/3/1/85.

132. For reports on the redundancies, see 'Motor cycle firm to sack 200 workers' *Daily Herald*, 26 April 1956 (contained in the Trade Union Congress news clipping archive, file 12915, MRC), 'More dismissals in Midlands', *Financial Times*, 2 June 1956 and 'Report for July and August 1956' prepared by A.N. Hall and dated 7 September 1956, contained in NA BT 177/634. Overall industry employment in October 1955 was estimated at 16,500. Among the firms, BSA employed 5,100, AMC 1,350 and Villiers 3,500 (not all these workers, however, were necessarily engaged exclusively in motor cycle manufacturing). See 'Notes on the location of

manufacturing industries – no. 10 Motor Cycles', particularly Appendix 4, dated October 1956 and contained in NA BT 177/621.

133. The letter, dated 27 September 1955, addressed to Peter Thorneycroft, the President of the Board of Trade, is attached to a memo entitled '405/55: Purchase Tax Etc', contained in Guardbook MRC MSS 204/3/1/81. A letter, dated 4 July 1956, from AMC Chairman Hogg to the company shareholders, blamed the imposition of higher hire/purchase restrictions (the minimum deposit on both new and used motor cycles had gone up from 33 1/3 per cent to 50 per cent) for a 40 per cent drop in sales over 1955. The letter, attached to the 1955 *Annual Report*, is on deposit in the Guildhall Library.

134. See letter to Thorneycroft, *op. cit.*

135. *Ibid.*

136. See, for example, minute no. 5 from 'C.J.', dated 14 November 1950 and report entitled 'Pedal cycles with motor attachments', prepared by G.F. Stedman, dated 9 May 1951, both contained in NA MT 34/468.

137. *Ibid.*

138. The expense accounts were mostly related to expensive clothing that Lady Docker (who was also on the board of one of Daimler's subsidiaries) had purchased for events associated with the launch of the new Daimler car models and which she then tried to charge to the company. Among the string of expensive cars used by the Dockers, which cost BSA tens of thousands of pounds, included at least one gold plated Daimler limousine outfitted with a lizard skin interior. The nepotism concerned Docker's brother-in-law, R.E. Smith (Daimler's General Manager) whom Sir Bernard had arranged to be elected to the BSA Group board. These, and Docker's other alleged misdemeanors, were featured in the extensive press coverage of

Docker's dismissal from the BSA Board. See, for example, 'Sir B. Docker and BSA', 1 June 1956, 'BSA Dispute: Appeal to Shareholders' 2 June 1956 and 'BSA Board Dispute' 1 August 1956, all in the *Financial Times*. See also Davenport-Hines, *op. cit.*, pp. 231–2.

139. The official account of the 31 May 1956 meeting is briefly explained in the Minute Book for that date. No agenda item number was provided. For the post-Docker Board's side of the problems prevalent before 1956 see 'Statement by the Board of Directors to the Ordinary Stockholders', dated 16 July 1956 and 'Reasons why Sir Bernard Docker's attempt for Secure Re-Appointment Should be Opposed'. These were prepared for distribution to shareholders at the Extraordinary General Meeting called by Sir Bernard in an unsuccessful attempt to regain his place on the Board of Directors. All these are contained in BSA Directors' Minute Book no. 16, MSS 19C/20. A separate and much lengthier account of the 31 May Board meeting, prepared by the Company Secretary, the so-called 'Secret Minutes', are contained in MSS 19C/30. A copy of Sir Bernard's defence of his chairmanship of the company, entitled 'To the Shareholders of the Birmingham Small Arms Co. Ltd' (no date but probably July 1956) is contained in Box 31/Folder 1 of the Hannon Papers on deposit at the Parliamentary Archives. Another published and highly partisan defence of Sir Bernard's leadership of BSA was subsequently made by his wife Norah. See Norah Docker *Norah – the Autobiography of Lady Docker*, London: W.H. Allen, 1969, especially p. 92 and pp. 214–28.

140. The Policy Committee was created at a Board meeting held on 13 March 1954. See agenda item 10539 contained in Director's Minute Book no. 16, *op. cit.*

Notes to Chapter 5: The window closes, 1956–1961

1. See 'Buyers' Guide' included in the 18 November 1954 edition of *The Motor Cycle*.

2. See 'BSA Scooter and Revolutionary 70 cc Ultra-Lightweight', *Motor Cycle and Cycle Trader*, 12 November 1955, p. 146. Prices are from the 1956 'Buyers' Guide', enclosed in the same issue.

3. See 'Scooters in Britain', *Financial Times*, 2 July 1955, contained in clipping book MRC MSS 204/10/1/3 and 'British Scooters Appear', *The Economist*, 19 November 1955, p. 683.

4. The Ambassador's electric start was included, one report claimed, specifically to attract women, who it was hoped, were now moving from the pillion

seat to the saddle: 'how do you expect a girl with high-heel shoes to operate a kick starter? … the answer is that with the Ambassador – you don't.' See *Daily Sketch*, untitled feature about the 1954 Show, 13 November 1956, contained in the Manufacturers' Union clipping book, MRC MSS 204/10/1/3.

5. See 'Cycle and Motor Cycle Show stages a Counter-attack on Continental Competition', *Board of Trade Journal*, 19 November 1955.

6. See leading article, 'World's Leading Producer', p. 171, 'Motor Cycle and Scooters for All Markets', pp. 180–4 and 'Motorised Cycles and Power Units',

pp. 193–4, all contained in *Motor Cycle and Cycle Export Trader*, December 1955. See also an untitled feature on the 1955 Show in the *Motor Cycle and Cycle Trader*, 12 November 1955, pp. 134–5.

7. See feature entitled 'Comment', *Ibid.*, p. 141.

8. See 'Motor Cycle Matters' by Francis Jones, *Motor Cycle and Cycle Trader*, 4 February 1956, p. 329. See also 'UK scooters enter fight for markets', *The Observer*, 13 November 1955. Other similar opinions were expressed elsewhere in the broadsheet press, see, for example, 'Now Cycle Firms are Worried', *Manchester Guardian*, 7 March 1956 and 'Export Challenge to UK Cycles', *Financial Times*, 16 March 1956, all contained in TUC press clipping file 12913, at the MRC. The concept of the larger motor cycles as 'masculine' was not simply theoretical. In 1954, the Manufacturers' Union protested at the participation of a German side-car rider, Inge Stoll-LaFarge, in that year's TT races. Their resolution informed the ACU that they were 'appalled' at the decision to allow Stoll-Farge to race. See minutes of the Manufacturers' Section meeting of 12 May 1954, contained in Guardbook MRC MSS 204/3/1/77.

9. See BSA Directors' Minute Book, MRC MSS 19C/20, meeting of 18 October 1956, agenda item 10881. See also Hopwood, *op. cit.*, pp. 131–4.

10. See letter to Shareholders, dated 4 July 1956, on deposit at the Guildhall Library, London.

11. See leading article, 'Motor Cycle Sales', *Motor Cycle and Cycle Trader*, 23 June 1956, p. 145.

12. See 'The Motor Cycle Export Battle', *Financial Times*, 28 May 1956, contained in clipping book MRC MSS 204/10/1/3.

13. In 1958, the FBI conducted an inquiry in conjunction with the Council of Industrial Design, about what measures were followed by manufacturers for product design. In response, a Director with AMC replied that, in general terms, 'appearance only enters into our products in the sense that good technical geometry produces the desired appearance, and to a degree even this is secondary to technical performance, road holding etc. What few embellishments are needed to bring about design attractiveness, arise from the opinions of higher management generally, with the occasional help of a consultant and even this help would usually be forth coming from manufacturers of badges and motifs etc.' See letter, A.A. Sugar to E.W. Goodale, FBI, dated 2 June 1958, contained in MRC MSS 200/F/3/Ts/12/15.

14. For Edward Turner's background, see Barbara Smith entry in the *Dictionary of Business Biography*, David Jeremy (ed.), London: Butterworths, 1986, pp. 565–70. A full account of Bert Hopwood's struggles to convince the Boards of various motor cycle companies to revamp design are in Hopwood, *op. cit.*, pp. 77–81, 194–6. AMC, for example, had great difficulties holding on to skilled design staff, see J.M. West interview, 23 November 1994.

15. See memo entitled '23/55: Germany', dated 20 January 1955, contained in Guardbook MRC MSS 204/3/1/79.

16. See 'Design and Development' by Edward Turner, *The Motor Cycle*, 9 October 1952, pp. 406–8.

17. See 'British Motor Cycles' by Hugh Palin, *Financial Times*, 15 October 1956, contained in clipping book MRC MSS 204/10/1/3.

18. *Ibid.*

19. The £500,000 was voted during a Board meeting held on 18 December 1953. See entry for that date, agenda item 10519. For the decision to buy Carbodies, see the Board meeting of 20 May 1954, agenda item 10552. The following year, BSA bought Hobbs Transmission at the cost of £150,000, again for the benefit of Daimler. See Board meeting of 24 March 1955, agenda item 10645. Expenditures at Triumph included a capital outlay of £116,916 for the period 1953 to 1956 and a special allowance of £94,000 for 1956. See Board meetings held on 22 January 1954 and 2 May 1956, agenda items 10529 and 10748 respectively. All references contained in BSA Directors' Minute Book no. 16, contained in MRC MSS 19C/20. The BSA output figures are contained in the BSA Management Committee Minutes, BSA Management Meeting Minutes, MRC MSS 19A/1/5. According to BSA's Service Manager John Balder, at no time after 1950 did the BSA factory utilise 100 per cent of productive capacity. See Balder interview, 18 November 1994.

20. See Chairman Hogg's speech at the Annual General Meeting of 7 February 1956, on deposit at the Guildhall Library. According to a circular sent out to shareholders dated November 1955, the entire building project was projected to cost 'over £900,000'. The initial £750,000 was raised through AMC's banks, a further £500,000 would be provided through a Convertible Debenture stock issue. See circular dated 25 November 1955, signed by company secretary W.A. Hildeth, copy kindly provided by J.M. West.

21. See 'New Type Light Engine Made', *Daily Telegraph* and 'New two-stroke engine' *Times*, both from 8 November 1956, and contained in TUC clipping file 12913, on deposit at the MRC.

22. See *British Cycles and Motor Cycles Overseas*, August/September 1951, 'Extension at Woolwich', p. 140. The general press also covered the work, see 'New type Light Engine Made. European

Markets' *Daily Telegraph*, 8 November 1956 and 'New Two-Stroke Engine', *Times*, 8 November 1956, both articles contained in the TUC's industrial news clipping file 12913, entitled 'Cycle and Motor Cycling', on deposit at the MRC. J.M. West, confirms the dissatisfaction with Villiers and noted that problems continued even after AMC had purchased 25 per cent of this supplier in an effort to improve delivery. The money for the expansion work would have been better spent, in his opinion, had it been used to purchase outright either Villiers or gearbox maker Burman. See J.M. West interview, 23 November 1994.

23. See Hopwood, *op. cit.*, p. 155.

24. A survey in 1958, comparing the running costs of a Austin A40 motor car and a Velocette 'LE' light weight motor cycle revealed that, on average, the Velocette cost 2s 26d per mile compared to the Austin's 7s 61d. See 'Costs per mile', *Motor Cycle and Cycle Trader*, 1 March 1958, pp. 304–5.

25. See Jonathan Wood, *Wheels of Misfortune*, chapter 5, pp. 95–133 and Martin Adeney, *The Motor Makers*, chapter 10, pp. 194–220.

26. Prices derived from the 'Buyers' Guide' contained in *The Autocar*, 11 November 1955 and 11 November 1960 and from the 'Buyers' Guide' contained in *The Motor Cycle*, 18 November 1954 and 17 November 1960.

27. The song is featured in a radio documentary entitled 'Hell for Leather', which was broadcast on BBC Radio 1 on 31 July 1993. Thanks to presenter John Peel and producer Wendy Pilmer for making a copy of this audio tape available, which is now on deposit at the MRC.

28. See, for example, 'Heavy going for Cycles', *Financial Times*, 6 June 1957 and 'Downhill drift in cycling', *Manchester Guardian*, 29 November 1958. See also 'Drift to cars hits cycle makers', *Coventry Evening Telegraph*, 29 January 1959. All citations contained in clipping volume MRC MSS 204/10/1/3.

29. See memo entitled '280/56: Director's Personal Report' dated 20 August 1956, contained in Guardbook MRC MSS 204/3/1/83.

30. See memo '357/57: Director's Personal Report', dated 7 August 1957. The statistics concerning Anglo-Italian trade were drawn from a letter Industry Association Director Hugh Palin had written to the Minister of State for the Board of Trade and is attached to the memo. Both documents are contained in Guardbook MRC MSS 204/3/1/86.

31. See draft memorandum, 'Bicycle and Motor Cycle Export Trade', dated 26 November 1957, contained

in Industries' Association Guardbook MRC MSS 204/3/1/87.

32. See 'Special Report: Milan Cycle and Motor Cycle Show' dated December 1957, prepared by H. Palin and contained in the Industries' Association Guardbook MRC MSS 204/3/1/87. It was also noted elsewhere that the Italians had a high tax placed on machines over 200 cc engine capacity, making demand for heavy weight models unlikely to be more than 1,000 per year. See memo (no date, but probably January 1957), entitled '127/57. Special Report, Milan Cycle and Motor Cycle Show, December 1956', pp. 9–10, contained in MRC MSS 204/3/1/85. See also 'Liberalising Trade', *Motor Cycle and Cycle Trader*, 12 April 1958, p. 2.

33. See Minutes of the Motor Cycle Manufacturers' Section, 9 October 1958, contained in Industry Association Guardbook series, MRC MSS 204/3/1/89.

34. See Scandinavian sales report, dated 17 July 1961, J.M. West personal papers. According to West, another cause of the decline of Nordic motor cycle sales was that 'the nights are long and cold in Sweden [and] you can't go courting on a motor cycle'. See West interview, 23 November 1994.

35. See minutes of the Motor Cycle Manufacturers' Section, held on 21 March 1952, contained in Guardbook MRC MSS 204/3/1/73.

36. See memo entitled '247/55: Australia', dated 2 June 1955, contained in Guardbook MRC MSS 204/3/1/80. This trend continued afterwards, see memo entitled '267/58: Australia: Motor Cycle Exports', dated 15 July 1958, contained in Guardbook MRC MSS 204/3/1//88.

37. In 1934, for example, 125 motor cycles were sold to Liberia compared with 37 machines sent to the USA, see 'Statistical Report 172/35' dated 16 September 1935, contained in MRC MSS 204/3/138.

38. According to Managing Director Edward Turner, when Triumph began exporting to the US in 1936, the initial reception by American consumers was not entirely favourable and the British imports were resented. Indeed, 'there were times when certain of the rougher elements were inclined to be quite militant about the situation'. See 'Through Edward Turner's Eyes', *The Motor Cycle*, 20 March 1947, pp. 180–1.

39. See, for example, Watling's report to the Manufacturers' Union Council, which expressed concern that government pressure to export to North America might be at the expense of trade in other areas, especially South America. However, Watling did not explain how they should deal

with South American tariff barriers and import quotas. See report dated 23 December 1949, entitled '458/49. The Dollar Drive', contained in MRC MSS 204/3/167.

40. See untitled news story *Motor Cycle and Cycle Trader*, 20 April 1951, p. 36, and 'Through the Eyes of Edward Turner', *op. cit.* Turner had written earlier in a popular motor cycle journal extolling the potential of the American market. See 'From Coventry to California', *Motor Cycling*, October 18, 1945, p. 436–7.

41. See 'We must 'sell motor cycling'' by Gilbert Smith, *Motor Cycle and Cycle Trader*, 5 May 1950, p. 174.

42. When he met with the Minister of Overseas Trade in 1951, Manufacturers' Union President F. Kimberley stressed the importance of British imports of the medium weight machines (350 cc to 650 cc engine displacement) the industry was sending to the USA: 'This type of machine was not previously made in the United States and British manufacturers felt that they had opened up a market for what was, to the Americans, an entirely new product.' See Document #38, entitled 'Export of bicycles and motor cycles', prepared by D. Simpson, 14 November 1951, NA BT 11/4452. See also 'US Light Weights Sales Rise', *New York Times*, 6 January 1949, p. 39.

43. Gilbert Smith, Managing Director of Norton Motors, noted that 'the success of British motor cycles in the United States results in part from members of the American Forces getting to like them when over in Britain'. 'Through a manufacturers' eyes', *The Motor Cycle*, 18 December 1947, pp. 478–9. This observation was confirmed by another report which appeared in the *Times*, 8 July 1948, 'Motor Cycling Boom in America'. For details on the importance of sporting activities among American motor cyclists, see Ivor Davies, *op. cit.*, p. 126 and Brooke and Gaylin, *op. cit.*, pp. 14–25.

44. See 'Johnson Motors in California', *British Motor Cycle and Cycles Export Trader*, May 1953, pp. 90–3. Triumph's development of the American market is given a detailed account in Ivor Davies, *op. cit.*, pp. 113–35.

45. West also expressed concern about the activities of the so-called 'milk bar cowboys' whose riding style, he claimed 'deters others from normal riding in view of the stigma they create'. See 'American Report', prepared by J.M. West, dated 17 December 1957, contained in J.M. West, personal papers.

46. See Minutes of the Manufacturers' Section, 24 September 1949, Guardbook MRC MSS 204/3/1/66.

47. See S.F. Digby, 'Advance of the British Motor Cycle Industry', *Financial Times*, 12 August 1952. See also 'Europe Puts Its Best Wheels Forward', by R. Stevenson, *Business Week*, August 1947, pp. 138–42, 'Motor Cycle Renaissance', 18 September 1949, *ibid.*, and 'In the United States' by Emmett Moore, *The Motor Cycle*, 13 November 1952, pp. 593–4.

48. In Hawaii, for example, formerly a strong hold for Harley-Davidson, British models such as the 650 cc BSA 'Golden Flash' had become a favourite of local motor cycle enthusiasts. Their popularity was believed to have been gained at Harley Davidson's expense. See 'Hawaiian Enterprise', *Motor Cycle and Cycle Export Trader*, March 1953, pp. 47–9.

49. See J.R. Nelson, *Bonnie. The Development History of the Triumph Bonneville*, Sparkford: Haynes Publishing Group, 1979, pp. 36–40 and *Triumph Tiger 100/Daytona*, Sparkford: Haynes Publishing Group, 1989, pp. 21–31.

50. See memo dated 26 January 1949, entitled '31/49 – USA: Motor Cycle Exports and the AMA', contained in Guardbook MRC MSS 204/3/1/64. When visiting the US in 1947, Norton Managing Director Gilbert Smith noted that 'trade and industry in the United States do not entirely welcome the importation of British motor cycles, especially when these machines are successful in competitions'. See also 'Through a Manufacturer's Eyes' by Gilbert Smith, *The Motor Cycle*, 18 December 1947, pp. 478–9.

51. See the minutes of the Motor Cycle Manufacturers' Section meeting of 24 September 1949, contained in Guardbook MRC MSS 204/3/1/66 and Ivor Davies, *op. cit.*, p. 119 and p. 123.

52. For background on the so-called 'outlaw' motor cycle gangs, particularly the 'Hells' Angels' motor cycle club, see Hunter Thompson, *The Hells' Angels*, New York: Bantam Books, 1965.

53. At the time the film *The Wild One* was considered so unsuitable for British film goers that it was only approved by the British Board of Film Censors for general release in 1968. See Maz Harris, *Bikers*, London: Faber and Faber, 1985, p. 23.

54. See, for example, 'Forty hours in Hollister' by John Durrance, *Cycle*, August 1987, pp. 39–44.

55. For F.G. Norman quote, see *British Motor Cycle and Cycle Export Trader*, July/August 1954, 'Continental Competition in American markets', p. 103. The information on Douglas is from the FBI file 'Dollar Exports Board, June 1949 to June 1950', document entitled 'Canada – current enquiries in the market and dossier of 'follow-up' letters', entry for Douglas (Sales and Service) dated 17 August 1949, contained in MRC MSS 200/F/3/DD1/42(1).

56. See Ivor Davies, *op. cit.*, pp. 113–34 and FBI Exports Report on motor cycle sales, dated August 1950, contained in MRC MSS 200/DEC/3/3/C149.

57. See 'BSA Expansion in North America', *British Cycles and Motor Cycles Overseas*, December 1949, p. 592.

58. See 'BSA factory branch in America', *Motor Cycle and Cycle Export Trader*, July/August 1954, p. 101.

59. Colonel Grantham, formerly of the Ministry of Supply and now on the staff of Brockhouse Engineering, represented the firm at a meeting of the Manufacturers' Union Motor Cycle Manufacturers' Section held on 24 September 1949 and outlined his company's plans for the American market. The minutes are contained in Guardbook MRC MSS 204/3/1/66.

60. See Peter Watson, 'Brockhouse: Why the British closed Indian', *Classic Bike*, June 1987, pp. 30–1 and 'Indian Sales Corporation, Named American Distributor of British Motorcycles', *New York Times*, 22 October 1949, p. 24. The arrangement, from Enfield's perspective, was outlined in the Chairman's speech to the Annual General Meeting, held on 30 January 1956. Copy of the speech is on deposit at the Guildhall Library, London.

61. See 'British Motor Cycles Fill Out US Maker's Line', *Business Week*, 5 November 1949, pp. 89–90, and a memo entitled 'Hambros Trading Corporation', dated 17 September 1949, contained in MRC MSS 200/F/3/4/8/83. For general information on distribution in the US see, *British Cycles and Motor Cycles – Interesting Facts and Figures and Some Useful Information*, published by the Manufacturers' Union in 1950, copy contained in Guardbook MRC MSS 204/3/1/68.

62. See Rogers, *The British Motorcycle Industry, 1945–1975*, pp. 27–8 and John Balder interview.

63. *Ibid.*

64. In total, the cost of opposing Harley-Davidson's application to the Tariff Commission cost £11,075. The Manufacturers' Union agreed to pay £5,536, see Minutes of the Council meeting of 3 July 1951, contained in Guardbook MRC MSS 204/3/1/71 and minutes of the Motor Cycle Manufacturers' Section meeting of 23 November 1951, contained in Guardbook MRC MSS 204/3/1/72. The balance was made up by individual manufacturers: BSA (£1,522), Ariel (£166), Brockhouse Engineering (£1,993) and Triumph Engineering (£1,858). See Triumph Engineering, Accounts Analysis books for 1952/1953, p. 102/31, contained in MRC MSS 123/2/1/2.

65. See minutes of the Motor Cycle Manufacturers' Section meeting of 17 June 1952, contained in Guardbook MRC MSS 204/3/173. The case been also discussed during the Section meetings of 16 December 1949 and 23 November 1951, minutes contained in Guardbooks MRC MSS 204/3/1/67 and MSS 204/3/172 respectively.

66. Harley-Davidson's application to the US Tariff Commission received nationwide press coverage, see for example, 'Motorcycles bump into trade amity', *New York Times*, 8 October 1951, p. 33. Ironically, the British employed the same tactics the Americans had used against them in order to stem the rising numbers of Czech and German imports into Australia. The Australian dealers protested, but evidently there was nothing illegal about this in Australian law. See 'Minutes of the Motor Cycle Manufacturers' Section', 16 December 1949, contained in Guardbook MRC MSS 204/3/1/67.

67. US Tariff Commission, *Motorcycles and Parts. Report on the Escape-Clause Investigation. Report no. 180. 2nd Series.* Washington D.C.: Government Printing Office, 1953, p. 3. The Commission also remarked on the role played by US service personnel stationed in Britain during the war, who later helped to popularise British motor cycles when they returned home after 1945.

68. *Ibid.*, pp. 4–5.

69. *Ibid.*, pp. 5–6.

70. See 'BSA Expansion in North America', *British Cycles and Motor Cycles Overseas*, December 1949, p. 592. See also 'Brothers build business on nerve; little capital', *Financial Post*, 12 October 1946 contained in NA BT 60/81/6, 'Canada: Trade and Missions from UK. Cycles and Motor Cycles'. Deeley, which also carried British cars as well as motor cycles, had been founded in Vancouver before the First World War, see Frank Hilliard, *Deeley – Motorcycle Millionaire*, Victoria, Canada: Orca Book Publishers, 1994, especially pp. 25–39, 76–101.

71. See Steve Koerner, 'Asleep at the Wheel? British Motor Vehicle Exports to Canada, 1945–75' contained in Phillip Buckner (ed.), *Canada and the End of Empire*, Vancouver: UBC Press, 2005, pp. 151–64.

72. See 'US market opening favourable', 29 May 1954, p. 120., *Motor Cycle and Cycle Trader*, 29 May 1954. British sports car manufacturers also exported a high proportion of output to North America at this time. Between 1945 and 1959 MG, for example, sent 85.4 per cent of its production there. Less than 10 per cent was sold in the British market. See Whistler, *op. cit.*, p. 259.

73. Turner's remarks were reported in 'Triumph

Corporation's New Premises in Baltimore', *The Motor Cycle and Cycle Export Trader*, May/June 1956, p. 67.

74. Despite their longstanding anxiety about the Germans, the British industry evidently turned down an opportunity to co-operate with a group of German industrialists to manufacture motor cycles of German design. Although Major Watling termed the offer 'genuine' evidently no British manufacturer ever followed it up. See Memo sent to AMC, BSA, Royal Enfield, Norton et al., entitled '116/50: Germany – Motor Cycle Manufacture', dated 28 March 1950, contained in Guardbook MRC MSS 204/3/1/67.

75. Further details of the German motor cycle industry during 1953 are outlined in memos '178/53: Germany – Information' dated 15 May 1953 ', Confidential Bulletin #4, dated 28 July 1953, both contained in Guardbook MRC MSS 204/3/1/75 and Confidential Bulletins #5 and #8 dated 18 September and 16 November 1953 respectively, contained in Guardbook MRC MSS 204/3/1/76.

76. In early 1949 Major Watling met with a Mr. Nieztsch, a Director of the NSU company and the current President of the German Motor Cycle Manufacturers' Association. The substance of their discussions is outlined in a memo entitled '83/49: Germany: Motor Cycle Exports', dated 8 March 1949, contained in Guardbook MRC MSS 204/3/1/65.

77. See 'Comment on Prices' by Edward Turner, *The Motor Cycle*, 18 September 1952, p. 333.

78. See, for example, 'The Factories in Germany' by Arthur Bourne, *ibid.*, 5 May 1949, pp. 352–5 and 'German Motor Cycle Design' by Bert Hopwood, *ibid.*, 13 December 1952, pp. 630–2.

79. These reports, 34 in total, commenced in May 1953 and were received regularly until October 1959.

80. See 'Confidential Bulletin no. 8, Developments in the German Cycle, Motor Cycle and Accessories Industries' dated 16 November 1953, contained in Guardbook MRC MSS 204/3/1/76 and 'Confidential Bulletin no. 3, Developments in the German Motor Cycle Industry', dated 15 June 1953, contained in Guardbook MRC MSS 204/3/1/75. The President of the German Association of Cycle and Motor Cycle Manufacturers said that his industry's production programme was 'mainly influenced by the need of the working classes to obtain cheap and efficient transport facilities'. See article entitled 'Cycle and Motor Cycle Industry', *Statist*, 23 June 1951, p. 21.

81. See 'UK Motor Cycles Abroad', *Financial Times*, 14 September 1955, contained in clipping volume MRC MSS 204/10/1/3 and 'Know Your Competitors, XXV – Von Heydekampf', *ibid.*, 16 May 1956, both contained in TUC clipping file 12913 and 'Confidential Bulletin #9', dated 8 January 1954, contained in Guardbook MRC MSS 204/3/1/76.

82. See memo entitled '193/55: Directors' Personal Report', dated 20 April 1955, contained in Guardbook MRC MSS 204/3/1/80.

83. When he visited a trade exhibition in October 1956, AMC Sales Director J.M. West observed a major change in the attitude of his German rivals: 'The smug satisfaction of a few years ago is conspicuous by its absence, open depression reigns.' In West's opinion, 'the current position of the German industry [is the] equivalent to someone in the middle of the Sahara without a compass'. The report, entitled 'The Frankfurt Motor Cycle Exhibition, October 1956', dated 21 October 1956, is contained in J.M. West's personal papers. For a general account of post-war German industry, especially motor manufacturing, see Simon Reich, *The Fruits of Fascism*. London: Cornell University Press, 1990.

84. See 'Confidential Bulletin no. 17 – Developments in the German Cycle, Motor Cycle and Accessory Industries', dated December 1954, and 'Confidential Bulletin no. 25 Developments …', dated August 1955, contained in Guardbooks MRC MSS 204/3/1/79 and MSS 204/3/1/81 respectively. See also 'German Motor Cycle Setback', *Financial Times*, 26 October 1957, contained in clipping book MRC MSS 204/10/1/3.

85. See memos dated 20 January 1955 entitled '23/55: Germany', contained in 204/3/1/79 and '357/57: Director's Personal Report' dated 7 August 1957, contained in Guardbook MRC MSS 204/3/1/86. After visiting the 1956 German motor cycle show, Industries' Association Director Palin identified a 'rapid increase in the standards of living' as well as bad weather as the main causes for declining motor cycle sales. He also noted hostile German press coverage, which had 'waged a systematic campaign against the motor cycle'. See 'Special Report. German Cycle and Motor Cycle Show – Frankfort 1956', dated December 1956, contained in Guardbook MRC MSS 204/3/1/84.

86. See Bulletin no. 32, 'Report on the German Cycle and Motor Cycle Industry', dated August 1957, contained in MRC MSS 204/3/1/86.

87. *Ibid.*

88. See Confidential Bulletin no. 3, 'Report on the German Cycle and Motor Cycle Industry', dated 29 May 1953, contained in MRC MSS 204/3/1/88 and memo '59/59 – Bulletin no. 33 – Report on the

German Cycle and Motor Cycle Industry' dated 18 February 1959, contained in Guardbook MRC MSS 204/3/1/90. For details on BMW at this time, see 'Shocked into Excellence', *Independent on Sunday*, business section, 28 June 1992, pp. 12–13.

89. See memo entitled '326/52: Japan – Motor Cycle Exports', dated 5 November 1952, which noted the popularity of foreign machines. The memo is contained in Guardbook MRC MSS 204/3/1/74. See also Document 47a, dated 30 September 1952 and entitled 'Motor Cycles' and document 47b, letter from N.S. Roberts, Minister, British Embassy Tokyo, to Nobuhiko Ushiba, dated 30 September 1952. Both documents are contained in NA BT 11/4452.

90. See memo, 'Japanese Competition', dated 19 April 1950, Guardbook, MRC MSS 204/3/1/68.

91. For the popularity of foreign motor cycles on the Japanese market, see memo entitled '326/52: Japan – Motor Cycle Exports', dated 5 November 1952, contained in MRC MSS 204/3/1/74.

92. See memo entitled '171/53: Japan – Motor Cycle Exports', dated 11 May 1953, contained in Guardbook MRC MSS 204/3/1/75. According to W. Rawson, BSA's Export Manager, 'In Japan there is a tremendous demand for motor cycles both domestic and imported, and the domestic manufactures far from being hurt by imported machines, are not able to fill more than a fraction of the total market. We ourselves could easily sell one hundred BSA motor cycles per month, judging from our waiting list, but the last allocation, which was only one tenth of our previous allocation, permitted us to bring in only 20 or 30 machines per month.' See Document 54, letter from W. Rawson to the Board of Trade, dated 31 October 1952. For the Japanese position, see Document 51a, N. Ushiba, Chief of International Trade Bureau, MITI, to N.S. Roberts, Minister, British Embassy in Tokyo, dated 8 October 1952. Both documents are contained in NA BT 11/4452.

93. See memo entitled '61/56: Japan – Motor Cycle Exports', dated 7 February 1956, contained in Guardbook MRC MSS 204/3/1/82 and memo '61/56: Japan – Motor Cycle Exports', dated 7 February 1956, contained in Guardbook MRC MSS 204/3/1/82.

94. Domestic production was 105,191 in 1955, and 79,870 in mid-1956. By contrast, imports were 13,855 in 1955 and had already reached 25,121 in mid-1956. See memo to the Council, dated 20 August 1956, entitled '280/56: Director's Personal Report', contained in *ibid*.

95. *Ibid*. Later that October, the Motor Cycle Manufacturers' Section unanimously voted against the same motion once more. See, minutes of the Motor Cycle Manufacturers' Section, 25 October 1956, contained in Industry Association Guardbook, MRC MSS 204/3/1/84.

96. The initial debate about membership took place on at a Council meeting conducted on 1 October 1958, see minutes contained Guardbook MRC MSS 204/3/1/89. The new membership category was adapted during a subsequent Council meeting held on 24 March 1959, while the Show rules were amended during a meeting on 26 May 1959. Both minutes are contained in Guardbook MRC MSS 204/3/1/59.

97. See memo (no date but probably autumn 1957) entitled '165/57: Director's Personal Report', contained in Industry Association Guardbook, MRC MSS 204/3/1/85. For reports of sales of imported foreign scooters see, for example, a Industry Association memo, dated 21 March 1958, which contains a protest to the Blackburn Police, who had recently bought Italian scooters, entitled '139/58: Director's Personal Report', contained in Industry Association Guardbook, MRC MSS 204/3/1/87. See 'More British motor scooters 'on way'' a story about the Birmingham City Police using Vespas, built under licence by Douglas, published in the *Birmingham Post* (no date, summer 1956) contained in the Industry Association news clipping book, MRC MSS 204/10/1/3. See also memo entitled '323/57: BOAC – Supply of Motor Cycles', dated 15 July 1957, which described how the airline was using German scooters for transporting aircrew and a series of stories in the *Motor Cycle and Cycle Trader*, about the Liverpool Police buying Vespas (19 February 1955), the Cambridge police doing the same (15 October 1955, p. 32) and the RAC using foreign scooters (15 March 1958).

98. See memo dated 24 September 1959 entitled '380/59. Director's Personal Report', p. 4. and letter from Palin to F.G. Bebb, editor Trader Publishing Co., dated 13 October 1959, both contained in Guardbook MRC MSS 204/3/1/91.

99. See memo entitled '32/56. Motor Cycle Publicity – The Technical Press', dated 17 January 1956, contained in Guardbook MRC MSS 204/3/1/82.

100. Turner also admitted that most British scooter manufacturing originated from smaller firms, which because of their relatively higher costs, were unable to compete with their Continental rivals' lower prices. See 'Scooters: A British Challenge to the Continentals', *Financial Times*, 20 October 1958, contained in clipping volume MRC MSS 204/10/1/3.

101. *Ibid.* The BSA/Triumph scooter was priced at between £220 and £250 (depending on specification) compared to between £195 and £230 for a Vespa.

102. See memo entitled '357/57: Director's Personal Report', dated 7 August 1957, contained in Guardbook MRC MSS 204/3/1/86.

103. In mid-1957, there had already been 24,000 Italian, 14,000 German and 6,000 French motorised two-wheeled imports. See memo dated 7 August 1957, entitled '357/57: Director's Personal Report', contained in Industry Association Guardbook, MRC MSS 204/3/1/86; see memo dated 21 March 1958, entitled '139/58: Director's Personal Report', contained in Industry Association Guardbook, MRC MSS 204/3/1/88. See also, 'Only Scooters Prosper', *Economist*, 14 August 1957, p. 577.

104. See '200 motor cycle men given notice', *Times*, 12 April 1958, contained in TUC clipping collection, file 12915, on deposit at the MRC.

105. This view was expounded by Hugh Palin in an article published in 1957. Palin accused the government of continuing to 'strangle the production and sales' of mopeds by treating them as the larger, more powerful motor cycles. Moreover, requiring drivers' licences and test were not only a deterrent to prospective consumers but also undermined 'the efforts of the manufacturers to found a moped industry on anything but a small scale'. See 'Two Wheeled Transport', *FBI Review*, October 1957, pp. 57–64. The Union's position was also produced in a popular format designed for wide distribution through retailers, see *Vehicle Legislation and the Moped*, dated March 1957. A copy of this pamphlet is contained in Guardbook MRC MSS 204/3/1/85.

106. This is the substance of remarks made by Industry Association Director Hugh Palin when he met E.I.R. MacGregor, an official at the Ministry of Transport's Road Safety Division, during a meeting of 27 February 1958, see MacGregor's report, dated 28 February 1958, contained in sub-file RS2/15/00, PRO MT 92/63, entitled 'Accidents. Mopeds. Licensing and Accidents rates'. Compulsory helmet use was not adopted at that time, on the grounds that such a law could not be effectively enforced. See draft letter dated 11 June 1956, Minister of Transport to Godfrey Nicolson MP, contained in NA MT 92/33.

107. See 'Ride that moped at 16 … and no L-tests', *News Chronicle*, 2 April 1957, contained in clipping volume MRC MSS 204/10/1/3 and memo from E.W. McCallum, Engineering Industries Division, Board of Trade, to C.P.F. North, Ministry of Transport and Civil Aviation, dated 17 April 1957 and contained in NA MT 92/63.

108. See 'Note of meeting with a Deputation from the British Cycle and Motor Cycle Industry Association', dated 29 May 1957, contained in *ibid.*

109. See brief prepared by E.I.R. MacGregor, Road Safety Division, Ministry of Transport, dated 28 February 1958, contained in *ibid.*

110. See memo 253/60: Director's Confidential Report' dated 13 May 1960, contained in Guardbook MRC MSS 204/3/1/93. Columnist Francis Jones believed the Bill had been 'torpedoed [because of] the accident panic … and nothing else, [combined with] the apparent inability of some MPs to see any difference between a motorised bicycle and a 100 mph road-burner'. See 'Motor Cycle Matters', *Motor Cycle and Cycle Trader*, 8 April 1960, p. 12.

111. See memo from E.W. MacCallum, Engineering Industries Division, Board of Trade, to C.P.F. North, Ministry of Transport and Civil Aviation, dated 17 April 1957, contained in *op. cit.*

112. According to Francis Jones, the reason that Villiers had not previously produced a moped engine was insufficient manufacturing capacity. Villiers had, however, absorbed its chief rival JAP in 1945 and thereby at least partially rectified this shortcoming. See 'Motor Cycle Matters', *Motor Cycle and Cycle Trader*, 7 December 1957, p. 134.

113. The joint BSA/Triumph gala took place at Grosvenor House, while the new Raleigh moped was unveiled at the Savoy Hotel. See 'Blare of Publicity Follows Pre-Show Presentations of New Models', *Motor Cycle and Cycle Trader*, 8 November 1958, pp. 66–8. See also 'The Lightweight Trend', *The Motor Cycle and Cycle Export Trader*, January/February 1958, p. 1.

114. See 'Motor Cycle Industry's strong position', *Export Trader*, January/February 1959, pp. 14–16.

115. In Jones' words, 'some makers are getting nearer to the original idea of the powered cycle, instead of trying to develop their products into super-lightweights. See 'A Show that inspires confidence', *Motor Cycle and Cycle Trader*, 22 November 1958, pp. 155–7.

116. In 1953 the top two positions in both the Senior and Junior TT were won by British machines (Norton) and riders. See Matthew Freudenberg, *The Isle of Man*, *op. cit.*, pp. 165–6.

117. See 'A Memorable TT', *Motor Cycle and Cycle Trader*, 26 June 1954, p. 173.

118. Ironically, most of the Gilera factory output was in the 150 cc class and its largest production model was only 300 cc. The machine that won the Senior TT was specially built for the race. See 'Britain must race to win', *Daily Sketch*, 2 July 1955, contained in newspaper clipping book MRC MSS 204/10/1/3.

119. See Massimo Clarke, *100 Years of Motorcycles*, New York: Portland House, 1988, pp. 82–92.

120. According to one national daily: 'It is not only in football that Britain is suffering a sporting eclipse. In the one field in which this country has for so long been supreme the foreigners are now setting the pace – motorcycling. [Except for a period during the 1930s] … motor cycles made in Britain, ridden almost without exception by British riders, were better than anything any other country could produce.' See 'Britain no longer leaders world motorcycling', *Evening Standard*, [no date, but probably October 1954], contained in the Manufacturers' Union newspaper clipping book, MRC MSS 204/10/1/3.

121. Gilbert Smith also commented on the great expense required to hire top class riders. He calculated that it would cost Norton £156,000 alone just to maintain three first class riders. See 'Norton and AJS quit racing', *Daily Herald*, 8 November 1956, contained in TUC clippings file 12913, on deposit at the MRC. For Heather's remark, see 'No Norton or AJS works entries', *Manchester Guardian*, 8 November 1956, contained in newspaper clipping book MRC MSS 204/10/1/3.

122. See 'Why Foreign Machines Won TT Victories', *Coventry Evening Telegraph*, 27 June 1957, contained in newspaper clipping book MRC MSS 204/10/1/3.

123. See Collier's obituary, *The Motor Cycle*, 2 September 1954, p. 311 and Peter Hartley, *Matchless – Once the Largest British Motor Cycle Manufacturer*, p. 152.

124. See J. M. West interview, 23 November 1994.

125. See Woollett, *op. cit.*, p. 264 and Smith's obituary, *Motor Cycle and Cycle Trader*, 7 August 1964.

126. See obituary, *ibid.*, 29 March 1958, p. 374.

127. See biographical piece prepared by R. H. Thomas, *The Export Trader*, June 1946, p. 332 and obituary, *Motor Cycle and Cycle Trader*, 15 December 1961.

128. See biographical piece prepared by R. H. Thomas, *The Export Trader*, December 1946, pp. 466–8 and obituary, *Motor Cycle and Cycle Trader*, 4 May 1962, p. 62.

129. See biographical piece prepared by G. E. Thomas, *Export Trader*, August 1946, pp. 395–6 and Ryerson, *op. cit.*, pp. 59–60.

130. See Hopwood, *op. cit.*, pp. 15, 25.

131. So is the opinion of John Balder, who was BSA's Service Manager during Turner's stint as Managing Director. Balder interview, 18 November 1994.

132. Hopwood noted that Turner 'flatly refused to allow any movement towards inter-company management collaboration and it is not surprising that, given this sort of encouragement, a barrier of mistrust grew which was, much later, almost impossible to remove'. See Hopwood, *op. cit.*, p. 128 and p. 132. See also Shilton, *op. cit.*, p. 147, Ryerson, *op. cit.*, pp. 153–8 and the entry on Edward Turner, prepared by Barbara Smith, contained in the *Dictionary of Business Biography*, pp. 564–9.

133. In early 1961, Turner wrote a journal article wherein he predicted that in 50 years' time motor cycles would be powered by thermo-nuclear generators. In fairness to Turner, the article may have been written in less than perfect seriousness. See 'A Turner forecast – the motor cycle of AD 2010', *Motor Cycle and Cycle Trader*, 13 January 1961, pp. 258–9; in John Balder's opinion, during the Turner years as Division Managing Director, there was little or no direction received by the subsidiaries. One manifestation of this lack of leadership was the fact that almost no new production development occurred under the Turner Directorship. See Balder interview, 18 November 1994.

134. The sale of the bicycle subsidiary was especially significant, insofar that its Montgomery St. factory had built the Group's clip-on bicycle engine unit, the 'Winged Wheel'. After the sale, BSA would do little development in this lightweight engine category for years to come.

135. Shilton, *op. cit.*, p. 88.

136. See the entry on John (Jack) Young Sangster, prepared by Barbara Smith, contained in *op. cit.*, pp. 55–9.

137. See Shilton, *op. cit.*, p. 88, Chairman's Statement, contained in the 1960 *BSA Annual Report*, p. 14, MSS 10A/4/38 and Balder interview, 18 November 1994.

138. See 'In the Summer of '59', by Peter Watson, *Classic Bike*, December 1986, pp. 32–6.

139. Total motorised two-wheeled production for 1959 was actually recorded as 248,900 units; however, 108,000 of these were mopeds and scooters of mostly Italian origin built under licence in Britain. A further 13,500 were three-wheeled machines. See *Business Monitor, Production Series, Motor Cycles, Three-Wheeled Vehicles, Pedal Cycles and Parts (1968)*. See also 'Half a million extra customers', *Motor Cycle and Cycle Trader*, 13 March 1959, p. 385.

140. The estimate of lightweight and scooter output was made by Ronald Price, a senior executive with Villiers Engineering, the company which supplied power units to most of the smaller British motor cycle and scooter firms. See 'How the British Motor Scooter Industry is Expanding', by Ronald Price, *Motor Cycle and Cycle Trader*, 11 March 1960, pp. 344–6.

141. *Ibid.*

142. See memo '4/59 – Director's Personal Report' dated 5 January 1959, contained in Guardbook MRC MSS 204/3/1/89.

143. Referring to the high accident rate, one newspaper put it: '*It is a horrifying record. If this is the price we pay for a long, fine summer – and the boom in a drive-yourself community – we wonder if its worth it.*' [Emphasis in the original]. See 'SOS', *The Sketch*, 10 November 1959, contained in newspaper clipping book MRC MSS 204/10/1/3.

144. See 'I spend a night with the 'Wild Ones' of Britain', *Reynolds News*, 16 August 1959, contained in the BSA Collection, MS 321/F, and a file entitled 'Anti-motor cycling comments' on deposit at the Birmingham Central Reference Library, Local History Archive.

145. See 'The Night Riders', by Martin Page, *The Guardian*, 11 March 1961. For much the same type of reporting, see also 'Dicing with Death' by Keith Waterhouse and John Edwards, contained in the *Daily Mirror* 'Shock Issue' of 9 February 1961. Both articles are contained in the BSA Collection, MS 321/F, Birmingham Central Reference Library. The *Daily Mirror* article especially antagonised the manufacturers. Hugh Palin was irritated sufficiently to make a reply to it in the trade press. See his 'Creating favourable publicity for motor cyclists', *Motor Cycle and Cycle Trader*, 7 April 1961, pp. 8–9.

146. See, for example, 'A grim new spectre stalks into the road casualty returns: Death on two wheels', *The Sketch*, 10 November 1959, 'Crash … Crash … Crash went motor cyclists. Nightmare night on A20', *Chronicle*, 19 November 1959 and Pillion girls hit 100 along murder mile', *News Chronicle*, November [no day indicated] 1959, all contained in clippings volume MRC MSS 204/10/1/3.

147. See memo entitled 'Motor cycle competitions and the FIM 'sports' motor cycle', dated 17 September 1957, contained in Guardbook MRC MSS 204/3/1/86. There is no record in the files explaining whether or not the industry ever responded to the Ministry's suggestion.

148. See memo dated 24 September 1959, entitled '380/59: Director's Personal Report', contained in Guardbook MRC MSS 204/3/1/91.

149. See memo entitled '253/60: Director's Confidential Report', dated 13 May 1960, contained in Guardbook MRC MSS 204/3/1/93.

150. See 'Anthony Eden opens the 1953 Show', *Motor Cycle and Cycle Trader*, 21 November 1953, p. 155.

151. See 'All this at Earls Court', *op. cit.*, 18 November 1960, p. 141.

152. In 1956, Palin had conceded to the Council that the industry did not have much support among MPs. See memo entitled '173/56: Director's Personal Report', dated 26 April 1956, contained in Guardbook MRC MSS 204/3/1/83.

153. Palin noted that he had agreed to invite Rodgers only after two more senior Ministers turned him down. See Minutes of the Council for 24 March 1959, contained in Guardbook MRC MSS 204/3/1/90. Rodgers' remarks at the opening were reported in 'New IA headquarters at Coventry opened by J.C. Rodgers, MP'. 29 April 1959, pp. 36–7, *Motor Cycle and Cycle Trader*.

154. In 1962, the Industries' Association approached Prime Minister MacMillan and Princess Margaret to see whether either of them would do the honours at that year's show. After they had been rebuffed, Palin advised Association members that, in his opinion, 'we need to find a public figure who whilst not being a politician would appeal to the crowds, without in any sense lowering the dignity of the occasion'. See memo entitled '229/62 – Director's Report', dated 9 July 1962, contained in Guardbook MRC MSS 204/3/1/99.

155. Turner's remarks were reported in 'Triumph export dinner', *op. cit.*, 22 November 1958, p. 162.

156. See 'Motor Cycle Matters' by Francis Jones, *Motor Cycle and Cycle Trader* 4 January 1958, p. 186 and 'As modern as the moment' by Francis Jones, *op. cit.*, 18 November 1960, pp. 153–6.

157. See memo '323/60: Confidential Report', dated 28 June 1960, contained in Guardbook MRC MSS 204/3/1/94.

158. See 'Confidential Report on the 41st Amsterdam Cycle and Motor Cycle Show, 26 February–8 March 1959', prepared by Hugh Palin, no date but probably March/April 1959, contained in Industry Association Guardbook, MRC MSS 204/3/1/90.

Notes to Chapter 6: The firms and their workers, 1960–1973

1. See 'Gloom among the motor cycles', *Financial Times*, 30 August 1961, contained in TUC clipping file 12913 and 'Motor cycles and 'Unhappy prospects', *The Economist*, 25 November 1961, p. 834.

2. See 'Triumph workers to be dismissed early next month', *Coventry Standard*, 1 December 1961, p. 1, contained in MRC MSS 123X/10/1/3.

3. See *Hansard*, [vol. 650], 1 December 1961, cols 890–900.

4. *Ibid.*, cols 891–2.

5. *Ibid.*, col. 893.

6. *Ibid.* plus cols 895–8, 900.

7. See 'Motor cycles look for markets' by David Jenkins, *The Statist*, 16 February 1962, pp. 516–17.

8. See 'Recession on two wheels', *The Economist*, 14 July 1962, pp. 172–3.

9. The leading article is contained in the *Motor Cycle and Cycle Trader*, 15 December 1961, pp. 143–4. The Design Commission was announced in an article entitled 'Comment', *Ibid.*, 12 January 1962, pp. 192–3. A letter to the editor from Maurice Edelman was published on page 281 of the 21 February 1962 issue of *ibid.*, which urged that the Commission also include consumers and worker representatives. Thereafter, no further mention of the Commission was published, either in the trade press or in the surviving archives of the Industries' Association, leading one to suspect it had become defunct very quickly.

10. See 'Slamming the Critics', *The Motor Cycle*, 11 January 1962. Rawson was particularly incensed over sensationalist press coverage of motor cyclists: 'The motor cyclist appears to be fair game for everyone.'

11. See minutes of the Publicity Committee held on 19 December 1961, contained in Guardbook MRC MSS 204/3/1/98.

12. See memo entitled '27/62: Motor Cycle and Scooter Publicity' by Hugh Palin, dated 9 January 1962, attached to the minutes of the Motor Cycle Publicity Committee of the same date, contained in Guardbook MRC MSS 204/3/1/93. In 1966 an unnamed sales director was quoted bemoaning the fact that 'people got the impression our job was selling lethal projectiles to morons'. See 'After ton-up kids, a labour shortage', *The Guardian*, 15 February 1966, contained in TUC clipping file 12913, on deposit at the MRC

13. Turner, who was President of the Industries' Association that year, was speaking at the Show on 8 November 1962. The text of his speech is contained in MRC MSS 204/3/T41.

14. The Committee also recognised that many traditional customers were now marrying and starting families earlier than before, 'which again struck a blow at our market' since 'the younger element of the public formed a substantial proportion' of sales. See minutes of the meeting of the Joint Advisory Committee, held on 3 July 1962. The minutes are held in the offices of the Motor Cycle Retailers' Association. The *Economist* observed that higher personal income among the British population now tempted 'potential [motor cycle] buyers to get a car instead – which bring more comfort as well as, perhaps, higher social esteem'. See 'Recession on two wheels', *op. cit.*

15. See 'Gloom among the motor cycles', *op. cit.*

16. See minutes of the Motor Cycle Manufacturers' Committee meeting of 19 January 1960, contained in Guardbook MRC MSS 204/3/1/95.

17. *Ibid.* See also 'Motor cycles look for markets' by David Jenkins, *op. cit.*

18. See 'The management skid in the two wheeled business', *Business*, May 1965, pp. 22–32.

19. According to a poll conducted by the *Birmingham Mail* at about the same time, parental opposition was identified as the major obstacle to motor cycle sales to young people. See 'Motor cycle survey', *Birmingham Mail*, 11 December 1963, contained in newspaper clipping book MRC MSS 204/10/1/4.

20. See 'The Management skid in the two wheeled business', *op. cit.*

21. See 'Tenterden trader must quit', *Kent Messenger*, 26 November 1965, contained in newspaper clipping book MRC MSS 204/10/1/6.

22. The levy was expected to raise approximately £10,000. See memo '445/63: The Motor Cycle and Scooter Publicity Campaign' dated December 1963, contained in Guardbook MRC MSS 204/3/1/102. A subsequent report, 'A memorandum on public relations' dated 4 July 1968 outlined the various programmes initiated by the Industries' Association over the past several years and is contained in Guardbook MRC MSS 204/3/1/113. The information on the 'National Essay Contest' is drawn from the minutes of the Joint Motor Cycle and Scooter Publicity Committee meetings of 6 February 1963 and 22 January 1967, contained in Guardbooks MRC MSS 204/3/1/113 and MSS 204/3/1/110 respectively.

23. See letter, J.D. Richards (Solex Ltd) to D. O'Neill (Permanent Under-Secretary, Ministry of Transport), 27 July 1961, contained in NA MT 92/63.

24. See minute dated 28 July 1961, prepared by C. North and letter, C.C. Nicholas (Board of Trade) to J.D. Richards, dated 18 December 1961, both contained in *ibid.* One estimate of the potential revenue loss should the tax be lifted on mopeds was thought to be approximately £450,000. See note prepared by J. Garlick (Road Safety Division, Ministry of Transport), contained in *ibid.*

25. See memo, P.A. Walker to Whipp, dated 4 January 1963, *ibid.*

26. See letter, Marples to Bolton, dated 17 December 1962, contained in *ibid.*

27. See Chairman's speech to the Annual General Meeting, held on 13 December 1962, contained in MRC MSS 19A/4/40.

28. See letter, Turner to Hannon, dated 10 September

1962, contained in Box 35, Folder 1, Hannon Papers on deposit at the Parliamentary Archives.

29. See Peter Hartley, *The Ariel Story*, Watford: Argus Books, 1980, p. 199, p. 209 and p. 230 and Wilson, *op. cit.*, volume 6, pp. 120–4. See also 'Buyers' Guide 1961', contained in *The Motor Cycle*, 17 November 1960, pp. 665–71.

30. See Wilson, *British Motor Cycles since 1950*, vol. 1, pp. 120–5.

31. See 'Letter to the Shareholders' written by Managing Director Donald Heather in response to a circular sent out by a group of disgruntled shareholders, dated 10 September 1959. Heather sent out a second letter entitled 'Adjourned Annual General Meeting', dated 10 March 1960 outlining the circumstances for the postponed meeting. Both letters are attached to the 1960 *Annual General Meeting*, on deposit at the Guildhall Library.

32. The nominees were Cyril Bird, William Gardiner and Oliver Smedley, MC.

33. A circular entitled 'Associated Motor Cycles Shareholders' Committee', dated 17 May 1961, which described the grievances of the rebels, is reproduced in Hopwood, *op. cit.*, p. 167. J.M. West, who was on the Board at the time, questioned the motives of the leaders of the Committee, terming them 'asset strippers', West interview, November 23, 1994. For press coverage of the AGM, see 'AMC Board unchanged by Stormy AGM', *Motor Cycle and Cycle Trader*, 11 August 1961, p. 257, and also *The Times*, untitled story, 1 August 1961, p. 15.

34. See Hopwood, *op. cit.* and *AMC Directors' Report* for the year ended 31 August 1954 and 31 August 1961, on deposit at the Guildhall Library. Cowell, who joined the AMC board in 1958, had been Assistant General Manager at Barclays Bank and was also a director of N. Burston & Co., merchant bankers. See *Motor Cycle and Cycle Trader*, 24, May 1958, p. 106.

35. See Chairman's Speech to the 1961 AMC Annual General Meeting, 23 March 1962, on deposit at the Guildhall Library, London. See also 'Cycle Firm Diversifies', *The Times*, 31 August 1961, p. 13 and 'AMC Sheerness plan dropped', *Motor Cycle and Cycle Trader*, 20 October 1961, p. 32.

36. As Cowell explained: 'The high rate of growth and profits during the expansion period of a sellers' market had the inherent penalty of vulnerability.' After the motor cycle market suffered the 1956 recession, 'the industry steadily became more competitive, of smaller volume and reverted to the pre-war pattern of extreme seasonal trading' leaving the AMC Group 'ill-equipped both as to specialised facilities and labour' to respond. See Chairman's Speech to the Annual General Meeting, delivered on 23 March 1962, copy on deposit at the Guildhall Library.

37. See 'Statement' by AMC Chairman Hulbert, dated 5 June 1962, on deposit at the Guildhall Library.

38. See Chairman's Speech to the Annual General Meeting, 4 April 1963, on deposit at the Guildhall Library. See also 'AMC Group's Big Loss', 26 January 1962, 'AMC Re-organisation', 20 April 1962 and 'Norton Motors to be moved to Woolwich' 27 July 1962, all in the *Motor Cycle and Cycle Trader*.

39. BSA was particularly interested in its US distribution network, which Edward Turner thought would be a 'very useful acquisition'. See Board meeting of 31 October 1957, agenda item 11105, contained in Minute Book no. 17, contained in MSS 19C/20. Negotiations between the two companies proved inconclusive.

40. See Peter Hartley, *The Story of Royal Enfield*, pp. 110 and 121. See also the Chairman's speech to the Annual General Meeting, 30 January 1961 and notice to shareholders, entitled 'Merger with E. & H.P. Smith' dated 1 November 1962, both on deposit at the Guildhall library.

41. See Wilson, *British Motor Cycles*, volume 4, pp. 19–20.

42. See *ibid.*, vol. 6, pp. 207–8. One explanation for the Viceroy's poor sales may have been its high specifications, which included its 250 cc engine, with power transmission provided by a shaftdrive, an unusual feature for a British machine, along with its price of £198. See untitled feature on the Viceroy, *Motor Cycle and Cycle Trader*, 21 October 1960, p. 37 and 'Veloce increases prices', *ibid.*, 21 September 1952, p. 295.

43. See Wilson *op. cit.* See also 'Velocette to phase out motor cycles', *Financial Times*, 25 June 1970 and a photo story of the final machine (an LE) produced, *Birmingham Post*, 3 February 1971, both in clipping book MRC MSS 204/10/1/7.

44. For an overview of these companies, see Roy Bacon's *Villiers Singles and Twins, The Postwar British Two-Stroke Lightweight Motor Cycle* and *British Motor Cycles of the 1960s*.

45. See 'The problem for the motor cycle makers how to lose an image and win a world market' by John Mills, *The Director*, September 1967, pp. 331 and 'Boom in mopeds and scooters', *Financial Times*, 25 February 1960, the latter contained in TUC clipping file 12913, on deposit at the MRC. See also 'New Raleigh Scooter', *The Times*, 4 November 1960, 'Scooter Prospects in 1960' 15 January 1960, p. 201 and 'Get into Moped market now', 27 July 1962, pp. 192–3. both from *Motor Cycle and Cycle Trader*.

46. See 'Raleigh taps new market with Wisp', *Financial Times*, 5 June 1967, contained in newspaper clipping book MRC MSS 204/10/1/6 and 'Raleigh drops out of moped market', *The Times*, 12 September 1969 and 'Sales fall forces Raleigh to stop producing mopeds', *Financial Times*, [no date, but probably September 1969] both contained in newspaper clipping book MRC MSS 204/10/1/7. See also 'Now Austrian firm is dominant force in moped market as Britain moves out' by Jack Hay, *Birmingham Post*, 17 November 1969, contained in newspaper clipping book MRC MSS 204/10/1/8.

47. For one of the more recent surveys of labour relations in the British automobile industry, see Anders Ditlev Clausager's chapter entitled 'Labour Relations', which is contained in Georgano et al., *Britain's Motor Industry*, pp. 184–209. See also, H.A. Turner, Garfield Clack and Geoffrey Roberts, *Labour Relations in the Motor Industry: A Study of Industrial Unrest and an International Comparison*, London: Allen and Unwin, 1967, Wayne Lewchuk, *American Technology and the British Vehicle Industry*, Cambridge: Cambridge University Press, 1987 and *The Automobile Industry and its Workers : Between Fordism and Flexibility*, Steven Tolliday and Jonathan Zeitlin (eds), Oxford: Berg Publishers, 1992.

48. For more detailed information on the settlement of the strike, see 'Report, re. Strike', dated 27 December 1911 (no author indicated), contained in the BSA Papers, MRC MSS 19A/7/PE/2/21.i.

49. *Munitions of War*, compiled by George Frost, published by BSA (no date is indicated but probably during 1919/1920). See especially the chapter entitled 'Welfare work in BSA factories'.

50. Alistair Cave interview, 15 and 22 August 1990; see also 'A laugh a line for the Doctor', a feature article about the Small Heath factory Dramatic Society, contained in issue no. 82 (May 1967) of the *BSA Group News*.

51. See BSA Management Minutes, entry for 25 June 1945, no. 7743, p. 3, BSA Papers, MRC MSS 19A/1/5/24.i; See also Cave interview, *op. cit.* who confirms that most labour-management discussions focused on peripheral issues such as cafeteria food; according to H.W. Robinson, who also worked at Small Heath during the period in question and who later became the National Union of Vehicle Builders and then Transport and General Workers' Union plant convener, the 1940s and 1950s was a time of 'weak and poor organisation', interview with H.W. Robinson, Small Heath, Birmingham, 18 September 1990.

52. See Cave interview, *op. cit.*

53. See BSA Management meeting of 25 June 1951, minute no. 9265, p. 1., MRC MSS 19A/1/5/110.

54. See, for example, AEU Coventry District Committee Minute Book, entry for a meeting on 24 November 1910, p. 39. Copy on deposit at the Coventry Records Office (hereinafter CRO) Accession 1243/1/4. See also Tom Donnelly and Martin Durham's *Labour Relations in the Coventry Motor Industry, 1896–1929*, Coventry: Coventry Polytechnic, Centre for Business History, n.d., for a more general description.

55. See Davenport-Hines, *op. cit.*, pp. 102–3.

56. See AEU Coventry District Committee Minute Book, entries for 10, 11, 12, 18, 26 191, CRO Accession 124/1/16; see also F.W. Carr, 'Engineering Workers and the Rise of Labour in Coventry, 1914–1939 (unpublished Ph.D. dissertation, Warwick University, 1978), pp. 183–6 for more details on the dispute.

57. National Union of Vehicle Builders, Coventry Branch Minute Book, SR IS (4), CRO Accession 1177/1/4.

58. Interview with Bert Hopwood, Torquay, 10 May 1990.

59. See Hopwood, *What ever Happened?*, p. 27; according to Ivor Davies, such was the employment situation in Coventry at that time that even with the wage cut Triumph workers 'were only too glad to still have jobs', see *It's a Triumph*, p. 52.

60. See Coventry District Engineering Employers' Association Book (volume for 1948–1954), item no. 1432, p. 32, on deposit at West Midlands Engineering Employers' Federation offices in Birmingham.

61. Several booklets and some correspondence relating to the Norton strike can be found within MRC MSS 309, Box 6. See, specifically, the 'Solidarity file'. Among these documents is a pamphlet published by the Norton Motors Strike Committee entitled *The Fight Against Redundancy* (September 1956). There are several newspaper clippings concerning the Norton strike contained in NA LAB 10/1445, 'Engineering – Standard Motor Car Co. Ltd, Coventry and the Confederation of Shipbuilding and Engineering Unions. Strikes over redundancy'. Harry Finch, who was the Norton shop stewards' convenor during the strike, was later listed as a leader of the Socialist Labour League in *Patterns of Trotskyism – A new form of subversion in Industry*. London: The Economic League Ltd (no date but probably 1960), which is contained in MRC MSS 200/F/5/53/5. A more reliable witness of this incident is Bert Hopwood, who had been appointed a Director of Norton just as the strike broke out and who provides a brief

description of the dispute in Hopwood, *op. cit.*, pp. 136–7.

62. The 'blacking' incident at the Show was described by Industry Association Director Hugh Palin in a memo dated 26 November 1956, entitled '367/56 – Director's Personal Report', contained in MRC MSS 204/3/1/84.

63. See 'Triumph Engineering Company and the Amalgamated Engineering Union, Transport and General Workers' Union and National Society of Metal Mechanics. Reference: Change in clocking Arrangements'. This file also contains CDEEA verbatim notes regarding a series of conferences held between the parties on 18 March, 18 April and 7 and 8 May 1959. File on deposit among the CDEEA papers, MRC MSS 66, File A17 (59/1).

64. *Ibid.*

65. See 'Gloom among the motorcycles', *Financial Times*, 30 August 1961, contained in TUC clipping file 12913 on deposit at the MRC.

66. See *Times* article dated 19 October 1961, TUC clipping file, *op. cit.* and 'Triumph workers to be dismissed early next month', *Coventry Evening Standard*, 1 December 1961, p. 1.

67. The relevant files for Triumph Engineering Ltd are contained in the CDEEA Collection at the MRC as MSS 66, A17 and A22 (59/1 to 59/29), A23, A55 and MRC MSS 66B-A17.

68. Under the provisions of the 1941 Agreement, skilled toolroom workers would receive the average earnings of skilled production personnel not just at their own factories but throughout the Coventry District. Under the wartime conditions that prevailed when the Agreement was signed, its purpose was to prevent excessive labour mobility between factories. However, after the war its effect was to act as a force to push up wages among Coventry engineering firms. See K.G.J.C. Knowles and D. Robinson's 'Wage Movement in Coventry', *Bulletin of the Oxford University Institute of Economics and Statistics*, vol. 31, no. 1 (February 1969), pp. 1–21 and William Brown's 'Piece-work Wage Determination in Coventry', *Scottish Journal of Political Economy*, vol. 18, pp. 1–30.

69. See Work's Conference, 'Re: Claim of Substantial Wage increase for Chargehand and Setters', dated 4 February 1964, contained in MRC MSS 66, A17, 59/5.

70. *Ibid.*

71. The 'Blue Book'(so described because of the colour of its cover) was published by the CSEU and officially entitled the *Handbook of National Agreements*. A January 1964 edition of the *Handbook* was kindly provided to the author by TGWU official Bill Lapworth.

72. See proceedings of an Informal Work's Conference of 10 August 1966, 'Reference: Piecework Job on the Capstan Section', contained in MRC MSS 66, A17, 59/6 and another Informal Conference of 13 March 1964, 'Reference: Enameling Department Wage Dispute', MRC MSS 66B, A17.1.

73. The comparison is slightly flawed insofar that 'Red Robbo' came to public attention ten years after Allsopp's heyday during the 1960s. According to John Walford, Triumph's General Works Manager between 1961 and 1971, Allsopp was reputed to have been, at an earlier stage in his career, the shop floor mentor of a young Jack Jones, future leader of the Transport and General Workers Union. Walford interview, 30 August 1990.

74. See Steve Wilson, *British Motor Cycles since 1950*, Volume 5, p. 102.

75. Allsopp was often the source of controversy at the Meriden factory. District Secretary Lapworth recalled an instance when, during one of the many unconstitutional stoppages, Allsopp was confronted by a CDEEA official who accused him of violating the procedures outlined in the 'Blue Book'. Allsopp is said to have found this remark quite amusing. 'Oh', he replied, 'we threw the "Blue Book" out the window here years ago.' Lapworth interview, Coventry, 23 April 1990.

76. See informal Work's Conference of 10 August 10, 1966, *op. cit.*

77. The *BSA Group News* carried two stories about labour troubles at Triumph's Meriden factory, see 'Triumph at a Standstill' no. 83, June 1967, p. 3. and 'Stoppage at Triumph', no. 93, May 1968, p. 3. However, one looks in vain, both in this publication or elsewhere, for stories about labour relations at the Group's other subsidiaries, motor cycle producers or not. Whether this was because there were no such disputes, or perhaps as a result of some other reason, is difficult to ascertain from the information available.

78. Presumably the White Paper in question was *Prices and Incomes Standstill*, London: HMSO, July 1966, Cmd. 3073.

79. See Informal Work's Conference, file 59/6, *op. cit.* In this instance the company would later admit that, while they may have 'misunderstood the intent' of the White Paper, from their point of view this was no excuse for the rash of illegal strikes at Meriden. Still, piece work rates kept on climbing, the White Paper notwithstanding, nor did the level of work stoppages appear to have significantly abated.

80. Nor does it cover labour stoppages, if they occurred, among industry component suppliers or to take into account factors such as shop floor

work jurisdiction rules which might have also affected BSAs (or, for that matter, any other motor cycle company's) ability to efficiently operate its factories.

81. See 'Double Tribute to Senior Shop Steward', *BSA Group News*, no. 9, July 1960s, p. 3. In contrast, H.W. Robinson, who became National Union of Vehicle Builders and later Transport and General Workers' Union Works Convenor for most of the 1960s and early 1970s, recalled Tidmarsh as a 'weak' leader who was unpopular with the stop stewards. Interview with H.W. Robinson, 18 September 199.

82. See WMEEA 'Minutes of the Management Board', volume for January–December 1966, Ref. 7340, Appendix 26, 'Claim for Improved Annual Holiday', advanced by the Association of Scientific Workers and the Draughtsmen and Allied Technicians' Association (this claim ultimately went to Central Conference in London for resolution) and volume for January–December 1968, Appendix 18, 'Increase for Males Earning in Excess of £950 p.a. and Females Earning in Excess of £650 p.a.' Both volumes are on deposit at the offices of the West Midlands Engineering Employers' Association in Birmingham.

83. See 'Review of the Wages Policy at the Small Heath Factory' submitted to BSA Motorcycles Ltd, by G.G. Field, 30 November 1964. Copy provided to the author by Alistair Cave.

84. *Ibid.*, p. 5. The consultants estimated that this level of turnover cost BSA some £30,000 yearly, presumably in additional training expenses.

85. *Ibid.*

86. *Ibid.*, pp. 8–9.

87. *Ibid.*, p. 10.

88. Interview with former Small Heath Works Manager Alistair Cave, *op. cit.*

89. See, for example Turner's remarks on 15 December 1960 and 10 December 1964 and again at the 1966 Annual General Meeting contained in MRC MSS 19A/4/38, MSS 19A/4/42 and MSS 19A/4/44.

90. Former Small Heath Works Manager Alistair Cave expressed especial concern about what he termed labour 'poaching' from the BSA plant by the motor car industry and of more skilled workers by the castings industry. Interview with A. Cave, 15 August 1990.

91. See 'After Ton-Up Kids, a Labour Shortage', *Guardian*, 15 February 1966, contained in TUC clipping file 12913 on deposit at the MRC.

92. Interview with Bert Hopwood, 10 May 1990, Torquay.

93. See Triumph Engineering Co. and the Transport and General Workers' Union, Informal Conference of 11 May 1967, 'Ref. To Discuss the Application of the Company's Indirect Bonus Scheme' contained in MRC MSS 66, A17, File 59/11.

94. See proceedings of Local Conference of 21 June 1967, contained in *ibid.*

95. See, for example, 'TEC and NSMM and AEU. Works' Conference of 28 September 1967. Ref. To Claim a Substantial Increase for all Male Inspectors with Pro Rata Increases for Female Inspectors', contained in File 59/13, *ibid.*

96. See 'TEC and NSMM, AEU and TGWU. Works' Conference of 28 September 1967, Ref: To Claim a Substantial Increase for Millwrights and Millwrights' Mates', File 59/14, contained in *ibid.*

97. At a Works' Conference held during March 1969, the company did recognise that the piece rate workers' wages had far outstripped those of the day workers and agreed to institute an annual review of those wages. It is unclear what happened subsequently. See 'TEC and AEU. Works' Conference of 28 March 1969. Ref: 'To Claim a Substantial Wage Increase for Two Members Employed as Testers', contained in *ibid.*

98. Information about this incident was supplied during interviews with John Nelson on 16 August 1990, who worked in the Triumph Engineering service department and ultimately became its manager and Triumph's then General Works Manager John Walford, *op. cit.*

99. Walford interview, *ibid.*

100. The company's dilemma is outlined in Barbara Smith's 'Production Relationships at BSA, 1963/64–1971/72' (unpublished paper on deposit at the Centre for Urban and Regional Studies, University of Birmingham).

101. The press coverage noted that this was the first recorded work stoppage in the past 25 years. See 'BSA factory shut by unofficial strike', *The Times*, 17 April 1969. Later that year there was another walk out prompted by a computer malfunction that disrupted the issuance of pay cheques. See 'Sacked? the computer that just couldn't do its sums', *Daily Mirror* 14 August 1969. These and other newspaper references cited relating to the events at BSA between 1969 and 1972 are drawn from Mr. A. Cave's personal file of news clippings deposited as part of the MRC's BSA collection.

102. See 'Plans to save BSA will cost 3,000 jobs' by Stewart Fleming, *Guardian*, 8 October 1971.

103. During the summer of 1971, the Upper Clyde Shipbuilders who employed some 8,000 workers was close to liquidation. In order to protect their jobs, trade union activists initiated a worker occupation of their employer's premises. The

occupation was ended early the following year when Conservative Prime Minister Edward Heath pledged public money in order to keep the UCS going, another one of his government's so-called 'U-Turns' away from previously stated economic policy. See John Foster and Charles Woolfson's *The Politics of the UCS Work-In*, London: Lawrence and Wishart, 1986.

104. See Cooper Bros, 'Report to the Board, re. Small Heath Rundown', dated 25 August 1971, signed by a David Frean. The report is contained in the BSA Collection at the Solihull Public Library, item no. 357.

105. See 'Unions speed up fight on jobs after BSA shock' by Alexander McDonald, *Birmingham Post*, 9 October 1971; 'Labour MPs to press for £18m overdraft from Barclays' by Peter Cartwright, *Financial Times*, 12 October 1971; "Rescue motor cycle giant' plea to Heath', by Kingsley Squire, *Daily Express*, 12 October 1971.

106. See '4,000 ask: 'Am I on the axe list?', 'The man who had 'a job for life" and 'Looking ahead in anger?' all contained in the 10 October 1971 edition of the *Sunday Mercury*; for coverage of the protest rally see, '5,000 take break for BSA protest park', *Evening Mail*, 14 October 1971 and 'BSA problem like UCS – Union Man', *Evening Mail*, 14 October 1971.

107. See 'BSA resistance abandoned', *Morning Star*, 29 October 1971 and 'BSA men drop work-in plan', *The Motor Cycle* 3 November 1971.

108. Interview with H.W. Robinson, *op. cit.* The total cost of redundancy payments made to the 3,000 worked affected came to some £750,000 according to the BSA Group's 1971 *Annual Report*.

109. See 'Lord Shawcross warns BSA workers: Co-operate or we go into liquidation', *Times* 23 October 1971, contained in TUC news clipping file 12916, on deposit at the MRC.

Notes to Chapter 7: The collapse of the British motor cycle industry, 1960–1975

1. The article featured a Japanese lightweight model which struck an observer as a copy of a current British model. See 'A Japanese two stroke', *The Motor Cycle*, 11 April 1946, p. 276.

2. See *Japan as an Automotive Market. (Special Agents' Series no. 217)*, Washington D.C.: Government Printing Office, 1922, pp. 59–60. This report also claimed that most motor cycles used in Japan during the early 1920s were from the USA.

3. See C.D. Bohan, 'Rikuo', *Cycle World*, April 1978. Details of the Harley-Davidson/Rikuo agreement are contained in Jerry Hatfield, *Inside Harley-Davidson*, Osceola, USA: Motorbooks International, 1990, p. 114. Thanks to Herbert Wagner for bringing this reference to the author's attention.

4. See US Strategic Bombing Survey, *The Japanese Motor Vehicle Industry*, Washington DC: US Government Printing Office, 1946.

5. See The Japan Automobile Manufacturers' Association, *The History of Japan's Automobile Industry*, Tokyo: The Japan Automobile Manufacturers' Association, 1997, p. 40.

6. For an overview of the Japanese motor cycle industry, see 'Appendix 11 – A Brief Description of the Production System of the Japanese Motor Cycle Industry', contained in Boston Consulting Group, *op. cit.*, pp. 213–24 and Didier Ganneau and Francois-Marie Dumas, *Motos Japonaises. 100 ans d'Histoire*, Paris: EIAI, 1997, especially pp. 9–20.

7. See Akira Kawahara, *The Origin of Competitive Strength: Fifty Years of the Auto Industry in Japan and the US*, Tokyo: (privately published), 1997, p. 10.

8. See Demizu Tsutomu, 'Technological Innovation in the Motorcycle Industry in Postwar Japan', *History of Industry and Technology in Japan, Marburger Japan-Reihe*, vol. 14/II, Marburg: 1995, pp. 297–300.

9. See 'The Japanese Motor Cycle Industry, 1945–1960', an unpublished paper jointly presented by the author and Jun Otahara to the September 1999 Association of Business Historians' conference held at the London School of Economics in London England.

10. Japan Automobile Manufacturers' Association, *op. cit.*, p. 59.

11. For background on this programme, see Nick Tiratsoo, 'The United States Technical Assistance Programme in Japan, 1955–62', *Business History*, October 2000, pp. 117–36.

12. See Sakiya, *op. cit.*, p. 85, pp. 115–16, 174; Jeff Clew, *Suzuki*, Sparkford: Haynes Publishing Group, 1983, pp. 31–4 and Ezra Vogel, *Comeback*, Tokyo: Charles Tuttle, 1985, p. 62. Access to and subsequent use of foreign technology was a common practice at this time with the Japanese automobile industry as well. See Michael A. Cusumano, *The Japanese Automobile Industry: Technology and Management at Nissan and Toyota*, Cambridge, MA: Harvard University Press, 1991, pp. 35, 40–5, 65, 83–111.

13. For background on the Yamaha YA–1, see Ted Macauley *Yamaha*, London: Cadogan Books, 1979,

pp. 5–7, GK Dynamics/Yamaha Motor Co., *Spirit of Yamaha Motorcycle Design*, Tokyo: Rikuyo-Sha Publishing, 1989, pp. 17 and 96 and Ganneau and Dumas, *op. cit.*, pp. 44–5. Further information about the company and its history was provided to the author during a visit to the Yamaha motor cycle factory between 14 and 15 October 1998.

14. Ganneau and Dumas, *op. cit.*, p. 38.

15. In 2001 Suzuki and Kawasaki reached an agreement to combine their motor cycle manufacturing operations. See 'Japan: Motorcycle Joint Venture', *New York Times*, 30 August 2001, Section W, p. 1.

16. See Jun Otahara, 'An Evolutionary Phase of Honda Motor. The Establishment and Success of American Honda Motor', *Japanese Yearbook on Business* History, 2000/17, pp. 109–10 and pp. 116–21; Tetsuo Sakiya, *Honda Motor, The Men, the Management and the Machines*, New York: Kodansha International, 1982 pp. 82, 85–6, 118, 175–6. See also 'Soichiro's Ladder – Twenty-five years of technical progress', by Kevin Cameron, *Cycle*, September 1985 and 'Soichiro Honda' by Graham Sanderson, *Classic Bike*, July 1998, pp. 50–66.

17. See Richard T. Pascale, 'Perspectives on Strategy: The Real Story behind Honda's Success', *op. cit.*, p. 52, Tetsuo Sakiya, *Honda Motor: The Men, The Management, The Machines*, Tokyo: Kodansha International Ltd, 1987, p. 62, Roy Bacon, *Honda – The Early Classic Motor Cycles*, London: Osprey Publishing Ltd, 1985, pp. 100–23 and 'Soichiro's Ladder – Twenty-Five Years of Technical Progress' *op. cit.*

18. See Pascale, *op. cit.*, p. 53.

19. See 'The case for lightweights' by Francis Jones, *Motor Cycle and Cycle Export Trader*, December 1952, pp. 237–42. Bill Johnson's comments are from 'Johnson Motors of California', *ibid.*, May 1953, pp. 90–3.

20. See 'Motor Cycle Matters', *Motor Cycle and Cycle Trader*, 6 July 1957, p. 1866.

21. See Pascale, *op. cit.*, p. 51.

22. See Boston Consulting Group, *op. cit.*, p. xiv.

23. See article entitled 'Technical Analysis: Honda 350 Four' by 'Europa', *Cycle World*, June 1964, contained in *Cycle World On Honda, 1962–1967*, Cobham, Surrey: Brooklands Book Distribution Ltd, 1988, pp. 30–3.

24. See 'Oriental look for motor cycles', *The Statist*, 6 April 1962.

25. See memo entitled '486/59: Trade with Japan, 1960/1961', dated 2 December 1959, contained in Guardbook MRC MSS 204/3/1/92.

26. See minutes of Council meeting held on 31 May 1960, contained in Guardbook MRC MSS 204/3/1/93. In a memo to the Council, Hugh Palin reported that the dismantling of the trading agreements, 'demolished the valuable scheme of trading that the industry has built up over a long period of years'. See memo dated 13 June 1961, contained in Guardbook MRC MSS 204/3/1/96.

27. See memo entitled '355/60. Director's Confidential Report', dated 19 July 1960, contained in *ibid.*

28. See minutes of the Motor Cycle Manufacturers' Section meeting of 20 July 1960 and the Council meeting of 21 July 1960, both contained in *ibid.*

29. See 'Imports from Japan. Mr. Maudling's Assurances', *Financial Times*, 7 September 1960, contained in newspaper clipping book MRC MSS 204/10/1/4.

30. See minutes of Council meeting of 20 September 1960, contained in *op. cit.*

31. See memo entitled '517/60. Confidential Report', dated 7 November 1960, contained in Guardbook MRC MSS 204/3/1/95.

32. *Ibid.*

33. See minutes of the Motor Cycle Manufacturers' Section meeting of 19 January 1960, contained in *ibid.*

34. Turner's report is reproduced in Ivor Davies, *It's a Triumph*, pp. 199–205. In an interview conducted afterwards, Turner claimed the rapid growth of the Japanese motor cycle industry was brought about by 'heavy home market consumption caused by the rising standard of living'. He also claimed that generous American financial aid had allowed Japanese motor cycle manufacturers, among others, to invest in factory and plant 'on a lavish scale'. See 'E. Turner visits Japan', *Motor Cycle and Cycle Export Trader*, December 1960, p. 160.

35. See Otahara, *op. cit.* as well as 'Kogata Jidousha No Ayumi 61', *Kogata Jidousha Shinbun Sha*, Tokyo, 1961, which contains an account of Turner's remarks made at a Japanese press conference, which were very kindly translated into English and provided to the author by Dr Otahara.

36. *Ibid.* The surviving BSA Group Board of Directors Minute books have a gap covering the period 1960 to 1969 and consequently no information is available about how any information Turner passed on to his colleagues may have been received or acted upon.

37. See *Government's Statement on the Anglo-Japanese Treaty*, London: HMSO, 1962.

38. See 'Brief for President's Visit to Japan, April 1962', contained in NA BT 11/5758. Much the same point about the priorities of the British government are made in Jim Tomlinson's 'British Industrial Policy in a Japanese Mirror: Why no MITI in Britain?', unpublished paper delivered at

the Fourth Anglo/Japanese Conference, London School of Economics, 14–16 April 1994.

39. See 'Draft Speech for the President to give to the Kansai Japan-British Society in Osaka, on May 1, 1962' contained in NA BT 11/5909. Another consideration held by British trade negotiators was the fact that the Japanese bargaining position had been 'greatly strengthened' by a 'substantial improvement' in the British balance of trade with Japan. This imbalance, one civil servant wrote, might create pressure on the British government to liberalise existing trade restrictions on items such as mopeds, even though such action would be undertaken 'with some misgivings'. See 'Annex C – Note on the Trade Negotiations with Japan, August–December 1961', contained in NA BT 11/5758.

40. See 'Director-General's Report', dated February 1961, attached to the FBI Grand Council minutes, 1961, contained in MRC MSS 200/F/3/S3/2/12.

41. According to Kipping's itinerary, he toured the Honda factory on 10 October 1961. A copy of the itinerary is contained in MRC MSS 200/F/3/D3/6/72. For a general account of Kipping's Japanese tour, see *A Look at Japan*, Federation of British Industries: London, 1961 contained in MRC MSS 200/F/4/76/17. In his memoirs, Kipping noted that, after his visit to Japan, 'we could see many gaps in the products on sale that could be filled by British exports, in a market that was rapidly absorbing western tastes and standards'. See Norman Kipping, *Summing Up*, London: Hutchinson & Co., 1972, p. 173.

42. See *The Japanese Economy*, London: Economist Intelligence Unit, April 1962. A copy of this report is contained in MRC MSS 200/F/4/77/5.

43. The agreement's formal title was *Treaty of Commerce, Establishment and Navigation*, signed on 14 November 1962. London: HMSO, 1962. (Cmnd 1874). For various reactions to the negotiations leading up to the signature of the treaty, see, for example 'More competition from Japan', *The Economist*, 31 December 1961, p. 1303, 'A Sun still rising', *ibid.*, 3 March 1962, pp. 786–7, 'Doing business with Japan' by Victor Sampson, *The Statist*, 23 November 1962, pp. 535–9' and 'Anglo-Japanese Trade Treaty is signed', *The Times*, 15 November 1962, p. 2.

44. See *Government Statement on the Anglo-Japanese Commercial Treaty*, London: HMSO, November 1962 (Cmnd 1875) pp. 4–9. The agreement was the subject of much discussion in the House of Commons, see 'Debate on the Anglo-Japanese Treaty', *Hansard*, [668], 5 December 1962, cols 1335–443. The Government's case was put by Alan Green, Minister of State for the Board of Trade, see cols 1336–37, 1341. There was little opposition expressed against the agreement, except from MPs representing textile districts in the north. See, for example, the remarks of Geoffrey Hirst, MP from Shipley, at col 1352.

45. See 'Misgivings felt by FBI', *The Times*, 15 November 1962, p. 12. See also a copy of the FBI press statement, dated 14 November 1962, entitled *Anglo-Japanese Commercial Treaty*, contained in MRC MSS 200/F/3/D3/6/72.

46. See minutes of the Joint Advisory Committee meeting of 27 September 1960, on deposit with the Motor Cycle Retailers' Association. See 'First Honda 50 cc sold in UK', *Motor Cycle and Cycle Trader*, 14 November 1960, p. 126.

47. See memo entitled '458/61. Director's Report', dated 15 November 1961, contained in Guardbook MRC MSS 204/3/1/97, see also 'Motor cycles for the UK', *Financial Times*, 20 July 1960, contained in clipping book MRC MSS 204/10/1/4.

48. See Chairman's speech, 14 December 1961, contained in MRC MSS 19A/4/39.

49. See 'Japanese Motor Cycle Company for Europe', 13 December 1961 p. 21 and "Honda European Works', 1 June 1962, p. 105, both in the *Motor Cycle and Cycle Trader*. At the time, Honda production in Japan was reported to be 70,000 units per month, of which 20 per cent was exported.

50. The Belgian factory was opened in September 1963: see 'UK Honda Sales Scope Limitless. First European Works Opened in Belgium', *Motor Cycle and Cycle Trader*, 20 September 1962, pp. 261–2. A brief news item about Harrisson being hired by Honda is contained in *ibid.*, 27 July 1962, p. 204. See also 'Biggest Two-wheeler Sales Drive Yet', *ibid.*, 9 August 1963, p. 196. For the quote about Honda, see 'Motor cycles – facing the 50 cc challenge', *Financial Times*, 17 October 1963, contained in clipping book MRC MSS 2/4/10/1/4.

51. See memo dated 26 April 1961, entitled '206/61: Director's Confidential Report', contained in Guardbook MRC MSS 204/3/1/96.

52. See 'Keep it up, Honda!', *ibid.*, 20 September 1963, p. 271. Other letters to the *Motor Cycle and Cycle Trader* are 'Honda Competition Enterprise', 23 August 1963 p. 233 and 'Well Done Honda', 6 September 1963, p. 251. One retailer in Sheffield, however, was less impressed with the Japanese. Referring to an upcoming tour of Japan, laid on for its dealers by Honda, he recalled that there had also been 'a trip made by many good men in 1942/44 who, due to some small oversight, forgot to return'. See 'Selling British – and All Right!' *ibid.*, 4 October 1963, p. 287.

53. See Minutes of the FBI Working Party on the Anglo-Japanese Commercial Treaty, dated 11 January 1963, contained in MRC MSS 200/F/1/1/217.

54. Belchem was hired as Sangster's Personal Assistant as of 12 January 1959. See agenda item 11342, BSA Board meeting of 22 January 1959, contained in Directors' Minute Book 17, MRC MSS 19A. See also memo dated 8 February 1963, entitled '45/60: Director's Confidential Report', contained in Guardbook MRC MSS 204/3/1/100.

55. See memo dated 24 October 1963, entitled '363/63: Director's Confidential Report', contained in Guardbook MRC MSS 204/3/1/101.

56. See minutes of the Council meeting of 29 October 1963, contained in Guardbook MRC MSS 204/3/1/102.

57. See minutes of Council meeting of 10 December 1963, *ibid*. In an article he submitted to the *Motor Trade Executive* at about the same time, Turner explained that Honda's success in the 50 cc engine displacement class could not be attributed to unfair trading practices. Their success was the result, he wrote, of the size and strength of the Japanese home market, 'which enabled them to build huge quantities' allowing them to make 'extremely substantial investment' in manufacturing facilities. This placed them, he concluded, 'in a very favourable position to attack world markets, which they are now doing with great success'. See 'The Next Five Years' by Edward Turner, draft copy dated 21 October 1963, contained in Guardbook MRC MSS 204/3/T91.

58. See memo dated 5 December 1963, entitled '423/63: Director's Confidential Report', contained in MRC MSS 204/3/1/102. Emphasis in original.

59. See Letter Palin-Belchem, dated 12 December 1963, entitled 'Re: Anglo-Japanese Treaty', contained in Guardbook MRC MSS 204/3/1/79.

60. See letter, Palin to Belchem, dated 3 February 1964, entitled 'Re: Treaty', contained in *ibid*.

61. See Minute #2, prepared by K. Taylor, dated 12 December 1963, contained in PRO BT 258/1889.

62. See letter, W.G. Onslow to D. Johnson (Customs and Excise), dated 24 December 1963, contained in *ibid*.

63. See memo entitled 'In Confidence. Motor Cycle and Scooters', no date or author indicated, but attached to a memo entitled 'Bicycles and Mopeds' and dated 17 December 1963, signed by C.W. Sanders, contained in *ibid*. This assessment was shared by an independent observer. Honda's success in the lightweight classes demonstrated that the Purchase Tax was less a deterrent to sales than the fact the market for the heavy weight models favoured by British manufacturers was simply too narrow and showed little likelihood of expansion. See 'Motor cycles facing the 50 cc challenge', *Financial Times*, 17 October 1963, contained in clipping book MRC MSS 204/10/1/4.

64. See letter to the editor, entitled 'UK-Jap Design Contrasts', from D. Rogerson, Manager of Rogerson's in Wigan, *Motor Cycle and Cycle Trader*, 1 May 1964, p. 52. BSA Production Manager John Balder termed the Beagle 'an utter flop'. In his opinion, the problem was that BSA tried to compete on the basis of price, which meant that 'everything was scrimped to the point in which it wouldn't work'. In contrast, the Japanese machines may have cost more but, thanks to their superior specification, were far more reliable. See John Balder interview, 18 November 1994.

65. See Hopwood, *op. cit.*, p. 197.

66. See 'The British-Jap motor cycle controversy', *Eltham and Kentish Times*, 19 February 1965, contained in clipping book MRC MSS 204/10/1/4.

67. See letter from Hugh Palin to J.F. Kelleher (Joint Managing Director, AMC), dated 1 July 1963, contained in Guardbook MRC MSS 204/3/T72. See also 'AMC to Distribute Japanese Motor Cycles', *Financial Times*, 26 June 1963 and 'Surprise at motor cycle link-up', *Birmingham Post*, 26 June 1963, both contained in clipping book MRC MSS 204/10/1/4 and 'AMC to handle Suzuki' *Motor Cycle and Cycle Trader*, 28 June 1963, p. 154.

68. See Chairman's speech, delivered on 27 April 1964, copy on deposit at the Guildhall Library. One dealer wrote that 'now we have the somewhat humiliating picture of [AMC] acting as distributing agent for one of the foreign machines – no doubt a wise commercial move. But the victories and honours could have been ours, surely?' See letter from K. Robert, entitled 'Not too late for UK lightweights', *Motor Cycle and Cycle Trader*, 26 July 1963, p. 190. In the first year of the agreement, some 17,000 of the lightweight Suzukis were shipped to Britain for distribution by AMC. See Jeff Clew, *Suzuki*, Sparkford, Yeovil: Haynes Publishing Group, 1980, p. 51.

69. See memo 363/63, entitled 'Director's Confidential Report', dated 24 October 1963 and the minutes of the Council meeting held on 29 October 1963, contained in Guardbooks MRC MSS 204/3/1/100 and MSS 204/3/1/102. See also letter, Hugh Palin to D.P. Cobb (Greeves Motor Cycles), dated 17 August 1964, contained in Guardbook MRC MSS 204/3/T80.

70. See Palin-Cobb, *ibid*.

71. See memo entitled '229/64: Director's Confidential Report', dated 4 June 1964, contained in Guardbook

MRC MSS 204/3/1/103. For more on the 'Mods and Rockers', who were young often combative young men who rode respectively, scooters and motor cycles, see Stanley Cohen, *Folk Devils and Moral Panics*, Oxford: Blackwells, 1993. See also Ian Harris, 'Myth and Reality in the Motorcycle Subculture', *op. cit.*, and Mike Clay, *Cafe Racers – Rockers, Rock 'n' Roll and the Coffee-Bar Cult*, London: Osprey Publishing, 1988.

72. See untitled memo to members of the Industries' Association Council, dated 9 February 1967, contained in Guardbook MRC MSS 204/3/1/109. In early 1968, the Industries' Association was still sensitive enough about public perceptions about motor cycles and motor cyclists that it opposed the much delayed release of the film 'The Wild One' in Britain. Their opposition was based on the grounds that the 15 year old movie might have a negative effect 'on the improved image of the industry'. See minutes of the Joint Motor Cycle and Scooter Committee meeting of 6 February 1968, contained in Guardbook MRC MSS 204/3/1/110.

73. For the reaction of one well-established Canadian motor cycle dealer, see Frank Hilliard, *op. cit.*, p. 121.

74. See memo '271/61. Director's Confidential Report' dated 5 June 1961, contained in Guardbook MRC MSS 204/3/1/96 and 'Japanese Competition helps British Motor Cycles. Paradox of US Sales Expansion', *Times*, 17 March 1963, contained in TUC file 12913, on deposit at the MRC.

75. See 'Late news from England' by B.R. Nicholls, contained in *Cycle World on BSA, 1962–1971*, Cobham, Surrey: Brooklands Book Distribution Ltd, 1987, p. 9.

76. See Sol Sanders, *Honda – the Man and His Machines*, Boston: Little Brown and Co., 1975, pp. 84–5, 96–7, and Tetsuo Sakiya, *Honda Motor*, pp. 124–5. See also Bacon, *Honda – The Early Classic Motorcycles*, pp. 23–26, Richard T. Pascale, *op. cit.*, pp. 47–72 and 'Thirty Years after Sunrise' by Art Friedman, *Motorcyclist*, July 1989, pp. 51–63.

77. See memo '307/64. Japanese Exports of Motor Cycles', dated 19 August 1964, contained in Guardbook MRC MSS 204/3/1/103.

78. See 'Japanese Competition helps British Motor Cycles. Paradox of US Sales Expansion', *Times*, 17 March 1963, *op. cit.*, 'Lightweight trade will increase', by Ted Wassell, *Motor Cycle and Cycle Trader*, 7 February 1964, p. 156 and 'Forward planning essential today', *ibid.*, 28 February 1964, p. 195. For more on the American perspective, see also 'Wooing the 'Mild Ones'', *Business Week*, 30 March 1963, pp. 26–7, 'How the 'Thunderherd' brought a Honda boom to the US' *Newsweek*, 6 July 1964, pp. 66–7 and 'Japanese cycles in high gear', *New York Times*, 20 October 1965.

79. See *Report of Mission to the USA, April–May 1966*, Coventry: British Cycle and Motor Cycle Industries' Association, 1966, p. 11. Bert Hopwood specifically cites this attitude as symptomatic of the complacency which ensured British manufacturers were ill-prepared to meet the Japanese heavy-weights when they became available several years later. See Hopwood, *op. cit.*, p. 183.

80. See Report, *op. cit.* The delegation came to the same conclusions about the Canadian market, although they noted that British manufacturers had great difficulty in supplying their dealers with sufficient numbers of machines.

81. See 'A change in two wheeled fortunes?', *The Statist*, 22 February 1963, p. 571, 'AMC building exports', *The Motor Cycle and Cycle Trader*, 27 November 1964, p. 116, Woollett, *op. cit.*, pp. 282–3 and 'Motor cycle exports continue to rise', *Financial Times*, 30 July 1965, contained in newspaper clipping book MRC MSS 204/1/10/1/4.

82. See 'AMC asks bankers to appoint receiver', 2 July 1966, 'The cost of failing to move with the times', both in *Financial Times*, and 'How America's Mr. Berliner could sway the fate of threatened AMC', *Sunday Times*, 7 July 1966. All references contained in newspaper clipping book MRC MSS 204/1/10/6.

83. See 'Associated Motor Cycles Resuscitated', *The Statist*, 22 November 1966, p. 1240. See also 'Villiers takes over AMC motor cycles', *Financial Times*, 14 September 1966 and 'Motor cycle exports should aid BSA earnings', *Daily Telegraph*, 22 May 1967 and 'Motor bikes ease into top gear' by John Mattison, *Sunday Times*, 9 July 1967, all three final references contained in *ibid.*

84. For information on the Daimler sale to Jaguar, see Jonathon Wood, *op. cit.*, p. 144. See also Chairman's Speech to the Annual General Meeting, delivered on 16 December 1960 and 14 December 1961, contained in MRC MSS 19A/4/38 and 39 respectively. Writing some years after the fact, Bert Hopwood noted that the money spent on Churchill 'would have been sufficient to enable British motor cycles to survive and compete if it had been injected into the BSA Motor Cycle Division [as it would become] together with a "no-nonsense" management'. See Hopwood, *op. cit.*, p. 186.

85. 'See 'Benefits of BSA motor cycle reorganisation', *Financial Times*, 29 April 1965, contained in newspaper clipping book MRC MSS 204/10/1/4. In early 1964, the Industries' Association had informed Maurice Macmillan, Economic Secretary

to the Treasury, that 'between 60 and 70 per cent of all production' was going abroad, a good proportion to the USA. See text of letter, which is included in the minutes of the Council meeting of 4 February 1964, contained in Guardbook MRC MSS 204/3/1/102.

86. See Ryerson, *op. cit.*, p. 162, 'Motor Cycle Division has a new look', *BSA Group News*, September 1964, p. 1, and 'BSA Group 'Fight Back' is on!', *Motor Cycle and Cycle Trader*, 18 September 1964, p. 210. Sturgeon ruefully admitted that there would be hard work ahead in order to increase sales: 'we had been too complacent ... the industry [is] beginning to learn that British products [are] not automatically the best nor the most saleable'. See *ibid.*

87. According to former Small Heath Works Manager Alistair Cave, the new system was intended to comprise five individual assembly lines which would be gradually phased in over time. By 1970 they mostly were although the entire process was evidently never entirely completed. Cave interview, 22 August 1990.

88. See Balder interview, 18 November 1994 and 'The computer as a tool for production, planning and control' by John Balder, contained in *Computer Case Histories*, S. Sumersbee (ed.), London: The Machinery Publishing Co. Ltd, 1970. See also 'Motor cycles – far from gloomy', *Financial Times*, 16 August 1967, contained in newspaper clipping book MRC MSS 204/10/1/7.

89. See 'Benefits of BSA Motor Cycle reorganisation', *op. cit.* See also 'Overseas sales prospects bright' by Lionel Jofeh, *Birmingham Post*, 16 January 1968, both contained in newspaper clipping book MRC MSS 204/10/1/7. See also Ryerson, *op. cit.*, pp. 162–3 and Shilton, *op. cit.*, p. 173. For improvements at Triumph during this time, see 'These factories are gearing up for "go"', July 1963, p. 3, 'Triumph clear the way for more machines', June 1966, p. 3 and 'Triumph change space to keep up exports', December 1966, p. 3, all in *BSA Group News*.

90. See 'How the 'Thunderherd' boss brought a Honda boom to the US', *Newsweek*, 6 July 1964, p. 66 and 'Top gear get away for BSA', *op. cit.* See also 'Cycle sales find road to success a bit bumpy', by Bob Thomas, *Los Angeles Times*, 9 April 1967, contained in newspaper clipping book MRC MSS 204/10/1/6. For the Queen's Award, see the 'Queen's Award Special Edition', *Birmingham Post*, 28 June 1967, p. 10, contained in MRC MSS 19A/5/1 and the BSA Chairman's Speech, delivered on 4 December 1968, contained in MRC MSS 19A/4/46.

91. The Viet-Nam war temporarily dampened the motor cycle market in the USA but did result in at least one extra sale for BSA in Britain. In 1968 the British Communist Party bought a 250 cc model and sent it to the Viet Cong to help in their struggle with the American armed forces. See untitled feature, *Morning Star*, 20 June 1968, contained in newspaper clipping book MRC MSS 204/10/1/6.

92. See Chairman's Speech, delivered on 6 December 1967, contained in MRC MSS 19A/4/45. Two years later, a representative of the advertising agency J. Walter Thompson told a group of British motor cycle industry executives that the key to the success of sales in USA was to present their products as 'fun vehicles', associated with the 'outdoor way of life' which, in contrast with the old hoodlum 'leather jacket' image, was now 'socially acceptable'. See minutes of the Motor Cycle Trade Group, held on 28 October 1969, contained in Guardbook MRC MSS 204/3/1/117. See also, 'BSA's American challenge', *Marketing*, February 1971, contained in newspaper clipping book MRC MSS 204/10/1/9.

93. See 'Heavyweight challenge from Japan', *Financial Times*, 16 June 1965, contained in newspaper clipping book MRC MSS 204/10/1/4.

94. See 'The optimistic two-wheeler industry' by Jack Hay, *Birmingham Post*, 8 November 1966, contained in newspaper clipping book MRC MSS 204/10/1/6.

95. See, for example, remarks made by BSA Chairman Eric Turner during an interview when he identified the 'average motor cyclist' as one who is 'very keen on the mechanical side and ... wants something different to pull apart'. See 'Top gear get away for BSA', *The Observer*, 27 July 1966, contained in MRC MSS 123X/10/1/3. It was also noted that British motor cycle manufacturers, unable to sell their machines on the home market, had been saved by 'the monied and blasé youth of America' who had 'turned to a more virile method of transportation'. See 'After ton-up kids, a labour shortage', *Guardian*, 15 February 1966, contained in TUC clipping file 12913, on deposit at the MRC.

96. As one reporter noted, although successful on the race track, the Trident was not a cheap motor cycle for American consumers. At $1,750 (US) it cost nearly as much as an economy car such as the British Leyland 1.3 litre saloon model or a VW Beetle. See 'Accelerated sales of motor cycles and bicycles', by Peter Cartwright, *Financial Times*, 28 January 1969, contained in newspaper clipping book MRC MSS 204/10/1/7. For details on the

planning of the 'Trident', see Hopwood, *op. cit.*, pp. 197–200, 212, 212–13, 229.

97. Despite earlier warnings, BSA's American sales representatives later admitted that the appearance of the new Honda caught them with their 'pants down'. See 'British motor cycles fight to get off the starting line', by James Poole, *Sunday Times*, 14 September 1969, contained in newspaper clipping book MRC MSS 204/10/1/7.

98. See 'Challenge to the speed men', by Clifford Webb, *the Times*, 8 July 1969, contained in newspaper clipping book MRC MSS 204/10/1/7. For contemporary reactions to the new Honda, see 'Honda's Fabulous 750 Four – The Ultimate Weapon in one-upmanship', *Cycle World*, January 1969, pp. 24–7 and 'Honda CB 750', *ibid.*, pp. 41–7, both contained in *Cycle World on Honda, 1968–1971*, Cobham, Surrey: Brooklands Book Distribution Ltd, 1988. It should be noted that the comparable Triumph/BSA model had a top-end speed comparable to the Honda but, for the average consumer, that was not really the point.

99. In the 650 cc class, too, the Japanese succeeded in pricing their machines much cheaper than the British competition. For example, in 1971 a Triumph T120 cost $1,579 (US), a BSA A65 Lightning $1,474 and a comparable Yamaha only $1,295. See 'Memorandum on the Birmingham Small Arms Company Inc.', dated 12 July 1971, prepared by Cooper Brothers and contained in MRC MSS 19B/TB3. Jofeh's remarks are contained in the article 'Overseas sales prospects bright', *op. cit.*

100. See Cooper Brothers Report, *op. cit.*, p. 6 and p. 34.

101. Points raised in both Steve Wilson, *British Motorcycles since 1950*, vol. 1, p. 24 and Roy Bacon, *British Motorcycles of the 1960s*, p. 13.

102. *Ibid.*; Hopwood's memoirs, *Whatever happened?*. is full of accounts of his repeated and unsuccessful efforts to convince the various companies he worked for between the 1930s and 1970s to thoroughly re-design their motor cycles. See especially pp. 111–15, 118, 275–90.

103. According to BSA's former Production Manager John Balder, relations between the industry and its suppliers had been aggravated by fact that the manufacturers' buyers had frequently 'screwed down' the price of the various components. The result was poorer quality components, a view point shared by J.R. Nelson, Triumph's former Service Manager. John Balder interview, 18 November 1994 and J.R. Nelson interview, 16 August 1990.

104. For figures of Triumph's planned and actual production totals for 1965, see information contained in the Triumph Engineering Accounts books, MRC MSS 123/2/3/20/1.

105. See 'BSA may sack up to 1,050 workers in Birmingham', 26 July 1969, and 'BSA jobs threat partly due to production snags', 29 July 1969, both by Peter Cartwright, *Financial Times*, contained in newspaper clipping book MRC MSS 204/10/1/7.

106. See 'Plan to streamline two wheel Assembly' in *BSA Group News*, no. 67, January 1966, p. 1. and 'New Plant best in Europe, contained in *BSA International*, no. 1, August 1967, p. 1.

107. Ryerson, *op. cit.*; see also 'Quiet Revolution puts Small Heath on the Air', *BSA Group News*, no. 84, July 1967, p. 3.

108. *Ibid.* See also Brooke and Gaylin, *op. cit.*, p. 71.

109. See 'March of the Piled Arms', produced by the BSA Group public relations department, published by BSA circa 1972. Copy on deposit in MS 321/E (file marked as 'Historical') at the Birmingham Central Reference Library.

110. . See Chairman's Speech, 4 December 1969, MRC MSS 19A/4/47. See also 'BSA to close Redditch motor cycle plant', by Clifford Webb, *The Times*, 28 November 1969 and 'BSA to close down Redditch motor cycle factory', by Peter Cartwright, *Financial Times*, both contained in newspaper clipping book MRC MSS 204/1/0/1/7.

111. See Hopwood, *op. cit.*, p. 207. One former BSA production worker, Tony Jeffries, who worked at Small Heath during the 1960s, when he was interviewed for the BBC Radio Four Programme 'Magic Moments', recalled that the factory was 'production mad'. He claimed that it cost the company more money than it was worth to stop the production line to correct a problem and, in any case, BSA believed it could sell whatever it made in the USA, defects notwithstanding. The 'Magic Moments' programme was broadcast on 4 November 1992.

112. See 'BSA 650 cc Lightning', May 1970, *Cycle World*, pp. 71–5, contained in *Cycle World on BSA – 1962–1972*, Cobham, Surrey: Brooklands Book Distribution, 1987, and Smith *op. cit.*, p. 36. Complaints from American dealers about weak frames on Triumph models had actually begun as early as 1960. And unreliable electrical components remained the enduring bane of many British motor cycle owners. See Brooke and Gaylin, *op. cit.*, pp. 63–64, 80.

113. See 'Notes of a meeting of the motor cycle industry', held on 16 September 1970, contained in Guardbook MRC MSS 204/3/1/120.

114. See Chairman's Speech, delivered on 8 December 1970, MRC MSS 19A/4/48.

115. See 'Britain's motor cycles fight to get off the starting line', by James Poole, *Sunday Times*, 14 September 1969, contained in newspaper clipping

book MRC MSS 204/10/1/7; Hopwood, *op. cit.*, pp. 93–199.

116. One later account of the 1971 range was that 'the "new" models were old ones titivated, though the improvements were substantial and it must always be arguable how much change is required to an old model before it can properly be described as a new one'. See Ryerson, *op. cit.*, p. 175.

117. See 'Ariel fun', *Financial Times*, 27 June 1970, contained in newspaper clipping book MRC MSS 204/10/1/7, Shilton, *op. cit.*, pp. 172–3, Ryerson, *op. cit.*, p. 168, document entitled 'Motor Cycle Division. Review of 1971/72 Sales Forecast', prepared by Cooper Brothers, dated 9 August 1971, p. 13, contained in MRC MSS 19A/TB3 and 'Notes on a meeting of members of the motor cycle industry', dated 16 September 1970, contained in Guardbook MRC MSS 204/3/1/120.

118. See John Nelson, *Bonnie*, Sparkford: Haynes

Publishing Group, 1989, pp. 53–6 and Boston Consulting Group, *op. cit.*, Appendix 10, 'A Brief Description of the Production System of the British Motor Cycle Industry', p. 206.

119. See Ryerson, *op. cit.*, pp. 175–6, Hopwood, *op. cit.*, p. 239, 249–50, Smith, *op. cit.*, pp. 36–7 and 'The Decline and Fall of the British Bike', by Tony Osman, *op. cit.*

120. However, before his departure, Jofeh was able to negotiate a generous 'Golden Handshake' in the amount of £35,518. See untitled memo dated 7 July 1971, listed as item #362 in the BSA Collection at the Solihull Public Library.

121. See Chairman's Speeches, delivered on 15 December 1971 and 5 December 1972, contained in MRC MSS 19A/4/49 and 50 respectively. See also 'How the British Bikes Crashed', by Tom Lester, *op. cit.*

Notes to Epilogue: The British motor cycle industry since 1973

1. Ivor Davies interview, 9 April 1990.

2. See Barbara Smith *op. cit.* for a general account of events after 1973 and especially Hopwood *op. cit.*, who describes the final years of BSA/Triumph in some detail. A more partisan account was written by NVT during the height of the Meriden factory takeover, see Norton-Villiers-Triumph, *Meriden – Historical Summary – 1972–1974*, London: Norton-Villiers-Triumph, 1974. See also Jock Bruce-Gardyne, *op. cit.*

3. There was a debate in the House of Commons over the issue of the Report and the end of funding to the industry. See *Hansard*, [897], 1974/1975, 7 August 1975, cols 734–77.

4. Several years later the Co-operative finally gained the ownership of the 'Triumph' name and the rights to sales and marketing.

5. For a more detailed account of the occupation of the Triumph factory and the subsequent creation of the co-operative, see Ken Fleet, 'Triumph Meriden' contained in K. Coates *et al.*, *The New Worker Co-operatives*, Nottingham: Institute for Workers' Control (Spokesman Books), 1976, Martin Fairclough, 'The Political Economy of Producer Co-operatives: A Study of Triumph Motorcycles (Meriden) Ltd. and Britain's Industrial Decline' (unpublished Ph.D. dissertation, Bristol University, 1986), John Tomlinson, 'The Meriden Co-operative' (unpublished MA dissertation, University of Warwick 1980).

6. For background on Harley-Davidson's recent history, see Mary Walton, 'Harley Roars Back', *Philadelphia Enquirer*, 29 November 1987,

pp. 24–37, Lindsay Brooke, 'Harley vs. Honda', *Automotive Industries*, May 1992, pp. 24–7, 60–1, Gary Slutsker, 'Hog Wild', *Forbes*, 24 May 1993, pp. 45–6, Peter Stanfield, 'Heritage Design: the Harley-Davidson Motor Company', *Journal of Design History*, vol. 5, no. 2, pp. 141–55 and Jonathan Fahey, 'Love into Money', *Forbes*, 7 January 2002, pp. 60–5.

7. See Lindsay Brooke, *Triumph Motorcycles. A Century of Passion and Power*, St. Paul, USA: MBI Publishing Co., 2002, pp. 155–6 and 'Interview with John Bloor' by Alan Cathcart, *Motorcyclist*, May 2002, pp. 74–80, pp. 102–3; there was a considerable amount of coverage on Triumph's re-launch from the non-motor cycle press, see, for example, 'At long last, a Triumphant return to form' by Roland Brown, *The Independent*, 1 December 1990, 'Triumph accelerates down long road to recovery' by Martin Whitfield, *ibid.*, 10 April 1993, 'Making a success out of Triumph' by Bill Goodwin, *The Engineer*, 14 October 1993 and 'The mild ones' by Justin Doebele, *Forbes*, 19 December 1994.

8. See Howard Lees, 'Triumph turns the tables on the Japanese', *Autocar & Motor*, 9 October 1991, pp. 18–19, Brooke, *op. cit.*, pp. 156–7; information provided to the author by Triumph public relations staff during a visit to the factory, spring 1994.

9. See Bloor interview, *op. cit.*, p. 74, 77–8.

10. Brooke, *op. cit.*, p. 170. Triumph has since gone on to produce a greater proportion of its components at the factory, although it did recently open a factory in Thailand to manufacture some motor

cycle parts. See Bloor interview, *op. cit.*, p. 77.

11. See 'A Triumph of British Engineering', *The Independent*, 31 January 2006 and Motor Cycle Industry Association, *Pocket Guide* (2005 edition) statistical table on Production, Imports and Exports, posted on the Association's website (http://www.mcia.co.uk).

Notes to Conclusion: The strange death of the British motor cycle industry

1. In fairness to the industry, as was described in chapter three, efforts to acquire greater competitive advantage via German reparations were often stymied by government policies as well as the rivalry of former war-time allies and that considerably limited the potential success of the entire programme.

2. See, most notably, Martin Wiener, *English Culture and the Decline of the Industrial Spirit, 1850–1980*, London: Penguin Books, 1987, especially pp. 127–54.

3. See, for example, D.S. Heather (the future managing director of AMC), 'A Survey of Current Motorcycle Design', *Proceedings of the Institution of Automobile Engineers* vol. XIII, pp. 247–72, Edward Turner (who was Technical Director at BSA Cycles at the time, before he returned to Triumph Engineering as Managing Director), 'Post War Motor Cycle Development', *ibid.*, vol. XXXVII, 1942–43, pp. 135–54, Joe Craig (Development Engineer at AMC at the time, before returning to Norton Motors), 'Progress in Motor Cycle Engines – with some Notes on Combustion', *ibid.*, vol. XXXIX, 1944–45, pp. 91–114 and R.A. Wilson-Jones, B.Sc (Eng.), 'Years of Development', *Proceedings of the Automobile Division of the Institution of Mechanical Engineers*, 1958–59, pp. 1–20. Wilson-Jones was the Chief Engineer of Enfield Cycles and, at the time, Chairman of the Institution's Automobile Division Council.

4. Thanks to Jim Bamberg for suggesting this point. See D.C. Coleman, 'Gentlemen and Players' *Economic History Review*, vol. XXVI (1973), pp. 93–116 and, more specifically for the automobile industry, see Whisler, *The British Motor Industry*, especially chapter five, 'Design and Development: The Practical Man and the Myth of Engineering Excellence', pp. 155–80.

5. See Francis Jones, 'Motor Cycle Matters', *The Motor Cycle and Cycle Trader*, 15 June 1951, p. 164.

6. A point well understood by the trade press. According to one journal: 'Past racing successes have done much to build and maintain the supremacy of the British sports motor cycle, and its racebred precision has brought it admirers in every overseas country.' See leading article, 'Selling for sport', *The Export Trader*, June 1947, p. 167.

7. See untitled biographical piece on AMC's Charles Collier and Donald Heather contained in *The Motor Cycle and Cycle Export Trader*, June 1948, pp. 243–5.

8. J.M. West interview, 23 November 1994. This is not to suggest that West's practice of attending such club meetings was exceptional. No doubt it was a common practice also followed by others in comparable positions with other firms.

9. The machines displayed at the National Motor Cycle Museum are a case in point. It has been observed, for example, that the collection there 'is heavily weighted in favor of large, glamorous machines, and small utilitarian cycles are seriously underrepresented'. See Rudi Volti, 'Exhibit Reviews. The National Motor Cycle Museum, Birmingham, England'. *Technology and Culture*, January 1987, p. 97. During subsequent visits to this museum during the 1990s, the author observed that nothing had appreciably changed since Volti wrote his above-noted article.

10. See 'The Motor Cycle Industry', *The Automobile Engineer*, January 1936, pp. 1–2.

11. 'The fitting being essential when components did not fit together automatically but needed careful adjustment and filing down.' See Smith, *op. cit.*, p. 23.

12. One popular journalist actually argued that a motor cycle could not, by its very nature, be adapted to a modern assembly track because it was 'too small for more than two men to cluster over it at one time'. See 'Ixion', 'Mass produced motor cycle', *The Motor Cycle*, 1 January 1953, p. 3.

13. The advertisement is contained in a separate leaflet attached to *The Motor Cycle and Cycle Trader*, 31 October 1953. A story contained in the same issue described how a Power-Pak was being ridden around the world by an ex-Chindit, as part of a publicity campaign designed to emphasis the robust construction of this machine. See 'Lee-Warner back from his world tour', *ibid*.

14. As Neil Cossons, then director of the Science Museum has commented: 'British craftsmanship is one of the weights around the neck of British industry. Craftsmanship is an excuse for things not working. It is hand-made therefore it is better. Actually, if it's handmade it's almost inevitably inconsistent and may well not work.' See *The Guardian*, 17 February 1992.

15. See Davies, *op. cit.*, pp. 186–92.

16. See 'Motor cycle design of today and tomorrow' [a précis of a paper delivered by Arthur Bourne, editor of *The Motor Cycle*, to a London meeting of the Automotive Division of the Institution of Mechanical Engineers], *The Motor Cycle*, 6 November 1947, pp. 354–5.

17. As AMC Sales Director J.M. West recalled: 'A 250 cc showed no profit, 350 cc a reasonable amount and 500 cc, which cost little more than a 350 cc made a substantial profit.' See letter, J.M. West to the author, 16 April 1995. BSA's Production Manager John Balder observed that the company's main profits were in the larger displacement machines, and 'that coloured everything.' John Balder interview, 18 November 1994.

18. As early as the nineteenth century, it has been noted that British industry in general, when 'faced with a challenge, [found it] easier and cheaper to retreat … rather than to meet competition face to face'. See E.J. Hobsbawm, *Industry and Empire*, London: Penguin Books, 1979, p. 191.

Select bibliography

1. Manuscript sources

A. National repositories

i. Modern Records Centre, University of Warwick
MSS 19A-C – BSA deposit
MSS 66 – Coventry District Engineering Employers'
  Association deposit
MSS 123 – Triumph Engineering Co. Ltd. deposit
MSS 125 – Maurice Edelman (MP) Papers
MSS 200 – Federation of British Industries deposit
MSS 202 – R.A. Etheridge Papers

MSS 204 – Motor Cycle Industry Association
Records (Previously British Cycle and Motor Cycle
Manufacturers and Traders' Union and then British
Cycle and Motor Cycle Industries' Association)
deposit
MSS 309 – Peter Nicholas Papers
The Trade Union Congress (TUC) Labour and
Industrial Press Clippings Collection

ii. The National Archives, Kew, Richmond
Ministry of Aviation papers
  AVIA 15
  AVIA 22
  AVIA 46
  AVIA 55
Board of Trade papers
  BT 11
  BT 59
  BT 60 BT 64
  BT 69
  BT 177
  BT 211
  BT 258
Home Office papers
  HO 192

HO 199
Ministry of Labour papers
  LAB 10
Ministry of Supply papers
  SUPP 14
Ministry of Transport papers
  MT 34
  MT 92
  MT 108
Premier's papers
  PREM 11
Treasury papers
  T 228
War Office papers
  WO 185

iii. Parliamentary Archives, London
Sir Patrick ('Paddy') Hannon Papers

B. Local repositories

i. Birmingham City Central Reference Library, Local Studies Archives
MS 321, BSA Deposit

ii. Coventry Public Library
Coventry and Warwickshire Collection

iii. Coventry Records Office
Amalgamated Engineering Union Papers
   Jack Wicks audio tape.

iv. Motor Cycle Retailers' Association, London
Files of the Joint Committee

v. Solihull Public Library, Local Studies Archives
BSA Deposit

vi. Mr. J.M. West, personal papers, Walmer, Kent

vii. West Midlands Engineering Employers' Association, Birmingham

2. Oral interviews and audio tapes

A. Interviews

John Balder, 18 November 1994, Coventry. Mr Balder was Service Manager and subsequently Production Manager at BSA's Small Heath factory between 1948 and 1968.

Alistair Cave, 15 and 22 August, 19 September 1990, Solihull. Mr Cave started work at BSA in the early 1940s and was Works Manager at the Small Heath factory during the 1960s and early 1970s.

Ivor Davies, 9 April 1990, Kenilworth. Mr Davies joined Triumph Engineering Co. in 1946. He was the company's Advertising Manager and later preformed the same duties for the BSA Group's Motor Cycle Division.

Bert Hopwood, 10 May 1990, Torquay. Mr Hopwood started as an Assistant Designer at Ariel Motors in 1930 and subsequently worked in a similar capacity with Triumph Engineering. He was later Chief Designer at Norton Motors, Chief Engineer at BSA, Managing Director at Norton and then General Manager at the Triumph factory at Meriden. From 1971 to 1973 he was a member of the BSA Group Board of Directors.

Bill Lapworth, 23 April and 27 July 1990, Coventry. Mr Lapworth was District Secretary for the Coventry District of the Transport and General Workers' Union and extensively involved with labour relations at Triumph both before, during and after the formation of the workers' co-operation in the mid-1970s.

J.R. (John) Nelson, 16 August 1990, Fiskerton, Nottinghamshire. Mr Nelson joined Triumph Engineering Co., in 1950. He was Service Manager there until 1971.

Hugh Palin, 28 March 1991 and 21 June 1994, London. Mr Palin was Director of the British Cycle and Motor Cycle Manufacturers and Traders' Union and the subsequently the British Motor Cycle and Cycle Industries' Association between 1953 and 1966.

H.W. Robinson, 18 September 1990, Small Heath, Birmingham. Mr Robinson started work at BSA in the 1940s and was the National Union of Vehicle Builders and subsequently the Transport and General worker' Union Work's Convenor at the Small Heath factory for the 1960s and early 1970s.

John Walford, 30 August 1990, Sulihull, West Midlands. Mr Walford was Works Manager at Norton Motors from the late 1950s up to 1961 when he became General Works Manager at the Triumph Engineering Co. factory at Meriden until 1971.

J.M. West, 23 November 1994, Walmer, Kent. Mr West was BMW's British Sales Manager (motor cycles) between 1935 and 1939 and AMC's Sales Manager and subsequently Sales Director between 1945 and 1961.

B. Audio tapes

British Broadcasting Corporation.
   BBC Radio 1: 'Hell for Leather', broadcast on 21 July 1991.
   BBC Radio 4: 'Magic Moments' (interview with Tony Jeffries), broadcast on 4 November 1992.
Turner, Edward and Page, Val, 'Recollections', no. 5, The British Motorcycle Industry. Editor, Ken Mellor. (Copies available through the National Motorcycle Museum, Solihull).

Wickes, Jack. Tape recording of reminisces of his career at Triumph Cycle Ltd and Triumph Engineering Ltd. Copy on deposit at the Coventry City Records Office.

3. Newspapers and periodicals

The Autocar
Autocar & Motor
The Automobile Engineer
Automotive Industries
Birmingham Mail
Birmingham Post
Bournemouth Daily Echo
British Cycles and Motor Cycles Overseas
BSA Group News
BSA News
Business
Business Week
Classic Bike
The Classic Motor Cycle
Coventry Evening Standard
Cycle
Cycle World
Daily Express
Daily Herald
Daily Mail
Daily Telegram
Daily Worker
The Economist
The Engineer
Evening Mail
The Export Trader

Financial Times
Forbes
The Garage and Motor Agent
Guardian
The Independent
The Independent on Sunday
Management Today
Morning Star
The Motor Cycle
Motor Cycling
Motorcyclist
Motor Cyclist Review
The Motor Cycle and Cycle Export Trader
The Motor Cycle and Cycle Trader
New Statesman and Nation
Newsweek
The New York Times
Observer
Post Magazine and Insurance Monitor
The Sketch
The Spectator
The Statist
Stock Exchange Gazette
Sunday Mercury
Sunday Times
The Times

4. Journals

Board of Trade Journal
British Industries
BSA International and BSA Group News
Bulletin of the Oxford University Institute of Statistics
Business History
California Management Review
Diplomacy and Statecraft
The Director
Economic History Review
International Journal of Motorcycle Studies
Japanese Yearbook on Business History
Journal of Design History
Journal of Transport History

Labour Research Bulletin
Management Today
Marketing
Midland Bank Monthly Review
National Defence
Proceedings of the Automobile Division of the Institution of Mechanical Engineers
Proceedings of the Institution of Automobile Engineers
Proceedings of the Institution of Production Engineers
Proceedings of the Royal Society of Medicine
Quarterly Journal (published by the British Cycle and Motor Cycle Manufacturers and Traders' Union)
Technology and Culture

5. Primary printed sources

A. Official publications

Board of Trade, *Committee on Industry and Trade, 1924–1927, Minutes of Evidence*, HMSO, 1928.

——, *Restraint of Trade, Report of the Committee appointed by the Lord Chancellor and the President of the Board of Trade to answer certain Trade Questions*, London: HMSO, 1931.

——, *Census of Production, 1935*, London: HMSO, 1936.

——, *The Government's Statement on the Anglo-Japanese Treaty*, London: HMSO, 1962.

——, 'White Paper on Prices and Incomes Standstill', London: HMSO, July 1966.

——, *Business Monitor, Production Series, Motor Cycles, Three-Wheeled Vehicles, Pedal Cycles and Parts*, London: HMSO, 1968.

Boston Consulting Group, *Strategy Alternatives for the British Motorcycle Industry – A Report Prepared for the Secretary of State For Industry*, London: HMSO, H of C., 1975.

British Intelligence Objectives Sub-committee (BIOS), *The German Motor Cycle Industry – Final Report no. 620*, London: BIOS, 1946.

——, *The German Motor Cycle Industry since 1938 – Final Report no. 654*, authored by S. du Pont, London: BIOS, March, 1946.

——, *Manufacturing Methods in the German Motor Cycle Industry Final Report no. 1318*, authored by R.B. Douglas, London: BIOS, 1946.

Department of Transport, *Department of Transport Road Accidents, Great Britain 1992*, HMSO, 1992.

House of Lords Sessional Papers, 1937–1938, *Report by the Select Committee of the House of Lords on the Prevention of Road Accidents together with the Proceedings of the Committee, Minutes of Evidence and Index*, London: HMSO, 1938.

Imperial Economic Committee, *Thirtieth Report: A Survey of the Trade in Motor Vehicles*, London: HMSO, 1936.

Ministry of Transport, *Road Traffic Census, 1936 Report*, London: HMSO, 1937.

——, *Return showing the number of Mechanically Propelled Road Vehicles, Great Britain*, London: HMSO, various years between 1928 and 1963.

——, *Highway Statistics*, London: HMSO, various years after 1964.

——, *Report to the Minister of Transport on Motor Cycle Accidents*, London: HMSO, 1952.

US Strategic Bombing Survey, *Report on the German Motor Vehicle Industry*, Washington: Munitions Division, 1947.

US Tariff Commission, *Motorcycles and Parts. Report on the Escape-Clause Investigation. Report no. 180, 2nd Series*, Washington D.C.: Government Printing Office, 1953.

B. Other

British Cycle and Motor Cycle Manufacturers and Traders' Union, *Annual Reports* (various years)

——, *Carry on by Side-car*, Coventry: BCMCMTU, 1927.

——, *Notes on the Cycle & Motor Cycle Trade in Canada and USA*, prepared by H.R. Watling, Coventry: BCMCMTU, June 1928.

——, *British Cycles and Motor Cycles – Interesting Facts and Figures and Some Useful Information*, Coventry: BCMCMTU, 1950.

——, *Vehicle Legislation and the Moped*, Coventry: BCMCIA, 1957.

——, *Report of Mission to the USA – April–May 1966*, Coventry: BCMCIA, 1966.

Confederation of Shipbuilding and Engineering Unions (CSEU), *Handbook of National Agreements*, Privately printed: January 1964.

The Economic League, *Patterns of Trotskyism – A new form of Subversion in Industry*, London: The Economic League Ltd, no date but probably 1960.

Federation of British Industries, *A Look at Japan*, London: Federation of British Industries, 1961.

Norton Motors Strike Committee, *The Fight Against Redundancy*, Birmingham: September 1956.

6. Secondary printed sources

A. Books

Addison, Paul, *The Road to 1945*, London: Quartet Books, 1975.

Adeney, Martin, *The Motor Makers*, London: Fontana, 1989.

Allen, G.C., 'The Concentration of Production Policy', in D.N. Chester (ed.), *Lessons of the British War Economy*, Cambridge: Cambridge University Press, 1951.

——, *British Industries and their Organisation*, London: Longmans, 1959.

Ansell, David, *Military Motorcycles*, London: B.T. Batsford, 1985.

Ayton, Cyril et al., *The History of Motor Cycling*, Norwich: Orbis Publishing Ltd, 1979.

Bacon, Roy, *Villiers Singles and Twins, The Post-War British Two-Stroke Light Weight Motor Cycles*, London: Osprey Publishing Co., 1983.

——, *Honda – The Early Classic Motor Cycles*, London: Osprey Publishing Ltd, 1985.

——, *British Motorcycles of the 1930s*, London: Osprey Publishing Group, 1986.

——, *British Motorcycles of the 1940s and 1950s*, London: Osprey Publishing Group, 1987.

——, *British Motorcycles of the 1960s*, London: Osprey Publications Ltd, 1988.

Balder, John, 'The computer as a tool for production, planning and control', in Sumerbee, S. (ed.), *Computer Case Histories*, London: The Machinery Publishing Co. Ltd, 1970.

Blaich, Fritz, 'Why did the Pioneer fall behind?',

contained in Theo Barker (ed.), *The Economic and Social Effects of the Spread of Motor Vehicles*, London: Macmillan, 1987.

Bower, Tom, *The Paperclip Conspiracy*, London: Paladin Grafton books, 1987.

British Cycle and Motor Cycle Manufacturers and Traders' Union, *Review of the British Cycle and Motor Cycle Industry*, Coventry: BCMCMTU, 1935.

Brooke, Lindsay, *Triumph Motorcycles. A Century of Passion and Power*, St. Paul, USA: MBI Publishing Co., 2002.

Brooke, Lindsay and Gaylin, David, *Triumph Motorcycles in America*, Osceola, USA: Motorbooks International, 1993.

Bruce-Gardyne, Jock, *Meriden – Odyssey of a Lame Duck*, London: Centre for Policy Studies, 1978.

Brunner, Christopher T., *The Problem of Motor Transport*, London: Ernest Benn Ltd, 1928.

Calder, Angus, *The Peoples' War*, London: Pimlico, 1992.

Carrick, Peter, *Vincent-HRD*, Cambridge: Patrick Stephens Ltd, 1982.

Caunter, C.F., *Motorcycles, A Technical History*, London: HMSO, 1982.

Chamberlain, Peter (and the staff of *Motor Cycling* magazine), *The 1951 Motor Cycling Year Book*, London: Temple Press, 1953.

Champ, Robert Cordon, *Sunbeam S7 and S8*, Sparkford: Haynes Publishing Group, 1983.

——, *The Sunbeam Motor Cycle*, Sparkford: Haynes Publications, 1980.

Chester, D.N. (ed.), *Lessons of the British War Economy*, London: HMSO, 1949.

Church, Roy and Miller, Michael, 'The Big Three: Competition, Management, and Marketing in the British Motor Industry, 1922–1939', in Barry Supple (ed.), *Essays in British Business History*, Oxford: Clarenden Press, 1977.

Church, Roy, *Herbert Austin. The British Motor Car Industry to 1941*, London: Europa Publications, 1979.

——, *The Rise and Decline of the British Motor Industry*, London: Macmillan, 1994.

Clark, Ronald, *Brough Superior – The Rolls Royce of Motor Cycles*, Norwich: Goose and Son, 1954.

Clarke, Massimo (ed.), *100 Years of Motorcycles – A Century of History and Development*, New York: Portland House, 1988.

Clausager, Anders Ditlev, 'Labour Relations', in Nick Georgano et al., *Britain's Motor Industry. The First Hundred Years*, Sparkford: G.T. Foulis & Co., 1995.

Clay, Mike, *Cafe Racers – Rockers, Rock 'n' Roll and the Coffee Bar Cult*, London: Osprey Publishing Company, 1988.

Clew, Jeff, *Suzuki*, Sparkford: Haynes Publishing Group, 1980.

——, *The Douglas Motorcycle*, Sparkford: Haynes Publishing Company, 1981.

——, *BSA Bantam*, Sparkford: Haynes Publishing Group, 1983.

Cohen, Stanley, *Folk Devils and Moral Panics*, Oxford: Blackwells, 1993.

Currie, Bob and Louis, Harry, *The Story of Triumph Motorcycles*, Cambridge: Patrick Stephen, 1978.

Currie, Bob, *Great British Motor Cycles of the Thirties*, London: Ivy Leaf, 1991.

Cusumano, Michael A., *The Japanese Automobile Industry: Technology and Management at Nissan and Toyota*, Cambridge, Mass.: Harvard University Press, 1991.

Cycle World, *Cycle World on BSA, 1962–1971*, Cobham, Surrey: Brooklands Book Distribution Ltd, 1987.

——, *Cycle World on Honda, 1962–1967*, Cobham, Surrey: Brooklands Book Distribution Ltd, 1988.

Davenport-Hines, R.P.T., *Dudley Docker. The Life and Times of a Trade Warrior*, London: Cambridge University Press, 1984.

Davidson, G.S. (ed.), *The Motor Cyclist Annual, 1939–1940*, London: H.E.W. Publications Ltd, 1939.

Davidson, G.S., *Racing Through the Century*, Coventry: W.W. Curtis, 1951.

Davies, Ivor, *Its a Triumph*, Sparkford: Haynes Publishing Company, 1982.

——, *Triumph – The Complete Story*, Swindon: The Crowood Press, 1991.

Debenham, Betty and Nancy, *Motor Cycling for Women*, London: Pitman and Sons, 1928.

Dintenfass, Michael, *The Decline of Industrial Britain*, London: Routledge, 1992.

Docker, Norah, *Norah – The Autobiography of Lady Docker*, London: W.H. Allen, 1969.

Dracket, Phil, *Speedway*, London: W. & G. Foyle Ltd, 1951.

Dunnett, Peter, *The Decline of the British Motor Industry, the Effects of Government Policy, 1945–1979*, Croom Hill, 1980.

Evely, Richard and Little, I.M.D., *Concentration in British Industry*, Cambridge: Cambridge University Press, 1960.

Fleet, Ken, 'Triumph Meriden' in *The New Worker Co-operatives* (Nottingham: Institute for Workers' Control Spokesman Books, 1976).

Freundenberg, Matthew, *The Isle of Man TT*, Bourne End: Aston Publications Ltd, 1990.

Fry, Robin, *The VW Beetle*, London: David & Charles, 1980.

Ganneau, Didier and Dumas, Francois-Marie, *Motos Japonaises. 100 ans d'Histoire* (French language text), Paris: EIAI, 1997.

GK Dynamics/Yamaha Motor Co., *Spirit of Yamaha Motorcycle Design*, Tokyo: Rikuyo-Sha Publishing, 1989.

Grant, Gregor, *AJS – The History of a Great Motor Cycle*, Cambridge: Patrick Stephens, 1969.

Grew, W.F., *The Cycle Industry. Its Origin, History and Latest Developments*, London: Pitman and Sons, 1921.

Harper, Roy, *Vincent Vee-Twins*, London: Osprey Publishing Company, 1982.

Harris, Maz, *Bikers*, London: Faber and Faber, 1985.

Harris, Nick, *The Motorcourse History of the Isle of Man TT Races, 1907–1989*, Richmond, Surrey: Hazelton Publications, 1990.

Hartley, Peter, *The Ariel Story*, Watford: Argus Books, 1980.

——, *The Story of Royal Enfield Motor Cycles*, Cambridge: Patrick Stephens, 1981.

——, *Matchless – Once the Largest British Motor Cycle Manufacturer*, London: Osprey Publishing Company, 1981.

——, *The Story of Rudge Motor Cycles*, Wellingborough: Patrick Stephens Ltd, 1985.

Hatfield, Jerry, *Inside Harley-Davidson*, Osceola, USA: Motorbooks International, 1990.

Heath, H. Frank and Heatherington, A.L., *Industrial Research and Development in the UK. A Survey*, London: Faber and Faber Ltd, 1946.

Hebdige, Dick, *Hiding in the Light*, London: Routledge, 1988.

Hilliard, Frank, *Deeley – Motorcycle Millionaire*, Victoria, Canada: Orca Book Publishers, 1994.

Hobsbawm, E.J., *Industry and Empire*, London: Penguin Books, 1979.

Holliday, Bob, *The Story of BSA Motorcycles*, Cambridge: Patrick Stephen, 1978.

Holt, Richard, *Sport and the British*, Oxford: Oxford University Press, 1990.

Hopwood, Bert, *Whatever Happened to the British Motorcycle Industry?*, Sparkford: Haynes Publishing Group, 1980.

Hough, Richard and Setright, L.J.K., *A History of the World's Motor Cycles*, London: George Allen & Unwin Ltd, 1966.

Irving, Phil, *An Autobiography*, Wahroongo, Australia: Turton and Armstrong, 1992.

Ixion (The Rev. B.H. Davies), *Motor Cycle Cavalcade*, London: Iliffe & Sons, 1951.

Japan Automobile Manufacturers' Association, *The History of Japan's Automobile Industry*, Tokyo: The Japan Automobile Manufacturers' Association, 1997.

Jeremy, D.J. (ed.), *Dictionary of Business Biography* (in five volumes), London: Butterworth, 1986.

Johnson, Gary, *Classic Motorcycles*, London: Boxtree Ltd, 1993.

Kawahara, Akira, *The Origin of Competitive Strength: Fifty Years of the Auto Industry in Japan and the US*, Tokyo: privately published, 1997.

Kipping, Norman, *Summing Up*, London: Hutchinson and Co., 1972.

Koerner, Steve, 'Asleep at the Wheel? British Motor Vehicle Exports to Canada, 1945–75' in Buckner, Phillip (ed.), *Canada and the End of Empire*, Vancouver, Canada: UBC Press, 2005.

Macauley, Ted, *Yamaha*, London: Cadogan Books, 1979.

MacDonald, C.A., *The United States, Britain and Appeasement, 1936–1939*, London: Macmillan, 1981.

Masters, A. St. John, *Motor Cycle Sport*, London: C. Arthur Pearson Ltd, 1958.

Maxcy, George and Silberston, Aubrey, *The Motor Industry*, George Allen & Unwin, 1959.

Mellors, Ted, *Continental Circus*, Coventry: W.W. Curtis, 1949.

Mercer, Helen, 'The Monopolies and Restrictive Practices Commission', in G. Jones and M. Kirby (eds), *Competitiveness and the State*, Manchester: Manchester University Press, 1991.

Morewood, Steven, *Pioneers and Inheritors: Top Management in the Coventry Motor Industry, 1896–1972*, Coventry: Coventry Polytechnic, Centre for Business History, 1990.

The Motor Cycle, *The Motor Cycle Book for Boys*, London: Illiffe and Sons Ltd, 1928.

——, *The Motor Cycle Overseas Annual and Buyers' Guide 1925*, London: Illiffe and Sons, 1925.

Motor Cycling, *The Motorcycling Year Book*, London: Temple Press Ltd, various years between 1952 and 1958.

Motor Cycle Industry Council, *1981 Motorcycle Statistical Annual*, Irvine, California, USA: Motorcycle Industry Council, 1981.

Nelson, J.R., *Bonnie: The Development History of the Triumph Bonneville*, Sparkford: Haynes Publishing Group, 1979.

——, *Triumph Tiger 100/Daytona*, Sparkford: Haynes Publishing Group, 1989.

Newcombe, T.P. and Spurr, R.T., *A Technical History of the Motor Car*, Bristol: Adam Hilger, 1979.

Newton, Scott and Porter, Dilwyn, *Modernisation Frustrated*, London: Unwin Hyman, 1988.

Nockold, Harold, *Lucas: the First Hundred Years. Volume I: The King of the Road*, London: David & Charles, 1976.

Norton-Villiers-Triumph, *Meriden – Historical Summary, 1972–1974*, London: Burrup, Mathieson & Co., 1974.

O'Connell, Sean, *The Car in British Society. Class, Gender, and Motoring, 1896–1939*, Manchester: Manchester University Press, 1998.

Plowden, William, *The Motor Car and Politics, 1896–1970*, London: The Bodley Head, 1971.

Plummer, Alfred, *New British Industries in the 20th*

Century, London: Sir Isaac Pitman and Sons Ltd, 1937.

Postan, M.N., *British War Production*, London: HMSO, 1952.

Reich, Simon, *The Fruits of Fascism*, London: Cornell University Press, 1990.

Rogers, Nick, *The British Motorcycle Industry, 1945–1975 – Programme Notes for an Epic still to be Written*, Birmingham: University of Birmingham, Centre for Urban and Regional Studies, 1979.

Ryerson, Barry, *Giants of Small Heath – The History of BSA*, Sparkford: Haynes Publishing Group, 1980.

Sakiya, Tetsuo, *Honda Motor – The Men, the Management, The Machines*, Tokyo: Kodansha International Ltd, 1987.

Sanders, Sol, *Honda – The Man and His Machines*, Boston: Little Brown and Co., 1975.

Sheridan, Clare, *Across Europe with Satanella*, London: Duckworth, 1925.

Shilling, Phil, *The Motorcycle World*, New York: Random House, 1974.

Shilton, Neil, *A Million Miles Ago*, Sparkford: Haynes Publising Group, 1982.

Shimokawa, Koichi, *The Japanese Automobile Industry. A Business History*, London: Athlone Press, 1994.

Smith, Barbara, *The British Motorcycle Industry, 1945–1975*, Birmingham: University of Birmingham, Centre for Urban and Regional Studies, 1983.

Society of Motor Manufacturers and Traders, *The Motor Industry of Great Britain*, London: SMMT, various years.

Stevenson, John, *British Society, 1914–1945* (London: Penguin Books, 1990).

Sucher, Harry, *Harley-Davidson – The Milwaukee Marvel* (Sparkford: Haynes Publishing Group, 1990).

———, *The Iron Redskin* (Sparkford: Haynes Publishing Group, 1990).

Supple, Barry (ed.), *Essays in British Business History* (Oxford: Clarenden Press, 1977).

The Times, *Accidents on the Road* (London: The Times Publishing Company, 1951).

Thompson, Hunter S., *The Hells' Angels* (New York: Bantam Books, 1965).

Thoms, David and Donnelly, Tom. *The Motor Car Industry in Coventry since the 1890s*. Beckenham, Kent: Croom Helm Ltd, 1985.

Thoms, David, *War, Industry and Society, The Midlands, 1939–1945* (London: Routledge, 1989).

Tiratsoo, Nick. 'The Motor Car Industry', contained in H. Mercer, W. Rollings and J.D. Tomlinson (eds), *The Labour Government and Private Industry. The Experience of 1945–1951*, Edinburgh: Edinburgh University Press, 1992.

Tiratsoo, Nick and Tomlinson, Jim. *Industrial Efficiency and State Intervention: Labour, 1929–51*. London: Routledge, 1993.

Tomlinson, Jim, 'A missed opportunity? Labour and the Productivity Problem, 1945–1951', in G. Jones and M. Kirby (eds), *Competitiveness and the State*, Manchester: Manchester University Press, 1991.

Ughanwa, D.O. and Baker, M.J., *The Role of Design in International Competitiveness*, London: Routledge, 1989.

Vogel, Ezra, *Comeback*, Tokyo: Charles Tuttle, 1985.

Walford, Eric, *Early Days in the British Motor Cycle Industry*, Coventry: British Cycle and Motor Cycle Manufacturers and Traders' Union, nd.

Wallach, Theresa, *The Rugged Road*, High Wycombe: Panther Publishing Ltd, 2001.

Ward, Donovan, *The Other Battle*, Birmingham: BSA, 1946.

Watling, H.R., 'The Cycle and Motor Cycle Industry', in H.J. Schonfield (ed.), *The Book of British Industries*, Edinburgh: Denis Archer, 1933.

Webster, Michael, *Motor Scooters*, Aylesbury, Bucks: Shire Publications Ltd, 1986.

Wensley, Robin, 'Marketing Strategy', contained in M.J. Baker (ed.), *The Marketing Book*, London: Heinemann, 1987.

Wherrett, Duncan, *Vincent*, London: Osprey Publishing Ltd, 1994.

Whistler, Timothy R., *The British Motor Industry, 1945–1994. A Case Study in Industrial Decline*, Oxford: Oxford University Press, 1999.

Wiener, Martin, *English Culture and the Decline of the Industrial Spirit, 1850–1980*, London: Penguin Books, 1987.

Williams, Karel, Williams, John and Thomas, Dennis, *Why are the British bad at manufacturing?* London: Routledge and Kegan Paul, 1983.

Wilson, Steve, *British Motorcycles Since 1950* (in six volumes), Cambridge: Patrick Stephens, 1982.

Wood, Jonathan, *Wheels of Misfortune*, London: Sidgwick & Jackson, 1988.

Woollett, Mick, *Norton*, London: Osprey Publishing Company, 1992.

Worthington-Williams, Michael, *From Cyclecar to Microcar. The Story of the Cyclecar Movement*, London: Dalton Watson Ltd, 1981.

Wright, Owen, *BSA – The Complete Story*, Ramsbury: The Crowood Press, 1992.

B. Articles

Anonymous, 'The Works of the BSA Co. Ltd – Methods in the Manufacture of Motor Cycle Engines', *Automobile Engineer*, November 1938, pp.434–439

Bowden, S.M., 'Demand and Supply Constrains in the Inter-War UK Car Industry: Did the Manufacturers get it Right?' *Business History*, April 1991.

Brown, William, 'Piece-work Wage Determination in Coventry', *Scottish Journal of Political Economy*, vol. 18.

Caudwell, E., 'The Engine of the side-car motor cycle', *Proceedings of the Institute of Automobile Engineers*, vol. XII (1918–1919).

Cenzatti, M., 'Restructuring in the motorcycle industry in Great Britain and Italy until 1980', *Environment and Planning*, vol. 8 (1990).

Coleman, D.C., 'Gentlemen and Players', *Economic History Review*, vol. XXVI (1973).

Dawson, R.F.F., 'Ownership of cars and certain durable household goods', *Bulletin of the Oxford University Institute of Statistics*, May (1953).

Heather, D.S., 'A Survey of Current Motorcycle Design', *Proceedings of the Institute of Automobile Engineers*, vol. XIII (1918–1919).

Hingston, W. Halcot, 'The Light Car and Motor Cycle and Side-car', *Proceedings of the Institute of Automobile Engineers*, vol. XVII (1921–1922).

Knowles, K.G.J.C. and Robinson, D., 'Wage Movement in Coventry', *Bulletin of the Oxford University Institute of Economics and Statistics*, vol. 31, no. 1 (February 1969).

Koerner, Steve, 'The British Motor Cycle Industry during the 1930s', *The Journal of Transport History* (March 1995).

Lee, J.A.H., 'Motor cycle accidents to male teenagers: A contemporary epidemic', *Proceedings of the Royal Society of Medicine* (May 1963).

Newton, Scott, 'The "Anglo-German Connection" and the Political Economy of Appeasement', *Diplomacy and Statecraft* (November 1991).

Otahara, Jun, 'An evolutionary Phase of Honda Motor: The Establishment and Success of American Honda Motor', *Japanese Yearbook on Business History* – 2000/17.

Overy, R.J., 'Cars, roads and Economic Recovery in Germany', *Economic History Review*, vol. XXVIII (1975).

Page, V., 'Developments in Motor Cycle Design', *Proceedings of the Institute of Automobile Engineers*, vol. XXXII (1937–1938).

Pascale, Richard T., 'Perspectives on Strategy: The Real Story behind Honda's Success', *California Management Review* (Spring 1984).

Potter, Christopher T., 'Motorcycle Clubs in Britain During the Interwar Period, 1919–1939: Their Social and Cultural importance.' *International Journal of Motorcycle Studies*, March 2005, posted on www.ijms.nova.edu/.

Sandes, E.W.C., 'The Evolution of the Motor Cycle', *The Royal Engineers' Journal*, vol. LIX (1945).

Shaker, Steven and Wise, Alan, 'Motorcycles', *National Defense* (September 1984).

Sigl, Robert, 'The Military Motorcycle', *Armor* (September–October 1982).

Stanfield, Peter, 'Heritage Design: The Harley-Davidson Motor Company', *Journal of Design History*, vol. 5, no. 2 (1992).

Teage, H.D., 'Motor cycle progress: Past, Present and Future', *Proceedings of the Institute of Automobile Engineers*, vol. XXVI (1931/1932).

Tomlinson, Jim, 'The Failure of the Anglo-American Council on Productivity', *Business History*, no. 1 (1991).

Tsutomu, Demizu, 'Technological Innovation in the Motorcycle Industry in Postwar Japan', *History of Industry and Technology in Japan. Marburger Japan-Reihe*, vol. 14/II (Marburg: 1995).

Turner, Edward, 'Post War Motor Cycle Development', *Proceedings of the Institute of Automobile Engineers*, vol. XXXVII (1942–1943).

Volti, Rudi, 'Exhibit Reviews. The National Motorcycle Museum, Birmingham, England.' *Technology and Culture* (January 1987).

Wallace, John, 'The Super-Sports Motor Cycle', *Proceedings of the Institute of Automobile Engineers*, vol. XXIV (1929–1930).

Wilson-Jones, R.A., 'Years of Development', *Proceedings of the Automobile Division of the Institution of Mechanical Engineers* (1958–1959).

7. Unpublished theses

Carr, F.W., 'Engineering Workers and the Rise of Labour in Coventry, 1914–1939', unpub. Ph.D. dissertation, Warwick University, 1978.

Fairclough, Martin, 'The Political Economy of Producers Co-operatives: A Study of Triumph Motorcycles (Meriden) Ltd and Britain's Industrial Decline', unpub. Ph.D. dissertation, Bristol University, 1986.

Harris, Ian, 'Myth and Reality in the Motorcycle Subculture', unpub. Ph.D. dissertation, University of Warwick, 1986.

Kelly, John, 'History of Veloce Ltd – Motorcycle Manufacturers, Hall Green, Birmingham', unpub. Ph.D. dissertation, Bradford University, 1978.

Koerner, Steve, 'Trade Unionism and Collective

Bargaining at Two British Motor Cycle Factories: a Study of BSA/Small Heath and Triumph/Meriden, 1951–73', unpub. MA dissertation, University of Warwick, 1990.

Turner, I.D., 'British Occupation Policy and its effects on the town of Wolfsburg and the Volkswagenwerk, 1945–1949', unpub. Ph.D. dissertation, UMIST, 1984.

Whisler, Timothy R., 'Niche Products in the British Motor Industry: A History of MG and Triumph Sports Cars, 1945–1985', unpub Ph.D. dissertation, London School of Economics, 1991.

8. Unpublished papers

Bettmann, Siegfried, 'Struggles: A Man of No Importance' (in three volumes), unpublished and undated, but probably circa 1938 and on deposit at the Coventry City Records Office.

Koerner, Steve and Otahara, Jun, 'The Japanese Motor Cycle Industry, 1945–1960', paper presented at the Association of Business Historians' annual conference, London School of Economics, London England, 2 September 1999.

Miller, Michael, 'The British Motor Cycle Industry before 1939' (University of East Anglia, n.d).

Smith, Barbara, 'Production Relationships at BSA, 1963/64–1971/72' (unpublished paper on deposit at the Centre for Urban and Regional Studies, University of Birmingham).

Tomlinson, Jim, 'British Industrial Policy in a Japanese Mirror: Why no MITI in Britain?' (paper delivered at the Fourth Anglo-Japanese Conference, London School of Economics, 14–16 April 1994).

Index